# PANZER LEHR DIVISION 1944–45

## Helion WWII German Military Studies Volume 1

Edited and translated by

Dr Frederick P. Steinhardt

Helion & Company Ltd

Helion & Company Limited
Unit 8 Amherst Business Centre
Budbrooke Road
Warwick
CV34 5WE
England
Tel. 01926 499619
Email: info@helion.co.uk
Website: www.helion.co.uk
X (formerly Twitter): @Helionbooks
Facebook: @HelionBooks
Visit our blog at https://helionbooks.wordpress.com/

Published by Helion & Company 2008. Paperback edition 2010, reprinted 2024
Designed and typeset by Mach 3 Solutions (www.mach3solutions.co.uk)
Cover designed by Paul Hewitt, Battlefield Design (www.battlefield-design.co.uk)
Editorial notes and linking commentary by Dr Frederick Steinhardt


ISBN 978-1-804516-51-5

British Library Cataloguing-in-Publication Data.
A catalogue record for this book is available from the British Library.

# CONTENTS

# LIST OF PHOTOS

# LIST OF MAPS

Publisher's note: Reproducing the maps from the original manuscripts was a huge challenge for everybody concerned with this project. The quality available to us was very poor indeed in most cases. We wanted to include as many of the maps as possible, aware of the importance of these to the manuscripts and to tracing the course of the unit's operations generally. Not only was the technical quality very poor, but many of the place names were incorrect. Editor Fred Steinhardt has done a superb job in assisting us in trying to clarify the maps. Working within technical limitations, we have done our best to reproduce the maps for the reader. Any errors that remain are our responsibility, not the editor's.

*Part I – Panzer Lehr Division in Normandy through to the Withdrawal from France*

**ETHINT 66**



**ETHINT 67**



*Part II – Panzer Lehr Division 130 in the Ardennes Offensive*

**A–941**

**A–942**



**A–944**



*Part III – Panzer Lehr Division 130 after Ardennes, before Remagen*

**D–322**



**B–768**



*Part IV – Panzer Lehr at Remagen and after*

**A–970**

# LIST OF TABLES

# FOREWORD

The series of interviews that are the focus of this book do not provide a continuous account of the history of the *Panzer Lehr Division,* nor do they provide the context in which the actions described took place. I have, therefore, tried to provide the missing continuity with a very brief history of *Panzer Lehr Division* 130 and descriptions of the relevant military situations.

The scope of this volume precluded great detail in the division history. For such detail, the reader is referred to Jean-Claude Perrigault's massive *La Panzer-Lehr-Division, Le Choc des Alliés Brise l'Arme D'Elite de Hitler*. Perrigault provides the definitive detailed history of the division, recognizing and utilizing previous histories along with extensive research in records and personal interviews and narratives. His account is richly rewarding reading. Helmut Ritgen's *Die Geschichte der Panzer Lehr Division im Westen 1944 1945* remains valuable. Ritgen's personal narrative, *Westfront 1944* overlaps his history of the division and has the advantage that it is also available in an English translation. Kurowski's *Die Panzer-Lehr-Division* provides some colorful anecdotes and glimpses of action but is light on the facts.

Discussion of the larger military context rests largely on those works mentioned in the attached bibliography.

# EDITOR'S NOTE

In general, I have approached this project with the viewpoint that these are essential source documents being made available through this publication. Therefore the style of translation has been scholarly in attempting to carefully preserve the original nature of the documents, including errors. That, in turn, required careful use of bracketed notes, even though that, at times, may interfere with ease of reading. This book includes a number of documents in their original form that did not require translation, either because they were originally written in (American) English or the original German was not available, in which case the available translation is given. Because these are 'source documents' and may be used as such, care has been taken to preserve the original spelling (including mis-spellings), punctuation, abbreviations etc. These documents were provided as photocopies of typed or mimeographed material. Thus, foreign terms were not italicized and German vowels with umlauts were rendered with an 'e', *e.g. ä* = ae, *ü* = ue, etc. In contrast with material translated for this publication, this was retained to preserve the original nature of the document. My apologies to those readers for whom this may reduce ease of reading. I can only assure them that there are others for whom this knowledge will provide reassurance that they can utilize these documents as printed here in their own work. Although it is incorrect to capitalize 'Von', as in von Choltitz, that error was so common that I did not insert the usual [*sic.*n ] to indicate that an error in the original document was preserved as such. Wherever the reader meets a capitalized 'Von', it can safely be assumed that it was so capitalized in the original document.

Because the German term, *Heer*, refers to 'the Army', as distinguished from *Armee*, the tactical unit, I insert the German original in brackets where there might otherwise be confusion.

In the area of Germany, Luxembourg and Belgium where the Ardennes Offensive occurred, geography frequency has names in several languages, names that differ slightly and whose current validity depends on the temporal accident of the present border location. In general, German military reports and documents usually use the geographical names and spellings on the maps serving as references for that action. Reports based on that action and subsequent reports on up the line carefully preserve those spellings, since they serve as location references on the maps specifically referred to as the basis for relevant operations orders and the like. Thus, a division history or historical study of an action may include a variety of spellings of place names, sometimes different names for the same place. When translating or writing for the general reader, it is customary to standardize place names and provide maps using those place names. However, when presenting material that may serve as 'source material' for later studies, there is a reason for preserving place names exactly as the original author presented them. With the sole exception of replacing *Lüttich* with Liège, to maintain conformity with the usage in the previously translated documents, that is the practice I have followed here, adding more generally accepted spellings in brackets where relevant, accepting Michelin maps as the standard in most cases. Generally, at the first mention, I have supplied the accepted current spelling in brackets, then continuing to use the author's variation. However, in a few instances where there is an error, as in Bayerlein's repeatedly saying Senonchamps, a village west of Bastogne, when actually referring to Benonchamps, a village east of Bastogne, I have appended a bracketed correction to each mention. Where it was a simple matter of a diacritical mark (*e.g.*e vs. é) I have simply bracketed the first use of the correct mark and then employed it without comment.

Bayerlein, or, in some cases, the person who recorded the interviews, used abbreviations for most formation and unit designations, some of which are non-standard. Frequently the abbreviation or idiosyncratic name varies from one line to the next. In documents that were already translated, I did my best to accurately transcribe them precisely as they were, since they are being presented as original source documents. In material that I translated, on the first appearance I used Bayerlein's (or other interviewee's) designation, followed by the bracketed standardized name, based, for *Panzer Lehr Division*, on those designations used in Helmut Ritgen's history of the *Panzer Lehr Division* and, for other units, either on Tessin's *Verbände und Truppen der deutschen Wehrmacht und Waffen SS im Zweiten Weltkrieg 19339 – 1945* or Bender and Taylor's *Uniforms, Organization and History of the Waffen-SS*. In subsequent mentions I replace the original abbreviated or non-standard designation with the standard designation. I did not see any reason to preserve the variable and idiosyncratic designations of elements and units for the sake of scholarly value in those documents which I translated. An initial experiment in so doing resulted in tedious and confusing proliferation of bracketed notes of explanation.

In giving dates, 13–14 January means on the thirteenth and fourteenth of January, whereas 13/14 January means during the night of January 13 and post-midnight hours on January 14.

Where German terms are retained in material I translated, I used German plurals, but used the nominative form, regardless of grammatical position in the sentence.

## Notes regarding translation

In the sections located in France, where there is no doubt as to the location intended, the spelling of all French place names has been corrected in accord with the 2002 Michelin Tourist and Motoring Atlas of France.

Massive blocks of text have been broken up into paragraphs to improve clarity and readability.

Familiar German terms have been retained, with a bracketed explanation upon first appearance. There is a complete glossary at the end. In some cases where an English term has been used the original German term has been included in brackets for added clarity.

# BRIEF HISTORY OF *PANZER LEHR DIVISION* 130 FROM ACTIVATION TO NORMANDY INVASION[1]

The interviews here translated represent, in each case, the views of the person being interviewed. In most cases that person was not in possession of his unit's records or maps and was depending largely on his own memory and what maps the interviewer could provide. As, at times, noted by the interviewer, the interviewee may have been biased for one reason or another. Therefore I have taken care that the history of the Division in which the interviews are embedded represents my own best understanding of the events in light of the full range of resources and sources available at this time.

When the nature of the future invasion by the Western Allies became apparent in 1943 Hitler designated the invasion as a danger and directed construction of coastal fortifications. There was an obvious need for additional mobile formations to combat the prospective invasion. *Generalinspekteur der Panzertruppen, Generaloberst* Guderian offered his *Lehrtruppen*, demonstration and instructional units at the various training schools. They were to be combined and organized into a newly constituted elite division whose main function would be to repulse the invasion.

Although the *Panzer Lehr Division* (properly *Panzer Lehr Division* 130) was not an old division, it comprised an abundance of officers and non-commissioned officers who had proven themselves on the Eastern Front. Those elements of the Division whose designation included the word *Lehr* could look proudly back on a history that began during the original period of activation and creation of the German *Panzertruppe* from 1935 to 1938. These elements took part in the early campaigns, in Poland, France and Russia, in varying attachments and assignments to regular divisions so that they could gain combat experience which they then brought back to the various troop-training schools. At the training school these units served to train, demonstrate and test new tactics and equipment.

The Division's activation order was issued 30 December 1943. It was to be constituted from the training/demonstration units (*Lehrtruppen*) of the *Panzertruppenschule*. *Oberbefehslhaber West* was to supply an artillery regimental staff, two artillery *Abteilungen* [ = battalions] and the requisite logistical elements. The organization of the Division was, at the start, somewhere between the 1943 standard and the 1944 standard, evolving in time closer to the 1944 standard *Panzer Division*. The T/O strength of the Division before September, 1944 was set

---

1 Note – This brief history of *Panzer Lehr Division* 130 is largely based on Jean-Claude Perrigault's *La Panzer-Lehr-Division, Le Choc des Alliés Brise l'Arme D'Elite de Hitler*, Helmut Ritgen's *Die Geschichte der Panzer Lehr Division im Westen 1944 1945* and, with limitations, on the interviews and questionnaires translated here. Considerable important and interesting additional material came from other sources listed in the bibliography.

at 449 officers, 3146 non-commissioned officers and 10,891 enlisted men, with a total strength of 14,634. After September 1944 the T/O strength was set at 492 officers, 3146 non-commissioned officers and 10,289 enlisted men with a total of 13,927.

The Division consisted, ideally, of:

Division staff (*Divisionsstab*), with its sections:

Ia First General Staff Officer and his aids, responsible for organization, command in combat and training.

Ib Second General Staff Officer and his aids, responsible for logistics.

Ic Enemy intelligence.

IIa Division adjutant, responsible for personnel.

III Military judge, dealing with all legal matters.

IVa Administration and rations.

IVb Division surgeon

IVd Chaplain

V Division engineer

W&G *Waffen und Gerät,* weapons and equipment, ammunition supply.

The division staff was generally organized in two echelons, the command echelon including those requisite for command in action of the division: the commander and his aide, Ia reinforced with radio and telephone squads of the reconnaissance battalion, and the Ic, IIa and IVb., often supplemented with the map section. The logistics echelon, Ib, attended to logistic support and included all elements of the staff that were not in the command echelon.

Division map section (*Divisionskartenstelle*) took care of and duplicated necessary maps.

Division escort company (*Divisions Begleit-Kompanie*) consisting of:

The company squad,

motorcycle platoon,

heavy machine gun platoon,

light machine gun platoon (later 120 mm mortar platoon),

light antiaircraft platoon (self-propelled),

heavy antitank platoon (three 7.5 cm antitank guns).

Military Police (*Feldgendarmerietrupp*)

An armoured regiment (*Panzer-Lehr-Regiment* 130) consisting of two *Abteilungen*:

I../*Panzer-Lehr-Regiment* 130 (1st *Abteilung, Panzer-Lehr-Regiment* 130).

II./*Panzer-Lehr-Regiment* 130.

The II *Abteilung* (*Panzer* IV) consisted of:

Staff

Staff company (including communications platoon) with 3 command vehicles (*Befehlswagen* IV). A reconnaissance platoon with five *Panzer* IV, a pioneer platoon on *SPW* (half-tracks). A motorcycle reconnaissance platoon and an armoured antiaircraft platoon with two quad–20mm *Flakpanzer Wirbelwind.*

Four (companies 5–8) *Panzer* companies, with 22 *Panzer* IV each

Supply company.

Including the vehicles of the staff company, the II *Abteilung* fielded 96 *Panzer* IV.

However, the I *Abteilung* was redesignated II *Abteilung*, since the equipment situation only permitted it to be outfitted with *Panzer* IV and the I *Abteilung* was to receive *Panzer* V, *Panther*. Replacing the I *Abteilung*, which was not, in fact, activated until July 1944, *Panzer-Lehr-Regiment* 130 received the I./*Panzerregiment* 6, which was attached to it until October. I./*Panzer-Regiment* 6, replaced the Division's own missing I./ *Panzer-Lehr-Regiment* 130 while it was still training with the new *Panther* tanks.

The I./*Panzer-Lehr-Regiment* 130 *(Panther)* finally reached the Division in February 1945, with two *Panther* companies, each with 14 tanks, and one *Jagdpanther* company.

A company of radio-controlled miniature tanks loaded with demolitions (*Funklenk-Kompanie* 316) was also included in *Panzer-Lehr-Regiment* 130. However, in the event, instead of the ten *Tiger* tanks to be used for control vehicles and the radio-controlled demolition carriers, the company ended up with nine *Sturmgeschütze*, with which it fought until they were all lost at Tilly and St. Lo, at which point the company was disbanded.

*Werkstattkompanie* 130. The tank repair company was part of the armoured regiment.

Two regiments of *Panzergrenadiere*.

*Panzergrenadier-Lehr-Regiment* 901. At the start of the invasion, the entire regiment, regimental units and the two battalions, were mounted on *SPW, Schützenpanzerwagen*, half-tracked lightly armoured personnel carriers, with an abundance of self-propelled heavy weapons, giving it high mobility, armoured protection and great firepower.

The regiment consisted of:

Staff and staff company, which included a total of 16 *SPW,* an armoured flame-thrower and a platoon of 7.5 cm heavy antitank guns (two guns);

three *Panzergrenadier* companies, each with 22 *SPW,* 29 machine guns, 17 of which were mounted on the vehicles, four heavy machine guns, two 8 cm mortars, three 3.7 cm antitank guns on the platoon leaders' vehicles and two *SPW* with short-barreled 7.5 cm guns;

a heavy weapons company with 19 *SPW,* six with 7.5 cm short-barreled guns, two light infantry guns and two 7.5 cm antitank guns. Although part of the initial plans, a heavy mortar platoon with four 12 cm mortars instead of the light infantry guns did not join the heavy weapons company until the fall of 1944 and

A logistics company.

The 9th (heavy infantry gun) Company had six heavy 15 cm self-propelled infantry guns;

The 10th Pioneer Company included armoured-flamethrowers and heavy antitank guns.

The 11th (antiaircraft) company had two platoons of single 2 cm and one platoon with quad–2 cm antiaircraft guns. Unavailability of the weapons delayed replacement of the above inadequate armament with 27 2 cm mounts on half-tracks (*Sd.Kfz. 251/17*) in each battalion until June 1944.

*Panzergrenadier-Lehr-Regiment* 902. At the start of the invasion it resembled *Rgt.* 901, except that it lacked an antiaircraft company.

*Panzeraufklärungs-Lehr-Abteilung* 130. Fully motorized, the reconnaissance battalion consisted of:

Staff

Reconnaissance elements including a communications platoon and two armoured reconnaissance companies, 1st and 2nd, the First Company with eight-wheeled *Puma* armoured cars, the Second with *Sd. Kfz. 250/9* half-tracks.

Combat elements consisting of two (3rd and 4th) armoured reconnaissance companies (*Panzergrenadier (gp)* companies) and one (5th company) heavy-weapons company.

Supply company.

*Panzerjäger-Lehr-Abteilung* 130. Far from its intended original equipment, in May 1944 the tank-destroyer battalion consisted of:

Staff and staff company with communications, pioneer and antiaircraft platoons.

Three mixed *Panzerjäger* companies, each with 9–10 *Panzerjäger* 39 (*Jagdpanzer* IV) and four towed 7.5cm antitank guns. The *Jagdpanzer* IV had the same gun as the *Panzer* IV, but a lower profile and thicker frontal armour.

Supply company.

Following reconstitution, the *Panzerjäger Abteilung* finally received 21 *Panzerjäger* 40, whose guns took the same ammunition as the powerful *Panther* main gun. At that time the towed guns were concentrated in the 1st company. Finally, at the end of March 1945 the *Abteilung* received an additional 18 *Panzerjäger* 40.

*Panzer-Artillerie-Regiment* 130. At the time of the invasion the artillery regiment consisted of:

Staff with staff battery (motorized)

I *Abteilung* with staff, staff battery and three batteries, each with four light towed 10.5 cm howitzers (*le F.H.* 18)

II. *Abteilung* (armoured howitzers) with staff, staff battery, two batteries, each with six light 10.5 cm self-propelled armoured howitzers (*Wespe*) and one battery with six heavy 15 cm self-propelled armoured howitzers (*Hummel*).

III *Abteilung* (heavy field-howitzers) with staff, staff battery and three batteries, each with four Russian 15.2 cm canon-howitzers (15.2 cm *Kanonenhaubitzen* 433/1).

*Heeres-Flak-Abteilung* 311, an army formation assigned as an integral part of the Division. The initial organization was:

staff and staff battery

Three batteries, each with six 8.8 cm, two 2 cm antiaircraft guns and four machine guns.

After reconstitution, the *FlakAbteilung* consisted of:

Staff and staff battery

One medium battery with nine 3.7 cm guns.

Two heavy batteries, each with three 2 cm and six 8.8 cm guns.

It should be noted that the other elements were also equipped with antiaircraft weapons, initially only 2 cm, later also 3.7 cm.

*Panzer-Pionier-Bataillon* 130 consisted of:

Staff and logistics company (communications, machine and survey platoon on *Schützenpanzerwagen,* logistics echelon),

three pioneer companies, each with 27–28 halftracks including two with 8 cm mortars and six armored flamethrowers,

One heavy bridging column.

*Panzer-Nachrichten-Abteilung* 130, with

staff,

telephone company, partially in light half-tracks, partly on wheeled vehicles,

radio company, partly half-tracked, partly on wheels,

light column (as of autumn, logistics echelon, motorized.)

*Sanitätstruppen* 130

two medical companies and three ambulance platoons.

*Panzerdivisions-Nachschubtruppen* 130

With a supply company (*Nachschub-Kompanie*) and six 90 ton truck companies (later four 120 ton companies) the transport tonnage was limited to start with. However, the worst part of the picture was the strange assortment of vehicles, totalling 96 types, 58% of which were of foreign manufacture, which produced a nearly impossible situation with respect to spare parts. At that time in the war there were no longer enough proper German-made military transport vehicles in existence, so the Division received whatever was on hand.

*Kraftfahr-Park-Truppen*

The three workshop companies and the motor-vehicle parts echelon were equipped to care for all but the armoured vehicles. Assigned armourers also cared for weapons and equipment. One company dealt primarily with short-term repairs, the second specialized in those that were expected to take more than 48 hours.

*Verwaltungstruppen* 130

Under the Division IVa the housekeeping troops included an administrative company, which took care of rations, pay, clothing and *Marketenderwaren* (like an American PX, but distributed at no charge), a bakery company and a butchering company.

*Feldpostamt* 130

Field post office with three officials, seven non-coms and eight men.

*Feld-Ersatz-Bataillon* 130

Initially with staff and replacement echelons for the most important combat specialties, as of fall of 1944 it became staff, three companies and a logistics company.

The field-replacement-battalion formed the Division's reserve for replacing officers and men, assembling replacements sent on from the replacement army and continuing their training for the conditions of the front. As conditions worsened, there was little opportunity for training, which, given the declining quality of replacements and of their initial training was doubly disadvantageous.

# PART I

## *PANZER LEHR DIVISION* IN NORMANDY THROUGH TO THE WITHDRAWAL FROM FRANCE

# ACTIVATION OF *PANZER LEHR DIVISION* 130, HUNGARIAN INTERLUDE AND FURTHER TRAINING PRIOR TO THE NORMANDY INVASION

In January 1944 the various *Lehrtruppen*, the training/demonstration units that were to constitute *Panzer Lehr Division* 130, assembled for the training and activation of the division in northeastern France, the various elements being quartered in Nancy, Verdun, Lunéville, Pont à Mousson and Toul.

Before training and activation had reached a useable level, the Division was warned for movement to the area of the 19th *Armee* near Avignon or Carcassone in southern France in fear of an Allied landing on the Mediterranean coast of France.

However, even as movement to southern France seemed imminent, on 6 March 1944 orders arrived that the Division would, instead, move to the Vienna area in Austria. This movement interrupted the process of organization and training. Rumours abounded. The facts were that the Division was to be employed as part of Hitler's plan to occupy Hungary. Hitler feared that Hungary's Regent, Admiral Horthy, was planning to jump ship, abandoning the foundering Nazi cause and taking Hungary out of the war or, even worse, switching sides. Hence the surprising change in plans for *Panzer Lehr Division* 130.

The Division's Hungarian interlude involved no combat and, while it interrupted training plans, it did provide valuable experience in functioning as a division and planning and executing movements. While in Hungary the division resumed training. The move to the east raised the danger that the Division might be sucked into the maelstrom of the Eastern Front.

According to *General* Warlimont, the acting Chief of the *Wehrmachtführungsstabe*, it was only with great difficulty that *Panzer Lehr Division* 130 and some of the other units detached from the West for this special operation in Hungary regained their original designation as reserved to counter the imminent Western Allied invasion.

On 29 April *Generalinspekteur der Panzertruppe* Guderian ordered that the Division, starting 1 May, was to return by rail to the area under *Oberbefehlshaber West*.

The Division war diary noted:

> The six weeks commitment in Hungary have, despite the, especially initial, difficulties, given the Division opportunity to bring the activation and training to a definite conclusion. Although training in cooperation of arms still needs more practice, the units have made good progress in individual and weapons training and the exercises have resulted in understanding of the particular forms of employment of the individual elements.

*Generalleutnant* Fritz Bayerlein, commander of *Panzer-Lehr* Division 130 from inception until late January 1945, and author of many of the reports presented in this book. Photo taken March 1944. (Bundesarchiv 146-1978-033-02)

The Division moved to the area west of Paris, the various elements billeted in the Chartres – Le Mans – Orléans area. Concern about increasing danger of air attack resulted in great dispersal and emphasis on camouflage.

Because of the danger from the air, barracks and cities were avoided, all units bivouacking in forests and farmsteads surrounding smaller communities. Daytime movement and activity was greatly restricted.

On 1 May *Generalmajor* Bayerlein was promoted to *Generalleutnant*. Personnel and materiel continued to arrive during May. Routes leading to probable areas of commitment were reconnoitered and determined. As of 1 June, the division was still short 487 (15%) non-commissioned officers but had an excess of enlisted men. The Division had, on that day, 229 tanks and tank-destroyers ready for action and 658 *SPW* (armoured half-tracks). It was rated as ready for any aggressive employment.

# THE NORMANDY INVASION

The Allied invasion of Normandy began on 6 June. At 0415 in the early morning the Division's troops were placed in readiness by telephone. As the troops feverishly prepared to move out, the Division received a preliminary order from *Oberbefehlshaber West, Feldmarschall* von Rundstedt:

> The *Panzer-Lehr-Division* is to hold itself in readiness in its assembly area to advance toward Caen – Bayeux. The Division will provisionally be attached to *Armeeoberkommando* 7 [Command of the German 7th *Armee*]. Further instructions [are to be received from] *Armee*headquarters in Le Mans. The Commander is to proceed there for briefing.

The Division commander, *Generalleutnant* Bayerlein learned about the situation in the landing zone. Subject to approval by the *Wehrmachtsführungsstab*, which had to release the divisions from its reserve, "The I *SS-Panzer Korps – General der Waffen-SS* Sepp Dietrich – is to attack with the 716th *Infanterie Division,* 21st *Panzer Division* and *12th* SS-Panzer Division, seal off the east bank of the Orne and throw the enemy [forces] that have penetrated west of the Orne back into the sea."[1]

At about 1430 hours the *Führungsstab* also released *Panzer Lehr Division* 130 for commitment against the beachhead. At 1730, due to the worsening situation at the bridgehead, *Panzer Lehr Division* 130 was attached to the I *SS-Panzer Korps*, of which *Generalmajor* Kraemer, interviewed below, was chief of staff.

*Generalleutnant* Bayerlein, the Division Commander, did his best to convince 7th *Armee* that the Division would be unable to complete the movement during the hours of darkness and that daytime movement would lead to serious losses due to Allied air attacks and, in fact, would not result in the Division arriving any sooner. His views were emphatically rejected. The Division would keep moving, day and night.

1 Note – *Obergruppenführer und General der Waffen-SS* Joseph 'Sepp' Dietrich was promoted to *Oberstgruppenführer und Generaloberst der Waffen-SS* on 20 April 1944.

Conversation between *Oberbefehlshaber West* Gerd von Rundstedt (left) and *Generalfeldmarschall* Erwin Rommel, commander Army Group B. Photo taken at the Hotel 'George V', Paris, December 1943. (Bundesarchiv 101I-718-0149-17A)

*Generalfeldmarschall* Hans-Günther von Kluge, successor to von Rundstedt as *Oberbefehlshaber West*, France 1944. (Bundesarchiv 101I-299-1823-12)

*Panzer Lehr Division* 130 moved out on three separate march routes: *Panzer-Lehr-Regiment* 130 and the Division staff proceeded via the center route, Nogent-le-Rotrou – Alençon – Argentan – Flers; *Panzergrenadier-Regiment* 901 marched via the northern route from Illiers to Thury-Harcourt. *Panzergrenadier-Regiment* 902 took the southern route from Vibray to Villers-Bocage.

From the very start the march turned into a nightmare as constant Allied air attacks left the route marked by columns of dark smoke rising from burning vehicles. Even at night, 'Christmas Tree' flares lit the scene for further attacks. Bayerlein's fears were amply realized. The ferocity of the enemy air attacks exceeded anything that had been imagined.

The Division sent a liaison officer to the headquarters of the 716th *Infanterie-Division* which had been defending at the coast. The 716th *Infanterie-Division* had already been reduced to a few isolated pockets of resistance. The morrow's attack by the 21st *Panzer Division* and 12th *SS-Panzer Division 'Hitlerjugend'* was discussed. The attack was to be launched at noon on 7 June. By the morning of 7 June *Panzer Lehr's Panzer* IV *Abteilung* (II./*Panzer-Lehr-Regiment* 130) was barely half-way on its 160 kilometre march, at the forest just north of Alençon, where it had to stop to refuel. While refuelling it was spotted and again attacked from the air, losing more tanks and wheeled vehicles.

The march continued, with greater spacing and in smaller groups, but losses continued to mount Ritgen (p. 106) states that the early report of the destruction of 5 *Panzer* IV, 84 *SPW* and prime-movers and 90 wheeled vehicles was exaggerated, but actual losses of precious vehicles, especially of the vital fuel tankers, were heavy and the time loss was even worse.

At this point the interviews below take over the account.

*Generalfeldmarschall* Erwin Rommel, commander Army Group B. (Bundesarchiv 146-1973-012-43)

# MS # B–814

## QUESTIONS TO FRITZ KRAEMER[2]

Translator's note: At first all that was available was a translation by an Army translator. Then the original turned up. Wording slightly differs on the page of 'Questions to be asked … ', nothing significant. Apparently questions were in German, so Kraemer could read them. The questions were then back-translated, apparently separately for the two versions of his answers, one in the original German, the other as translated by an army interpreter.

Although, in general, the army interpreter did well, several significant errors emerged when his version was compared with the German original. Therefore I discarded his version and worked directly from the German.

These questions were in English and are copied precisely.

## QUESTIONS TO BE ANSWERED BY KRAEMER[3]

1. When did 12th SS Pz Division begin moving from the Durex [Dreux] area? How far did it get 6 June? Did it have tanks in position to attack on the morning of 7 June?

2. What were the first orders given to Panzer Lehr Division? When were they received? When was Panzer Lehr ordered to move? What was its designated assembly area? What was its mission? What elements did it have in position to attack on the morning of 7 June? What elements were ready on 8 June?

3. What happened during 8 June? Apparently I SS Panzer Corps had scheduled an attack west of Caen for the morning. It also seems that no such attack took place. Apparently Panzer Lehr Division did not move from its assembly areas near Thury-Harcourt during the day. At the end of the day 12th SS Panzer Division was holding a line northwest of Caen roughly from Authie to Carpiquet. Did 12th SS Panzer Division try to attack? Did it become involved immediately in defensive battles? What tanks did it have in action?

## MS # B–814 – ANSWERS BY FRITZ KRAEMER

Translated by Frederick P. Steinhardt. German unit designations standardized for uniformity.

Fritz K R A E M E R Landsberg, 28.4.48

I) 12th *SS-Panzer Division 'Hitlerjugend'*

2 See explanatory note following this pair of interviews for background and context of *Panzer Lehr's* movement to the Normandy invasion front and activity there.

3 Translator's note: *Generalmajor* Fritz Kraemer was a regular army officer attached to the *Waffen–SS* as Chief of Staff of the I *SS-Panzer Korps*.

1. The 12th *SS-Panzer Division 'Hitlerjugend'* moved out, on 5 June, from its billeting area northwest of Paris toward the mouth of the Seine. *Oberbefehlshaber West* [the Commander in Chief, West, *Feldmarschall* von Rundstedt] issued the order [for this movement] through the *General der Panzertruppen West* [*General* Geyr von Schweppenburg].

   Basis: Assembly for defence against expected enemy landings west of the mouth of the Seine.

   Departure of the Division in the evening of 5 June.

   Intense aerial attacks during the movement until darkness fell.

2. The 12th *SS-Panzer Division 'Hitlerjugend'* was attached to the I *SS-Panzer Korps* effective 1500 hour, 6 June, and was immediately diverted to an area between Falaise and Caen.

   Mission: Concentration and assembly for attack west of Caen in conjunction with the 21st *Panzer Division* (This division had, for some time, already been stationed in the area on both sides of and south of Caen.)

   Ia: *Oberstleutnant i. G.* von Berlichingen.[4]

   The leading elements of the 12th *SS-Panzer Division 'Hitlerjugend'* arrived in the intended area in the morning of 7 June.

   *SS-Panzer-Aufklärungs-Abteilung* 12, commanded by *Sturmbannführer* Brettmer, established contact on 7 June with the 21st *Panzer Division* and an infantry division stationed at the coast (command post in a big command-bunker at the west edge of Caen).

   The Division's armour did not arrive until evening of 7 June. The Division had no enemy contact on 7 June.

   The commander of *SS-Panzer-Regiment* 12, *Obersturmbannführer* Wünsche (in English captivity) has, certainly, prepared extensive reports.

II) *Panzer Lehr Division* 130

By orders of the 7th *Armee*, *Generalmajor* Pemsel[5], the Division was set in march to an area southwest of Caen and attached to the I *SS-Panzer Korps* during the night of 6/7 June.

The Division Commander, *Generalleutnant* B e y e r l e i n [*sic.*], can give details.

III) The I *SS-Panzer Korps* was attached with staff and corps troops to the 7th *Armee* at about 1500 hours on 6 June.

Mission: The I *SS-Panzer Korps* was to attack the enemy that had landed near Caen and throw him back into the sea.

---

4 Translator's note: The abbreviation '*i.G.*', *im Generalstab*, means that the officer so designated went through special training for general staff duties.

5 Translator's note: Pemsel was chief of staff of *General* Dollmann's 7th *Armee*.

Attached to the corps were the 21st *Panzer Division*, 12th *SS-Panzer Division 'Hitlerjugend'* and, in anticipation [of its arrival], *Panzer Lehr Division* 130. The attack was to begin on 7 June, the time to be reported. The corps staff and corps units (communications section [*Abteilung*], one heavy tank battalion [*schwere Panzer Abteilung*], one artillery *Abteilung*[=battalion]) were set in march on 6 June. Their last elements arrived during the night of 7/8 June.

On 7 and 8 June (mornings) only the 21st *Panzer Division* attacked, conducting localized thrusts.

During the afternoon of 8 June the 21st *Panzer Division* (right) and elements of the 12th *SS-Panzer Division 'Hitlerjugend'* (left) were committed in an attack west of Caen in order to gain a usable assembly area for the combined attack of the 12th *SS-Panzer Division* and *Panzer Lehr Divison*130. In addition this (locally limited) attack was intended to prevent any further advance of the English to extend their beachhead.

Due to the unheard-of strength of enemy aerial attacks, the Division's movements to the areas specified on 6 June took longer that foreseen by the superior commands. Daytime movements were practically excluded. The German *Luftwaffe*, unfortunately, was not visible during those days.

The 21st *Panzer Division* and 12th *SS-Panzer Division 'Hitlerjugend'* went over to the defence late in the evening of 8 June in the positions attained. It was necessary to wait for the arrival of the entire *Panzer Lehr Division* 130.

I can no longer give locations and lines without maps.

About 50 tanks of the 21st *Panzer Division* and 60 tanks of the 12th *SS-Panzer Division 'Hitlerjugend'* took part in the attack. Elements of the 21st *Panzer Division* were employed east of Caen. There was no intention of remaining on the defensive.

During 7 and 8 June it became evident that the infantry division that had been stationed at the coast had been almost entirely destroyed (the number of the division is no longer known).

Signed: Fritz K r a e m e r

## MS # B–814 – ADDITIONAL QUESTIONS TO BAYERLEIN

Translated by Frederick P. Steinhardt.

23 April 1948
Additional Questions. [to Fritz Bayerlein]

1. (Questions 1 – 5). *Panzer Lehr Division* 130 remained in the Nogent le Rotrou – Chateaudun – Vendom area starting 8 May as *OKW* [*Oberkommando der Wehrmacht*] reserve. Routes for movement into the presumptive landing areas were reconnoitered and determined.

a. In Normandy – Caen, Bayeux and St. Lo areas.

b. In Brittany – Brest area and south thereof.

a. [tr. note- The original document repeats 'a' and 'b', as given here, with no break, heading or explanation.]

From *Oberbefehlshaber West* at 0400 hours in the morning: 'The Allies have landed between the Orne and the mouth of the Vire. *Panzer Lehr Division* is to prepare to move out.'

b. From *Oberbefehlshaber West* via *Panzer Gruppe West* at 0600 hours in the morning: '*Panzer Lehr* is to assemble to advance toward Caen – Bayeux by 1700 hours in the Nogent le Rotrou – La Ferte Bernarde – Montfort area along the Chartres – Le Mans road. The Division will be attached to the 7th *Armee*. Further instructions in *Armee Hauptquartier* Le Mans. Division Commander [is to proceed] there for briefing.'

From the 7th *Armee* at 1730 hours the Division received the following orders:

'The *Panzer Lehr Division* 130' is immediately to depart from its Nogent – Le Mans assembly area. It is to depart immediately via the line Argentan – Mortain and reach the Thury Harcourt – Aunay – Benie Bocage area by a night march. The Division will be attached to the I *SS-Panzer Korps*, with which it is to establish immediate contact.'

Note: No attention was given to the Division Commander's opinion that this objective could not be attained during the night and that a daytime move would result in extremely heavy losses due to the expected constant enemy air attacks and also would not result in any significant savings in time.

2. (Question 6) The mission was merely to reach the Thury Harcourt area. The I [*SS-Panzer*] *Korps* was to issue further orders. These orders were to read something like: Attack the enemy forces that had landed near Bayeux – Caen, destroy them and eliminate the beachhead.

The Division Commander tried throughout the entire night of 6/7 June to find the corps staff in order to get orders. However, the staff was nowhere to be found.

3. (Question 7) In the morning of 7 June the leading elements of the Division march-column were roughly in the line Argentan – Domfront. The Division was considerably spread-out in depth. The Division was thus still far distant from a jump-off position for an attack. There was still no sort of attack order nor assembly position for an attack issued by the corps.

In the afternoon of 7 June, at the headquarters of the I *SS-Panzer Korps*, which had, at last, been located southeast of Thury Harcourt, the Division received the following orders: '*Panzer Lehr Division* 130 is to reach the Norrey – Brouay area (west of Caen, at the Caen – Bayeux railroad line) by the morning of 8 June and be in readiness there to attack to the coast between Courseulles sur Mer and Arromanches. The attack will be conducted along with the 12th *SS-Panzer Division 'Hitlerjugend'* with the objective of crushing and eliminating the bridgehead.'

4. In the morning of 8 June at 0700 hours the following units were ready to attack on the line Norrey – Brouay (at the Caen – Bayeux railroad line):

   One battalion of *Panzergrenadier-Regiment* 901 at Norrey,

   one battalion *Panzergrenadier-Regiment* 902 at Brouay,

   two artillery *Abteilungen* [ = battalions],

   no tanks, since, due to the lengthy approach march, they could not yet be present.

   *Panzeraufklärungs-Lehr-Abteilung* 130 and *Panzer-Pionier-Bataillon* 130 were already committed in the Tilly area as flank protection.

5. (Question 8.) The attack order was not initially carried out in order to await the arrival of the armour. After they had captured Brouay, the troops of *Panzergrenadier-Lehr-Regiment* 902 were, themselves, attacked by strong English forces and had difficulty holding the place. The following order from I *SS-Panzer-Korps* arrived in the afternoon: 'Do not carry out the attack. The Division will be withdrawn from the Norrey – Brouay sector of the front and shifted during the night of 8/9 June to the Tilly area, where it will attack in the morning of 9 June along the Tilly – Bayeux road with the objective of capturing Bayeux.

6. (Question 9) *Kampfgruppe* 901 was pulled out of the front in the evening of 8 June. *Kampfgruppe* 902, on the other hand, had to remain in Brouay since it had already been cut off by the English (Its extraction did not succeed until the next day). During the night of 8/9 [June] the II *Bataillon* of *Panzergrenadier-Lehr-Regiment* 902 and one *Panzer Abteilung* arrived in the Tilly area, so the attack along the Tilly – Bayeux road could be carried out in the morning of 9 June with the II.*Bataillon* of *Panzergrenadier-Lehr-Regiment* 902, *Panzeraufklärungs-Lehr-Abteilung* 130 and one *Panzer Abteilung*. By noon the attack reached Ellon (south of Bayeux) as orders arrived to halt the attack, hold in the line Tilly – Lingevres – la Belle Epine and go over to defence.

   In the event of additional questions or if more extensive answers are required to the questions, I await orders.

Signed Fritz Bayerlein

# *PANZER LEHR DIVISION* 130 AND THE JUNE 7–9 COUNTERATTACKS AGAINST THE NORMANDY INVASION

A key element in understanding this confused and confusing series of events is that the confusion started at the top and received little clarification at other levels. As Hubert Meyer makes clear in *Die Kriegsgeschichte der 12. SS-Panzerdivision 'Hitlerjugend'*, (pp. 89ff.), the destruction of communications resulting from the pre-invasion air-strikes combined with mandatory radio silence during movements and the effects of constant air-attacks on the moving units resulted in misinformation and misunderstanding at all levels. As a prime example, at 0400 hours in the morning of 7 June Rommel's Chief of Staff informed him that the three *Panzer* divisions attached to the I. *SS-Panzer Korps* were already in their assembly positions, ready to counterattack with all available forces. In fact, the 21st *Panzer Division* was, at that time, in contact with the enemy, west of the Orne, on the defensive. The other divisions were still *en route* and unable to report their whereabouts or condition due to radio silence. The description that follows is based largely on Ritgen's account in *Die Geschichte der Panzer Lehr Division im Westen, 1944 1945,* Jean-Claude Perrigault's *La Panzer-Lehr-Division* and Hubert Meyer's *Die Geschichte der 12. SS-Panzer-Division 'Hitlerjugend'.*

When *Generalleutnant* Bayerlein, the commander of *Panzer Lehr Division* 130, finally located the command post of the I *SS-Panzer Korps* in the afternoon of 7 June, he learned the 7th *Armee* was calling for, the elimination of the enemy beachhead west of the Orne river in a decisive armoured attack by the I *SS-Panzer Korps* that was to take place on 8 June.

The resultant Division attack order for 8 June 1944 read:[6]

1. Enemy forces that landed from the sea are established in the Cherbourg – Caen – Caen-Bayeux highway area. [ed. note- Ritgen gives this paragraph as 'Enemy airborne troops … , which appears to be in error, so I have followed Perrigault.]

2. German strongpoints are still holding at the coast and in the enemy landing area.

3. *I. SS-Panzer Korps* with attached 21st *Panzer Division*, 12th *SS-Panzer Division* and *Panzer Lehr Division* is to attack the beachhead from the Caen – St Croix area and attain the line St. Aubin – Vauvres – Creully. In addition it is to screen the left flank in the line Carcagny – Ellon –Trungy with reconnaissance forces.

4. *Panzer Lehr Division* is to position itself during the night of 7/8 June 1944 in the Bretteville – St. Croix area by 0300 hours on 8 June in readiness to attack when ordered toward Courselles [Courseulles].

---

6 This differs between Ritgen and Perrigault, each including portions the other skips. Also, Ritgen appears to be in error in para 1, referring to enemy airborne troops.

5. *Panzergrenadier-Lehr-Regiment* 901 is to be ready on the right, *Panzergrenadier-Lehr-Regiment* 902 on the left.

   Boundary line: Le Mesnil-Patry – Putot (902) – Sequeville (901) – Lantheuil (902).

   Front line of the assembly area is the road to Bayeux.

6. Routes of advance: for *Panzergrenadier-Lehr-Regiment* 901: Thury-Harcourt – Curcy – Evrecy – Moudrainville [*sic.*] – Cheux.

   [tr. note – The type font used for place names on the detailed map of Normandy that the Germans used is peculiar in that frequently a lower case 'u' and lower case 'n' are easily confused. What seemed, at first, to be inexplicable mis-spellings of some French place names in a variety of sources, particularly in Kurt Meyer's [*'Panzermeyer's'*] account, *Panzergrenadiere*, suddenly became comprehensible upon close examination of that map. Hence the probable explanation for the mis-spelling here of Mondrainville. A good photocopy of that map which survives considerable photographic enlargement is *Karte 1* in the map section of Herbert Meyer's *Kriegsgeschichte der 12. SS-Panzer-Division 'Hitlerjugend.*]

   for *Panzergrenadier-Lehr-Regiment* 902: Villers-Bocage – Juvigny – Fontenay.

7. *Panzer-Artillerie-Regiment* 130 is to take position in the assembly area such that it can cover the assembly area and the attack, with *Schwerpunkt* [point of main emphasis] on supporting *Panzergrenadier-Lehr-Regiment* 902. *Schwere Artillerie Abteilung* 992 will, for movement purposes to the assembly area, be attached to *Panzergrenadier-Lehr-Regiment* 902.

8. *Panzer-Aufklärungs-Lehr-Abteilung* 130 is to advance to the northwest via Villers-Bocage, attaining the line Le-Douet – Ellon – Trungy, thereby securing the left flank of the Division. *SS-Panzer Aufklärungs Abteilung* 12 is to continue securing the line, in contact, to the east to the assembly area of the Division. Boundary: Tilly – Bayeux road (to *Panzer-Aufklärungs-Lehr Abteilung* 130).

9. *Panzer-[Pionier]-Bataillon* 130, to which the *Divisions-Begleit-Kompanie* is attached for march purposes, is to attain the Rauray – Tessel area at 0500 hours on 8 June.to be available to the Division.

10. *Panzer-Lehr-Regiment* 130 and *Panzerjäger-[Lehr]- Abteilung* 130 are to close up behind *Panzer-Pionier-Bataillon* 130 to be available to the Division.

11. *Heeres-Flak-Abteilung* 311 … .

12. Medical units …

13. Command post in the Cheux area.'

These orders were far removed from the reality of the situation, but did determine the organization of the Division for the upcoming battle.

*Obergruppenführer und General der Waffen-SS* Joseph 'Sepp' Dietrich, commander I *SS-Panzer-Korps*. Photo taken in 1944. (Bundesarchiv 183-J27366)

According to Perrigault (p. 160), *SS-Obergruppenführer und General der Waffen-SS* Dietrich, commanding the I *SS-Panzer-Korps* realized the necessity of launching the 8 June attack with the forces actually on hand. Since *Panzer Lehr's* two *Panzergrenadier* regiments had not arrived, he modified his plan of attack, assigning *Panzer Lehr's* original zone to 12th *SS-Panzer-Division 'Hitlerjugend's' Panzergrenadier-Regiment* 26. That regiment also had many delays in its approach march, arriving west of Caen in the evening of 7 June. Its 1st *Bataillon* occupied the village Cheux, which had been specified in *Panzer Lehr's* attack order as *Panzer Lehr Division* 130's command post.

When the leading elements of *Panzer Lehr Division* 130 began to arrive, they found *'Hitlerjugend'* troops already in their assigned assembly area, which partly coincided with that already assigned to 12th *SS-Panzer-Division 'Hitlerjugend's' SS-Panzergrenadier-Regiment* 26.

Hubert Meyer suggests that, perhaps, I *SS-Panzer Korps* intended to shift *'Hitlerjugend's'* 26th *Panzergrenadier-Regiment* to the right, in conformity with its sister regiment, thereby clearing its former assembly area for *Panzer Lehr*. If so, neither division involved was so informed. Nor was *Panzer Lehr* informed that the enemy was already into the front of its assembly area.

When the first elements of 12th *SS-Panzer Division 'Hitlerjugend'* arrived, *Standartenführer* Kurt Meyer, generally known as '*Panzermeyer*', commanding *SS-Panzergrenadier-Regiment* 25, set up his command post in one of the towers of the Abbaye d'Ardennes on the northwest fringe of Caen. He immediately saw that Canadian forces were advancing dangerously fast and committed his reinforced regiment to an attack, thereby committing *SS-Panzergrenadier-Regiment* 25 on the right of *'Hitlerjugend's'* sector.

The progress of the Division's elements was delayed during the second night of their movement by detours which tracked vehicles had torn up to the point where wheeled vehicles got stuck and by difficulties getting through bombed cross-roads-communities. Bayerlein's vehicle was knocked out in an aerial attack that left him with minor wounds but killed his driver.

There is confusion regarding *Panzer Lehr Division* 130's actions on 8 June. The Canadian 3rd Infantry Division had already crossed the Caen – Bayeux road, which had been specified as the front of *Panzer Lehr's* assembly area. In the area specified for *Panzergrenadier-Lehr-Regiment* 901 the Royal Winnipeg Rifles occupied Putot-en-Bessin by noon of 8 June, the Regina Rifle Regiment in Bretteville l'Orgueilleuse, with companies in position south of Norrey-en-Bessin and at Villeneuve. Canadian outposts were on both sides of the railroad and south of the Caen – Bayeux highway with loose contact with the British 50th (Northumberland) Division to the west. The Canadians planned to continue their attack toward Buron.

The 12th *SS-Panzer Division 'Hitlerjugend's* 8 June attack achieved little, barely hanging on to Brouay. After changing hands several times, Putot ended up Canadian and Norrey remained so. Before even reaching the specified assembly area from which it was to launch the attack, *Panzergrenadier-Lehr-Regiment* 901 was thereby halted right after passing through Cheux, where it awaited orders that never came.

The leading elements of *Panzergrenadier-Lehr-Regiment* 902's II *Bataillon* reached the Fontenay – Tilly area, its I *Bataillon* still lagging far behind. *SS-Panzeraufklärungs-Abteilung* 12 (*'Hitlerjugend'*) secured in front of the sector in the general line Brouay – railroad line – le Douet.. Isolated elements of the battered 352nd *Infanterie Division* conducted a valiant fighting retreat before superior enemy forces.

As *Panzergrenadier-Lehr-Regiment's* II *Bataillon* reached the railway line near Brouay and le Bas d'Audrieu it found a melee of German and hostile troops with leading elements of enemy forces advancing on both Brouay and le Bas d'Audrieu. The Nottingham Yeomanry tank battalion bypassed Loucelles to the west, capturing the railroad crossing and Point 103. That evening the Dorset infantry and tanks of the 4/7 Dragoon Guards took Loucelles and the Audrieu area, Audrieu itself remaining divided between the two sides during the night.

*Panzergrenadier-Lehr-Regiment* 902's II *Bataillon* held onto the railway crossing at Brouay initially, setting up the regimental command post in the nearby chateau's park, where British tanks rolled up to the park entrance and shot up the command post and vehicles. An observation plane then directed naval gunfire on the hapless scene, exacting heavy losses in men and equipment in the Brouay area and to its south.

With *Panzergrenadier-Lehr-Regiment* 902's II *Bataillon* caught up in the British 8th Armoured Brigade Group's advance there could be no hope of a concerted attack by the divisions of the I *SS-Panzer Korps* on 8 June.

The long-awaited II/*Panzer-Lehr-Regiment* 130 languished since early morning of 8 June in the Monts chateau park awaiting orders for the scheduled attack that never came..

During the night of 8/9 June *Panzergruppe West* (*General* Geyr von Schweppenburg) took over command of the Calvados sector from 7th *Armee*. The *Panzergruppe* ordered preparations for the joint counterattack during the night of 10/11 June to divide the British bridgehead. But now it is necessary to go back to 7 June.

On 7 June the British 50th (Northumbrian) Division occupied Bayeux after patrols of the 2nd Battalion of the Essex Regiment of the 56th Infantry Battalion had found little opposition there the previous evening. The German command realized there was a major opening for a British advance south through Bayeux with little hindrance to the south, southwest and southeast. Therefore the emphasis now shifted to recapturing Bayeux before *General* Geyr von Schweppenburg's *Panzergruppe West*, controlling the three *Panzer* divisions, could launch the major armoured attack.to the coast.

Accordingly, I *SS-Panzer Korps* redirected *Panzer Lehr Division* 130 to shift west, assemble on both sides of the Tilly – Bayeux highway and recapture Bayeux. With some of its elements already involved in combat, others yet on the approach march, the *Panzer-Lehr Division* was less than enthused about the new mission.

Nevertheless, those elements of the Division that were available were in position in the morning of 9 June to launch the attack: *Panzergrenadier-Regiment* 901, reinforced with *Panzerjäger-Abteilung* 130 was on the right, straddling the Seulles River; on the left was *gepanzerte Gruppe Schönburg* (II/*Panzer- Lehr-Regiment* 902 and I/*Panzergrenadier-Lehr-Regiment* 902.) The remainder of *Panzergrenadier-*

*Lehr-Regiment* 902 was still hotly engaged in Brouay. *Panzeraufklärungs-Lehr-Abteilung* 130 continued to secure the Division's left flank in the line Ellon – Trungy.

At this point *Generalleutnant* Bayerlein had to look to his right flank. Enemy pressure mounted near Tilly. Audrieu went lost. Bayerlein ordered *Panzergrenadier-Lehr-Regiment* 901 to forego the attack on Bayeux and concentrate on holding Tilly.

Late in the morning of 9 June *Gruppe von Schönburg* launched its attack northward, its first objective, the village of Ellon. *Generalleutnant* Bayerlein accompanied the assault group. Ellon fell without resistance, but, as the force exited Ellon to the north, enemy armour was spotted to the northeast. Bayerlein then ordered the attack be held up, whether on his own initiative or on orders from higher up is, according to Ritgen's account, unclear.

The entire sector of the front was under pressure. *Panzergrenadier-Lehr-Regiment* 901 was having a hard time hanging on to Tilly. New enemy forces were attacking from Hill 103, while 12th *SS-Panzer Division 'Hitlerjugend'* was under attack at Cristot.

The armour was pulled back to its jump-off position. As Ritgen puts it (p.112),

> … the only classic armoured attack conducted by the *Panzer Lehr Division* in Normandy was at an end. At the same time, the attempt to thwart the enemy that had landed back in to the sea and regain the initiative finally failed.

At this point the Allied air forces also put an end to *Panzergruppe West's* impending attack that was to split the British position. On 11 June, the Royal Air Force wiped out *General* Geyr von Schweppenburg's mobile headquarters, killing most of the general's staff, though he, himself, escaped with wounds. At the time the Germans believed it was the result of *General* Geyr's complete failure to camouflage his headquarters. However, according to Ralph Bennet, *Ultra in the West*, the RAF had been notified of its whereabouts from an Ultra intercept. It was the end of June before *Panzergruppe West* was back in action as a functioning command entity. Thus, *Panzergruppe West's* control of the three armoured divisions was short lived. Command reverted to *Obergruppenführer und General der Waffen-SS* Sepp Dietrich. Dietrich immediately put a hold on the three-*Panzer*-division attack *General* Geyr had planned.

# BATTLE IN THE BOCAGE – THE BATTLE FOR VILLERS-BOCAGE, THE ODON RIVER CROSSINGS AND THE EVRECY HILLS

General Montgomery had looked for the fall of Caen on the first day. Caen was critical. It controlled access to the good tank-country of the Caen-Falaise plain, obvious route of advance toward Paris. The air forces wanted the existing and potential airfield sites on the high ground around Caen. The British were stymied by stubborn German defence in their frontal assault on Caen.

Bayeux, on the other hand, fell with little effort, revealing an as-yet undefended sector beyond *Panzer Lehr Division* 130's left flank. As noted above, the German command responded to this revelation of vulnerability, the I *SS-Panzer Korps* redirecting *Panzer Lehr Division* 130 to recapture Bayeux. Now, however, pressure on *Panzer Lehr's* right flank forced it to give up the attack on Bayeux and concentrate on defending the Tilly area.

Montgomery, thwarted in the direct, frontal assault on Caen, next envisioned a two-pronged envelopment, which would begin on 10 June with two simultaneous attacks. The left arm of the pincers would move out of the small bridgehead east of the Orne, the right arm would be the British 30th Corps, which would move south down the Seulles River valley, capturing Villers-Bocage (originally seen as a D-Day objective). Villers-Bocage, located at the head of the Seulles River valley was at the hub of the entire road network of the region, controlling access to the Odon River valley and Caen, to the east, and to Mont Pinçon, ten miles to the south, the commanding height on a rugged plateau. The British forces would then turn east and link up with the British 1st Airborne Division which was to be dropped in the Odon Valley, near Noyers and Evrecy and prevent the German forces in Caen from escaping.

Montgomery's plan for the air-drop was blocked by Air Chief Marshal Leigh-Mallory. Bad weather in the Channel delayed landing the 51st (Highland) Division and 4th Armoured Brigade, the forces that were to provide the muscle for the left hook. A German attack on the small bridgehead east of the Orne then involved the 51st Division in two days of heavy fighting, assisting the 6th Airborne Division.

With the left arm of the pincers eliminated, Montgomery now put all his hopes on the right arm. The British 30 Corps was to thrust via the Tilly – Norrey area to advance down the Seulles River Valley, capture Villers-Bocage, win crossings over the Odon River, gain the high ground near Evrecy. and cut in behind Caen.

As *Panzer Lehr* suffered severe attrition holding against the frontal attack during the period from 9 – 13 June, British forces elsewhere discovered a gap in the German defences, west of the Aure River. American forces were advancing, almost unopposed, toward Caumont. This inviting gap in the German line of defence appeared to extend all the way from the remaining fragments of the 352nd *Infanterie-Division* retreating before the American thrust to the west flank of *Panzer-Lehr Division* 130's position. The British 7th Armoured Division's commander, General Sir George 'Bobby' Erskine discovered this opening which invited a fast armoured thrust via Caumont and Villers-Bocage. The high ground around Villers-Bocage controlled access to the valley of the Odon River which, in turn, would allow an armoured force to cut in and around, behind the hard-fought Tilly – Norrey sector, west of Caen, cutting the city off from the rear. One of the first effects of that advance would, of course, be to undermine *Panzer Lehr's* position, forcing it to retreat or be cut off.

The British Second Army Commander, General Miles Dempsey and the 30th Corps Commander, Lt.-General G. C. Bucknall, agreed to the proposal, but took

24 hours to react, which turned out to be a critical 24 hours. While the British 50th (Northumberland) Division fixed *Panzer Lehr Division* 130 in eventful frontal fighting, the 22nd Armoured Brigade advanced through the gap around its western flank, meeting practically no resistance. It spent the night of 12 June in Caumont, then moved on to Villers-Bocage. Part of the force continued on through the town to occupy Hill 213, a few miles past Villers-Bocage toward Caen.

Unfortunately for the British, the German 2nd *Panzer Division* had already been alerted to move up from its positions near Amiens and plug this gap. Thanks to the 24 hour delay, the armoured reserve of the I *SS-Panzer Korps* had already started to arrive. The 1st and 2nd companies of *SS-(schwere) Panzer Abteilung* 101 were already in position near Villers-Bocage. *SS-Obersturmführer* Michael Wittmann of the 2nd *Kompanie* spotted the British force, acted immediately and, in a brilliantly conducted, brief action, Wittmann and his company scuttled the British effort, knocking out about 25 of the vaunted British 7th Armoured Division's armoured vehicles, shooting up the accompanying infantry and dealing a severe blow to the morale and reputation of the famed 'Desert Rats'.

The 22nd Armoured Brigade fell back to new positions for the night and requested reinforcement from 30th Corps. Bucknall, commanding 30th Corps, failed to detach the needed reinforcements from the 50th Infantry Division, thinking that the infantry division would break through *Panzer Lehr's* defence, thereby making its way to Villers-Bocage. *Panzer Lehr Division* 130 continued its hard-fought defence and held the British 50th Infantry Division. Bucknall's action, or lack thereof, lost the British their chance. The 22nd Armoured Brigade might well have held its fall-back positions with adequate reinforcement, but, in the event, had to pull back to the previous British lines. The German 2nd *Panzer Division* plugged the gap in the German defences.

Henceforth the British would have to fight their way through the hard way, a lengthy process that would take many lives. *Panzer Lehr's* part in this stubborn defence was less spectacular than Michael Wittmann's, but was significant in denying the British their hoped for access to the Orne River crossings and the back-door to Caen. From *Panzer Lehr's* viewpoint, the attempted British end-run via Villers-Bocage and its scuttling was marginal to the Division's continued battle to 'hold the line'.

For nearly four weeks *Panzer Lehr Division* 130 would discover the difficulties and defensive opportunities unique to fighting in Normandy's *bocage*, the terrain of hedgerows growing out of massive, three to four foot high, root-bound earthen ramparts, sometimes single as simple field boundaries, sometimes lining both sides of sunken, narrow lanes. The landscape was compartmentalized by the hedgerows into thousands of small fields, each sealed off from its neighbour, each a separate combat problem. Armour ceased to manoeuvre. Tanks became armoured pill-boxes, dug in for concealment, their crews afraid to exist during daylight for fear of being spotted, painstakingly maintaining the perfection of their camouflage. Enemy artillery employed sensitive fuses to achieve tree-bursts that drove deadly hails of steel fragments down into trenches below. Cut by streams and rivers, with steep hills and woods, the *bocage* offered tremendous opportunities for skilled and stubborn defence, but was punishing for defenders and attackers alike.

Where the country was more open, stone-walled farmsteads provided natural fortresses with good fields of fire.

The Allies found the terrain greatly favoured the German defence, but German armoured commanders were frustrated by the degradation of their once-mobile forces to static defence. Until taken out of the line into *Heeresgruppe* reserve, whence it was called farther west to counter the American bridgehead over the Vire River and Vire-et-Taute Canal in the U. S. push of St. Lô, *Panzer Lehr Division* 130 took part in blocking the British 30th Corps push down the Seulles River Valley to capture Villers-Bocage and gain the crossings of the River Odon and the high ground near Evrecy. *Panzer Lehr Divison* 130 departed the area as, on 2 July, the British Operation 'Epsom' opened the next phase of the major series of battles for the Odon River crossings that made 'Hill 112' infamous in some of the fiercest, horrendously interminable fighting for a commanding piece of ground in the war. *Panzer Lehr* defended the Rauray Ridge in the preliminary phases of Epsom but was then withdrawn to *Heeresgruppe* reserve.

But now back to 9 June.

As noted above, the intended left arm of Montgomery's pincers attack on Caen was stalled by the German 21st *Panzer Division* attack on the 6th Airborne Division, which drew in the 51st (Highland) Division, that division having been intended, with the 4th Armoured Brigade, to provide the main impetus for that arm of the attack.

The British western arm of the pincers involved the 7th Armoured Division attacking on 9 June through the 50th Infantry Division between the Seulles and Aure Rivers with Hottot as the initial objective. The 8th Armoured Brigade Group, initially attached to the 50th Infantry Division, later to the 7th Armoured Division, was to advance via Tilly south to Villers-Bocage.

Late in the morning of 9 June elements of *Panzer Lehr Division* 130 attacked, the Division Commander himself leading the attack at the head of detachments of *Panzeraufklärungs-Lehr-Abteilung* 130. The reconnaissance battalion bypassed Ellon at noon, reaching Argenchy, a small village southwest of Bayeux. At the same time, the tanks of the II./*Panzer-Lehr-Regiment* 130, under Prince von Schönburg-Waldenburg advanced toward Ellon, where they came up against the 56th Infantry Brigade, which was attached to the 49th (West Riding) Infantry Division. The Germans took the village, establishing an excellent basis for the next phase of the attack. However, at that point the attack order was rescinded, the elements involved called back to the Tilly-sur Seulles area.

While *Panzer Lehr* had been attacking north, the British 8th Armoured Brigade Group had launched its own attack in parallel but opposite direction, gaining entry to the village of St. Pierre, the eastern suburb of Tilly-sur-Seulles, thus threatening *Panzer Lehr's* right flank. *Panzer Lehr Division's* I./*Panzergrenadier-Lehr-Regiment* 901 continued to hold the bridge over the Seulles River, but at high cost. That evening *Panzergrenadier-Lehr-Regimenter* 901 and 902 on both sides of the Tilly – Bayeux highway, just north of Tilly-sur-Seulles, 901 on the right, 902 on the left.

Following the cancellation of *Panzer Lehr's* attack to regain Bayeux, *Generalleutnant* Bayerlein reported to I *SS-Panzer-Korps* headquarters where *SS-Obergruppenführer und General der Waffen-SS* Sepp Dietrich made it clear that it was no longer a matter of throwing the enemy into the sea, but of going over to the defensive. The Division was ordered to occupy a line of resistance Cristot – Tilly-sur-Seulles – Verrières.

During the night of 9/10 June *Panzer Lehr Division* 130 (less I./ *Panzerregiment* 6, which had not yet arrived), occupied a 17 kilometre line of resistance extending southwest from Cristot – skirting south of St. Pierre –Tilly-sur-Seulles – Verrières – just north of la Senaudiere – south of la Belle Epine – then bending south along the east bank of the Aure River. Division headquarters, painstakingly camouflaged, was established at the Sermentot farmstead, southwest of Tilly-sur-Seulles.

On 10 June the British 7th Armoured Division planned to advance between the Aure and Seulles Rivers on Villers-Bocage. An early-morning British barrage pounded *Major* Uthe's I./*Panzergrenadier-Lehr-Regiment* 901, and the British achieved some local gains, but a spirited counterattack by three companies of Uthe's battalion (I./ *Panzergrenadier-Lehr-Regiment* 901) broke into both the village of St. Pierre and the positions near Point 103. With great difficulty and with strong support from artillery, armour and naval guns, the British hung on to their positions on Point 103 and in the northern part of St. Pierre.

North of Tilly-sur-Seulles and west of the I *Bataillon* positions, the II./ *Panzergrenadier-Lehr-Regiment* 901 was also severely hammered by artillery. In the adjoining sector the 3rd *Kompanie* of *Panzergrenadier-Lehr-Regiment* 902 was on ground where a rocky layer prevented them from properly digging in. Some of the men started to break and run under the fire, but were halted, encouraged and sent back to their positions.

After the barrage the British 22nd Armoured Brigade attacked down the main Bayeux – Tilly road. Infantry support restored movement when the point elements were held up at Jérusalem by combat outposts of the I./ *Panzergrenadier-Lehr-Regiment* 902.

Five British tanks broke through, endangering the command post of the I./ *Panzergrenadier-Lehr-Regiment* 101. Fortunately for the commander of the I./902, the 1st *Kompanie* of *Panzerjäger-Lehr-Abteilung* 130 was nearby and proved its new *Panzerjäger* IV tank-destroyers by knocking out the British tanks.

Partly to prevent other such surprises, *Generalleutnant* Bayerlein embarked on a personal terrain reconnaissance. At this point, after mopping up German resistance in Jérusalem, the 22nd Armoured Brigade resumed its advance. South of Bucéels the British brigade unknowingly intersected Bayerlein's recce. Bayerlein estimated the unsuspecting force as regimental in size. The General immediately dispatched his aide, *Hauptmann* Hartdegan, to bring back whatever he could find, especially a couple of 8.8cm guns.

Hartdegan returned, half-an-hour later, with two 8.8's and four tanks. With the advantage of surprise, the little German force took excellent firing positions and made a shambles of the British unit. The British artillery response was punishing and forced the little German force to fall back to its own lines without loss. The British regiment, whose assembly for the attack had been disrupted, withdrew.

During the afternoon, another German reconnaissance patrol spotted a Scottish brigade forming up for attack and dispersed it by calling down heavy fire from their supporting 15 cm infantry guns.[7]

The above description typifies the the kind of action *Panzer Lehr Division* 130 was involved in until its withdrawal to *Heeresgruppe* reserve, which began on June 26. The remainder of its commitment in the Tilly-sur-Seulles area was equally eventful, with massive artillery preparations and intense British attacks. Again and again local penetrations were cleared up in fierce counterattacks, but, gradually and as the result of severe attrition, sections of the line were forced back. Perrigault provides much fascinating detail, but since such detail is not needed to follow the material covered in the interviews, only a few highpoints will be mentioned.

On 11 June a heavy British attack caused only minor rearrangements of the line, attacks and counterattacks costing lives but ending up with few significant alterations in who held what.. The commander of II./ *Panzer-Lehr-Regiment* 130, Prince Schönburg-Waldenburg, was killed in a counterattack. On the Division's left, la Belle Epine was lost, drawing attention to the weakness between *Panzer Lehr's* left and the 352nd *Infanterie-Division*.

On 12 June heavy fighting continued, again with little net change in the line. The British 22nd Armoured Brigade launched its ill-fated thrust toward Villers-Bocage, halting for the night in Livry.

On 13 June the British 22nd Armoured Brigade continued to Villers-Bocage, lead elements continuing past the town to Hill 213. As detailed above, Michael Wittmann and his company of *Tiger* tanks tore up the British force and put an end to its advance.

A surprised *Panzer Lehr Division* 130 reacted, its II./*Panzer-Lehr-Regiment* 130 was ordered to immediately block the north exits from Villers-Bocage and stand by for a counterattack, while the Division Ia hastily assembled a force of all available soldiers from the Division staff and other elements to likewise occupy a line along the northern edge of the town.

The commander of the II./*Panzer-Lehr-Regiment* 130 put together a force utilizing tanks from the Division repair shop at Parfouru and successfully counterattacked the British on Hill 213. As the *Panzer Lehr* counterattacks developed, the leading elements of the approaching 2nd *Panzer Division* cut the British route of advance in several places and turned toward Villers-Bocage, causing the British to fall back to the high ground near Tracy-Bocage.

While engaged in cleaning up the British penetration on its flank and in its rear, *Panzer Lehr Division* 130 was fully engaged on its front as the attack of the British 50th Infantry Division mounted in intensity. With massive support from artillery and air and against furious defence, after a full day of heavy eventful fighting the British ended up holding part of Lingèvres and taking la Senaudière.

The British 7th Armoured Division was ordered to pull back its force from the positions near Tracy-Bocage which, in light of the newly arrived 2nd *Panzer Division*, had become a liability. Thus ended the British attempt at an end-run around *Panzer Lehr's* left flank.

---

7 In addition to divisional artillery, German infantry regiments had their own light and heavy infantry gun-companies. *Panzer Lehr Regimenter* 901 and 901's 9th companies each had four heavy (15 cm) guns.

*General der Panzertruppen* Heinrich Eberbach, who took over the Caen sector in Normandy on 28 June 1944. (Bundesarchiv 146-1976-096-08)

*SS-Obersturmbannführer* Otto Weidinger, commander of *Kampfgruppe* Weidinger from 2 *SS-Panzer-Division 'Das Reich'*, attached to *Panzer-Lehr* on 27 June 1944, in Normandy. (Bundesarchiv 146-1984-101-05A)

By now both sides were exhausted. *Panzer Lehr Division* 130 had to shorten its left wing, evacuating Lingèvres. The arrival of the 2nd *Panzer Division* on *Panzer Lehr's* left allowed the battered remnants of *Panzergrenadier-Lehr-Regiment* 902 to be pulled out of the line for reconstitution near Sermentot while *Panzergrenadier-Lehr-Regiment* 901 extended its lines westward.

On 15 June the British also caught their breath as the 49th Infantry Division prepared to relieve the British unit east of Tilly-sur-Seulles.

16 June saw a British penetration to the Hottot – Torteval road cleaned up in a hasty counterattack. As a result of the heavy attrition in the Division's front lines, the 12th *SS-Panzer-Division 'Hitlerjugend' Divisions Begleit Kompanie* was attached to *Panzeraufklärungs-Lehr-Abteilung* 130.

Several days of relative quiet on the front were utilized to strengthen the positions, laying mines and improving field fortifications.

On 18 June an extremely heavy artillery preparation helped launch a new British attack. After a day of further heavy, eventful fighting and unsuccessful counterattacks, St. Pierre was lost and, after mining, Tilly evacuated. The main line of resistance was pulled back to the Montilly–Sagy line.

On 19 June, after a quiet morning followed by another intense artillery preparation that started at 1500 hours, the British 50th Infantry Division launched another heavy attack on the boundary of the two regiments. *Panzergrenadier-Lehr-Regiment* 902 cleaned up all penetrations with hasty counterattacks, but its sister regiment was forced back to the edge of Hottot, a counterattack by the reinforced *Panther Abteilung* resulting in only partial success.

By now severe attrition had resulted in casualty numbers exceeding the number of soldiers fighting in the line, leaving only a skeletal cadre of old-hands among the replacements, some of which had to come from the 2nd *Panzer Division's* field replacement battalion.

At this point the great storm that broke up the American artificial 'Mulberry' harbour and severely damaged the British one, dumped heavy rains inland, reducing the battlefield to a morass and cutting off the flow of supplies to the invading Allies. The resultant let-up in the fighting lasted until 24 June. The boundary with the 2nd *Panzer-Division* was shifted, shortening the Division's sector. The exhausted troops made good use of the break in the fighting for reorganization and refitting.

The great storm in the English Channel forced the British to postpone Operation 'Epsom' to 25 June. According to Chester Wilmot (*The Struggle for Europe*, p. 342), in Operation 'Epsom':

> The plan was that the VIII British Corps (O'Connor) should make the main thrust midway between Tilly and Caen. The 15th Scottish Division was to seize a bridgehead across the Odon and create a firm base on the broad ridge between that river and the Orne. Then, while the 43rd Division helped the Scotsmen to consolidate their gains, the 11th Armoured Division would attack south-east, cross the Orne and establish itself astride the Caen – Falaise road on the high ground between Bretteville-sur-Laize and Bourguebus ... In preparation for O'Connor's attack, the 49th Division (of XXX Corps) was to capture Rauray ridge on the previous day, and thus protect the right flank of 15th Scottish.

The preliminary attack to capture Rauray ridge on 25 June was preceded by yet another massive artillery preparation that began at 2000 hours on 24 June. Attacking in heavy ground-mist that lasted for hours and obscured positions, the 49th Division's attack took the Bas de Fontenay at the Division's left boundary and made it to the north edge of the hilltop woods about a kilometre west of Tessel. After extremely heavy fighting and reinforcement with another battalion, the British finally forced the last Germans out of Fontenay and Juvigny. However, the Rauray ridge remained in German hands.

*Panzer Lehr* planned and initiated a counterattack which was cancelled on *Korps* orders.

On 26 June enemy forces concentrated on capturing the Odon crossings and Rauray ridge.

On 27 June they did capture an undamaged Bridge and the village of Rauray. *Panzergrenadier-Lehr-Regiment* 901 was ordered to establish a strong blocking position south of the Tessel Woods to protect *Panzer Lehr's* right flank, endangered by the British breakthrough.

The Division was reinforced on 27 June by *Kampfgruppe Weidinger* of the 2nd *SS-Panzer Division 'Das Reich'* and a company of tank destroyers. Also on 28 June command of the German Front was rearranged. *Panzergruppe West,* later redesignated as the 5th *Panzer Armee,* under *General der Panztertruppen* Eberbach took over the Caen sector, 7th *Panzer Armee,* henceforth under *General der Waffen-SS* Hausser the western sector.

Now it is time to return to the interviews.

# ETHINT 66 – (ML–1079)

7–9 August 1945

**AN INTERVIEW WITH**
**Genlt Fritz Bayerlein**

**PANZER LEHR DIVISION**
**JAN–28 JULY 1944**

[For reasons explained in the introductory letter below, none of the material in this section was translated by Fred Steinhardt]

**DEPARTMENT OF THE ARMY**
**HISTORICAL DIVISION**
**WASHINGTON, D. C.**

[(*sic.*) added by F. Steinhardt to indicate errors preserved from original document]

12 July 1949

Note to: ETHINT 66
By: Kenneth W. Hechler
Major, Infantry (Res)

This oral interview with General Bayerlein was held over a period of 3 days, while General Bayerlein was confined in the hospital at Bad Nauheim with heart trouble. At times General Bayerlein was able to sit up during the oral interview, but some of it was held with him while he was resting in bed. He was extremely eager to talk–infact [*sic.*], one of the main difficulties of the interview was to get him to stop talking in order to clarify some points which he had made. I constantly had to prod the interpreter, Sergeant Kiralfy, to stop and interpret General Bayerlein's rapid flow of language, so we could not only clarify what he had said through further questions, but also to take adequate notes of the points that he was making. We had no German documents or maps with which to assist *General* Bayerlein, but adequate American maps were available and we briefed him on Americans [*sic.*] operations as he went along. He appeared to have no difficulty in recalling any of the details of operations in Normandy.

As noted elsewhere in annotation of Generals[*sic.*] Bayerlein's remarks, he was at times a little anxious to please the questioner by saying complimentary things about American troops. This should be taken into consideration when weighing the credibility of his statements. I see no reason, however, to question General Bayerlein's statements regarding the general tactics, plans and operations of his own division.

No record in German was made at the time of this oral interview, inasmuch as Sergeant Kiralfy, the interpreter, and myself both took copious notes as we went along. Sergeant Kiralfy also took a few notes in German, and these appear parentheticaly [*sic.*] throughout the oral interview report.

This was probably the most exhaustive oral interview which I held with any German commader [*sic.*], and it nearly caused Sergeant Kiralfy to go AWOL because he was so sick of taking notes, interpreting and typing. However, I am certain that although he felt this strongly during the compilation of this report, it did not interfere with his efficiency in interpreting faithfully, and in helping me prepare a very complete report of General Bayerlein's remarks.

I believe that the only other step that we can now take in order to guarantee the authenticity of this report is to have General Bayerlein check it through and make annotations of his own.

## ETHINT 66 – (ML–1079)

| | |
|---|---|
| Title: | Pz Lehr Div (Jan–28 July 44) |
| Source: | Genlt Bayerlein, Fritz |
| Position: | Cmdr, Pz Lehr Div |
| Date: | 7–9 Aug 45 |
| Place: | Bad Nauheim, Germany |
| Interviewer: | Maj Kenneth W. Hechler |

**Foreword**

This interview is one of a series conducted by the Historical Section, ETOUSA[8], and its successors. Unfortunately, only a typed record in English is available for editing. It is not known whether a record in German was made at the time of the interview, nor, if one was made, can the accuracy of the translation be determined. Therefore, no absolute guarantee can be given as to the authenticity and completeness of detail of this version of the interview. Only obvious errors in spelling, punctuation, and grammatical construction have been corrected. All quoted remarks and parenthetical statements, except those of the interviewer and editor which are identified as such, are as they appear in the available record. The sketch referred to in this interview has been reproduced and a copy is included in each copy of ETHINT 66. The original sketch is enclosed with Copy 1.

(signed)
LE ROY S. STANLEY
Capt. Inf.
Historical Editor
Jun 22 1948

[Editor's note– One of the problems in dealing with interviews and reports from captured German officers is that some of them are only available in translated form. Some of the translations, done at the time by U. S. Army translators, leave doubts that could only be resolved by reference to the German originals, which are not always available. Having translated many German unit histories, memoirs and other military history for publication I have developed an awareness of quality in translations, a feel for something that rings true to the original, versus one that is suspect.

Because this interview is a precious source document and, as the letter of introduction states, is not available in the original German because even the original notes were taken in English, I feel that it is worth passing on to the reader my own feeling of total confidence in the accuracy of the translation. It 'rings true'.]

8 Translator's note – European Theater of Operations, U. S. Army.

# ETHINT 66

[remarks contained in parentheses prefaced by 'Ed:' are remarks made by the original editor of the interview in the Historical Division of the U. S. Army. Notes by the editor and translator of this book, Frederick Steinhardt, will be bracketed and prefaced by 'FPS Ed:' or 'tr. note']

1. Q: When Pz Lehr Div moved to Hungary in the spring of 1944, was it understood that it would return before the time of the Invasion?

   A: The Division was activated in France at the end of Jan or beginning of Feb 44. It was completely new, and had completely new equipment. The occupation of Hungary intervened and, as no other division was available, it was thought that the Division could be activated (Ed: organized and trained?) Just as well in that country as in France.

2. Q: Was there any fighting in Hungary which caused the Division losses in personnel or equipment?

   A: No. It was a peaceful occupation. Its real object was to interest Hungary in further war activity by impressing them with German strength.

3. Q: Did this long movement handicap the state of maintenance of the vehicles?

   A: Yes, of course it did. A long movement requires a lot of time, and my main task was to weld my Division together. It was adversely affected by this loss of time.

4. Q: Did this handicap show up in the subsequent battles in Normandy? Can you point to any specific way the Division suffered because of its trip to Hungary?

   A: No, I cannot think of any specific example of this.

5. Q: Was it definitely understood that the Division was to return to France from Hungary?

   A: I had had 3 Pz Div (the 'Berlin' Division) in Russia during the withdrawal from the Donets (Donjesis) and, following this, was recalled to headquarters in East Prussia to see Genobst Guderian (Ed: then Inspector General of Panzer Troops). Guderian told me that a new division was to be activated specifically to meet the Invasion in the West, and that I had been appointed its commander because of my experience in fighting the English and Americans (Ed: in North Africa).

6. Q: Did Guderian give you any instructions as to the technique to be employed by this new division? Why was this division selected as being specially suitable?

   A: Guderian had fought only in Russia and had no experience of any kind in fighting the English and Americans. He miscalculated the whole matter and committed an error of judgement. OKH and Guderian had not adequately

*Generalinspekteur der Panzertruppe* Heinz Guderian (right).
(Bundesarchiv 101I-139-1112-17)

estimated the value and fighting ability of the English and Americans (see my report to the Ninth US Air Force). This error applied to the Allied armor, air force, and infantry, and explains the actions taken by the Germans in the Normandy campaign.[9]

When I assumed command of Pz Lehr Div, Guderian told me in East Prussia on 26 Jan 44, 'With this division alone, you must throw the Allies into the sea. Your objective is the coast – no, not the coast, it is the sea.' ('Mit dieser Division allein muessen Sie die Ango-Amerikaner in das Meer werfen. Ihr Ziel ist die Kueste, nein, nicht die Kueste – es ist das Meer.')

7. Q: Is this map (Interviewer's Note: map of German dispositions in [FPS Ed: U.S.] Twelfth Army Group publication, 'The Destruction of the German Armies in Western Europe') correct as to your location on D-Day?

   A: Yes. We were in the vicinity of Nogent le Rotrou.

8. Q: When did you return to France from Hungary?

   A: We started back on 1 May 44 and arrived 15 May 44. The movement was very difficult as the railroads were partly destroyed. Under normal circumstances, the journey would have taken not more than four days. As early as Mar 44, you had begun to destroy the transportation system behind the Atlantic Wall – the bridges, railroad stations and connections, marshalling [*sic.*] yards, and all forms of transportation. Our troops also suffered losses from night bombing.

9. Q: Was there any hold-up by the French resistance movement through blown bridges, etc?

   A: No. The French did not figure in it at all. On the contrary, the center of FFI resistance was in southern France. [tr. note – FFI = French Forces of the Interior.]

10. Q: Did you use any special security measures for protection against the French resistance movement?

    A: No. In general, there was an order that all troops in France must carry weapons with them, even in the cinema; this rule, however, was already in force, and no special security measure was ordered for my Division.

11. Q: What was the general condition of your Division?

    A: The Pz Lehr Div was the best equipped Panzer-Division that Germany ever had. It was 100 percent armored; even the infantry was completely

9 FPS Ed: *OKH, Oberkommando des Heeres* had been the headquarters and staff for the Commander in Chief of the Army until December 1941, when Hitler took direct command of the Army, at which point it was directly subordinated to him. Although, for some purposes, *OKH* was nominally subordinate to *OKW*, (*Oberkommando der Wehrmacht*, Armed Forces High Command), in general *OKH* commanded ground forces on the Eastern Front, while *OKW* was in control of the remaining theatres of the war.

*Generalfeldmarschall* Gerd von Rundstedt, *Oberbefehlshaber West*, photo taken 1942. (Bundesarchiv 146-1987-047-20)

*Generalfeldmarschall* Rommel shown on a visit to the Atlantic Wall shortly before the invasion, 1944. (Bundesarchiv 101I-719-0223-20)

armored so that in case of counterattack they would not suffer casualties from splinters and shrapnel, artillery, or infantry weapons. The armored infantry traveled in Schuetzenpanzerwagen (half-tracks). All this was because of our unique mission of throwing the invading Allies back into the sea. It was planned to make this the best Panzer-Division that existed.

The big mistake of the higher headquarters was that the half-tracks were not armor protected against aerial attack and, as they would have been exposed to attack from the air, the armored infantry was never used as such during the campaign. These vehicles were left about 60 km behind the line, and the men used as ordinary infantry.[10]

12. Q: Between 26 Jan 44 and 1 May 44, were any additional or new instructions given regarding defense of the coast or throwing back invading forces?

A: Intentionally, everything was planned on a big scale. There were two contradictory ideas. One, the idea of OKH[11], *OB WEST*[12], and of von Geyr (General of Panzer Forces, West)[13], was to allow the enemy to land and launch a counterattack only after he had penetrated a short distance inland. This idea was approved by Hitler, OKW [*Oberkommando der Wehrmacht*], Keitel, Jodl, Guderian, and all higher headquarters (who did not know the English and Americans and thought if they were allowed to land we could easily destroy them. Their opinion was reflected in Goebbels' sneer, 'Er soll nur kommen. Warum kommen Sie nicht?' ('Let them come. Why don't they come?')) They did not take into account the power of the air forces, did not understand the fighting methods of the Allies, and miscalculated the quality of the American commanders.

The other idea was to keep the reserves as far forward as possible and attack immediately when a beachhead was started. This was the view of Rommel. He felt that the coast should be the main line of resistance with the reserves kept very close to the coast in order to counterattack immediately.

Von Rundstedt was undecided as to which of the ideas was the better.

[FPS Ed: Both philosophies had their advantages and disadvantages. Rommel's preference of having the armoured divisions stationed close to the coast, where they could have pitched right into the invasion forces at their most vulnerable time, as

10 FPS Ed: The German *SPW* half-tracks were only lightly armoured, proof against small arms only. The tops were open, so that the infantry within could observe in all directions. That, however, left the occupants vulnerable to all sorts of projectiles and fragments coming from overhead, whether from aircraft, mortars, aerial-bursts, tree-bursts, hand grenades or fire from elevated terrain. The Allies made good, and extensive, use of artillery shells with sensitive fuses in the hedgerow country of the French *bocage* to produce tree-bursts, a problem frequently mentioned in German accounts as producing numerous casualties.

11 FPS Ed: *Oberkommando des Heeres,* Army High Command.

12 FPS Ed: *Generalfeldmarschall* Gerd von Rundstedt, *Oberbefehlshaber West.*

13 FPS Ed: *General der Panzertruppen* Leo, *Freiherr* Geyr von Schweppenburg, *Panzer Gruppe West.*

they disembarked, would have shortened the attacking German divisions' exposure to allied air attack as they moved up, but would have placed them within range of the big naval guns of the assault armada, which turned out to be a terrifically important factor. Rommel had experienced the terrible destructive power of the Allied Air Forces in Africa.

The opposing view was championed by Geyr von Schweppenburg, commander of *Panzergruppe West* who was also extremely experienced armoured commander, though his experience was on the Eastern Front, where he had never met the American and British Air Forces. His plan was to hold the armoured forces so far back that, not only would they would be safe from the naval guns, but they would be able to wait until the enemy had actually landed his forces, know where the real landing was, and then take advantage of the proven German expertise in planning and fighting battles of movement to then defeat the invading forces when they were farther inland. This strategy would keep the armoured forces out of reach of the big naval guns and take advantage of the German's proven superiority, to date, in battles of movement. The big question mark, however, would be whether the Allied air superiority would have negated this advantage by pinning down and destroying the German armoured divisions before they could become effective.

After the fact, in light of the failure of the option chosen – which was a bit of both and sufficient of neither, it is easy to decide that 'something different' would have been better. Most such discussions tend to favour Rommel's point of view with an 'If only he had been given a free hand to concentrate more of the *Panzer* Divisions forward … ' and fail to point out that Rommel showed no signs of certainty as to precisely where the invasion was going to land. In fact, as Bayerlein makes clear in his answers to question 16, Rommel, himself, (and Bayerlein) was still holding out for a 'main invasion' in the 15th *Armee* area. Bayerlein's reply to Question 14, below, may seem to raise questions about this assertion. However, even if Bayerlein is correct in saying that Rommel wanted these two divisions stationed directly behind the beaches, while it would have allowed those two divisions to intervene sooner, would still have left the remaining armoured divisions in other sectors of the coast, subject to the problems discussed below.

Therefore, if Rommel actually had been given the free hand he desired, it is quite likely that he would not have had all the *Panzer* divisions facing Normandy's Calvados – Cotentin coast where the invasion came ashore. He would have had the two divisions in question there, and divisions that were stationed in other sections of the coast, particularly the 15th *Armee* sector east of the Seine, would, similarly, have been positioned close to their respective beaches.

In that case, lateral movement of a division concentrated close to the wrong section of the coastline might have taken as long as or longer than moving it from a position farther to the rear. Lack of Seine bridges would have forced divisions moving from the 15th *Armee* sector to go far inland to cross the Seine before they could head back toward the actual invasion coast. That, in turn, would both have greatly delayed their arrival in the invasion zone and would have lengthened their exposure to the very air-attack that Rommel wished to avoid.

If, however, the divisions in question had been placed directly under Rommel's command, presumably there would not have been the long delay in obtaining the release of the divisions from *OKW* reserve. Rommel would still have been absent, but his Chief of Staff could have acted in his absence. If 12th *SS-Panzer Division 'Hitlerjugend'* and *Panzer Lehr Division* 130 had been positioned near the coast and were free to act on *Heeresgruppe* orders, they might have struck sooner and caused considerably more problems in the British zone. Further speculation about whether the 21st *Panzer Division* would have been divided and under a confusing command structure goes beyond this consideration. Opinion, in general, seems to be that the landing would still have succeeded.]

13. Q: What orders did you give, based on these ideas?

A: The OKH idea was adopted, with the result that the reserves (12 SS Pz[14] and Pz Lehr Divs) were too far behind the coast. They had a long distance to cover to reach the coast, and, owing to the enemy's air superiority, were unable to reach it. Everything was wrongly calculated and these operational reserves were unable to reach the line in time.

14. Q: Did these disagreements handicap the repulse of the Invasion?

A: Yes. Rommel demanded that these two divisions be right up at the coast and suggested for their position the very spot where the Allied airborne landings later occurred. Of course, we did not know that this place had been selected by the Allies for the landing of their airborne troops, but the recommended position happened to be that same area in the English sector around Caen – Bayeux.

15. Q: Did OB WEST have a Normandy plan in case of an invasion east of the Cotentin Peninsula?

A: I had no specific orders from higher up. On my own initiative, I personally reconnoitered the area in front of my Division, the area where the landing later occurred. I studied the methods of approach for my troops.

16. Q: What made you expect a landing there?

A: We really thought it would come northeast of the mouth of the Seine, or, next most likely, in Brittany; Normandy was considered the third most probable site. The preponderant opinion favored the other locations.

At this time, 2 and 116 Pz Divs were across the Seine, 12 SS Pz and Pz Lehr Divs behind Normandy, and 17 SS Pz Gren Div[15] in Brittany.

17. Q: In the original plan, was Pz Lehr Div to move up to where the actual landing later took place?

A: I personally went as far as Caen and Avranches. Although it was forbidden for me to go into the Atlantic Wall, I went to it and discovered that there were no workmen at one part of it. I did not really anticipate that the Invasion would come there.

---

14 FPS Ed: 12th *SS-Panzer-Division 'Hitler Jugend'*.

15 FPS Ed: 17th *SS-Panzergrenadier-Division 'Götz von Berlichingen'*.

My Division was to move north or west as the situation required. There was no original order to move into the area into which I later did move. I simply investigated and reconnoitred methods of approach. My Division was an OKW reserve, and, as such, could be sent anywhere depending on the circumstances.

18. Q: Did the Division move immediately on 6 June 44?

A: I was alerted on the night preceding the Invasion but did not move until the afternoon of 6 Jun 44.

19. Q: What information did you get before the Invasion started?

A: I was warned by telephone at 0300 on 6 Jun 44 of airborne landings being started somewhere near Caen and Bayeux.

20. Q: Was the Invasion a tactical surprise?

A: Certainly. The moment of time was a surprise. We estimated that the Invasion was about due, but had no information as to the exact time it would come.

The Division moved on the afternoon of 6 Jun 44. This was a mistake as it exposed us to bombing from the air; in fact, the troops were bombed in the assembly areas before the movement even started.

21. Q: Did you experience difficulty as a result of bad roads?

A: No. The roads were fairly good. There were six roads leading up to the beachhead. I only had to tell my regimental commanders to assemble the troops at certain points and take the roads indicated.

I was ordered to report to Seventh Army at Le Mans. Enroute, I saw burning vehicles, etc. Genobst Dollmann, who commanded Seventh Army, told me I was to advance as part of the Army, and, when I had reached the front line, was to form part of 'Sepp' Dietrich's Corps (Ed: I *SS Pz* Corps).

The nights were very short in France in Jun 44. We could move a maximum of only 10 or 12 km per hour, and could cover a total of only 60 to 70 km during the hours of darkness. As we had 140 km to cover to reach the coast, we had to move during the day and, as a result, suffer heavy losses from the air. I proposed that we rest during the day and resume the march the next evening, but Genobst Dollmann, who underestimated the Allied air forces, said we had to keep moving. (This problem of time of movement was another good reason why the Division should have been nearer the coast.)

It took two days and one night to reach the Caen front, and, on 7 Jun 44, I lost 85 or 86 armored vehicles, 123 trucks of which 80 were special gasoline trucks, 5 tanks, and 23 prime movers (Zugmaschinen), all through air bombings by Jabos (fighter bombers).[16]

16 FPS Ed: Ritgen, in his division history (p. 106), remarks that these numbers are probably in excess of reality.

22. Q: Did this lead to a change in the direction taken?

    A: No.

23. Q: Or any change in the plan of attack?

    A: It did delay us.

24. Q: Did French resistance play any part in delaying your movement to the beachhead?

    A: No.

25. Q: On what date did you first make contact with the British?

    A: On the morning of 8 Jun 44. We were ordered to take Bretteville l'Orgueilleuse and break through to the coast at Courseulles-sur-Mer.

26. Q: What comparison would you make of the American and British forces, for example, what tactical contrast?

    A: There was a big difference, but I did not realize it so much at that time. I must say very frankly that my judgement at that time, based on the experiences of the African Campaign, was that the English were better led and used better methods. (They had more of a routine.)

27. Q: Can you recall any particular good points about the British?

    A: On 7 Jun 44, my opinion, based on my experiences in Africa where I fought both the British and Americans, was as I have stated. The American Army was new at the time of the Tunisian fighting. Toward the end of Jul 44, when I was withdrawn from the English sector to be moved to the US sector, I thought, 'I don't believe we will have it quite so rough now.' (See my report to Ninth US Air Force,) Actually, however, we got from the frying pan into the fire. As early as the St Lo fighting, I had begun to change my opinion of the American Army, especially as regards leadership; later, I changed my opinion completely. I had a 24-page questionnaire from the Royal Air Force in which they asked me a similar question. I explained very clearly that in leadership especially, the American generals were completely different from the British. I did not want to offend the British, and later I was afraid they might take this as a slight. I asked the colonel from Ninth US Air Force to tone it down a bit ('Abschwaechen').

28. Q: Was Pz Lehr Div committed near Caen because it was generally anticipated that that would be the main point of the attack?

    A: Yes. The beachhead on the first day was much larger on that side and more airborne landings had taken place there. The Caen area was the most important point. We saw more troops landing near Caen and assumed it was the main point of attack.

29. Q: Were any of the generals of the opinion that we might try to break through near St Lo?

A: I cannot say. With my single Division, I was just 'small fry.' They seem to have considered Caen the most dangerous area. It was not a question of the British being in one sector and the Americans in the other. At the time we moved, they did not know which one was where. Of course, from reports of troop concentrations in southern England, we knew that the British would land farther east and the Americans farther west. But for all we knew, the whole Normandy Invasion was American and the British would land east of the Seine or the Normandy Invasion was British and the Americans would land in Brittany.

30. Q: Did these British attacks in the Caen area prevent the redistribution of reserves to the west of Normandy?

A: Yes, but politics also entered into it. The I SS Pz Corps, under Dietrich in the Caen area, had everything while Seventh Army had only poor equipment. Dietrich had Tiger tanks and heavy artillery and got everything he wanted.

31. Q: How did Dietrich enjoy such a good position with OKH?

A: He was a personal friend of Hitler, and a very ardent Nazi. If Dietrich wanted 100 tanks from Speer (Minister of Armaments), he got them, even if no one else got any.

32. Q: Was there any difference between I and II SS Pz Corps at that time?

A: Yes. The I SS Pz Corps got more. There is no question about that. The I SS Pz Corps was to have the glory of repelling the Invasion.

33. Q: Was this a personal order from Hitler?

A: Not officially or in so many words, but it was generally understood from the other orders that were given.

The Seventh Army sector was west of Caumont and Fifth Pz Army, then under Gen Frhr von Geyr, was east of Caumont. This demarcation corresponded to that between the American and British Armies.

34. Q: What were Dietrich's plans? What instructions did he give you?

A: I don't believe he had any clear view. He ordered us to break through to Courseulles-sur-Mer. Owing to the air attacks, my troops just trickled through ('Tropfenweise') with the artillery lagging behind them. On the afternoon of 8 Jun 44, I was told not to attack toward Courseulles-sur-Mer, but to withdraw to Tilly-sur-Seulles and attack toward Bayeux. These orders show confused thinking. Had we actually gone through Bretteville l'Orgueilleuse, I believe Pz Lehr and 12 SS Pz Divs could have cut through to the coast. Dietrich, however, was afraid the British would drive in behind us, and of course we would have suffered heavily from naval shelling and air attack. The British had advanced beyond Bayeux and our left flank would have been in danger.

35. Q: We had the feeling that you had too few reserves behind the line. Was this due to transportation difficulties?

A: The reserves for the most part were destroyed. After three weeks of fighting the British near Tilly-sur-Seulles, my Division was used up ('fertig'), due principally to artillery fire.

36. Q: Could you not get reserves from other fronts? Did air bombings prevent your moving up reserves? Was this front not considered important?

A: This front was considered of the greatest importance. We moved 2 Pz Div, 17 SS Pz Gren Div, and many other divisions, including 2 SS Pz Div, up to the area. This movement, however, was impeded by the destruction of the bridges over the Loire and the Seine. This was all part of the preparations for the Invasion made by the Allies. There were tremendous transportation difficulties. I had to haul my fuel from a point east of Paris (railhead) and my ammunition from south of the Loire.

37. Q: Did you have insufficient reserves directly behind the line? How did that handicap the defense of the entire sector?

A: In general, around 21 Jul 44, there were more reserves near Caen than farther west, but these reserves already were worn out. By no means did we have sufficient reserves, nor were the divisions themselves at full strength.

38. Q: Did you appeal for reinforcements?

A: Yes. After fighting for nearly four weeks against the British, my Division was shifted to western Normandy as if it were a fresh, new ('nagelneu') division. There, I was ordered to advance across the Vire Canal with my little, bedraggled remnant ('laecherliches Haeufchen'). There were simply no reserves to be had ('Es gab keine mehr.')

39. Q: Was your defense only linear, or did you have depth to your defense?

A: There was little depth in the defense. It was a line; there was no more.

40. Q: How did you organize the defense of your division sector after you moved to the St Lo area?

A: On the basis of my experience near Caen, I did not believe we could do anything with tanks; therefore, we simply used them as armored antitank guns or armored machine guns. The terrain was unsuitable for tanks, especially the Mark V[17], so we camouflaged them, and, with the crew still inside, fired our weapons when attacked. There was no possibility of moving on the battlefield; they had to stand and fight. Air attack contributed largely to this. A whole company of tanks was shot up, one after the other, near St Jean de-Daye (near Carentan) while they were hemmed in on the road. The long barreled guns impaired the maneuverability of the tanks.

[Tr. note – Conditions for crews cooped up in such immobilized tanks for long periods in hot weather were extremely punishing. The men were forced to sit, hour after hour for days on end, on seats and in positions that led to cramps, circulatory

17 FPS Ed: *Panther.*

problems and nervous problems. They were unable to go outside the tanks for fear of giving away the positions. There were no sanitary facilities in the tanks, empty shell-casings being used for makeshift urinals.

The *Panther* tank had particular problems in the narrow lanes bounded by massive hedgerows in Normandy because of its long gun. Due to the barrel length, the turret could not be rotated in the narrow lanes.]

41. Q: How did you employ the armored infantry?

A: Just like any other infantry.

42. Q: Were they dug in along the hedgerows?

A: Each tank was surrounded by a group of armored infantry. The defense was built up around the tank like a string of pearls (*'Perlenschnur'*). The men kept close to the tank, and, if it started its engine, they feared they would be left behind and became panic-stricken. There were mortars behind the tanks.

43. Q: Did the Panzer-Divisions and the infantry divisions use different methods of defense?

A: No. The Panzer-Divisions could not use their normal methods of fighting by movement because of your air force and artillery. Your air-directed artillery at times was worse than the bombers.

44. Q: Was it a mistake to leave the armored divisions on the line?

A: Yes. But when you have no other forces and you know the Panzer-Divisions have the best troops, what else can you do?

45. Q: Jodl [*Generaloberst* Alfred Jodl, *Chef des Wehrmachtsführungsstab* (Chief of Operations, *Wehrmacht* High Command)] said he wanted to withdraw the armored divisions and replace them with infantry. Did you hear this plan discussed? Why was it not carried out?

A: We ourselves made this proposal. It came from the panzer force ('Truppe'). We wanted good infantry with attached tank battalions to be used. Without some armored support, no unit by this time could hold its ground.

46. Q: Did you have separate tank battalions or would you have had to break up regular armored units? Did you have any GHQ armored units?[18]

A: We had some Tiger tank battalions; Dietrich had the 500 SS Tiger (Ed: probably battalion).[19]

47. Q: Why could the infantry not replace the armor in Normandy?

18 FPS Ed: armoured elements held at the corps or army level to be attached where needed.

19 FPS Ed: This is an error. The unit referred to, *schwere SS-Panzer-Abteilung 101* ( *Tiger*), was attached to the I *SS-Panzer Korps 'Leibstandarte'* under *Obergruppenführer* Dietrich. Following the Normandy fighting its remnants were reconstituted and redesignated as *schwere SS-Panzer Abteilung 501* in September 1944.

A: We had no good infantry divisions, and the Panzer-Divisions were then the best units left in the German Army. I say that not because I am a panzer general, but because it is clear that they got the best recruits, etc. The poor infantry could be put in some sectors of the Eastern Front, but under the severe artillery fire of Normandy, we needed divisions of the best caliber; we no longer had any.

[FPS Ed: There were still good infantry divisions on the Eastern Front. France, however, was another story. When better divisions had been sent to the Eastern Front, they had been replaced with divisions of lower combat effectiveness. For years the infantry divisions in France had been regularly combed through for any men fit for duty on the Eastern Front. Replacements were generally underage, overage, or physically unfit men. Many of the divisions in France were static divisions, lacking reconnaissance battalions and with reduced artillery. Many had been reduced from three regiments to two regiments, without sufficient transport to change positions, sometimes lacking sufficient horse-drawn transport to even bring up their own supplies, depending on local French civilians for delivery.

New divisions went through the activation process in France and were counted as divisions. Remnants of infantry (and armoured) divisions that had been burnt out in the bitter fighting on the Eastern Front were sent back to France for refitting and reconstitution. As soon as they were fit for action (and, frequently, before) they were sent back to the Eastern Front.

In response to the looming Allied invasion threat, Hitler's *Führer* Directive No. 51, issued 3 November 1943, emphasized substantially strengthening defences in the West and declared that there would be no more weakening of the West in favour of other theatres. Although intended to put an end to the practice of stripping the forces in France of all troops who could, in any way, be seen as fit for duty on the Eastern Front, the continued pressure of the war forced some exceptions.

Despite Bayerlein's disparaging remarks, it is amazing how staunchly many of the German infantry (such as the 352nd *Infanterie-Division*, which caused the Americans such grief at Omaha Beach and later) fought.]

48. Q: When did you make the proposal to Jodl?

A: About three weeks after the start of the Invasion.

49. Q: Did you see Jodl personally or go through channels?

A: Through channels ('auf dem Dienstweg'), that is, through Rundstedt, C-in-C West.

50. Q: What did Jodl think of this idea?

A: Jodl had no idea of British or American methods of fighting. He doesn't understand them to this day. They (Ed: probably OKW) were never on those fronts.

51. Q: What do you think of the Commander of Seventh Army, Genobst Dollmann?

A: Dollmann also knew nothing about these methods. He was a blank ('Null'). He later poisoned himself. He had lived a life of luxury and had grown soft. Hausser (*SS*-general) (Ed:Ogrf[20]) replaced him about 2 or 3 Jul 44. Dollmann poisoned himself in Le Mans (he was not an air raid victim). He had probably been reproved for the loss of Cherbourg. That was the last straw ('Cherbourg hat ihm den Rest gegeben') and OKW reprimanded him.

You will be interested in Hitler's opinion of Allied commanders, as quoted in the Frankfurter Presse of 12 A Gp. [*sic.*] In a speech on 30 Sep 42 in Berlin Sportpalast, he said, 'Wenn ich einen Gegner von Format haette, von militaerischen Format, dann koennte ich mir ungefaehr ausrechnen, wo er angreift. Wenn man aber militaerische Idioten vor sich hat, kann man nicht wissen, wo sie angreifen. Aber es ist ganz gleich, wo Churchill sich den naechsten Platz für die zweite Front aussucht. Er kann ueberall von Glueck reden, wenn er neun Stunden an Land bleibt.' ('If I had an opponent of proper schooling, I could calculate just about where he would strike; but when you are faced with military idiots, you can never guess where they will attack. But it is immaterial anyway where Churchill selects the place for the Second Front. He can consider himself lucky if he is still on dry land after nine hours.')

52. Q: What was the condition of the German infantry divisions?

A: Their condition was extremely bad. They had been in France for two to three years, and were completely spoiled. France is a dangerous country, with its wine, women, and its pleasant climate. Troops who are there for any length of time become bad soldiers. They had done nothing but live well and send things home. It is very painful to have to say it, but this was the opinion of all the troops which suddenly were transferred to France from the Russian Front. The troops in France had been in the rear zone for years ('Etappe') and, when thrown into combat, failed utterly. Furthermore, the best troops recruited had gone to the Luftwaffe, Paratroopers, and the SS, and no good replacements were ever sent to the infantry divisions. That is one reason why good panzer units had to be kept in the front line for an excessive length of time.

53. Q: Were not several panzer units also in France for long periods?

A: For shorter periods for rehabilitation. The 2 Pz Div had been in France quite a long time, but 9 and 116 Pz Divs were there only for rehabilitation and Pz Lehr Div was just activated there. The infantry, on the other hand, was used as occupation troops and as coastal defense forces, and had been inactive since 1941.

54. Q: How do you rate the German general in the West?

A: Only two, Rommel and myself, were experienced in battle with the British and Americans. Rundstedt, Dollmann, Dietrich, Geyr, Eberbach (Geyr's successor), von Kluge, Funck (XLVII Pz Corps), and Model (Kluge's successor as Cmdr, A Gp B), were without experience except on the Eastern Front.

20 FPS Ed: *Obergruppenführer.*

At the time he relieved von Kluge on 18 Aug 44, Model said we were a pack of cowards, that it was much easier to fight the Western Allies than the Russians, and that he would see that matters were changed. Model was then at La Roche Guyon with the General Staff (Ed: *A Gp B* Staff?) I was present, as Pz Lehr Div was being pulled back at that time.

55. Q: Can you point out any specific handicaps suffered by those generals who had fought only on the Eastern Front?

    A: The fighting was very different out there. I was in Russia in 1941, in Africa from 1941 to 1943, and, after Tunisia, was again in Russia, so I am well able to compare the differences. The Allied troops are much more intelligent fighters. The Russian is a very primitive fighter, yet the German troops fought less well against the Russians. After 1942, they were mortally afraid of the Russians, especially of being taken prisoner by them. When we were advancing, Hitler ordered prisoners to be fed and treated badly, and all Kommissars to be shot. When the tables were turned, our men feared being mistreated upon capture. Their fear of the Russians was colossal and inspired their devotion to their duty.

56. Q: Then you feel that the German troops fought better in the West?

    A: I must first add something. The cooperation of artillery and aircraft was not nearly so effective in the East as in the West. The Russian Air Force is not to be compared with that of the Allies.

57. Q: Can you show in what ways Model and the others were handicapped in dealing with the operations in the West?

    A: The main thing is that they did not take the Allied air force sufficiently into account. With an imposing paper array of Panzer-Divisions, an advance to cut off Patton's Army looked simple on the map, and cutting off the bottleneck to Avranches also looked extraordinarily easy on the map. Actually, however, the artillery and air force of the Allies made it impossible.

58. Q: Did this defect appear in Kluge, Funck, and Eberbach?

    A: In their judgments, yes. Funck, after fighting near Caen, had gained some experience, but Eberbach and Kluge were completely new. Not only were we attacked by your tactical air force when we moved on Avranches, but our men were attacked while still assembling for the attack ('Bereitstellungen').

    I can cite an order from OKW to A Gp B to the effect that the last chance of throwing back the enemy was a rapid advance on Avranches to annihilate Patton's Army and turn the scales in our favor on the Western Front. This proves how little OKW understood the real situation.

59. Q: What do you think were some of the main German errors in the battle of Normandy?

    A: First, false judgement as to the fighting ability and tactical and strategical leadership of the American forces.

*Generalfeldmarschall* Hans-Günther von Kluge, *Oberbefehlshaber West* in a photo taken whilst he was visiting the Channel coast shortly before the invasion, 1944. (Bundesarchiv 146-1995-002-09A)

*Generalfeldmarschall* Walter Model (front passenger seat) during a visit to the battlefront near Aachen, October 1944. Model succeeded Kluge as commander of Army Group B and *Oberbefehlshaber West*. (Bundesarchiv 183-1992-0617-506)

60. Q: Which American generals in your opinion were especially capable?

A: In the beginning, I thought Patton was the best because of his quick and fearless exploitation of opportunities and his breakthroughs with armored forces. From our reports, we later learned to respect Bradley even more as a cool, clear, and determined commander with more directional genius. Hodges also was considered good.

61. Q: Can you point out any particular American tactics you thought superior?

A: Outstanding, in my opinion, and the best strategic and tactical achievement in the whole campaign was the breakthrough at St Lo, the advance to Avranches, the breakthrough of the Third US Army, the feigned advance toward Brest so that we thought you were heading west, and the cool thrust to the Seine while the British pinned down strong units near Caen so that they could not be withdrawn to stop the American armor.

[tr. note – The American advance on Brest was, of course, not a feint. The original Overlord plan was predicated on the development of the Brittany ports to support the American forces in what was expected to be a lengthy, methodical battle, forcing the Germans back out of France. Possession of the ports and of the Brittany peninsula as a secure operating base appeared essential.

That plan continued to be the genuine Allied plan until a combination of circumstances made it apparent that it was no longer necessary. The surprising effectiveness of the Allied deception plans caused the Germans to keep the 15th *Armee* waiting for the invasion that never came in the Pas de Calais far longer than anticipated while the lengthy period of severe attritional fighting in Normandy wore down the German forces there. During that fighting German forces in Brittany were seriously reduced to provide replacements and reinforcements for the fighting in Normandy. Continued severe attrition developed a brittleness of the German defence such that, when the American Operation 'Cobra' breakthrough developed into a real breakout, it turned out there were no significant German forces left in Brittany that seriously threatened the American western flank and, at the same time, there were few forces to oppose a drive toward the Seine, the Paris – Orleans gap and the interior of France.

As noted in the discussion that follows these interviews, on 3 August General Bradley made a momentous decision that changed the entire course of the campaign as he announced that, abandoning the earlier plans for a methodical and orderly campaign to clear the Brittany Peninsula and seize and open its ports, Patton was, instead, to leave minimal forces to do the job there and turn the rest of his forces to drive eastward, south of the German armies that had defended Normandy and go all the way to the Seine. ]

62. Q: What about American strategy and tactics before St Lo? Did they mislead you as to American ability?

A: Yes. From 16 Jun 44 to 24 Jul 44, your aim was to wear down the German forces ('Ermattungsstrategie'). It was a long, slow destruction of our strength. I am familiar with the British tactics subsequent to El Alamein, and know that once they have the enemy worn down and weakened, they launch a sudden breakthrough with a big concentration of forces at one point.

63. Q: Did you anticipate that we would try to break out of the Cotentin Peninsula or that we would continue to press slowly forward and thus wear you down?

A: The commanders below division level felt you would break out, but the higher commanders did not. They were happy that the German divisions had held up so long, not realizing that what was happening was good strategy for the Allies.

64. Q: If this steady pressure had kept up, would it have achieved the same results later?

A: Yes, as our forces could not get replacements; however, it would have taken a much longer time.

65. Q: Would you care to make a general estimate of the length of time this wearing down might have taken?

A: It is hard to say, but probably would have required two months or until, say, Sep 44. I always think of three battles, El Alamein, Salerno, and Nettuno. The German higher command had still not learned anything from the last two battles; the lesson had not been appreciated. On a small scale, they were precursors of the Invasion. A small bridgehead or beachhead is built, the edges are mined, tanks and antitank guns are moved into it, and it becomes a difficult objective to attack. True, it has no depth, but the naval guns take the place of the artillery and the beachhead needs no depth. If you do not reduce it immediately, you find you cannot do anything, and it slowly grows and becomes wider and deeper.

The attack was intense and narrow, and a front of two km was attacked only after 60,000 to 70,000 rounds had been poured into it. It was then mined and tanks brought in. The German High Command thought the bridgehead unimportant because there was no defense in depth. They should have learned that even the smallest beachhead or bridgehead must be eliminated immediately, and, therefore, that reserves should be near the coast.

66. Q: Why did OKW want to admit the Allied troops inland? Was it in order to 'suck them in' and destroy a larger force?

A: Yes. That was the theory which was propounded in all strategic manuals from Von Schlieffen's time. It is a weak moment for the enemy when he has landed his men and has yet to gain depth. You attack him from both sides and drive him back into the sea.

67. Q: What were some of the other main German errors in connection with the battle of Normandy?

A: Completely wrong evaluation of the effects of the Allied air operations. The reserves, therefore, were too far away and a counterattack could not be made in time. As there was a failure to appreciate the danger, no supply preparations had been made. In addition, our rail and road nets were disrupted. We should have had supply dumps right in Normandy and, had we had them, we could have got munitions and fuel up to the front; however, nothing had been prepared. They believed that at the proper time, supplies could be brought up during the battle by road and railroad. Your air forces made this impossible. Some supplies could be brought up during the short hours of darkness, but roads were destroyed, and such communication centers as Argentan, Domfront, Conde, and Falaise (the main road junctions) were knocked out for the passage of supplies.

Rommel had a keen sense of such elements ('Fingerspitzengefuehl') and as early as 15 May 44 told me in a discussion, 'Uns wird es hier in der Invasionsschlacht gehen genau so wie in Nordafrika (bezueglich der Versorgung). Die Verkehrswege werden zerstoert sein und nichts wird ueber den Rhein herueberkommen, wie nichts ueber das Mittelmeer gekommen ist.' ('We will have the same experience with supplies in the Invasion battles as we had in North Africa. The supply lines will be destroyed and we will get nothing across the Rhine as we then got nothing across the Mediterranean.') In fact, nothing arrived from the other side of the Seine and Loire. We were on a transportation island.

Among mistakes made during the actual battle was the lack of a system for issuing orders. The higher command had no clear plan as to stopping the Invasion; they were not sure whether to drive them back or lead them on. Corps would give one order, and then conflicting orders would come from somewhere else. OKW and Hitler issued orders involving minor details. Instead of one clear order being issued, too many people were giving orders ('Hineinbefehlen').

68. Q: What caused this break in the chain of command?

A: This practice had become normal since 1941. Hitler upset the old principle by his insistence on having his say in the Russian campaigns.

69. Q: Was the situation in Normandy different in this respect than the fighting on the West Wall or in the retreat across France?

A: Rommel ordered an attack on 8 Jun 44, but OKW issued orders that we were to let the enemy in, assemble our forces farther south, and then attack; our forces were not to be expended in the meantime. I did not know which to do; it was a big decision to make. Dietrich had ordered me to attack toward Courseulles-sur-Mer, but Rommel decided we should first reduce Bayeux. On 8 Jun 44, I was already attacking Bretteville l'Orgeuilleuse and had to stop, withdraw my forces, and then attack through Tilly-sur-Seulles toward Bayeux. A lot of time was lost in this movement.

70. Q: Can you think of any other examples after you were moved to the American sector?

A: No, but perhaps later I will think of some. I want to explain the mistakes of the German command. There was no clear decision concerning a counterattack. They did not understand the attrition ('Abnuetzung') of the division committed there. This was also the reason for Pz Lehr Div later being given a mission farther west for which it had insufficient strength. Our G–2 information (Ed: possibly Div G–2 section) (Ic Dienst) was poor, and we had no enemy information.[21]

71. Q: How did bad intelligence handicap you specifically?

A: We had no aerial reconnaissance, none at all. We did not know where, how, or what might come there. We did not know about the strength of the enemy, what type of equipment he had, or where he would attack. The British and American intelligence was excellent; they seemed to know everything exactly as it was. They knew the location of every single machine gun position and were familiar with all the terrain features.

72. Q: Did you underestimate the possibilities of our artificial ports?

A: We did not know anything at all about them; they were a big surprise. You used things in the Invasion of Normandy which had never been used in Sicily, Nettuno, or Salerno.

73. Q: After the Invasion started, do you recall any specific instances where lack of intelligence caused you to be surprised?

A: We were surprised at the speed with which tanks came ashore. Armored vehicles were ashore immediately in the British sector. The artillery was excellently supplied with ammunition. From my command post in Tilly-sur-Seulles, I saw the cargo gliders land right behind the artillery positions.

74. Q: What handicaps were experienced through lack of intelligence after Pz Lehr Div moved west?

A: When I arrived there, I did not know which divisions had crossed the Vire Canal, nor their strength. In addition, no information as to the enemy situation could be furnished by the local commanders, as they knew nothing. ('Ueber das Feindbild konnten diese Kommandeure nichts sagen, weil sie nichts wussten.') We had 265th Inf Div there, plus remnants of 2 SS Pz Div Kfgr.

---

21 FPS Ed: The division's *Ic* officer (*3. Generalstabsoffizier*) was responsible for knowledge of the enemy situation (*Feindlage*), counterintelligence (*Abwehr*) and security (*Sicherheit*).

75. Q: When the breakthrough came on 25 Jul 44, did you anticipate this advance or was the failure to anticipate it due to your faulty intelligence?

A: I myself had not expected it; we did not know. I arrived on 8 Jul 44, and the breakthrough occurred on 25 Jul 44. During this time, I got a clear picture from reconnaissance and prisoners. I knew you had three infantry and two or three armored divisions there.

76. Q: Then why did you not expect a breakthrough?

A: As early as 2 Jul 44, there had been one attack across the Vire Canal, so I did not particularly expect a breakthrough. I did not believe there would be a breakthrough at that point, but felt that the main effort would be in the British sector between Caen and Bayeux and would be directed toward the southwest. I did not think it would head southeast as I felt that the base of the Peninsula must come next. In addition, I did not expect such a big operation, but rather something like those I had seen at El Alamein and Nettuno, that is, small sectors being attacked at one time. ('Mosaikarbeit bis ein grosser Brueckenkopf erzielt ist.' ('Patchwork until a large bridgehead is gained.')

77. Q: Do you have any further information on the details ordered by Hitler in regard to the coast?

A: The attack on Bayeux was Hitler's idea. We were ordered to give suggestions as to what we could do to concentrate our forces and destroy the bridgehead. Dietrich was pessimistic because of your air force and the shelling of your navy. He felt that an attack would be possible only if we had four or five units of ammunition and several units of fuel. Due to transportation difficulties, however, it was impossible to bring up such quantities of supplies. (Interviewer's Note: One unit is the normal supply of munitions and fuel.) Hitler also ordered the destruction of the bridgehead across the Orne. After the failure of Bayeux, he did not issue so many orders, and asked the others for their ideas.

78. Q: In what other respects did you have greater strength in the Caen sector?

A: I believe OKW expected the attack to head southeast from Caen, as most of the artillery (Ed: probably German) was massed near Caen. The British sector had been better equipped by the Germans than that opposite the Americans. Tiger tank battalions, for example, were committed against the British, as were heavier guns, 170 mm guns and 210 mm siege mortars.[22]

79. Q: Can you think of any other cases where you were surprised by American leadership?

A: The sudden capture of Cherbourg. I was then convinced that the push would come southward when the American forces, released by the fall of

22 FPS Ed: German nomenclature classified heavy howitzers of 210 mm or larger as *Mörser*, such as the 21 cm *Mörser 18*.

Cherbourg, were set free on the Peninsula. I still did not realize, however, that there would be a breakthrough at the place where it actually came. People later pointed accusing fingers at me because the breakthrough occurred in my sector. The II FS Corps[23] thanked God it had not happened in their sector..

[tr. note – Due to the amount of information involved, to avoid interrupting the questions the lengthy note on the Vire, Vire et Taute Canal bridgehead is at the end of ETHINT 66.]

80. Q: Then did you move to western Normandy and counterattack toward the Vire Canal?

A: I was relieved at Tilly-sur-Seulles by an infantry division toward the end of Jun 44.[24] We started moving about 4 Jul 44, leaving on the night of 4/5 Jul 44. We were ordered to take the ground southwest of St Lo during the same night. Our movement, however, was not completed until 7 Jul 44 (taking three nights). It had been contemplated that it would be completed in one night. The reason for the delay was that we believed the enemy was aware of our movement. During the night, we suffered a heavy aerial attack which delayed our movement by destroying the roads.

81. Q: Why did you move to the west at all?

A: The Division originally was to be used as a mobile reserve of A Gp S [*sic.*], with no mission yet being assigned to it.[25] At that time, however, you launched your surprise attack over the Vire Canal. It was a coincidence for us. The 275th Inf Div (a poor division) was there as was the Seventh Army Engineer School and a lot of other scraps thrown together. The attack took place on 3–4 July 44, and the Division there was swept aside.

82. Q: Did you think this was the beginning of a major offensive?

A: No, because an attack with a limited objective also took place near La Haye du Puits.

83. Q: Did you believe this was part of a coordinated offensive?

A: After the fall of Cherbourg, we expected a general advance toward the south. We believed there would be a slow, steady advance all along the front in accordance with Montgomery's special tactics. Montgomery originated this tactic and used it everywhere right up to the end. It is his special value ('Es I sein Wert'). The sector had not interested me so long as I was in the Caen sec-

23 FPS Ed: II *Fallschirmjäger Korps*.

24 FPS Ed: The relief by the newly brought up 276th *Infanterie-Division* started on 26 June, lasting several nights until the 276th *Infanterie Division* took command in the former *Panzer Lehr* sector at noon, 5 July.

25 FPS Ed: According to Ritgen, *Die Geschichte der Panzer Lehr Division*, p. 147, 'Initially the troops of the *Panzer Lehr Division* that were relieved from the front formed the corps reserve { XLVII *Panzer Korps*}. Effective 5 July the division – minus the elements attached to the 276th *Infanterie Division*, was the reserve of *Heeresgruppe B*.'

tor; it was just part of the general picture. As I told Rundstedt, however, I preferred to get away from the British to the American sector.

84. Q: Was there any other reason for your movement to the west?

A: The Division was withdrawn in order to be used as a reserve. At that time, you launched your successful attack across the Vire Canal with the use of smoke (according to rumors, phosphorus was being used). The 275 Inf Div could not stand it; the situation was critical and we had to go in.

85. Q: You knew where you were going at the start of the movement?

A: After the movement had started, but not before.

86. Q: Where were you to be stationed as reserve for A Gp B?

A: In the vicinity of Villers-Bocage, north of Aunay-sur-Odon. We were to be ready behind the infantry, which, they feared, could not hold there.

87. Q: Can you give the dates for this movement?

A: On 29 Jun 44, we moved out of the line (but I had to recommit half my armor (one tank battalion) and half the artillery there.) On 30 June 44, we assembled in the area north of Aunay, and, on 1 July 44, I had to attack again. The British had observed our relief by sending out reconnaissance. The next day, we heard on their radio, Soldatensender Calais (Ed: British propaganda station), about the movement of our Division out of the line. The British penetrated very deep, and on 1 Jul 44, we had to recommit an armored infantry battalion. The main body of the Division was brought up north of the Caen – Villers-Bocage road. You then launched your Vire Canal attack, and, on 4 Jul 44, we were taken out and ordered to move to St Lo (Canisy area, west of St Lo). I drove ahead, but it took the remainder of the Division until 7 Jul 44 to complete the move. We arrived just behind the line on 7 Jul 44, and made contact with the enemy on the following day. Seventh Army had an advance position there, and Ogrf Hausser was present.

88. Q: Whose idea was it to move Pz Lehr Div?

A: Rommel (A Gp B), Through Gen von Choltitz, Cmdr, LXXIV Inf Corps. A month later, on 17 or 18 Aug 44, I saw Von [*sic.*] Choltitz dressed in civilian clothes on the Champs Elysees in Paris. He complained that he had nothing with which to defend Paris. I had discovered six *Tiger* tanks belonging to the 12 SS Pz Div ('Hitlerjugend') at the Arc de Triomphe, bound for the front, and had taken them over. I wanted them myself, but gave them to Choltitz.

89. Q: Who gave the specific order to attack on 8 Jul 44?

A: Seventh Army. Hitler considered us to be a fine new division, and not tired. He felt it would be easy for us to make an attack like this.

90. Q: Did he tell you in which direction to attack?

A: For this attack, I came under the LXXXIV Inf. Corps. I drove to the Corps Command Post which, following a bombing, had been pulled back into the woods southwest of Lozon (370662). The Americans in that sector were weak and our line had held well. I was told that I could make a breakthrough and that the American division there was not good. I later got to know your 29 Inf Div much better. I believe you also had 30 Inf Div there and elements of your 3 Armd Div. At that time, however, no one knew your identifications. I drove forward to a point north of Pont-Herbert to see the Commander of 275 Infanterie-Division. A strong kampfgruppe of 2 SS Pz Div was in the woods directly south of le Desert and west of La Platriere (Ed: probably la Platiere), while a kampfgruppe of 17 SS Gren Div was located near Touroudes, southwest of le Desert. Between these two forces was a small but good kampfgruppe of the II FS Corps Reconnaissance Battalion. Also at this point was the Seventh Army Engineer School.

91. Q: How many troops in all did you have along the whole line?

A: Although we had had heavy losses, I estimate there were about 2,000 troops in that sector. The *SS* troops had 12 assault-guns. Few tanks, if any, were there.

92. Q: Any other artillery?

A: Relatively, quite a lot. About three battalions with 105 mm and 150 mm guns

93. Q: Would you describe this front as comparatively strongly or weakly defended? What was the general condition and fighting spirit of your troops?

A: Miscellaneous 'splinter groups' were thrown in after 275 Inf Div retreated. The front was then fairly well defended. The intention was to use my two armored infantry regiments (my 901 and 902 Pz Gren Regts) to relieve these other units.

The American attacks continued slowly but surely on 6 Jul 44. My first aim on 8 Jul was to stabilize the situation. The line was falling back and melting. With my adjutant, I reconnoitered on a tracked motorcycle, and then went to Rauline and le Desert; the use of cars was impossible because of the danger of the fighter-bombers. We then proceeded on foot toward the line. Physically and morally, the troops near Cavigny were through. The SS troops around Rauline were still fairly good. Ostbf (Obstlt) Wisliczeny, Commander of the 2 SS Pz Div Kfgr stood behind the line with a stick and beat anyone who tried to run back; he was a giant, brutal man. The 17 SS Pz Gren Div was also in a poor state and had no will to fight; the paratroopers, however, were good.

On 5 Jul 44, I went to see Hausser and Von Choltitz. On 6 Jul 44, after reconnoitering, I reported to Choltitz's headquarters again and told him the situation was bad. I also warned against an attack as half my Division was still at Tilly-sur-Seulles and had had four weeks severe fighting with the British. I explained the condition of my Division and that, so far as strength was concerned, it was not in a position to make a counterattack. At Tilly-sur-Seulles,

*General der Infanterie* Dietrich von Choltitz, commander of LXXIV *Korps* for much of the fighting in Normandy 1944. Bayerlein did not rate him highly! (Bundesarchiv 183-R63712)

we had been attacked every second day, and had been continually subjected to artillery fire. My Division had been opposed by three very good British divisions (49, 50, and 7 Armd). I knew these Divisions from Africa, especially 7 Armd Div which had seen action in Africa as early as 1941. Despite my explanations, Choltitz told me that I, like all Panzer-Division commanders, was a liar and that I must attack anyway.

I assembled my regimental and battalion commanders at my command post in Quibou on the evening of 6 Jul 44. I told them everything was all right, to keep up their spirits, and that our first mission was to stabilize the situation. Hausser agreed when I told him we could not relieve the other troops and that they must remain in the line.

94. Q: Did Hausser or Choltitz give any other instructions?

A: Just to gain the Vire Canal line. The next target would be Carentan and the third step was to reach the sea. This last possibility, however, was not even seriously mentioned.

95. Q: Were the commanders of the other miscellaneous units in the line represented at the meeting?

A: The commanders of those units were not present. They were at the front.

96. Q: You commanded a task force which included the 'splinter units'?

A: I refused to assume responsibility for the sector immediately, and took over the sector only on the evening of 7 Jul 44. I would not be responsible before that.

97. Q: Were you instructed to commit the entire Division?

A: Yes, with the exception of the force remaining farther east. This latter force comprised one tank battalion, one antitank company, and a 150 mm artillery battalion.

98. Q: How many men did you have in your Division?

A: I had the following: two armored infantry regiments with a total of 1500 men, one tank battalion of my Pz Lehr Regt with 300 men and 30 tanks, one reconnaissance battalion of 150 men, one antitank battalion (two companies) with 20 antitank guns, one engineer battalion with 300 men, one flak battalion, and one 105 mm and two 150 mm artillery battalions with a total of 36 guns (Ed: further details of the last five units not given).

A tank regiment has 1000 mechanics, repair and supply men behind the line, and about 200 men actually in combat.

99. Q: What was the total strength of your Division?

A: 10,000. You will be astonished at the big difference between combat strength and total strength. I had 2200 men back at Tilly-sur-Seulles. 17,000 is the normal strength. We had lost 5,000 men (all losses were suffered by the small fraction in combat, so that is a terrible figure). Combat troops form about one-third of the total.

The *S* and parachute 'splinter forces' had about 2000 men. The plan (see sketch) was to attack in three formations, that is, three combat commands each with its own tanks. Attacking from Pont-Hebert were I and II Bns of 902 Armd Inf Regt, with one battalion of 20 tanks; attacking from Les Touroudes toward le Desert were I Bn of 901 Armd Inf Regt and 11 Panther tanks were to attack from La Haye du Puits.

The Panther tanks all got stuck. I had been told that the terrain near St Lo was better suited for tank operations than that around Caen. Although I could have taken either the Mark IV or Mark V (Panther), I relied on what I had been told and took the latter. Actually the Mark IV would have been more suitable; the Mark V has too long a barrel and is not maneuverable. It was too wide and had too low a slope to negotiate the hedged dikes; it had to stick to the roads. Meanwhile, things went much better with the advance from Pont-Hebert.

During the entire Invasion, there was only one real close (Ed: mass?) tank attack. It took place at Bayeux, where the terrain was suitable for tank fighting. On all other occasions, the tank was auxiliary to the infantry which surrounded it. In real tank tactics, the tanks should be the dominating factor.

I discussed with the commanders how to conduct the attack (see sketch). We were to attack on the flanks and leave the middle as a pocket which would be cut off by a junction of our forces. Only my own commanders were present; the others were notified of the decisions made.

100. Q: What information did you give the commanders about the situation?

A: I explained to them that the tanks could not be employed in the usual ways, as the terrain was not what had been represented to me. We were to attack the next morning.

101. Q: What tank tactics did you employ?

A: We could only knock out enemy tanks at a maximum range of 200 yards, as the hedges concealed everything farther away. The German tanks are built for long range firing in the desert and on the Russian front. We could not use the Mark V cross-country in Normandy. The British Cromwell tank had a sharper angle of approach and, therefore, could scale the hedgerow dikes. We believed it had been specially built for use in Normandy, where the terrain is similar to that in southern England.

102. Q: Were the tactics prescribed for the tank operations?

A: They were to attack in small attack groups consisting of from one to three tanks and corresponding groups of infantry as assault troops, with fire support from stationary tanks. The rear tanks would support the advance of the forward tanks, which in turn would support the advance of the rear (leap-frogging). The distance between the tanks was not controllable as they had to follow the roads in column.

103. Q: Did you have any devices to cut down hedges and open a path?

A: No, although we knew that Normandy was like that. We took Normandy in 1940, and, in 1944, after four years of occupation, we still had taken no interest in the terrain. We knew there would be an invasion, but did not expect it in Normandy; we had made no preparations to adapt ourselves to the terrain. We considered the repulse at Dieppe as proof that we could repel any invasion.

I consider Dieppe as a feint aimed at keeping German forces in France which might have been sent against the Russians, and as an experiment for the coming invasion. Had it had unusual success, it might have been followed up.

104. Q: Did you use the same tank tactics you had used around Caen?

A: Based on my experience in fighting with the British and my repeated small counterattacks at Tilly-sur-Seulles, I now changed my tactics.

105. Q: What were your previous tactics?

A: In Russia and on other fronts, the whole tank battalion moved forward in a broad wave. On one occasion, I conducted a genuine tank attack in open country at Ellon (north of Tilly-sur-Seulles and south of Bayeux) on 9 Jun 44. The terrain was not ideal, but still it was a good tank country. I also made six successful counterattacks along the road at Hottot. (Ed: south of Tilly-sur-Seulles).[26]

106. Q: Would you return to the details of the conference with your commanders?

A: On the basis of my knowledge of the country, I told them in detail how to conduct the attack. There was to be a preparation by heavy GHQ (Ed: probably Heer, Army) artillery firing behind the enemy front north and east of St Jean de Daye and on this side of the Canal. The divisional artillery was to be laid on the front and on the bridges across the Vire Canal. The heavy artillery included a 170 mm battalion. As soon as the first shot was fired, we then intended to proceed with the assault groups ('Gruppentaktick [*sic.*]-verfahren') which consisted of a couple of tanks and a few infantrymen. We requested mortar fire on the enemy line to support the attack. In the attack, our first objective for the right flank was Cavigny, while the objective of the center was the road crossing south of St Jean de Daye (471747). The objective for the left flank was Le Mesnil (Ed: probably la [*sic.*] Mesnil-Vernon [le Mesnil Vernon]). All groups were then to meet on both sides of St Jean de Daye (Ed:

26 FPS Ed: The six counterattacks referred to were, presumably, local counterattacks during the bitter fighting in which the *Panzer Lehr Division* successfully defended Tilly-sur-Seulles.

the exact meaning of 'meeting on both sides of St Jean de Daye' is unknown.)[27]

The right flank was assigned the task of occupying the still intact bridge across the Vire at Aire [FPS Ed: Airel] (505748). This was on 6 July 44. Each regimental and battalion commander was ordered to drive forward during the night, to reconnoiter personally the sector assigned to him, and then occupy it. The next conference was held at 1200 on 7 Jul 44 in my command post at la Grembert. During the conference, fighter-bombers attacked the command post. Although none of the commanders was hurt, the attack depressed the morale of the conference.

All the commanders agreed to my plan, but all the troops had not yet arrived. The commanders reported on the situation of their units. The plan was not changed; as 275 Inf Div flooded back and the front was breaking up, stabilization of the front remained the mission.

107. Q: Did you receive any further instructions from LXXXIV Inf Corps?

A: Corps had no interest in my difficulties and issued no further orders. The tanks rolled forward that evening. They had been held back as long as possible to keep the attack secret from the fighter-bombers. The tanks arrived at dusk on 7 Jul 44.

The American artillery fired at every point and even used 150mm and 240mm guns. British artillery fire is concentrated on a few points and is terribly intense. We considered artillery and American bombing the worst experience. On this particular occasion, the American fire was nearly as bad as the British. The British lay 500 to 800 rounds on a few points, such as battery positions, while the Americans fire 20 or 30 rounds at a large number of targets, including small road crossings, etc.

Nothing unusual happened during the night. At 0530 on 8 Jul 44, the attack began. Le Desert was No Man's Land, not clearly possessed by either side. We captured le Desert. That sounded good in my report, anyway. It would keep Corps quiet. The left flank made good progress toward St Jean de Daye in a fluid advance. The situation on the right flank was not clear as it was a hesitating advance toward Cavigny. This was a question of how much defense the enemy could put up. Our troops were about equal in quality. The best commanders, such as Oblt Phillipps, were on the left flank. The allied defense was very strong on the eastern flank.[28]

---

27 FPS Ed: See extensive note preceding next interview giving details relating to St-Jean-de-Daye attack and placing it in larger context.

28 FPS Ed: Ritgen (p.153) refers to '*Bataillon Philipps* (I./901) as advancing from le Hommet to St. Jean, reporting at 0630 hours its position three kilometres behind enemy lines. It surprised the American artillery positions, cut wire communications, captured the command post of the Third Battalion of Infantry Regiment 39 of the 9th Division, caused great confusion among the enemy and took many prisoners.'

As our right flank advanced, it received an attack from your center and we had to divert II Bn of 902 Pz Gren Regt to halt your advance. We took Cavigny at 1200 and captured 12 prisoners. We encountered numerous road blocks, minefields, and dug-in tanks northeast of le Desert, where the attack came to a halt and heavy losses were incurred. The last report from the left flank stated that they had reached the heights on a level with le Mesnil at 1100, but had not been able to enter the village itself. Although the artillery observer reported at 1200 the most forward elements of the left wing had reached the outskirts of St Jean de Daye, I personally never heard from that battalion again. I believe it was destroyed by your 29 Inf Div. Later, 14 men of the tank company returned and reported that they had lost all of their tanks. They said they were rolling along on a road lined with trees when the first and last tank had been shot up thus leaving the rest helpless in a trap. The 17 SS Pz Gren Div[29] and other units were still on the left flank, but the attacking force for that flank had been wiped out. I was at le Hommet d'Arthenay. I could not leave the battalion cut off, so I tried to move the center units forward to St Jean de Daye. They, however, were stopped dead by the obstacles. The American tanks were so well dug in and fired so well that I lost many tanks there. The right flank held Cavigny, but could not move any farther forward. Our forces were too weak, the tanks shot up, and the men lost.

108. Q: After the attack bogged down, were any other plans made on 8 Jul 44 to continue the attack?

A: During the afternoon, and on my own initiative as things had turned out so badly, I ordered the evacuation of Cavigny and withdrawal of my troops to the original line of departure. This concluded the attack.

On 9 July 44, we held the same line. I had to take out part of the SS troops. I was reprimanded by the LXXXIV Inf Corps for the failure of this attack. This was the worst blow I ever experienced. Von Choltitz said in effect that if an infantry division could hold so well, he could at least expect a Panzer-Division, which thus far had suffered so little, to execute successfully a trifling attack like this. He said that the infantry must be better than the panzer troops.

109. Q: Were any additional orders given by Corps for the future?

A: No. I spoke to Hausser, who was a sensible, approachable man. Although an SS Ogrf, he was a good leader and was always in front of his men. I told him that for four weeks we had fought at a key point and that he could read the Wehrmachtsberichte (Official OKW Report to German people) and see how hard and how well we had fought there. I told Hausser that it was impossible for Von Choltitz to judge me as he had for not succeeding with such worn out forces, and that he could release me and give the Division to anyone else as under these circumstances it would surely be destroyed anyway. ('Diese Division wird doch noch zu Grunde gehen.') The next day Von Choltitz came and apologized.

29 FPS Ed: 17th *SS-Panzergrenadier-Division 'Götz von Berlichingen.*

While simply holding the line (near Caen), we had lost 60 men a day from the artillery, and lost 300 to 400 men on a front of two km in every attack made by the British. My front line would be completely destroyed. One could forecast it through simple mathematics and predict when the last man would be gone.

110. Q: What were the total losses in men and tanks in your attack of 8 Jul 44?

A: Twenty tanks and tank destroyers and 500 to 700 men. This was a 50 percent loss of effectives, an extraordinarily high rate. It was attributable to the refusal of the high command to understand the continual attrition of our men ('Sie hatten kein Verstaendnis fuer abgenuetzte Divisionen.') All they saw were pins on the map representing divisions. They did not appreciate the losses these units had suffered.

111. Q: Did Hausser or Choltitz give any new orders for the future?

A: No. I said I would try to hold the line, but was of the opinion that the American advance would continue. We had hardly any troops (a few *SS*) to hold a wide sector, and in time, the troops would have to give way and the Americans would go through. The American attacks continued on 9 and 10 Jul 44, and we lost ground each day.

112. Q: Was there a counterattack by Pz Lehr Div on 11 Jul 44?

A: We made small counterattacks on various occasions, especially 902 Pz Gren Regt and Kfgr Wisliczeny. The object was to stem the force of your attack. By using the maximum energy, all we could achieve was to weaken its force and delay its progress.

113. Q: Did you not have a counterattack on 11 Jul 44? Did you notice that our 9 Inf Div had come into the line?

A: We recaptured Chateau Esglandes near Pont-Hebert. Although we did not know its identity, we knew there was a third division there as well as your 29 and 30 Inf Divs. Through taking a few prisoners, you normally discover the presence of any new division; however, the American soldiers almost never talked.

114. Q: What was the objective of the attack of 11 Jul 44?

A: The same as always. The object was to regain the original line. You know Hitler's general order never to give up a foot of ground. ('Fuehrerbefehl, keinen Fussbreit Boden aufzugeben.')

115. Q: What kind of defense die Pz Lehr Div have along the line after the counterattack of 8 Jul 44?

A: Typical Normandy hedgerows. The tanks were very well camouflaged as houses and trees. When I went up there myself, I could not see them although I knew that they must be there. So far as I know the tanks were about 20 meters apart, and were used as armored machine guns to rake the hedges with interlocking fire and also to cover the hedges. The infantry was about four to six meters ahead of the tanks (with some also behind the tanks). The tanks almost leaned against the hedges or were hidden by the walls; otherwise there was no chance to camouflage them. We could fire over them. Some tanks and mortars were to the rear. Some mines were laid in front where the road ran up to the front. Both Teller mines and antipersonnel mines were used. We had a small reserve behind the line for use with a couple of tanks in a possible counterattack. To constitute this reserve, it was necessary to keep the front line thinly manned.

This was certainly a primitive defense. For a tank man it was a degradation. The tank is not a defensive weapon.

116. Q: Did you advocate withdrawing the Division and relieving it after 1 Jul 44?

A: I always proposed this, but it was hopeless. We were ordered not to yield a foot of ground. Our small counterattacks were very often successful where they had good leaders.

117. Q: What tactical significance did you attack [*sic.*] to St Lo?

A: It was important as a traffic center and road junction, but Pont-Hebert was a more important place for me. The bridge was still intact, and if you got over it, you could fan out and prevent our withdrawal.

118. Q: Had Hausser or Von Choltitz spoken of the importance of St Lo?

A: That was the II FS Corps sector. I put in three tanks on the east bank to secure the Pont-Hebert bridge as the paratroopers had no tanks. I did this even though I personally did not think there would be an attack by your divisions across the bridge. Army and Corps kept telling me not to lose the bridge under any circumstances as it would open the way for a further attack on St Lo. St Lo had less a strategic than a prestige value.

119. Q: How would you summarize the activity of your Division between 11 Jun 44 and 24 Jul 44? Were there any high points?

A: It was a fluctuating situation, but we always lost a little ground. I had a parachute regiment from the 'famous' 5 FS Regt (Ed: probably 5 FS Div) as reinforcements. They all ran away at once.

120. Q: Did you make any organized attack like that of 8 Jul 44?

A: We made counterattacks, but no large scale attack like that one. We had limited objectives ('begrenzte Ziele.')

121. Q: Was Pz Lehr Div taken completely out of the line during that time?

A: Never. Had they been withdrawn, you would have flooded through thus making the later breakthrough unnecessary. I told Hausser the Division would be destroyed. Our crews were in the tanks day and night and could not come out. They were cramped in there and could not venture out for fear of artillery and bombing. They had no latrine facilities. Their knees swelled and legs stiffened.

122. Q: What line did the Division hold on 24 Jul 44, just before the breakthrough?

A: See attached 1:50,000 map (Ed: Map not attached to available record.)

As part of your preparation for the attack, the road crossings were smashed. I committed the remnants of 275 Inf Div. On my left flank was the combined division formed out of 2 SS Pz and 17 SS Pz Gren Divs. The 5 FS Div was no longer there.

123. Q: What reserves did Pz Lehr have?

A: One regiment was in reserve. The rest was in the line.

124. Q: Did you anticipate that the breakthrough would occur on 25 Jul 44?

A: I did not anticipate a big, concentrated attack. I thought there would be a slow wearing through ('durchfressen'). We did not know of preparations for a large-scale attack and had no hint of it. On 22 Jul 44, we heard that the Caen front had been attacked by big bombers. I said I hoped that would not happen to us, as I had experience of these planes on the Mediterranean. The big attack itself was beautifully concealed ('tadellos Verschleiert [*sic.*]').

125. Q: Did anyone else in headquarters mention the possibility of attack?

A: Von Choltitz never came to us. Hausser came and told me about the Caen attack. All eyes were focused on St Lo. It was a good move to take St Lo first as a feint ('demonstration') to divert attention from the area. We expected an attack at Caen, and later expected it at St Lo. I had been reproved for losing the Pont-Hebert bridge as 'all the Allied forces will now come over to St Lo,' so Hausser told me. Von Choltitz telephoned me to the same effect. The Americans were reported by our paratroopers to be marching over the bridge in force ('Gruppenkolonnen').

[tr. note- Bayerlein attributes a secondary 'feint' motivation to what was, in fact, a genuine and substantial American objective, the capture of St.Lô. Martin Blumenson, in the U.S. Army official history, *Breakout and Pursuit* states (p.148): 'Because of its location at the apex of the Coutances – St. Lô – Lessay road triangle, the city was specifically important to General Bradley's emergin plan for achieving more rapid advance in the Cotentin. A premise of the new plan was American possession of St. Lô, a need that by mid-July imparted a sense of urgency to the battle for the city.'

126. Q: On 24 Jul 44, when some bombs were dropped in the vicinity of Marigny – St Gilles, did you feel a major attack was coming in this sector?

A: On about 22 or 23 Jul 44, Hptm Alexander Hartdegen, my aide, anticipated that four-motored planes would attack our sector and that a big attack would come; he felt something was imminent. At 1200 on 24 Jul 44, the first squadron appeared, followed by more and more. It was slightly cloudy, and I thought they were going farther toward our rear and would not attack us. After 15 to 30 minutes, after they had circled around about us, they began to bomb. I immediately went to my command post at le Mesnil-Amey. The command post was located in an ancient castle with very thick walls (412623). A series of carpets were laid in a crisscross pattern. From the tower of the castle and under the protection of the thick walls, I observed the whole bombardment. No bomb fell on le Mesnil-Amey itself the first day, but the ground was heaped onto itself. Artillery positions were blasted. The front line was wiped out. We thought this was part of your planned attack, and were surprised that you did not follow it up the same day.

127. Q: Our line withdrew to avoid being bombed. It is reported that your troops advanced to escape the fire.

A: Perhaps a reconnaissance outfit did.

128. Q: What orders did you give the Division after the bombing on 24 Jul 44?

A: All communications were completely destroyed and there was no possibility of moving along the roads.

129. Q: Were you still under LXXXIV Inf Corps?

A: Yes.

130. Q: Did you receive any orders from Gen Choltitz or Hausser?

A: No. He could not give any more orders; everyone had to look out for himself. I have been at all the hotly contested points on various fronts, but these three days by St Lô were the worst I have ever experienced. It was impossible to issue any orders. All you can do is crawl into a hole and pray that the next carpet will miss you.

131. Q: What did you lose in men and tanks?

A: One hundred percent casualties in the front line.

132. Q: How many men did you have there?

A: Two-thirds of the whole force. Thirty-five tanks and 15 tank destroyers were destroyed. The whole place looked like a moon landscape; everything was burned and blasted. It was impossible to bring up vehicle [*sic.*] or recover the ones that were damaged. The survivors were like madmen and could not be used for anything. On 24 and 25 Jul 44, I lost about 2000 men either dead or missing from the bombing. On the evening of the first day, I collected the few reserves we had north of la Chapelle-en-Juger, and tried to reestablish the old line. I had received more infantry, and put about 800 to 1000 men in the line. The next day, they too were destroyed. I don't believe hell could be as bad as what we experienced.

Your air force must have known everything about the artillery positions. There had been good advance reconnaissance. Only four or five bombers where shot down, and my flak battalion had one and one-half batteries destroyed.

133. Q: What were the next orders you received from Von Choltitz after this?

A: I tried to contact my own troops by runners. I ascertained what losses we had. The attack was not followed up on the afternoon of 24 Jul 44 (it stopped about 1230). I sent messengers to investigate the situation. I drove to St Gilles, but then had to walk. I visited the command post of 902 Pz Gren Regt in Bernardier, one km north of St Gilles. The commander had nothing left and I started to reestablish the situation. I had the commander of 901 Pz Gren Regt with me at the time of the attack. I walked toward Hebecrevon and found that 275 Inf Div was wiped out; no men or guns were left. A few survivors had escaped toward the north. I then returned to my command post between Canisy and Quibou (during the attack I had been at the command post of 901 Pz Gren Regt). I telephoned Choltitz toward the evening of 24 Jul 44. They had seen the bombing from the rear. I told him how things were and said that I could not hold the front without reinforcement of another regiment. Choltitz said he had nothing and could not send anything. I said he should withdraw some units from the fronts that had not been attacked, but Choltitz would not do it;

134. Q: What did Choltitz report about the rest of the front?

A: The left flank had also received the diversionary attacks near La Haye du Puits. We thought the attack on Periers was very important. My sector was intentionally neglected as less important. The attack was expected on Periers, but not on my sector. They never believed Pz Lehr Div needed anything anyway.

135. Q: Is it possible that the other fronts were better protected because they had great confidence in you?

A: The other divisions were infantry and we were armored and thus suppose to be stronger. They had not considered our five weeks of heavy fighting before this.

136. Q: Even after the bombing the higher command still did not expect a breakthrough?

A: They probably did, but did nothing about it. The SS did not want to take their men out. I was expected to hold without help. Hausser was an SSman. We did not dare to take anything from the SS.

137. Q: After the first contact, what did Choltitz say about a general plan for this area after the bombing?

A: He said to hold and not let them break through, but gave no explanation as to how we were going to do it (in his telephone conversation). Hausser never came after the evening or late afternoon of 24 Jul 44 when Choltitz made his last call. On 25 Jul 44, Choltitz sent a courier and again on the evening of 25

Jul 44 he telephoned (which rarely was effective because of the destruction by the fighter-bombers).

At this point, there was additional bombing, and my new line, which had been withdrawn slightly, was again wiped out. The bombing on 25 Jul 44 was much worse than the other, and went farther back.

138. Q: How important was the bombing in the success of the breakthrough?

A: The bombing was of decisive importance to the breakthrough, as otherwise we could have got reinforcements and tanks, etc, in the meantime. Everything was smashed in one blow and created the gap through which your tanks would run.

139. Q: Did you realize we were attacking southwest in order to cut off LXXXIV Inf Corps?

A: It was not recognized before 27 Jul 44. We thought the attack on the left flank of the Vire would proceed southward.

140. Q: After the period 25–27 Jul, what conversation did you have with Von Choltitz concerning the future role of Pz Lehr Div?

A: On the evening of 26 Jul 44, I received orders from Von Choltitz to assemble the remaining troops (nine remaining tanks (Panthers) of an original 40 and a parachute regiment from the 'famous' 5 FS Div) and to cut through toward the woods (north of Soulles) on 27 Jul 44. The troops were supposed to assemble in the area around (4057) and advance in a southeasterly direction toward le Mesnil Herman (to cut off the US forces advancing southwest). The order, however, could not be carried out The SS Panther battalion never arrived. That was my last conversation with Choltitz.

The next day, your attack was launched and the fighter-bombers destroyed about 1100–1200 men between Carantilly – Cerisy la Salle, and on the Canisy – Dangy roads. The main point of attack was clearly designated by the fighter-bomber target area. The Americans advanced southward in the best American attack I have ever seen. Very little artillery was used, but there was excellent tank-airplane cooperation. Fifty to 60 tanks liquidated my position north of Dangy and continued in three groups, one on Cerisy la Salle, one on Pont-Brocard, and one on Soulles. My divisional command post was located at (395520).

141. Q: What do you mean by 'liquidated?'

A: Tanks shot up and men killed or captured.

142. Q: How many men were left in Pz Lehr Div?

A: I had a kampfgruppe at Pont-Brocard; all others were annihilated. A Panzer-Division is echeloned in depth, so there are always men farther to the rear.

143. Q: How many men were in the front line?

A: The whole 901 Pz Gren Regt, consisting of 200 to 300 men, 12 tanks (all that were left) and six self-propelled guns. Part of my engineer battalion and some antitank guns were located around Pont-Brocard.

144. Q: You lost about 200 to 300 men only?

A: That was all I had. One hundred men and three antitank guns were at Pont-Brocard, and at Soulles there were still two companies of the 901 Pz Gren Regt, with from 25 to 150 men in the two companies. There also were four or five 88mm flak guns.

145. Q: Where did you then withdraw?

A: The US attack first headed toward Soulles, but then turned and headed for my command post. The lead planes would detect resistance at various points and would direct the advancing troops which way to move.

I could not move and had to stay where I was. At 1800, one column passed my command post on the left and one on the right. I had believed no tanks could get across the swampy Soulles creek. Three tanks suddenly appeared and the fighter-bomber activity stopped.

I was cornered by the tanks in the command post but hid and escaped several hours later. I reached Percy and, at midnight, I found a radio station of my unit (panzer radio station and crew). The Americans were then north of the road. I radioed LXXXIV Inf Corps that my Division was destroyed and that I had nothing to lead. This was the night of 27/28 Jul 44. The breakthrough went northwest of Percy. I found eight Mark V tanks in a repair shop near Villebeaudon, south of Percy, and began to form a unit from these tanks.

146. Q: What was the plan of LXXXIV Inf Corps?

A: They had written me off as a total loss and gave no orders. I picked up remnants of a reconnaissance battalion. On my own initiative, I took over the Percy sector and tried to defend it with what remnants I had.

# COUNTERATTACK AT ST JEAN-DE-DAYE

To avoid interruption to the above questions, the following note picks up the Division's history at the time it was pulled out of the line briefly into *Korps* reserve, then, on 8 July, committed in a counterattack on St. Jean-de-Daye against the Americans. (See questions 80 ff above, in ETHINT 66.)

As *Generalleutnant* Bayerlein noted above, *Panzer Lehr Division* 130 was relieved by the 276th *Infanterie-Division* on 26 June. As the individual units were relieved, they moved to the Aunay area for refitting. By 5 July the 276th *Infanterie Division* had taken over all of *Panzer Lehr's* former sector. *Panzer Lehr's Panzer* IV *Abteilung* (II./*Panzer-Lehr-Regiment* 130), the main body of *Panzerjäger-Lehr Abteilung* 130 remained behind temporarily to help the new division get established, as did the heavy artillery, *schwere Artillerieabteilung* 992, which had supported the Division for the last few weeks. Those elements that had been relieved went, for the time being, into *Korps* reserve while being refitted.

Within a few days of the fall of Cherbourg on 28 June, the American First Army under General Bradley used the troops that had been freed up to extend its attack at the foot of the Cotentin Peninsula. The base of the Cotentin Peninsula was nearly cut off from the mainland by large areas of marsh and poorly drained terrain. On the west side the area between the marshes and the coast was hilly, which, with the large Mont-Castre Forest, controlled the critical road junction of la Haye-du-Puits. The Germans had organized a strong main line of resistance protecting this seaward flank.

To the east slow, sluggish streams converged on Carentan from the south and southwest. Subject to the combination of tidal flooding and flooding due to the tidal effects on the rivers, since Roman times these low-lying areas had gradually been drained for farming. Their wide, marshy flood-plains, criss-crossed by innumerable drainage ditches, were devoid of cover. The Germans had destroyed the floodgates that controlled tidal effects on the rivers, flooding these low areas as a defensive measure. There were only two, relatively narrow corridors of passable ground, one along the axis of the Carentan – St Jean-de-Daye – St Lô highway, the other along the Carentan – Périers road.

The 17th *SS-Panzergrenadier Division 'Götz von Berlichingen'*, in particular, had come to know this area well and was prepared and able to put up an extremely stubborn, skilled and flexible defence.[30]

The limitation of movement to these narrow corridors favoured the German defence. Until Bradley's American First Army could get past this constriction, it could not deploy its powerful forces to full effect and assert its increasing superiority in men and materiel.

---

30 Their three-volume division history, *Due Sturmflut und das Ende*, by Hans Stöber and Helmut Gunther, is one of the finest and most readable unit histories I have ever studied. Its massive first volume is entirely devoted to the fighting in France, from the Normandy invasion through the retreat to the Seine.

First Army's attack in early July was planned to start on the western end near the sea and progress eastward in a series of blows. VIII Corps would open the offensive on the west, aiming at la-Haye-du-Puits and the Mont-Castre Hills. Next, on Army order, the VII Corps would attack with the American 83d and 4th Infantry Divisions, with the 9th Infantry Division awaiting sufficient room to join in. Finally, XIX Corps would attack in the zone including the Vire and Taute Rivers, with St. Lô and the adjacent high ground as its objective.

The series of attacks, starting on 3 July in the la Haye-du-Puits sector increasingly strained the German 7th *Armee*, which had already been feeling the need to pull some of its battered units, such as the 17th *SS-Panzergrenadier Divison 'Götz von Berlichingen'* and the 352nd *Infanterie Division*, out of the line for refitting or reconstitution even before the new offensive. All such plans fell by the wayside in the frantic effort to reshuffle forces to meet the new threat.

On 7 July XIX Corps launched its attack, initially west of the Vire. On 7 July the American 30th Infantry Division crossed the Vire et Taute canal. The immediate objective was the area of St.-Jean-de-Daye, the important crossroad just south of the village and the small elevation to the east. Capture of the road junction would give access to the two main highways leading west and south in the area north of the hills that begin at Hauts-Vents.

The crossing was successful and, despite problems with the special conditions of fighting in the hedgerows of the Bocage normal to any unit, even one that had trained well for this terrain, St.- Jean-de-Daye was taken and the division established a firm bridgehead. It would, however, turn out to be inadequate in size and depth for what was about to be pushed into it.

General Bradley was sufficiently encouraged by the afternoon of 7 July to order the American 3rd Armored Division to cross the Vire River at the Pont-de-Fromond bridge just west of Airel during the night of 7/8 July and begin its drive after advancing to the crossroads south of St.-Jean-de-Daye.

Combat Command B (CCB) began to move into the bridgehead that evening while Combat Command A (CCA) moved into an assembly area at Ste. -Marguerite d'Elle awaiting developments.

The 113th Cavalry Group entered the bridgehead on 7/8 July, moving to the right of the 30th Infantry Division to cover its right flank. After stiff fighting developed with both the German 639th *Ostermark Bataillon* and the 38th *SS-Panzergrenadier Regiment* of the 17th *SS-Panzergrenadier Divison 'Götz von Berlichingen'*, the cavalry group took up defensive positions on a north – south line based on Goucherie – le Mesnil-Véneron. Effective midnight 8 July, the 113th Cavalry Group was attached to Combat Command A of the 3rd Armored Division. During the day Combat Command A had crossed the Vire River, taking the Airel road toward le Désert, thus strengthening the Corps' right (west) flank.

The 3rd Battalion of the 30th Infantry Division's 120th Infantry Regiment had attacked during the day toward the southwest from a position near St-Jean-de-Daye to gain high ground north of le Désert, successfully repulsing a German counterattack. Concerned at the stiff resistance the 113th Cavalry Group had run into and anxious about the vulnerability of its right flank, XIX Corps released to the 120th Infantry Regiment its 2nd Battalion, which had been held in Corps reserve. The 30th Infantry Division now had a strong west flank astride the important highway through le Désert road.

Trouble developed as Combat Command B of the inexperienced armored division tried to pass through troops of the inexperienced infantry division in what was fast becoming a very congested bridgehead. The congestion was about to worsen as the 30th Infantry Division brought in the 3rd Battalion of its 119th Infantry Regiment. Neither the armor nor the infantry included the other in its plans. In some cases the infantry units had no idea American armor was coming through.

Despite these complications, the American bridgehead was strong, and expanding aggressively. The German command was unaware of the strength of the American forces they were hoping to crush.

The German 7th *Armee* had expected an attack on the Vire sector, but, as mentioned above, was also having to deal with a situation it felt was more pressing west of the Taute River. Reserves were being committed from the 2nd *SS-Panzer Division 'Das Reich'* to help the 17th *SS-Panzergrenadier Division 'Götz von Berlichingen'*, which was under heavy pressure from the attack of the U. S. VII Corps. Seventh *Armee* hoped to hold the American XIX Corps attack on 8 July with a mobile brigade and a last battalion from the 2nd *Fallschirmjäger Korps'* reserve.

However, the Germans anticipated stronger American efforts along the Vire. 7th *Armee* proposed pulling units of the 2nd *SS-Panzer Division 'Das Reich'* out of the la Haye-du-Puits sector, at the risk of weakening that critical sector. *Heeresgruppe* B finally decided to commit the 5th *Fallschirmjäger Division*, moving it up from Brittany to the Lessay sector and to bring in *Panzer Lehr Division* 130, which was to assemble between Périers and St. Lô and strengthen the sector from the Vire River westward.

On 9 July, in light of the increasing size of the bridgehead, plans were made to bring in VII Corps' 9th Division, which would make temporary use of XIX Corps' gains, 'borrowing' some ground on the western flank of the bridgehead, from which it would then fight its way back into the main VII Corps' zone. By so doing it would add to the security of XIX Corp's right flank. This would, also, place it in position where *Panzer Lehr's* counterattack would run into this experienced division two days later.

The American immediate objective on 9 July was the high ground around Haut-Vents, about 4000 yards from the 30th Division's forward positions. A long ridge stretching southward between the Vire and Terrette Rivers began at Haut-Vents (Hill 91). This ridge provided excellent observation for the Germans over a wide stretch of country toward St-Jean-de-Daye.

The Germans launched a counterattack on 9 July with the *Pionier* battalion of the 2nd *SS-Panzer-Division 'Das Reich'*, supported by *Panzer* IV tanks which caused more excitement than real damage to the Americans. The German 7th *Armee* said that the counterattack 'disintegrated under heavy artillery fire.' (Quote from *St. Lô*, American Forces in Action Series, p. 34)

By the night of 9 July the 9th Infantry Division had assembled in its jump-off positions for the next morning's attack toward the west and southwest. The 9th Infantry Division was under VII Corps, but it would be operating in the same

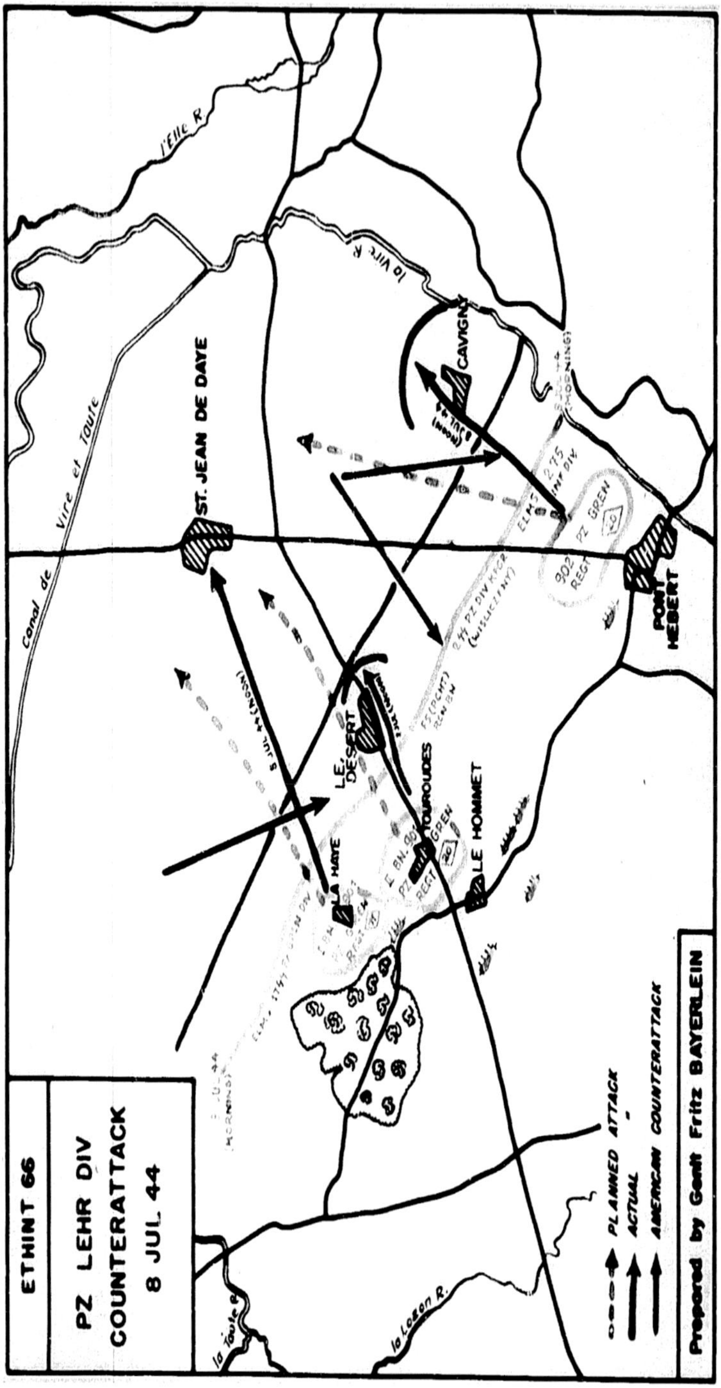


*Panzer-Lehr* Division counter-attack 8 July 1944

tactical zone as the 30th Infantry Division. The two divisions would operate in close association in coming days. XIX Corps sector was narrowed considerably.

By evening of 10 July, prior to the *Panzer Lehr* counterattack, the 9th Infantry Division, in hard fighting, pushed the western flank to a minor north-south road extending almost due south from Graignes and just east of the Bois du Hommet, where its line bent east to where its 39th Regiment held le Désert, on the road leading southwest from the St-Jean-de-Daye crossroads. However, there was a gap of almost 1000 yards between the 47th and 39th Infantry Regiments. A gap through which a minor road led back to the northeast to la Charmenerie. *Panzer Lehr* would send one force of its 901st *Panzergrenadier-Regiment* up that road the next day, another toward le Désert while the 902nd *Panzergrenadier-Regiment* struck north from Hauts-Vents and Pont-Hebert on the Vire River.

The line of defence of the 30th Infantry Division on the evening of 10 July continued only a little east of due south to le Rocher (inclusive), then bearing southeast, with Combat Command B of the 3rd Armored Division less than one thousand yards north of Hauts-Vents and infantry passing just north of Belle-Land and Pont-Hébert to the Vire River. The 113th Cavalry Group was about a mile west of St-Jean-de-Daye, Combat Command A of the 3rd Armored Division a little less than a mile southeast of St-Jean-de-Daye, northeast of the important road junction south of St-Jean-de-Daye.

The German counterattack on 11 July was the first major attack to hit XIX Corps since it crossed the Vire River and Vire et Taute Canal. Had the *Panzer Lehr* attack come a day or two earlier, as originally intended, it would have hit the XIX Corps flank when it was only held by a thin screen of the 113th Cavalry Group. Now, however, the VII Corps' veteran 9th Infantry Division held that sector with Combat Command A of the 3rd Armored Division close at hand. Although the II./*Panzergrenadier-Regiment 901* found initial easy passage through the gap between 9th Infantry Divisions 47th and 39th Infantry Regiments, the I./*Panzergrenadier-Regiment* 901 ran into the 1st and 2nd battalions of the 9th's 39th Infantry Regiment at le Désert. 902nd *Panzergrenadier-Regiment's* 1st *Bataillon*, striking north from Hauts-Vents found the 3rd Battalion of the 30th Infantry Division's 120th Infantry Regiment firmly holding le Rocher, with Combat Command B of the 3rd Armored Division close at hand. The 902nd's 2nd *Bataillon*dvanced northeast from Pont-Hébert along the west bank of the Vire River.

From the German viewpoint, when XIX Corps first crossed the Vire River and the Vire et Taute Canal, the Germans reacted to counter the obvious threat to St. Lô, throwing in a *Kampfgruppe* of the 2nd *SS-Panzer Division 'Das Reich'* under *Obersturmbannführer* Wisliceny, followed by *Panzer Lehr Division* 130, to attack and eliminate the bridgehead.

Despite the immediacy of the 7 July order, it took several days for *Panzer Lehr Division* 130 to complete its move 50 kilometres to the area west of St Lô where it would be attached to 7th *Armee*. Accordingly, the counterattack that had been scheduled for 7 July was put off until 11 July. Wisliceny's '*Das Reich' Kampfgruppe* attacked le Desert on 9 July causing local disruptions and damage, but were quickly driven off by heavy defensive fire.

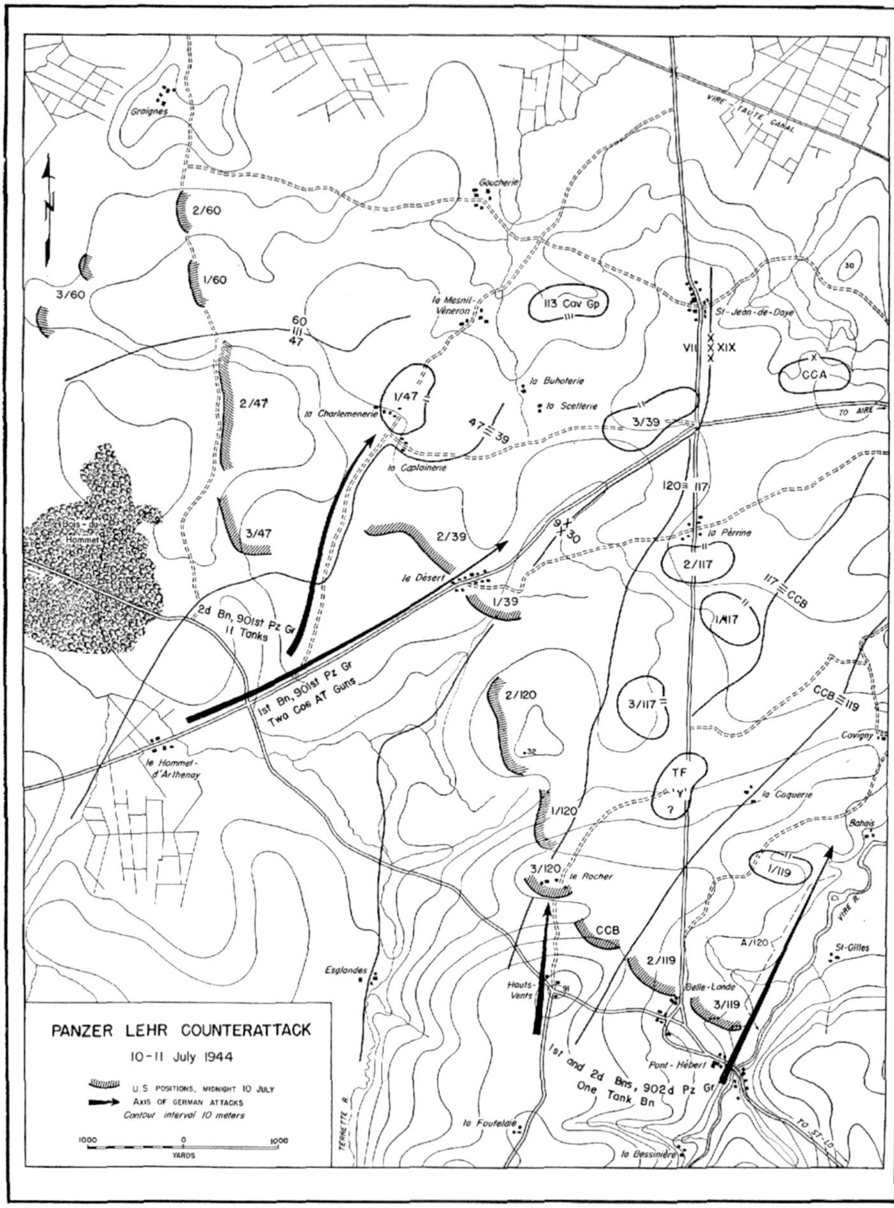


*Panzer-Lehr* counterattack 10–11 July 1944
(map taken from *American Forces in Action series: St Lo (7 July–19 July 1944)*,
Historical Division, War Dept, Washington DC, 1946).

*SS-Obersturmbannführer* Günther-Eberhardt Wisliceny, commander of *Kampfgruppe* Wisliceny in the sector between the Vire and Taute rivers, attached to *Panzer-Lehr Division* 130 during July 1944. Photo taken in July 1943, when Wisliceny held the rank of *SS-Sturmbannführer*. (Bundesarchiv 101III-Zschaeckel-210-08)

On 10 July *Panzer Lehr Divison* 130 assumed command in the sector between the Vire and Taute Rivers. In addition to its own units were a *Kampfgruppe* of the 275th *Infanterie Division* with about 500 men, the *'Das Reich' Kampfgruppe Wisliceny*, a reinforced *Panzergrenadier* battalion, a reconnaissance *Abteilung* [= battalion] of the II *Fallschirmjäger Korps* with about 300 men, elements of the 17th *SS-Panzergrenadier Division 'Götz von Berlichingen'* and elements from *Pionierschüle Frankreich*. These units and elements were attached to *Panzer Lehr's* two *Panzergrenadier* regiments and employed for flank protection and cleaning up enemy remnants. *Panzer Lehr Division* 130 was also supported by a heavy artillery unit, *schwere (21 cm Môrser) Artillerie-Abteilung* 628.

The Division issued an attack order during the night of 10/11 July for an 11 July attack to capture the high ground between Airel and St. Jean and block the Vire River crossings near Airel and north of St. Jean.

In the afternoon of 10 July the American advance intended to capture Hill 91 [Hauts-Vents] ran into the security for *Panzergrenadier-Lehr-Regiment* 902's assembly position for its forthcoming attack. Failure to aggressively push the advance cost the American General Bohn his command. Thanks to the delay, *Panzer Lehr* had moved in. It was now clear the Germans had plugged the gap in their lines. The Americans did, however, interfere with the German assembly and thereby delay the *Panzer Lehr's* attack from its planned 0145 jump-off to a pre-dawn start.

After a short artillery preparation, *Panzer Lehr* launched its attack, its two assault groups passing on both sides of Combat Command B's position. *Panzergrenadier-Lehr-Regiment* 902 attacked on the right, the I./902 with an attached company of *Panzer* IV advancing up the Vire River, through Pont-Hébert toward Cavigny and, eventually, the bridge at Airel. The I *Bataillon* got no further than Bahois. According to Ritgen (p. 153) the II./ 902, with one company of attached tanks and pioneers, ran head-on into a counterattack of the American 3rd Armored Division's Combat Command B and the 30th Infantry Divisions 120th Infantry Regiment and had trouble holding its ground.

*Panzer Lehr's* left assault group, *Kampfgruppe* 901, got off to a better start. *Panzergrenadier-Lehr-Regiment* 901 achieved two shallow penetrations of American lines, the II/ 901 along a minor road through the gap between the 39th and 47th Regiments, the I/901 through le Désert, close to the boundary between the American 9th and 30th Infantry Divisions. An infantry battalion command post was overrun, there were some local withdrawals and confusion behind the lines, but, after daylight, the American response quickly took effect. Intense aerial attacks tore into the German columns, which were tied to the roads because heavy rains had softened the adjoining fields. By mid-afternoon of 11 July the 9th Division had contained the attack. An American counterattack then regained all ground lost.

Bayerlein regretfully recognized that the attack had failed and called the remnants of his attack-forces back to their jump-off positions. Three of the four assault-groups made it back. *Bataillon Philipps* was cut off and destroyed. All attempts by *Panzer Lehr* to relieve it were repulsed.

Lost was the entire I./*Panzergrenadier-Lehr-Regiment* 901 with staff, three companies of *Panzergrenadiere*, the heavy weapons company and one company of tanks with ten *Panther* tanks. Only 7 non-commissioned officers and 23 enlisted men escaped with their personal weapons and six light machine-guns.

*Panzer Lehr*, suffered serious losses. *Generalleutnant* Bayerlein estimated them at about 5–700 men, possibly higher. In addition to the *Panther* company and tanks lost with *Hauptmann* Philipps' I. *Bataillon*, eight *Panzer* IV were lost.

*Generalleutnant* Bayerlein, as he stated in the interviews, was given essentially no information about the forces he faced. The attack was launched with no preliminary reconnaissance, the assault forces advancing blind. Unbeknownst to the German command, as outlined above, the Americans had brought strong forces over the bridge at Airel. Although the 7th *Armee* had hoped that *Panzer Lehr's* counterattack would annihilate the American bridgehead over the Vire River and the Vire et Taute Canal, the unexpectedly strong American forces in the bridgehead rapidly sealed off the penetrations and eliminated the German forces that had made their way behind the American lines. The American estimate was that about one day of progress had been lost while dealing with *Panzer Lehr*. The American 9th Infantry Division sustained about one hundred casualties.

During the subsequent nearly two-week period prior to the American Operation 'Cobra', *Panzer Lehr Division* 130 fought a constant, gruelling battle of attrition against massively superior American forces. The American 9th and 30th Infantry and 3rd Armored Divisions suffered extremely heavy losses. Ritgen (pp. 158–9) cites American losses during the 14-day period for the 30th Infantry Division as 3934 and, for the period of 10–20 July for the 9th Infantry division, about 2000. During that period *Panzer Lehr* lost somewhere between 1200 and 2000. The difference was that the Americans could replace their losses. *Panzer Lehr* could not. *Generalleutnant* Bayerlein described the American tactics as 'a strategy of attrition' ('*Ermattungsstrategie*')

Ritgen, (p. 160), says that the German artillery had proven effective in defence against American attacks, but that the heavy field-howitzer *Abteilung* (III./130) was experiencing a severe shortage of ammunition for the captured Soviet 15.2 cm guns with which it was equipped. Accordingly, *Heeres-Flak-Abteilung* 311 was ordered to position itself so that it could also take part as artillery support in ground action. Even worse than the ammunition shortage was the fuel shortage, which was so limited that the amount on hand merely sufficed to displace a single mortar battery or move individual tanks.

The hedgerow fighting was much like that near Tilly – or worse – with isolated nests of resistance built around two or three tanks concealed in hedgerows, their crews unable to move for days. A bit to the rear, a few more tanks, some mortars and a handful of *Panzergrenadiere* served as the 'local reserve'. Gradually, as counterattack followed attack, but invariably the force of the American superiority battered the German lines back, *Panzer Lehr Division* 130's line of defense was beaten back nearly to the St. Lô–Périers road, where it was on the eve of Operation 'Cobra'.

# OPERATION 'COBRA'

So much has been written and is readily available on the American Operation 'Cobra' that little needs to be added here, except that *Panzer Lehr Division* 130 was unfortunate enough to be precisely located in the neatly outlined rectangle where over 4,000 tons of bombs were to fall, blasting a way for what was hoped would be the breakthrough (hopes did not yet envision a 'breakout'). The capture of St. Lô, to which the crossing of the Vire River and Vire et Taute Canal were marginal, placed the American forces out of the swamps at the base of the Cotentin Peninsula and poised to move forward on hard ground.

The American 9th and 30th Infantry Divisions, followed by the 4th Infantry Division, would open a corridor through which the 2nd and 3rd Armored Divisions and the 1st Infantry Division ('The Big Red One') would thrust, exploiting the gap and then swinging westward to the sea, seizing Coutances and cutting off the German forces in the Cotentin Peninsula. The long-term plan was that the American forces would clear the Brittany Peninsula, opening its precious ports, then pivot on St. Lô and swing eastward to advance toward the Seine River with the British and Canadian forces on their left.

After initial postponement from its original date of 20 July due to rain on 20/21 July, based on predictions that the weather would be favourable for ground operations and moderately satisfactory for air, Air Chief Marshall Leigh-Mallory set H-Hour at 1300 hours, 24 July. Low clouds that would interfere with visibility for bombing resulted in a mid-morning decision to postpone another 24 hours. However, the bombers were already in the air. Although the first formation aborted because of poor visibility, about 35 of the second formation and 300 of the third dropped their loads, totalling nearly 700 tons of bombs.

A tragic accident, the inadvertent release of part of its bomb-load by the lead-bombardier of of a heavy-bomber formation, led the remaining fifteen planes of the formation to drop theirs. These bombs fell on American troops killing 25 and wounding 131 members of the 30th Infantry Division.

However, the bulk of the bombs dropped fell on *Panzer Lehr's* positions. American troops, which had pulled back from their front lines to provide a (inadequate) safety zone were then ordered to move forward and reoccupy their former positions to prevent the Germans from taking them over. Cobra' was rescheduled for 25 July. German troops had already advanced into these positions, so regaining them involved some hard fighting.

The Germans interpreted the events of 24 July as a full-scale American attack, preceded by a frighteningly heavy bomb attack. Reduced though the scale of the bombing was, the Germans still lost 350 men and about a dozen tanks and tank-destroyers. The German soldiers prided themselves in having held their existing positions against what they took to be a full infantry attack. Bayerlein, expecting resumption of the American attack on the morrow, pulled his outposts that were north of the St. Lô–Périers road back into his main positions, south of the road. That, of course, inadvertently positioned those troops inside the area outlined for the massive 'carpet-bombing' on the 25th.

On the eve of Operation 'Cobra' *Oberstleutnant Freiherr* von Hauser's *Panzergrenadier-Lehr-Regiment* 901 adjoined the 5th *Fallschirmjäger Division* at Point 40, east of le Mesnil-Eury, its front running along the St. Lô – Périers highway to the Terrete Stream. *Oberstleutnant* Welsch's *Panzergrenadier-Lehr-Regiment* 902, with attached *Fallschirmjäger-Regiment* 14, held the sector on the right, stretching from the Terrette Stream to the LXXXIV *Korps* boundary with the II *Fallschirmjäger Korps*, east of the village of Hébécrevon, where it adjoined a *Kampfgruppe* of the 352nd *Infanterie-Division* on the west bank of the Vire River, where the German line met the sharp elbow of the river. *Kampfgruppe Heintz*, of the 275th *Infanterie Division*, held five positions near Hébecrevon, each at reinforced-infantry-platoon strength with a few tanks or tank-destroyers and light anti-tank guns.. The II./ *Panzer-Lehr-Regiment* 130 was behind *Paznergrenadier-Lehr-Regiment* 902, near Hébécrevon, *Panzerjäger-Lehr-Abteilung* 130 backing *Panzergrenadier-Lehr-Regiment* 901 on the left. *Kampfgruppe Brosow* of the 2nd *SS-Panzer Division 'Das Reich'* was scheduled to be withdrawn on 24 July from the Division's zone for refitting near le Mesnil-Villeman, five kilometres southeast of Gavray.

At 1140 hours on 24 July American fighter-bombers opened the bombing attack, followed by the heavy bombers that dropped their loads in spite of poor visibility. The Americans may have suffered heavier casualties than the Germans from the supposedly-cancelled bombing attack that day, but the German *Ländser* still found it a harrowing experience.

During the night of 25 June 16 *Panther* tanks of the I./*Panzer-Regiment* 6 relieved the dozen *Panzer* IV's, which were sent back to Dangy as Division reserve.

At about 0800 hours, American front-line troops again pulled back to establish another, again-inadequate, safety zone for the bombing. This time the full-scale bombing added another 4150 tons of bombs to the previous day's 700 tons. Again bombs fell on American troops, this time adding, according to Georges Bernage (*La Guerre des GI*, p.95) 101 more dead and 463 wounded. Among the dead was Lieutenant General Lesley J. McNair, commanding general of the Army Ground Forces and *pro tem* commander of the U. S. First Army Group, the fictitious entity still being maintained in England to sustain German faith that 'the real invasion' was yet to come in the Pas de Calais. General McNair was an onlooker. His death was kept secret, to maintain the deception, the funeral attended by only a select few generals.

*Generalleutnant* Bayerlein felt that *Panzer Lehr Division* 130 had been obliterated. At least half of what was left of the division had been destroyed or disabled, the landscape transformed into a cratered moonscape.

Bayerlein was not too far from the truth. While a later assessment revealed fragmented remnants that survived and, by evening most of the American penetration seemed to have been more-or-less sealed off, as Ritgen described it, the *Panzer Lehr Division* had lost its infantry fighting capabilities and its cohesiveness. The Division was still able to put together two companies of armour, each with 7–8 *Panzer* IV tanks and send one to what was left of each of the two *Panzergrenadier* regiments. But '[The Division's] lines were like a rubber-band stretched to its breaking point, ready to snap at the slightest additional pressure.'

The Americans, however, were not that confident. In *Panzer Lehr's* sector, shortly after 1100 hours, a heavy artillery preparation followed the immense aerial bombardment. American infantry moved out on a broad front. After the overwhelming, awesome power of the aerial bombardment, many expected a walk-through. To their amazement they ran into enough isolated pockets of steadfast resistance so that they had to carefully work their way forward.

However, German communications had been totally destroyed, so there was no coordination. Artillery that had been outside the zone of obliteration fired what ammunition it had in pre-arranged fire-plans, but even that was risky, since American and German troops were interspersed. There was no resupply of ammunition.

The American attack on Hébécrevon – St. Gilles was brought to a standstill. A three company attack with armoured support cost the Americans three Sherman tanks. Envelopment likewise failed and it was only much later that the three German *Panther* at the heart of the resistance were finally knocked out and the block eliminated The entrance to Hébécrevon was mined and the minefield covered by fire from *Kampfgruppe Heintz*. By the end of the day *Kampfgruppe Heintz* was entirely wiped out. The town finally fell by midnight.

The American 4th Infantry Division required 18 Sherman tanks in support of a battalion attack to take out a German strong-point north of La Chapelle-en-Juger, in the centre of the sector. Another German strongpoint with two armoured vehicles remained defiant. La Chapelle-en-Juger remained German at the end of the day.

On the left, the American 9th Division advanced toward Marigny, but also ran into fierce opposition from the embattled *Fallschirmjäger* in the cratered landscape. To the GI at the fighting edge, made wary by sad experience of German skill and tenacity in defence, little seemed to have changed, except that the front line had been bumped forward another mile.

In actual fact, however, Ritgen's description was accurate. Within the bombed zone, there were enough survivors to interfere with the advance, to require 'spot-treatment'. But that was all. Though the units adjoining on either side of the bombed-zone rapidly realized they had not been hit and fought fiercely, there were no German reserves. Nothing at all backed up the front lines. The Americans had just neutralized all that was left. The next day they started to realize that there was a difference. By the day after that, they were out in the clear and on the move.

The story of the American advance, of the genuine 'break-out' that gave meaning to the world of that new term, can be found elsewhere. We shall restrict this narrative to following the battered remnants of a once-powerful elite division, reduced to such pitiful fragments that it now played a very marginal role in the events leading to the Falaise pocket and the retreat to the Seine.

On 26 July the American infantry divisions had to broaden the penetration, none of them having fully achieved their D-day objectives, and get out of the way of the armoured divisions that were to exploit the breakthrough. The German units adjoining the bombed zone fought with undiminished tenacity. What was about to evolve into the breakout was to achieve its spectacular success precisely because the Germans had 'everything in the shop window'. Aside from very minimal, very local reserves, nothing at all was immediately available to contest the American advance once it had broken through the hard, thin crust of the German defences. The massive bombardment had put the final breaking-stress on *Panzer Lehr Division* 130 and the regiment of the 5th *Fallschirmjäger Division* that came under the bombs. Such fragments as survived put up amazingly effective resistance, but they were overwhelmed by the mass and power of the American forces. Once they were gone, the way was open to the interior.

German reaction was crippled by the failure of communications. LXXXIV *Korps* commander von Choltitz committed part of his *Korps* reserve, a reinforced regiment of the 352nd *Infanterie Division* from its assembly area south of Périers to move eastward and secure la Chapelle-en-Juger, while Hausser, at 7th *Armee* level committed from his limited reserve a regiment of the 275th *Infanterie Division* also to move toward la Chapelle-en-Juger from its assembly area near Canisy. These two forces were to converge and seal off the penetration.

Choltitz optimistically launched a counterattack in the Marigny area with a company of tanks and a company of infantry of the 2nd *SS-Panzer Division 'Das Reich'*. That force ran into American armour and infantry.

What Hausser, at 7th *Armee*, did not know was that, while the one regiment that 5th *Fallschirmjäger Division* controlled was able to hold the western flank of the penetration, the other *Fallschirmjäger* regiment and *Panzer Lehr Division* 130, with the units attached to it, had, essentially, been totally destroyed. The regiment of the 275th *Infanterie Division* that Hausser had committed was wiped out *en route* to la Chapelle-en-Juger by American fighter-bombers.

That left the 352nd *Infanterie-Division* holding just east of the bombed zone with an open left flank which that division was simply too weak to handle.

26 July started out with the arduous completion of the previous day's infantry missions, but by the end of the day General Collins was confident enough that the penetration was a fact so that he told his infantry divisions to fight on through the night. As will be discussed below, on 26 July General Collins also committed two of his three armoured columns earlier than originally planned in order to secure Marigny and St. Gilles, road junctions essential for later armoured exploitation of the penetration.

Again, Operation 'Cobra' was almost entirely within *Panzer Lehr's* sector. On the German left, the west flank of the penetration, the American 330th Infantry Regiment of the 83rd Infantry Division fought hard against determined opposition from the *Fallschirmjäger* and failed to achieve the road junction that was its original D-Day objective. However, by late evening the 330th Infantry crossed the Périers–St. Lô highway and they formed a secure right flank for the American penetration.

General Eddy's 9th Infantry Division removed itself from the Marigny road and took positions almost two miles west of that road, reaching about two and a half miles south of the road, facing the German 353rd *Infanterie Division* which was attacking VII Corps' right flank in its attempt to recapture la Chapelle-en-Juger. The American 4th Infantry Division's 8th Infantry Regiment captured la Chapelle-en-Juger and continued its southward advance, overrunning part of the German 353rd and *Panzer Lehr* artillery positions, cutting the Coutances–St. Lô highway and ending the day about five miles south of their original Cobra line of departure.

During the night of 26 July, the American infantry divisions essentially completed all of their D-Day assignments except the singularly resistant road junction that was still denied to the 330th Infantry Division on the west flank and the two vital road hubs, Marigny and St. Gilles.

Also during the night of 26 July the Germans ordered slight withdrawals, in one of which the 352nd *Infanterie Division* withdrew from the loop of the Vire River, allowing elements of the American 30th Infantry Division to fully occupy that loop.

26 July had been the critical day for the Americans, the day when General Collins decided to commit some of his armoured forces, even though the infantry had not yet captured the two essential road junctions of Marigny and St. Gilles, both of which were critical prerequisites in granting access to the road network the armour required to exploit the penetration. General Collins thus committed two of his three armoured columns to capture Marigny and St. Gilles earlier than originally planned, holding off on committing the third armoured column to reduce the danger of congestion in the limited area.

Brigadier-General Maurice Rose's Combat Command A of the American 2nd Armored Division crossed the St. Lô–Périers road at 0700 hours and, with the 22nd Infantry Regiment, advanced south, objective St. Gilles. A weak blocking position set up by *Oberstleutnant* Welsch, the commander of II./*Panzergrenadier - Lehr-Regiment* 902 consisting of a few *Panzer* IV of *Panzer-Lehr-Regiment* 130, some artillery and remnants of *Fallschirmjäger Regiment* 15 was soon eliminated. The force entered St. Gilles by 1300 hours. As CCA continued its advance south toward Canisy it ran into another position set up by *Oberstleutnant* Welsch, this time a handful of grenadiers and a few *Panther* tanks of the 4th *Kompanie* of *Panzer-Regiment* 6. Fighter bombers helped CCA break through in hard fighting. As darkness descended, Canisy fell to the Americans. CCA did not stop there. South of Canisy it split into two columns, one heading toward le Mesnil-Herman, the other toward St. Sampson de Bonifossé.

In the centre, the 8th Infantry Regiment occupied la Chapelle-en-Juger at about midnight. Of July 25/26. Continuing south along the Terrette stream it crossed the St. Lô–Coutances road at about 1800 hours, reaching the area north of Quibou.

To the west, Major General Huebner's 1st Infantry Division committed its reinforced 18th Infantry Regiment (Colonel George Smith, Jr.) with Colonel Boudinot's Combat Command B of the 3rd Armored Division toward Marigny. Losing heavy infantry casualties to small roadblocks and resistance from defended hedgerows, the force advanced with CCB west of the road, the 18th Infantry Regiment to the east.

Northeast of Marigny, at about noon on 26 July, the advancing force ran into the I *Abteilung* of *Panzer-Artillerie-Regiment* 130. The *Panzer Lehr* artillerymen fought valiantly, with heavy casualties, until about 1830 hours, when the survivors fell back to the south.

As it approached Marigny the 1st Division troops ran up against the German 353rd *Infanterie Division* and two companies of the 2nd *SS-Panzer Division 'Das Reich'*. CCB tried unsuccessfully to envelop the town to the west. It required a tactical air strike for armoured elements to reach the north edge of Marigny. The enveloping forces closed up for the night west of Marigny. The 18th Infantry Regiment assumed from the presence of American armour in the northern outskirts of Marigny that the town had been captured by CCB. Accordingly, the regiment sent a battalion to bypass the town on the east. That battalion became disoriented in the dark and Marigny remained, for the most part, in German hands. The 18th Infantry finally cleaned out Marigny in the morning of 27 July.

During the night of 26/27 July those surviving elements of *Panzer Lehr Division* 130 that had been cut off north of the St. Lô–Coutances road broke contact and made their way south. In the morning of 27 July the remnants of the II./ *Panzergrenadier-Lehr-Regiment* 902 reached Quibou with seven *Panzer* IV.

27 July marked the start of the spectacular American advances that turned the hoped-for breakthrough into the genuine breakout. General Hobbs exulted, 'This thing has busted wide open!' (Blumenson, *Breakout and Pursuit*, p. 251.)

Returning to *Panzer Lehr Division* 130, 27 July was the final day of the breakthrough and breakout. All that was left of *Panzer Lehr Division* 130 were scattered fragments, out of contact with each other and higher levels. Outflanked to the east, though they fought hard in their isolation, there was little they could do except gain a little time. As the fighting passed them by, such as were able to straggled southward in its wake. As the Americans continued to advance south through Canisy, their aircraft continued to harry anything that moved on the battlefield.

During the preceding night all elements of the Division that could be contacted and the non-combat-worthy elements were sent to the Percy area. The Ib (logistics) headquarters moved to Montbray. The tank-repair shop in Cerisy-le-Salle was able to pull out with its invaluable personnel and most of its equipment, but lack of towing-capacity and congested highways meant that most of the 30 tanks that were under repair had to be left behind.

The exhausted *Panzergrenadiere* of the II./ *Panzergrenadier-Lehr-Bataillon* 902 and a few *Panzer* IV of the II./ *Panzer-Lehr-Regiment* 130 whose breakout is mentioned above dug in near Quibou. Pounded since morning by American artillery and hammered by constant fighter-bomber attacks, their resistance collapsed by noon under a frontal attack by the American 82nd Reconnaissance Battalion.

The German high command had yet to realize that *Panzer Lehr* had effectively ceased to exist. 27 July was the day that *Generalfeldmarschall* von Kluge's son appeared at *Generalleutnant* Bayerlein's command post.

During the afternoon of 27 July, General White's CCB of the 2nd Armored Division entered Dangy in the tracks of the 82nd Reconnaissance Battalion, and then moved on toward Pont Brocard. *Generalleutnant* Bayerlein had attempted to erect another line of defence, the 'Red Line', in the sector near the small Soulles River. His command post was by the stream.

Remnant elements of *Panzer Lehr Division* 130 established contact with the 17th *SS-Panzergrenadier Division 'Götz von Berlichingen'* on the Division's left, but there was a gap of approximately ten kilometres to the 352nd *Infanterie Division* on the right. While reconnoitering these positions *Generalleutnant* Bayerlein's *Schwimmwagen* was attacked by fighter-bombers. Bayerlein again escaped but lost his fifth driver to such an attack since 7 June.

At about 1630 hours word arrived at the command post that American armour was only 300 yards away, on the other side of the stream. As the first incoming rounds arrived, the surprised staff discovered that the back windows onto the courtyard had iron bars. Most of the command echelon, including *Generalleutnant* Bayerlein, escaped from the burning building between bursts of enemy fire, abandoning their gear, but the command bus with all the files and radio apparatus went up in flames.

At this point, as the American armour moved through and beyond the penetration area the story of *Panzer Lehr Division* 130 fades back into the wings of the great drama. We shall leave that drama of the breakout to others and follow the Division's remnants far from center stage.

Paul Carell (*Sie Kommen*, p. 201):

> As dusk fell he could be seen, marching alone toward Percy, the commander of the renowned *Panzer Lehr*, the division of which, three months earlier, Guderian had said, 'With this division alone you will throw the Anglo-Americans back into the sea.' Now he made his way on foot. In the *Führer* headquarters, however, one little flag was removed from the great situation map.

*Generalleutnant* von Choltitz ordered disengagement during the night of 27/28 July in an effort to save a portion of the LXXXIV *Korps*.

During the night of 27/28 July and during the day a significant number of dispersed elements of the division and vehicles made their way safely back to Percy by widely varying circuitous routes.

In the morning of 28 July the American 330th Infantry Division finally advanced against practically no resistance to rejoin its parent 83rd Infantry Division, the crossroads it had fought so hard for now falling in its lap. As far as the infantry units that had opened the way were concerned, Operation 'Cobra' was over.

Enemy pressure let up on *Panzer Lehr Division* 130 on 28 July. Rain gave a break from aerial attack. Reinforced with a few repaired *Panther* tanks, *Panzeraufklärungs-Lehr-Abteilung* 130 established a new security line in a strong position near Villebaudon, about five kilometres north of Percy, which repulsed an afternoon attack by the 2nd Armored Division's CCA. After an afternoon of hard fighting, the Americans took the village that evening.

General Bradley recognized, on 29 July, that the breakthrough was reality. Although General Patton was not scheduled to take over command with the Third Army until 1 August, on 29 July General Bradley asked Patton to serve as his deputy for the forces on the right and instructed him to supervise VIII Corps operations. As Blumenson puts it (*Breakout and Pursuit*, p.310):

> Though Patton remained in the background of command to the best of his ability, his presence was unmistakable, and his imprint on the operations that developed was as visible as his shadow on the wall of the operations tent.

VIII Corps would, upon activation of Third Army, pass under Third Army control. At the same time, in preparation for the activation of 12th Army Group, which Bradley would command, with Third and First Armies, General Hodges, who would assume command of First Army, was to 'keep close track' or the three corps on the American left VII, XIX and V Corps..

During the night of 29/30 August all of *Panzer Lehr's* forces were pulled back to the high ground at Percy, where a continuous line of defence was established.

*Kampfgruppe Wisliceny* of the 2nd *SS-Panzer Division 'Das Reich'* adjoined on the left, the newly arrived 116th *Panzer Division* of the XXXXVII *Panzerkorps* on the right.

The XXXXVII *Panzer Korps*, under *General* Hans *Freiherr* von Funck, was transferred from the *Panzergruppe West* front to take control of the 2nd *Panzer Division* (note that now both the 2nd *Panzer Division* and the 2nd *SS-Panzer Division 'Das Reich'* are present) and the 116th *(Windhund) Panzer Division* to plug the spreading gap between the LXXXIV and II *Fallschirmjäger Korps* and launch a counter-attack to cut the American lines of communication on the line Villebaudon–Notre-Dame de Cenilly–Coutances. Hard fighting ensued, but in the evening of 29 August new orders suspended the XXXXVII *Panzer Korps* attack to the northwest, redirecting it directly west with a new objective, to link up with *Panzer Lehr Division* 130 and the 2nd *SS-Panzer Division 'Das Reich'*.

The 2nd *Panzer Division* became heavily engaged in fighting off strong American attacks on its northern flank. Its first objective being to cut the St. Lô–Percy road, the 2nd *Panzer Division* soon was caught up in an eventful struggle for control of the la Denisière crossroads on that route. The contest ended, on 1 August with the destruction of the German *Kampfgruppe* 304 of the 2nd *Panzer Division* that had captured and held the crossroads, temporarily cutting off elements of the 175th Regiment of the American 29th Infantry Division that were at Villebaudon. The German *Kampfgruppe* 304, itself, in turn was intermittently cut off in la Denisière by the 116th Regiment of the American 29th Infantry Division. The German 116th *Panzer Division* was caught up in the struggle for the hills around Percy, Villebaudon and Beaucoudrays and proved unable to carry out its projected role in the westward attack.

So much for the effort to reestablish contact with *Panzer Lehr* and *'Das Reich'*, and also a glimpse of the confusing complexity of the larger battle to whose sidelines *Panzer Lehr* was now relegated.

Otto Weidinger, in his history of the 2nd *SS-Panzer Division 'Das Reich'* (p 263) noted:

> In Percy tanks of the *Panzer Lehr Division* provided weak security. There was no contact with the LXXXIV *Armee Korps*. The overall situation and the situation before the front was unknown.
>
> During the course of the morning orders arrived attaching [the 2nd *SS-Panzer Division 'Das Reich'*] to the XXXXVII *Panzer Korps*.
>
> At 1300 hours the 16th *Kompanie* of SS-Panzergrenadier *Regiment 'Deutschland'*, supported by a few tanks of the *Panzer Lehr Division* took positions on Mont Robin (two kilometres northeast of Percy). The enemy soon attacked, but was repulsed after the *Panzer Lehr Division* knocked out six enemy tanks.

The new position withstood attack on 29 July by a reinforced armoured battalion of the American 2nd Armored Division. However, the Americans gained the commanding heights overlooking Percy. Fierce fighting raged throughout the day. *Panzer Lehr* was severely weakened by the attack, the 116th *Panzer Division* having to take over a part of *Panzer Lehr's* sector.

Finally, in the morning of 30 July the American 29th Infantry Division fought its way into the outskirts of Percy, despite fierce resistance by the 116th *Panzer Division*. The city was not fully cleared of its defenders until 2 August.

Also, on 30 July, it is necessary to cross the American – British army boundary and note that General Montgomery, perceiving the lack of armour facing the British in the Caumont sector, had ordered General Dempsey to launch a British attack, Operation 'Bluecoat' south from Caumont., Operation 'Bluecoat' came too late to prevent the German 2nd and 116th *Panzer* divisions from moving west across the Vire River against the Americans, but it achieved its other objective of capturing the high ground around Mont Pinçon which the Germans might have used as a pivot to swing their left flank back to Avranches. As noted below, it also had British armoured forces approaching Vire.

On 31 July American forces broke through at Avranches, on the west coast of the Cotentin Peninsula. The bridge at Avranche provided access to the Brittany Peninsula and to the interior of France. Now General Patton's American Third Army entered the fray, its dramatic advances changing the whole complection of the war.

On 1 August the XXXXVII *Panzerkorps* fell back as ordered to the Vire-sector –Pontfarcy–Villedieu line.

On 2 August the *Korps* was forced back to the la Raballiere–Forêt de St. Severe line. *Panzer Lehr Division* 130, or, more correctly, its remnants, were ordered to cover the *Korps'* southern flank between Sourdeval and Barenton, a task far beyond its existing capabilities.

The British 11th Armoured Divison approached Vire on 2 August. Vire, however, was just over the British-American force boundary putting it in the American zone. On 4 August the American 2nd Armored Division also approached Vire, endangering the assembly area for German forces about to launch *Unternehmen Lüttich* (Operation Liège), Hitler's great assault that was intended to cut off Patton's Third Army at Avranches.

The Americans saw Vire as entry to a critical area of high ground that the Germans might utilize in erecting another line of defence, and as a key road-junction that would provide the American First Army with a pivot for the wheeling movement that would turn 1st Army to the east and permit Patton's Third Army to enter Brittany. The capture of Vire, however, required hard fighting until it finally fell to the American 29th Division on 7 August.

All combat-worthy elements of *Panzer Lehr Division* 130 were assembled into *Kampfgruppe Panzer Lehr* under *Oberstleutnant* von Hauser, commander of *Panzergrenadier-Lehr-Regiment* 901. (*Kampfgruppe Panzer Lehr* will, henceforth, be referred to as *Kampfgruppe von Hauser* to avoid confusion with the later *Kampfgruppe Panzer Lehr* referred to below.) *Kampfgruppe von Hauser* amounted to a few companies of *Panzergrenadiere*, which was all that was left of the two *Panzergrenadier* regiments, a weak company of *Panzer* IV tanks and an *Abteilung* of artillery with two batteries of 10.5 cm and one battery of 15.2 cm guns. The remainder of the Division, mostly train elements, were sent to the Alençon area, where they would shortly form the nucleus of another *Kampfgruppe Panzer Lehr*.

The staff of *Panzergrenadier-Lehr-Regiment* 902 was also sent to Alençon to reconstitute the regiment from replacements and returning stragglers.

*Armeeoberkommando 7* attached *Kampfgruppe von Hauser* to II *Fallschirmjäger Korps*, which was defending Vire and the northern flank of the XXXXVII *Panzer Korps* as it prepared for *Unternehmen Lüttich*.

Elements of *Panzer Lehr*, including *Panzeraufklärungs-Lehr-Abteilung* 130, were left to secure the southern flank of the XXXXVII *Panzerkorps*. The reconnaissance battalion defended a section of line between Barenton and Mortain, facing south.

Also on 2 August, Hitler sent *Oberbefehlshaber West* the directive ordering von Kluge to launch a powerful armoured thrust via Mortain to Avranches, a thrust that would cut off Patton's Third Army. The concept might have been brilliant, had the German resources been there to support it. As it was, it hit Kluge like a thunderbolt since he knew there was no way he could carry it out. The attempt would strip the armour from the Normandy fronts and they would collapse. Whatever forces were committed to the thrust toward Avranche would be exposed to being, themselves, cut off and destroyed. It was a shortcut to disaster.

On 3 August the American 1st Infantry Division easily entered Mortain, routing *Panzer Lehr's* weak forces, which again took heavy casualties, despite their reinforcement with the 2nd *Panzer Division's Panzeraufklärungs-Abteilung* 2. The 1st Infantry Division would be replaced in Mortain by the American 30th Infantry Division on the eve of the German offensive.

Also on 3 August, out in the larger world of the war, General Bradley made a momentous decision that changed the entire course of the campaign and engulfed the microcosm that was the remnants of *Panzer Lehr* in more great events, as he announced that, abandoning the earlier plans for a methodical and orderly campaign to clear the Brittany Peninsula and seize and open its ports, Patton was, instead, to leave minimal forces to do the job there and turn the rest of his forces to drive eastward, south of the German armies that had defended Normandy and go all the way to the Seine. From this plan, which would have penned the German forces against the lower Seine, whose bridges had been destroyed, developed the shorter-term southern arm of the encirclement that created the Falaise pocket.

*Panzer Lehr Division* 130 was in the unenviable position of having elements involved in the defence of both the northern and southern flanks of what would finally evolve into the Falaise pocket, as the XXXXVII *Panzer Korps* attacked Mortain in what it hoped would be the start of a thrust to Avranches and the American and British forces fumbled their way toward cutting those forces off.

On August 5 the American XV Corps' 90th Infantry Division captured Mayenne and crossed the Mayenne River. The American thrust was already advancing east of where the German XXXXVII *Korps*, to the north, was about to launch its attack on Mortain in hopes of driving to Avranches and the sea.

By August 6 German forces had to give up Vire after heavy fighting, which included hard-fought but fruitless counterattacks by *Kampfgruppe Panzer Lehr* (von Hauser), and fall back to a new line of resistance to the south.

On 6 August *Oberbefehlshaber West* directed *Armeeoberkommando* 7 to pull *Panzer Lehr Division* 130 and two other divisions out of the front for reconstitution. On 8 August *AOK* 7 ordered the Division staff, without any other elements of the Division, to go to the LXXXI *Armee Korps* near Alençon.

The German *Unternehmen Lüttich* began during the night of 6/7 August with an attack by *2nd SS-Panzer Division 'Das Reich'*, and one column of the 2nd *Panzer Division*. The other column of the 2nd *Panzer Division* attacked at dawn. The German offensive was off to a ragged start.

The American 30th Infantry Division in Mortain was hit hard and the 2nd *SS-Panzer Divison 'Das Reich'* forced its way through the town, but the American division battled desperately. One battalion, though cut off and surrounded, valiantly hung on to the critical commanding Hill 317, just east of Mortain, whence, with excellent observation, they called down heavy artillery fire stalling the German advance.

The morning dawned clear. The experienced German soldiers knew, as soon as the morning dawned clear, what would come and immediately dispersed and camouflaged their vehicles, found cover and dug in. German movement came to a complete halt. British Hurricanes and rocket-firing Typhoons pounded the German forces. Fortune favored the American defenders in the availability, sometimes apparently by pure good luck, of divisions that could rapidly be pulled in as reinforcements. Within 24 hours the American VII Corps controlled a total of seven divisions, two of them armoured. Heavy fighting continued, but the German advance was solidly brought to a dead stop. There would be more hard fighting, but no more German advances after the morning of 7 August.

Hitler, however, maintained lofty hopes that *Unternehmen Lüttich* would not only reach Avranches, but then would bring about the collapse of the Allied Normandy front. He accordingly ordered that additional forces be withdrawn from the remainder of the front and thrown in. Until the renewed attack was ready, those forces already involved were to hold in the positions they had attained.

1st *SS-Panzer Division 'Leibstandarte SS Adolf Hitler'* and the 116th *Panzer Division* joined the fray in the afternoon of 7 August, but they merely added themselves to the forces that would end up in the pocket.

For, also on 7 August, the First Canadian Army launched a major offensive, Operation 'Totalize' which was to advance down that Caen – Falaise plain toward Falaise. The combination of the unexpected German westward thrust toward Avranches and the American XV Corps eastward advance along the Mayenne/Laval–le Mans–Nogent–le-Rotrou axis gave new meaning and scope to Operation 'Totalize'.

7 August also saw the American XV Corps' 79th Infantry Division capture Laval, further south of Mayenne on the Mayenne River, while spearheads of the American 5th Armored Division reached the Sarthe River, south of le Mans, which had long been the location of German 7th *Armee* headquarters. The 5th Armored Division spearhead bypassed the city and crossed the river during the night.

The American 79th Infantry Division entered its part of le Mans on 8 August while the 5th Armored Division spearhead swung up around its eastern outskirts, cutting off the remaining exits.

The 90th Infantry Division entering the northern part of LeMans on 9 August. Le Mans is about 47 miles almost directly south of Alençon.. Alençon is about 35 miles east of Mortain, where the German forces were still attempting to get past the American 30th and 35th Infantry Divisions.

XV Corps' three hard-hitting divisions were now 85 air-miles southeast of the Germans at Mortain, still headed toward its objective, the Paris–Orleans gap and the Seine River. At this point, however, the military objective of destroying the enemy forces eclipsed the former geographical objective of reaching the Seine.

Returning to *Panzer Lehr Division* 130: on 10 August the Division was split up among three corps. *Panzeraufklärungs-Lehr-Abteilung* 130 was still attached to the XXXXVII *Armee Korps*, which was in charge of the German assault on Avranches, participating in the defence of the southern flank of the assault force. *Kampfgruppe von Hauser* was attached to LXXXIV *Armee Korps* in the Vire area, defending the northern flank, and the staff and rear elements had been sent to the LXXXI *Armee Korps* for reconstitution.

*Armeeoberkommando* 7 reported that, for the time being, it would be impossible to withdraw *Panzer Lehr Division* 130 for reconstitution.

While Hitler's orders kept the forces of the 5th *Armee* and 7th *Armee* committed to the failed Mortain offensive, securing the southern flank of the German 7th *Armee* in the Domfront–Alençon–Mamers–Nogent-le-Rotrou sector became the mission of the newly arrived LXXXI *Armee Korps*. Defending a 180 kilometre sector of front was totally beyond the capabilities of *Korps'* forces, which consisted of the fought-out 708th *Infanterie Division* on the right, *Kampfgruppe Panzer Lehr Division* (see below) in the center, and the 9th *Panzer Division* on the left.

*Panzer Lehr Division* 130's assembly area for its battered staff and logistic elements was between the 708th *Infanterie Division* and the 9th *Panzer Division,* near Alençon. As untrained reinforcements arrived, *Oberst* Gerhardt commenced reconstitution of a *Kampfgruppe* which gradually gained strength as stragglers returned and the Division workshops labored long, coming up with a few *Panzer*.

The resultant *Kampfgruppe Panzer Lehr Division* included elements of *Panzergrenadier-Lehr-Regiment* 902, I./*Panzer-Regiment* 6, *Panzer-Artillerie-Regiment* 130, *Panzer-Pionier-Bataillon* 130 and *Panzeraufklärungs-Lehr-Abteilung* 130. Attached were the I./*Grenadier-Regiment* 11 and *Sicherungs-Regiment* 1.

On 9 August the Division staff arrived in la Fresnaye sur Sarthe, 14 kilometres south of Alençon, also the site of the 9th *Panzer Division* headquarters. The new *Kampfgruppe Panzer Lehr* was assigned the line Jublains–St. Gemmes–the hills south of Sillé (le Guillaume)–Conlie, centered on Sillé. It was to use mobile tactics to deny the enemy access to Alençon.

The American 80th Infantry Division attacked just as the *Kampfgruppe* reached the important Sillé-le-Guillaume crossroads. By evening the *Kampfgruppe* had to fall back to the commanding hills to the north.

Also on 9 August, Canadian progress in Operation 'Totalize' bogged down on the third day of hard fighting after about eight miles advance, with nearly that much left to go to Falaise.

On 10 August, as noted above, the American XV Corps was now diverted from its Orléans – Paris gap geographical objective to a more immediate military objective of destroying the enemy forces, a move that would affect *Kampfgruppe Panzer Lehr*. Attacking north from le Mans the American 5th Armored Division, the French 2nd Armored Division and the 79th and 90th Infantry Divisions outflanked the German 9th *Panzer Division*. Through a 25 kilometre breach the Americans advanced on Alençon.

The LXXXI *Korps* command post, southeast of Alençon, was overrun. As American armor pushed into Alençon both *Panzer Lehr* and 9th *Panzer Division* staffs had to flee. Although the *Kampfgruppe Panzer Lehr* had no enemy contact, it was ordered to fall back to the north behind the Merderau River to shorten the front and economize on forces.

On 11 August there was only reconnaissance activity on *Kampfgruppe Panzer Lehr's* front. However, as American forces approached Alençon the trains and logistical elements fled in disorder.

Also on 11 August *Generalfeldmarschall* von Kluge at last obtained permission from Hitler to temporarily transfer *Panzergruppe Eberbach* from Mortain to attack the American XV Corps spearheads that were moving north toward Alençon. This was, of course, presented to Hitler as a temporary matter necessary to clear the flank so that *Unternehmen Lüttich* could be resumed on a larger scale. (The renewed attack toward Avranche was to involve eight divisions, exceeding the command capabilities of a corps. Accordingly, Hitler insisted that *General* Heinrich Eberbach be transferred from command of what had been *Panzergruppe West* to command the Mortain force, which would now include XXXXVII *Panzer Korps* and LVIII *Panzer Korps,* and would be known as *Panzergruppe Eberbach.* Eberbach's former command, *Panzergruppe West* was now designated 5th *Armee* under *SS-Obergruppenführer und General der Waffen-SS* Sepp Dietrich. *General* Eberbach was disgruntled at what he viewed as a demotion.)

In preparation for Eberbach's projected attack on XV Corps, the German 7th *Armee* began to withdraw eastward from Mortain during the night of 11 August.

The pace of events outstripped German plans. On 12 August the Americans captured Alençon and Sées, thereby depriving 7th *Armee* of its supply base, whereby it became entirely dependant on 5th *Armee* for logistical support. Eberbach was forced to prematurely commit the forces he intended to employ at Alençon in a futile attempt to defend Argentan.

As the American forces continued their northward advance via Alençon, Sees and Nonant-le-Pin. *Kampfgruppe Panzer Lehr* fell back on a parallel track. The Division was ordered to hold the line Pré-en-Pail–St. Denis on 12 August, its reserve, *Kampfgruppe Eltrich*, consisting of one company each of pioneers and armour, secured the deep left flank. *Grenadier-Regiment* 728 of the 708th *Infanterie Division* was attached.

*Kampfgruppe von Hauser* reported back to the division from its employment at Vire the night of 12 August. It was sent to the Fontainebleu area where the Division was again to be reconstituted.

The French 2nd Armoured Division on the left and American 5th Armored Division on the right approached Argentan from the south. The French, at one point, utilized the road east of the Forêt d'Ecouves that was assigned to the American division, delaying that division's advance for six hours, which gave the Germans time to add an armoured unit to their defence of Argentan, preventing what probably would have been an easy capture.

When the American advance resumed, *Kampfgruppe Eltrich* and advance elements of the 116th *Panzer Division* attacked the American 5th Armored Division in its approach to Argentan at Montrée, about 23 kilometres southeast of Argentan. *Kampfgruppe Eltrich* suffered heavy losses, but further delayed the American drive toward Argentan.

The advancing French 2nd Armored Division overran *Panzer Lehr* forces securing the line east of Pré-en-Pail. Attempts to establish a new front facing south were only partially successful.

On 13 August, as enemy pressure increased in the area south of Argentan, pressure let up on *Kampfgruppe Panzer Lehr Division* in the Carrouges – Boucé line. Contact was lost with the LXXXI *Armee Korps*

In the evening of 13 August *Kampfgruppe von Hauser* reported that it had been attached to the newly arriving 331st *Infanterie-Division* and committed in the defence of Gacé, facing south.

Also on 13 August, the final outcome of allied indecision regarding whether or not the American forces would be permitted to continue their northward advance into what had, originally, been specified as territory assigned to the British, General Patton ordered XV Corps to call back any of its forces that were north of Argentan and hold on the agreed boundary, the Carrouges – Sées, a few miles south of Argentan.

As enemy forces crossed the Argentan– l'Aigle road encirclement loomed. In light of the fact that, on 6 August, *Generalfeldmarschall* von Kluge had ordered *Panzer Lehr Division* 130 withdrawn from the line until 12 August for a period of reconstitution, which order the 7th *Armee* had declared impossible due to circumstances, *Generalleutnant* Bayerlein, on his own initiative, decided to leave *Kampfgruppe Kuhnow* behind and turn the Division's sector over to the 728th *Infanterie Regiment* of the 708th *Infanterie Division*.

In the morning of 13 August *Kampfgrupe Panzer Lehr* was at Habloville, about six kilometres northeast of Putanges. With its vehicles parked in the woods and along the margins of the roads, the *Kampfgruppe* was suddenly hit by intense air attacks that lasted from 0900 to 1400 hours and caused heavy losses, especially in vehicles.

Nevertheless, the Division staff and remaining elements reached the area east of Argentan on 14 August, thereby escaping the developing Falaise pocket.

It is now time to return to *Kampfgruppe Kuhnow,* which was left near Carrouges, and events in the developing pocket.

*Kampfgruppe Kuhnow*, at the time it was left behind, consisted of the remnants of *Panzergrenadier-Lehr-Regiment* 902, a company of tanks and a battery of howitzers.

On 14 August the enemy captured Carrouges, forcing *Kampfgruppe Kuhnow* back to the northwest. Losing contact with the 708th *Infanterie Division, Major* Kuhnow attached his unit to the XXXXVII *Panzer Korps*. As part of the XXXXVII *Panzer Korps* the *Kampfgruppe* was encircled in the Falaise Pocket. On 17 August *Major* Kuhnow found the command post of the 12th *SS-Panzer Division 'Hitlerjugend'*. At about 1800 hours on 19 August Allied forces met near Chambois and closed the Falaise Pocket.

The commander of the 7th *Armee, SS-Oberstgruppenführer* Hausser, set the night of 19/20 August for the general breakout of the encircled German forces. During the night of 19/20 August the remnants of *Kampfgruppe Kuhnow* joined the remnants of *'Panzermeyer's' 'Hitlerjugend'* division and the remnants of *Panzeraufklärungsabteilung* 21 in successfully breaking out of the pocket. After an eventful and exhausting odyssey, the remnants of *Kampfgruppe Kuhnow* crossed the Seine at Elboeuf and, in the evening of 21 August, rejoined the remnants of *Panzer*

*Lehr Division* 130 where it was bivouacked near Senlis. The following day *Panzergrenadier-Lehr-Regiment* 902 was transferred to the Soissons area for reconstitution near the front.

Now let us return to *Kampfgruppe Panzer Lehr* on 14 August. The delay in the American push northward occasioned by the decision to honor the boundary line noted above gave *Kampfgruppe Panzer Lehr* opportunity to regain contact with LXXXI *Armee Korps* and to establish a new line of resistance between le Bourg- St. Leonhard and Nonant-le-Pin.

That evening the *Kampfgruppe* was assigned to block the roads leading north from Argentan to Gacé. *Kampfgruppe von Hauser* was returned to the Division for that task.

Canadian forces entered Falaise on 16 August. The next day, 17 August, they cleared out the last Germans.

On 17 August leading elements the 344th *Infanterie-Division*, arriving on the Normandy Front fresh from the 15th *Armee,* relieved the *Kampfgruppe Panzer Lehr*.

Also on 17 August General Bradley released American forces from restriction to the Overlord lodgement area so that they could advanced to the Seine River. Since most of the German forces that avoided or escaped the Falaise Pocket and those retreating before the advancing Canadian forces were concentrated in the area west of the lower Seine River and north of Paris, this extended the lower jaw of the Allied pincers movement, trapping these forces with their backs against the river. Allied air had destroyed all but one of the lower Seine bridges. Forcing most of those German forces that made it across the Seine to cross by ferry.

On 18 August, effective immediately, *Oberbefehlshaber West* attached *Panzer Lehr Division* 130 to *Armeeoberkommando* 1 for reconstitution near Fontainebleu. That day *Generalfeldmarschall* Model replaced *Generalfeldmarschall* von Kluge. Paul Carell (*Sie Kommen,* p. 220) describes the scene as *Generalleutnant* Bayerlein reported at *Heeresgruppe* B headquarters.

> As [*Generalfeldmarschall* Model] came out of the map room from his first conversation with Kluge, *General* Bayerlein ran into him. 'What are you doing here?', asked Model. 'I am here to take leave of *Feldmarschall* von Kluge because the remnants of my division are to be withdrawn from the front for reconstitution', answered Bayerlein. Model's reply reeked with the merciless nature of the war in Russia: 'My dear Bayerlein, in the East divisions are reconstituted at the front, and, in the future, that is how things will be here. You and your units will remain where you are.'

According to Ken Hechler (*The Bridge at Remagen*, p. 150), 'Bayerlein looked him in the eye and said that if that was the way the German army had operated in Russia it evidently had not been too successful.' As Helmut Ritgen sums it up (p. 185), 'Nevertheless, the withdrawal order remained in effect. The situation was stronger than the *Feldmarschall*.'

# FROM THE SEINE TO THE WESTWALL

Reconstitution of the Division remained more dream than reality. The non-combat-worthy elements of the Division assembled on 13 August at Fontainebleau, 60 kilometres southeast (all distances from the center) of Paris, but then, on 17 August, *Heeresgruppe* B ordered that the reconstitution was to take place at Senlis, 40 kilometres north of Paris; the next day the Division was attached to 1st *Armee*, which specified Fontainebleau.

Nevertheless, the Division was transferred, first to Senlis, then to Laon, 90 kilometres northeast of Paris, as 1st *Armee* reserve. Then, as thoughts turned to defending the Seine River, the Division was ordered to move by 24 August to Provins, 75 kilometres east-southeast of Paris.

Three battalions of former cavalrymen were sent to the Division as replacements, along with a few guns and tanks, but that hardly started to cover the Division's needs. *Generalleutnant* Bayerlein reported the division's combat strength as: (Ritgen, p. 187.)

| | |
|---|---|
| *Panzergrenadier-Lehr-Regiment* 901 | 800 men on *SPW,* inadequate weapons |
| *Panzergrenadier-Lehr-Regiment* 902 | 300 men on trucks, inadequate weapons |
| *Panzer-Lehr-Regiment* 130 | About 20 *Panzier* IV and V |
| *Panzeraufklärungs-Lehr-Abteilung* 130 | about 5 *Panzerjäger* (tank destroyers) |
| *Panzer-Artillerie-Regiment* 130 | 6 – 10.5 cm light howitzers, 2 15.2 cm heavy howitzers [corrected as per Perrigault, p.313] |
| *Panzer-Pionier-Bataillon* 130 | 150 men |
| *Heeres Flak Abteilung* 311 | Unfit for service |

The division had, therefore, about one-quarter of its authorized strength in *Panzergrenadiere* and artillery, one-eighth its tanks and tank-destroyers. The rear elements in the Soissons area had about two-thirds their personnel, but only half of the motor-vehicles were serviceable.

On 23 August *Oberst*Gerhardt assumed command of the Division when *Generalleutnant* Bayerlein went on leave to recover from multiple wounds and to receive the Swords to the Oak Leaves of the Knight's Cross [*Schwerter zum Eichenlaub des Ritterkreuzes*].

On 24 August 22 new *Panzer* IV with crews unloaded at Sézanne and were assigned to the Division. However, the tanks were in such poor condition that they required inspection and work before they could go into action in the 5th *Kompanie* of *Panzer-Lehr-Regiment* 130.

Defence of the Seine River, with its deep meanders, was problematical from the start. German plans to defend the Seine were lost in the rush of events as the Allies crossed the river, first, as men of the American 79th Infantry Division walked single-file across a dam near Mantes in the rainy night of 19 August. The following day the engineers built a treadway bridge, allowing a full-scale crossing. By 23 August a Bailey bridge was in operation.

At the same time that the American V Corps' 79th Infantry Division crossed the Seine, the American 5th Armored Division, with special permission from Montgomery to cross army boundaries, started its drive up the west bank of the

Seine to Louviers and Elbeuf. Louviers was 30 miles down river from Mantes. The mission was to cut German forces off from crossing sites where the Seine was relatively narrow and force them toward the broad, lower tidal estuary of the river where crossing would be far more difficult. By this time, however, hard-working *Waffen-SS* officers had put together *Kampfgruppe Mohnke* out of remnants of the 17th *SS-Panzergrneadier-DIvision 'Götz von Berlichingen'* and elements of the 1st *SS-Panzer Division 'Leibstandarte SS Adolf Hitler'*. The American 5th Armored Division had five days of hard fighting to advance twenty miles to its first objective at the loop of the Seine near les Andelys.

On 23 and 24 August the American 5th Infantry and 7th Armored Divisions of Third Army's XX Corps crossed the Seine at Monterau. Also on 23 and 24 August a small bridgehead was established by the American 3rd Armored Division of First Army's VII Corps at Ponthierry, about seven miles downstream from Melun, which allowed crossing of two combat commands of armor and, on 25 August, the capture of Melun, 25 miles south of Paris, and establishment of a crossing there.. Also on 25 August, the American Third Army's XII Corps' 4th Armored Division reached the outskirts of Troyes, 140 kilometres southeast of Paris, also on the Seine River. The American forces crossed the Seine there that evening.

Thus, by 25 August the American Third Army had four bridgeheads on the upper Seine River south of Paris between Melun and Troyes, while the American First Army had a bridgehead north of Paris on the lower Seine River at Mantes-Gassicourt.

Also on 25 August the surrender of Paris, as noted below, provided another bridgehead over the Seine River.

Since the German command had never constructed any lines of defence, nor set forces aside for defence in interior France, the battered remnants of divisions that made it out of the Falaise Pocket or back before the advancing Canadian forces were, if fortunate enough to find some way across the nearly bridgeless river, hastily gathered up and thrown into immediate counterattacks with little if any time to catch their breath, let alone for reconstitution.

The uprising in Paris, which began on 19 August, triggered the dispatch of a *Kampfgruppe* from *Panzer-Lehr* under *Hauptman* Hennecke to fight its way into the city from the east during the night of 24/25 August. The *Kampfgruppe* consisted of a single, weakly armed battalion, the I./*Panzergrenadier-Lehr-Regiment* 901, reinforced with a platoon of heavy (15 cm) infantry guns and one company of *Panther* tanks (from the I./*Panzer-Regiment* 6).

American forces had already entered the eastern, French forces the western portions of Paris before *Kampfgruppe Hennecke* even got to the city,. The *Kampfgruppe* ran into increasing numbers of barricades as it entered the city, lost several tanks and *SPW's* and suffered many casualties due to the vulnerability of the open-topped *SPW's* to fire from buildings lining its route. The German city commander, *General* von Choltitz, rejected an ultimatum, but was captured less than two hours later, at 1500 hours on 25 August, and surrendered the city, whereupon *Hauptmann* Hennecke fell back to Villeparisis, where his *Kampfgruppe* was surrounded by French resistance forces on 26 August. *Kampfgruppe Hennecke* broke out with heavy losses. On 27 August *Kampfgruppe Hennecke* secured the Soissons – Villers-Cotterêts road.

Among the fragments of German forces opposing the Allied advance, the remnants of *Panzer Lehr's Kampfgruppe Ritgen'*, the II./*Panzer-Lehr-Regiment* 130, with all of 22 *Panzer* IV tanks (a single company's T/O strength) and *Kampfgruppe* 902 constituted *Armeeoberkommando* 1's 'operational reserve'.

At this point *Panzer Lehr* was no longer functioning as a division, but as a scattering of weak *Kampfgruppen* caught up in the maelstrom of the confused and headlong German retreat across France to the *Westwall*. For the reader who so desires, Jean-Claude Perrigault provides such detail as is available for this period.

The *Westwall* was not what it had been in 1939. Weapons, barbed wire, obstacles, even the steel doors for the bunkers had been removed and taken to the *Atlantikwall*. Furthermore, what might have seemed imposing in 1939 was obsolete. The concrete was not thick enough to withstand 1944's bombs. The weapons emplacements, designed in the days when 37mm anti-tank guns and the German MG 39 were the standard weapons, could not mount the 7.5 cm anti-tank guns and MG 42 machine guns of 1944. Gaps had been blown in the dragon's-teeth obstacles.

Nevertheless, even though the numbers of German troops were far too few to fully man the line (Ritgen says only one-fifth of the bunkers were occupied), the pursuing American forces were at the end of a long and over-stretched supply line and were exhausted by their rapid sweep across France. The fortifications of the *Westwall* were a morale boost for the German troops, as was the feeling that they were now defending the borders of their homeland. Also, as the Allies learned to their sorrow, the German soldier had a phenomenal ability to make good use of any natural or artificial aid to forming a strong defensive position.

*Kampfgruppe von Hauser* played an admirable part in eliminating the American 5th Armored Division's penetration near Wallendorf, southwest of Bitburg. Although the Germans were amazed that the American bridgehead over the Saur River was not enlarged, General Eisenhower's orders and the strained logistics situation forced the American V Corps' General Gerow on 16 September to order the forces in the bridgehead to go over to the defensive.

After the failure of the first German counterattack on 19 September, a stronger attack on 20 September reduced the size of the bridgehead. Under heavy German artillery fire, the American forces withdrew from the little bridgehead which, on 22 September, was entirely eliminated. *Kampfgruppe von Hauser* played a creditable role in this defensive success. *Oberstleutnant* von Hauser was awarded the Oakleaves to his Knight's Cross (*Eichenlaub zum Ritterkreuz)* for his part and in recognition of the *Kampfgruppe's* valour.

The interviews that follow cover the actions of *Panzer Lehr Division* 130 from the start of Operation 'Cobra', the American breakout in Normandy, action in Lorraine through the collapse in France with additional discussion on the Division's actions in Lorraine, at the Remagen bridge and in the Ruhr Pocket.

Additional material on the Division's involvement in Lorraine, at Remagen, and in the Ruhr Pocket will follow this interview.

# ETHINT 69 – ( )

25 Nov 45

**AN INTERVIEW WITH**
**Genlt Fritz Bayerlein**

**PZ LEHR DIV**
**AT THE**
**START OF OPERATION 'COBRA'**

**Office of the Chief of Military History**
**Department of the Army**
**Washington 25, D. C.**

EUCOM : HD : OHG2 Copy 1

**DEPARTMENT OF THE ARMY**
**HISTORICAL DIVISION**
**WASHINGTON 25, D. C.**

12 July 1949

Note to: ETHINT 69
By: Kenneth W. Hechler
Major, Infantry (Res)

No record in German was made at the time of this oral interview, inasmuch as the interview was held entirely in English, notes were made by Major Franklin Ferriss, and Major Ferriss dictated the attached report following the completion of the oral interview. The overlay to which Major Ferriss refers in his report is probably included in the [illegible, 'VII??'] Corps section of the EUCOM historical records covering the preliminary narrative prepared by the 'Operation Cobra' section.

There are more detailed accounts of the losses of the Panzer Lehr Division which General Bayerlein prepared, (see, for example, MS # A–902). For this reason, this brief oral interview must be read in conjunction with the other interviews and reports of General Bayerlein in order to get the full story on the bombing of 24 and 25 July 1944.

## ETHINT 69 – ()

| | |
|---|---|
| Title: | Pz Lehr Div At The Start Of Operation 'Cobra' |
| Source: | Genlt Bayerlein, Fritz |
| Position: | Cmdr, Pz Lehr Div |
| Date: | 26 Nov 45 |
| Place: | St Germain-en-Laye, France |
| Interviewer: | Maj Franklin Ferriss |

[tr. note- Since the German original was not available, this is presented exactly as is. Notes marked 'Ed.' were made by the army editor at the time. Notes marked 'FPS

Ed' or 'tr. note' were made by the present editor and translator, Frederick Steinhardt.]

**Foreword**

This interview, consisting apparently of a paraphrase of Genlt Bayerlein's remarks, is one of a series conducted by the Historical Section, ETOUSA, and its successors. Unfortunately, only a typed record in English is available for editing. It is not known whether a record in German was made at the time of the interview, nor, if one was made, can the accuracy of the translation be determined. Therefore, no absolute guarantee can be given as to the authenticity and completeness of this version of the interview. Only obvious errors in spelling, punctuation, and grammatical construction have been corrected.

The original initialed copy of the available record is inclosed [*sic.*] with Copy 1 of ETHINT 69.

(signed)
LE ROY S. STANLEY
Capt, Inf
Historical Editor
May 31 1948

1. Prior to the American bombing of 24 Jul 44, Genlt Bayerlein, then commanding Pz Lehr Div, had his main line of resistance a little north of the St Lo – Periers highway, as indicated on the attached overlay (Ed: overlay not included in available record). He had also prepared a second and a third line south of the highway. In preparing those alternate lines, the troops had actually dug foxholes and antitank and artillery positions, as well as positions for regimental and division reserves. However, none of these lines was more than a series of strongpoints, nor, due to the shortage of troops, were they close enough to be mutually supporting.

2. Genlt Bayerlein was not happy about the proximity of his lines to the St Lo – Periers highway, as he felt that this road constituted a fine marker for American planes. He had requested permission to withdraw his front line to a line through la Chappelle [FPS Ed: la Chappelle-en-Juger(?)], but higher authority had denied his request.

3. The bombing on 24 Jul 44 resulted in many casualties to Genlt Bayerlein's troops – both those in the main line of resistance north of the highway, and the battalion and regimental reserves, which had been in the second line of positions south of the highway. After this bombing, Genlt Bayerlein decided that in view of the danger of another such attack, which he felt would be concentrated on the German positions north of the highway, it would be safer to place the main body of his troops in the second line south of the highway. Hence, except on the Division's right flank, only outposts held the former main line of resistance north of the highway on 25 Jul 44; the tanks also were pulled back to the second line. The paratroopers on the Division's left pulled their main line of resistance south at this time to conform to the one now occupied by Pz Lehr Div.

4. Although the American bombing on 25 Jul 44 hit the new main line of resistance south of the highway very hard, the regimental and division reserves, which were south of this new line, were not badly hit, nor were the outposts north of the road. Most of the resistance on 25 July 44 was by these reserves, which were committed immediately after the bombing.

5. Total casualties in the Division on 24 and 25 Jul 44 were approximately 2000, of which two-thirds were suffered on 25 Jul 44. About 50% of the total casualties were due to bombing, about 20% to artillery, and the remaining 30% to ground action.

# MS A–902

***PANZER LEHR DIVISION***
**24–25 July 1944**

**DEPARTMENT OF THE ARMY**
**HISTORICAL DIVISION**
**WASHINGTON 25, DC**

12 July 1949

Note to: MS # A–902
By: Kenneth W. Hechler
Major, Infantry (Res)

This manuscript was prepared by General Bayerlein during his stay at St Germain in October 1945. General Bayerlein had prepared a previous account of the Normandy operation, including the bombing, and he had also been interrogated on this subject (see for example ETHINT 67, ETHINT 69 and MS # A–903.)

After General Bayerlein was brought to St Germain, the writers in the 'Operation Cobra' Section discovered that they needed some more detailed material on the precise effects of the bombing on 24 – 25 July 1944, and General Bayerlein was accordingly asked to prepare this more detailed material which he did in MS A–902.

Alfred Zerbel Koenigstein/Ts., 30. 5. 50

**INDEX FOR**
**MS # 902.**
**(*PANZER LEHR DIVISION* (24–25 JULY 1944))**

**[SIGNED] Alfred Zeerbel**
**(Alfred Zerbel)**

**[translated by Fred Steinhardt]**

BAYERLEIN
*Generalleutnant.*

## *PANZER LEHR DIVISION*
## 24–25 July 1944

MS # A–902 [these questions are, of course, in the original American English and were not translated by Fred Steinhardt]

### PANZER LEHR DIVISION, 24–25 June 1944

We have considerable information of a general nature on the bombing of 24 – 25 July, but would like additional and more specific information, if you are able to supply it, on the following points:

1. Estimate casualties due entirely to air attacks or due entirely to artillery preparations. In other words, which was the worst? Our air force figures estimate that because the German front lines were well dug in, casualties were no more than 10% along the front lines; I have a feeling this is too low a percentage. Nevertheless the American troops suffered many casualties and had a difficult time getting through the German line; therefore there was a great deal of opposition;

2. What was the effect of the bombing on German morale. [*sic.*]

3. How great was the shock effect of the bombing as distinguished from those actually killed or wounded?

4. In some detail, what was the effect of the bombing on German positions. [*sic.*]

5. What was the effect on German communications. [*sic.*]

6. Were the German forces hit any harder in the center of the Panzer Lehr Division sector? If not, where?

**MS # A–902 [*General* Bayerlein's replies translated by Frederick Steinhardt]**

1. Losses due to air attacks – artillery.

a. The main losses were a result of the carpet bombings, followed, in decreasing importance by artillery, then armour and lesser weapons.

   Actual losses in dead and wounded were attributed:

   to bombing: 50%

   to artillery: 30%

   to other weapons: 20%

   these are, however, estimates.

b. The good cover of the infantry (well dug in) proved useless, providing no protection from the carpet bombing, since the terrain that fell under the carpet bombing was transformed into a crater-field. Overhead protection was smashed and the personnel buried, most of whom could not be rescued. The same happened to guns and tanks. Losses on 24 and 25 July, therefore, were not only due to fragments, but also – very many – from burial. It also seemed to me that a number of people who had survived the carpet-bombing, (as a result of the great effect on morale), either quickly surrendered to the attacking infantry or fell back to the rear from their positions.

c. The front line was destroyed by the [aerial] bombardment. If, despite this, the attacking infantry ran into resistance, that was because the reserves of the battalions, regiments and the division, which were positioned directly behind the main line of resistance and, in part, escaped the effects of the bombardment, could be committed immediately to oppose the attacking infantry or attack the enemy forces that had penetrated in hasty counter-attacks. This primarily happened on 24 July, but was also the case on 25 July. Stubborn resistance was still offered particularly by artillery and *Flak* batteries employed in infantry service, as well as garrisons of built-up areas in the area behind the main line of resistance. All of these positions had to be taken in combat by U. S. armour and infantry.

2. Effect of the Bombardment on Morale.

The approximately three hour bombardment on 25 July – after the weaker bombardment on 24 July – had a destructive effect on the attitude of the physically and psychologically weakened troops, who had already been in the most extremely heavy, unbroken defensive fighting for 45 days. The long duration of the bombardment without any possibility for defense against it produced depression and the feeling of helplessness, of personal weakness and inferiority. As a result of this the combat morale of the majority of the men effected, to the extent that they survived the carpet-bombing, was reduced to a point where they either surrendered in the conviction that the battle was hopeless, crossed over to the enemy or fled from the combat zone. Only those with particularly strong nerves and devotion to duty were able to endure the nervous pressure.

3. The Shock-Effect.

   [The shock effect] was approximately equal to the physical effect (dead and wounded). Many men went crazy during the three hour bombardment or were crippled and incapable of action. I, myself, was in the center of the bombardment on 24 and 25 July and can bear witness to the powerful effect on morale. I had served in all theatres of this war at the hot spots of the fighting and this was the worst that I ever experienced.

4. Effect on the Positions.

   The well dug in infantry were smashed in their positions and earthen bunkers by the heavy bombs, killed by the air pressure or buried. The positions (infantry or artillery) were crushed. The entire bombarded area was transformed into a field of craters (or into a moonscape) in which there were no living beings. Tanks and guns were destroyed, damaged and turned over, and could no longer be recovered from the crater-field, since all roads and byways were also destroyed.

   Naturally, in the entire battlefield there were still areas that had escaped bombardment. There were still reserves and positions there with heavy weapons and artillery that resisted the attacking infantry and armour to the extent that their moral condition still permitted.

5. Effect on Communications.

   At the very start of the bombardment all wire communications were eliminated. Since almost all the command posts were in the area covered by the carpet-bombing, <u>radio communication</u> was nearly impossible. Communications were limited to <u>messengers</u> (on motorcycles), but that, too, was complicated, since the roads were soon severed and the journeys, themselves, were extremely dangerous and time-consuming during the period of the bombardment.

6. The centers of the bombardment were:

   a. The *main line of resistance* in its entire breadth.

   b. The <u>areas</u> around Hebecrevon [Hébécrevon], Le Manois [le Manoir], St. Gilles, La Chapelle on Juger [la Chapelle-en-Juger], Les Mesnil Amoy [le Mesnil-Amey], Montreuil [-sur-Lozon] and north of Marigny.

Signed. BAYERLEIN

# MS # A–903

## *Panzer Lehr Division*
## 15–20 July 1944

**DEPARTMENT OF THE ARMY**
**HISTORICAL DIVISION**
**WASHINGTON 25, D. C.**

12 July 1949

Note to: MS # A–903
By: Kenneth W. Hechler
Major, Infantry (Res)

After General Bayerlein had been orally interviewed and had prepared the initial accounts [Citation] of the operation of the Panzer Lehr Division in Normandy (see ETHINT 66 and 67, and MS # A–901 and MS # A–902) we brought General Bayerlein from Oberursel to St Germain, France, for further interrogation and writing.

In October and November 1945, when the 'Operation Cobra' section was engaged in writing a preliminary account of the First Army attack commencing 25 July 1944, we found that we needed some more precise information on the enemy situation, strength, losses as a result of the First Army attack, and enemy reaction to the attack. Accordingly, General Bayerlein was asked to prepare this information. He had access to more complete sources than he had had when he wrote his initial account in Oberursel. For example, we were able to give him a complete set of 1 to 15,000 and 1 to 50,000 American maps, as well as excerpts from the German Seventh Army War Diary. We were also able to brief him in a rather detailed fashion on the American operation.

Alfred Zerbel Koenigstein/Ts., 30 May 1950

**INDEX FOR**
**MS# 903**

***PANZER LEHR DIVISION***
**15–20 July 1944**

[signed] Alfred Zerbel
(Alfred Zerbel)

INDEX FOR MS # A–903 [translated by Frederick Steinhardt, bracketed notes by F. Steinhardt]

Fritz BAYERLEIN
*Generalleutnant*

## *Panzer Lehr Division*
## 15–20 July 1944

MS # A–903 [questions in original American English, bracketed notes by F. Steinhardt]

## PANZER LEHR DIVISION
## 15–25 July 1944

Major K. W. HECHLER

## ADDITIONAL QUESTIONS FOR GEN. BAYERLEIN ON NORMANDY

1. What was the total strength in man [*sic.*] and tanks of the various elements of Panzer Lehr Division and attached units on the line on 24 July 1944? How did this strength compare with the strength of the division when it first moved into this sector? How did it compare with full strength?

2. Can you draw the front lines of Panzer Lehr and its attached units on both the 1:25000 and 1:50000 maps as of 24 July? Please indicate, as you did before, boundaries, and which units were on your right and left, and boundary between the LXXXIV [Corps] and II Parachute Corps.

3. An American estimate published on 17 July 1944 summarized the strength of your front-line units as follows:

**5 Para Div.**

| | |
|---|---|
| Co. 12 Ren [reinforcement] Bn. | 150 |
| Regt. 13 Para. | 1500 |
| 1 Bn. 14 Para Regt. | 500 |
| 3 Bn., 14 Para Rgt. | 500 |
| Bn. II Para Ren [*sic*] | 300 |

**130 Pz. Lehr**

| | |
|---|---|
| Bn. 130 Engr. | 300 |
| 1 Bn. 130 Arty. | 200 |
| 4 Co. 130 Pz Ren [*sic.*] | 100 |
| Regt. 901 Pz Gren | 700 |
| Regt. Pz Gren 902 | 700 |

**2 SS Pz. Div.**

| | |
|---|---|
| Bn 2 SS Engr. | 400 |
| 3 Bn SS Deutschland | 200 |

**3 Para Div.**

| | |
|---|---|
| 1 Co. 5 Para Regt. | 200 |

**265 Inf. Div.**

| | |
|---|---|
| 2 Bn 894 Regt. | 300 |
| 517 Mob [Mobile, =*Schnelle*] Bn. Remnants | 50 |

What important corrections in the names of units present, and number of troops of front-line type, would you make in the above list?

4. At what points were your local regimental or division reserves located, and under what circumstances did you plan to commit them? How strong and in what condition were these reserves? Where were corps and army reserves located, and what strings were attached to their commitment?

5. What kind of a defense did you have along the front line on 24 July?

6. In a previous interview, you stated that you estimated a loss of about 2000 men and 35 tanks on the two days of bombing. How many of these losses would you estimate were sustained during the first day of the bombing?

7. In a previous interview, you stated that on the evening of the first day the bombing occurred, you received more infantry and were able to re-establish your old line. What outfit was this infantry from, and did LXXXIV Corps send them? How many were there? How many tanks and armored vehicles did you have left after the first day's bombing?

8. After the heavier bombing on the second day, what orders for withdrawal were issued? Were any casualties caused by American tank or small-arms fire?

9. What supply shortages or other difficulties did you have 24 July?

NOTE: From information contained in the captured German Seventh Army War Diary, the following may be of assistance:

9 July: Arrival of 5th Para Div. To relieve 77 Inf.

Evening of 10 July: Pz. Lehr takes over Combat Team Heinz [Heintz] of 275 Div.

13. July: A request that 14 Para Regt. support Pz. Lehr Div.

Late evening of 15 July: 1 Bn., 14th Para, put under Pz. Lehr. 2 Bn. Of 14 Corps reserve; 3 Bn already on the line.

16. July: St. Lo – Moon Road made boundary between 3d Para Div. and 352 Div.

17 July: It is doubtful whether the counterattack planned for Pz. Lehr Division can actually take place.

It is planned to employ another Panzer-Division transferred from Armored Group West.

21 July: 1800: 5th Para Div. Goes in between Pz. Lehr and 17th SS Pz. Grenadier Division.

22 July: 353d Div. Moved to Hautteville – St. Martin d'Aubigny.

25 July: 985th [Regt.] put under LXXXIV Corps and deployed in Pz. Lehr Division sector; 2 of 985 under II Para Corps, behind left flank of 352d Div.

# MS # A–903

## 1. <u>Staerken (strength) Panzer Lehr.</u>

(put before all numbers the word "about")

| *Elements* | *Full strength* | | *Strength, when moving in U.S. sector* | | *Strength on July 24* | | *Losses on July 24, 25* | | *Explanations* |
|---|---|---|---|---|---|---|---|---|---|
| Panzer Regt. | *Men* | *Tanks* | *Men* | *Tanks* | *Men* | *Tanks* | *Men* | *Tanks* | * the strength (in action) depends on the number of fit tanks. |
| | 2200<br>800 | *183 | 400 | 65 | 300 | 32 | 150 | 25 | |
| Panzer Gren. Regt. 901 | *Men* | *S.P.M.* | *Men* | *S.P.W.* | *Men* | *S.P.W.* | *Men* | — | 400 men (supply) came in the beginning of July |
| | 2600<br>1800 | 205 | 600 | 140 | 250* | 120 | 200 | – | * 1 Bn. was in rear for restoration |
| Panzer Gren. Regt. 902 | *Men* | *S.P.W* | *Men* | *S.P.W.* | *Men* | *S.P.W.* | *Men* | — | 300 men (supply) came in the beginning of July |
| | 2600<br>1800 | 250 | 700 | 160 | 300 | 130 | 250 | – | |
| Artillery | *Men* | *Guns* | *Men* | *Guns* | *Men* | *Guns* | *Men* | *Guns* | — |
| | 1700<br>1200 | 42 | 900 | 26 | 800 | 23 | 200 | 12 | |
| T.D's Bn. (Panzer-Jaeger) | *Men* | *T.D's* | *Men* | *T.D's* | *Men* | *T.D's* | *Men* | *T.D's* | — |
| | 400<br>220 | 31 | 140 | 20 | 120 | 12 | 70 | 10 | |
| Panzer Ron. Bn. | *Men* | *Armored vechicles* | *Men* | *Armored vechicles* | *Men* | *Armored vechicles* | *Men* | — | * The whole Ron Bn. was in rear area for restoration near Percy. |
| | 800<br>500 | 88 | 220 | 65 | 100* | 60 | | – | |

| | | | | | | | | | |
|---|---|---|---|---|---|---|---|---|---|
| Engr. Bn. | *Men* | — | *Men* | — | *Men* | — | *Men* | — | On July 24 Div. Reserve near CarantDly |
| | 600 | – | 200 | – | 120 | – | – | – | |
| | 450 | | | | | | | | |
| Flak Bn. (antiaircraft) | *Men* | *Guns* | *Men* | *Guns* | *Men* | *Guns* | *Men* | *Guns* | — |
| | 500 | 12 | 250 | 9 | 220 | 8 | 80 | 5 | |
| | 350 | | | | | | | | |
| Supply troops 5000 | | | | | | | | | |
| Summary 16400 (7120) | | | 3410 = 50% | | 2210 = 30% | | 950 men | | |
| | | | | | | | 37 tanks and T.D's | | |
| 14. Para Regt. | | | *Men* | | *Men* | | 350 | | |
| | | | 1000 | | 500 | | | | |
| Combat Team Heinz | | | *Men* | | *Men* | | | | |
| | | | 700 | | 450 | | 400 | | |
| Combat Team Wissliczeny (2 SS Div.) | | | *Men* | *Assault guns* | | | | | 20 July rejoined 2 SS Div. |
| | | | 600 | 10 | | | | | |
| Bataillon 985 Infantry (362 Div.) | | | | | 600 | | 400 | | |
| Moerser Abtlg. (21 cm) | | | *Men* | *Guns* | *Men* | *Guns* | | | |
| | | | 150 | 6 | 130 | 4 | | 50 | |
| Summary | | | | | | | | 2150 | |

2. Maps: 1:25000 and 1:50000[31]

Explanations:

- Front Line (*HKL* [*Hauptkampflinie*, main line of resiststance])

- *Panzer* strong point

- Sector boundary between [ *Panzergrenadier-Lehr-Regimenter* ] 901 and 902

- Division boundary, right, with II Para [II *Fallschirmjäger-Korps*] (352nd *Infanterie-Division*) left, with 5 Para Div [5th *Fallschirmjäger-Division* ]

- (rear-) Strong points in the battlefield, built around the heavy weapons (mortars, 2 cm guns and anti-tank guns {*Pak*].

- Reserves. Sector reserves of *Kampfgruppen* 902 (south of Hébecrevon) / 901 (near la Chapelle en Juger and of the division (southeast of la Chapelle en Juger) and northeast of Carantilly (*Pionier* battalion).

Artillery positions for one battalion [*Abteilung*] each, (2 – 3 batteries),at the same time, organized as a strong point.

Positions of the *Flak* battalion [*Abteilung*] (8.8 cm batteries), at the same time, organized as a strong point.

Command Post (C.P.) Of the sector commanders [*Panzergrenadier-Lehr-Regimenter*] 901 and 902 as well as attached *Fallschirmjäger-Regiment* 14 [of 5th *Fallschirmjäger-Division*].

Division command post west of Canisy and near Le Mesnil-Amey (advanced command post).

## MS # A–903
## 3. Strength of the front line on July 17

| *Estimated strength* | | *Important corrections* |
|---|---|---|
| *5 Para Div.* | | |
| Co 12 Bon Bn | 150) | were not under Panzer Lehr |
| | ) | |
| Regt 13 Para | 1 500) | But under 2.SS Div. |
| 1 Bn 14 Para Regt | 500) | correct |
| | ) | |
| 3 Bn 14 Para Regt | 500) | |
| Bn II Para Ron | 300 | on July 10, removed to II Para. |
| *Panzer Lehr.* | | |
| Bn 130 Engr. | 300 | only 120 |
| 1 Bn 130 Arty | 200 | not only 1 Bn but 3 Bn.s: 800 men |
| 4 Co 130 Pz Ron | 100 | correct, but 3 and 4 o. |

31 Annotations referring to maps absent from the manuscript.

| | | |
|---|---|---|
| Regt 901 Pz. Gren. | 700 | only about 300 men |
| Regt 902 Pz. Gren. | 700 | only about 350 men |
| 2.SS Ps.Div. | | |
| Bn SS Engr. | 400) | together 400 men and 10 T.O.'s, |
| | ) | |
| 3 Bn SS Deutchland | 200) | on July 20 rejoined 2 SS Div. |
| 3. Para Div. | | |
| 1 Co 5 Para Regt. | 200 | not in the front line of Pz. Lehr |
| 265. Inf. Div. | | |
| 2 Bn 894 Regt. | 300 | I don't know |
| 517 Mob Bn Resnants 50 | | not clear what it means! |
| | | Additional: Combat team Heinz* (275 Infantry Div.) about 500 men and Army Eng. School about 100 men. |

* 'Combat team Heinz' should read 'Combat Team Heintz' (with a 't').

[bracketed notes added by F.Steinhardt. Regardless of bizarre grammar and, at times, confusing wording, the current section has been preserved as in the original translations by U. S. Army translators at the time.]

4. Reserves: (See the sketch, next sheet!)

   a. Battalion reserves: small combat teams (20 – 30 men, 2 – 3 tanks or tank destroyers (Panzerjäger).

   b. Regimental reserves: Combat teams consisting of about one company (80 men) Panzergrenadiere, 5 tanks or tank destroyers (Panzerjäger).

   It was planned to commit the reserves a. and b. for barring enemy's break-in [in] the front line and for carrying out counter attacks. These reserves were located so that they were able to start for counter-attacks immediately, when the enemy succeeded in breaking into the front line.

   Location near the front line see the sketch!

   c. Division reserves:

      1. A combat team, consisting of one company (Divisions Begleit Kompanie [guard company for division HQ] and 6 tanks. Location so, that the team was able to be committed in the sectors of [Panzergrenadier-Lehr-Regimenter] 901 and 902, in case of need, if the regimental reserves should not be sufficient to drive back the enemy.

      2. Ingr. Bn. (Panzer Pionier Lehr Bataillon [*Panzer-Pionier-Bataillon* 130], located near Carantilly for several cases of barring an imminent

break-through in both sectors of counterattacking-as shown on the sketch.

d. Corps and Army Reserves: I don't know.

5. Type of Defense:

Strong point type defense of *Panzergrenadiere* along the entire division front.

Tanks formed the backbone of the position and were – well dug in – employed as armoured antitank guns or armoured machine guns (aside from tanks used in counter attacks). Tank destroyers [*Panzerjäger*] were employed in the same fashion as tanks.

The *Panzergrenadiere* or infantry were grouped around the tanks to protect them from tank-killer squads. Tank crews who no longer had tanks were employed for the same purpose.

Heavy weapons (antitank guns, mortars, 2 cm guns) of the *Panzergrenadier*-regiments were employed in strong points behind the front line in the depth of the battlefield and also for defense as infantry (with rifle, machine gun, machine pistol and *Panzerfaust*) in addition to the mission of supporting the defense with the heavy weapons (final protective fire, fire for destruction). The greatest possible care [was employed] in camouflage of all weapons, and, especially, of armour against both ground and air [observation]. Tanks were transformed into bushes.

*S.P.W.* Of the *Panzergrenadiere* were all pulled far to the rear (about 50 kilometres behind the front), since they could not move about on the battle field (due to the air situation). They were used at night to transport personnel and ammunition in the artillery fire zones to speed those transports and avoid losses due to artillery fire.

Mines were employed on roads and byroads (*T* [*Teller*] mines) and in the hedgerows (*S* mines [Since the abbreviation, *S-Minen,*could apply to *Schrapnellminen*, *Springminen* and *Schützenminen*, it cannot be expanded automatically, as with *T-Minen*.])

Artillery: In addition to missions as artillery (final protective fire and harassing fire) it was employed as the second combat position. The gun positions were fortified as strong points and defended [by the artillerymen] as infantry (with rifle, machine gun and *Panzerfaust*).

*Flak* battalion [*Abteilung*], employed as anti-aircraft defense and, at the same time (as with the artillery) employed in ground combat in strong point-type positions defended as infantry.

*Pionier* battalion and *Aufklärungsabteilung* employed as *Panzergrenadiere*.

Reserves: Battalion and regimental reserves (see section 4) kept far enough forward so that they could automatically and immediately counterattack in the event of a penetration.

Command posts set up to also serve as strong points for infantry defense.

General: For reasons of terrain and the situation in the air the *Panzer-Division* had to be employed as an infantry division with attached tanks. Movement by day was totally out of the question except during rainy weather (but even then with extreme caution).

6. Losses of elements attached to the division (14 Para Rgt. [*Fallschirmjäger-Regiment* 14], *Kampfgruppe Heinz* [*Heintz*] and the battalion of the 363rd [*Infanterie*]-*Division* are included in the loss of 2000 men on 24 and 25 July.

   Losses on the first day (24 July) were approximately 300 – 400 men and (definitely) 10 tanks or tank-destroyers. The main losses took place on the second day, where nearly all of the tanks and tank-destroyers committed on the battlefield were either destroyed or could not be extracted from the field of craters and ruins of the bombarded area.

7. a. The losses of the first day in the front lines were replaced by committing part of the reserves of the regiments and division and by committing elements of the 275th *Infanterie-Division*, which were positioned behind the *Panzer Lehr* [*Division*] and were driven forward so that the front line had been restored by the morning of 25 July.

   b. The infantry of the 275th [*Infanterie* ] -*Division* were only equipped with rifles and machine guns. The strength was about 200 men.

   c. They had not been at the disposal of the 84th *Korps* but were brought up as a result of direct arrangements between myself and the commander of the 275th [ *Infanterie* ]-*Division*.

   d. After the first day (24 July) the following tanks and armoured vehicles were still available:

   Tanks: 25
   Tank-destroyers: 10
   Armoured motor vehicles (*SPW* and armoured cars): 310. These *SPW* and armoured cars had been parked in the rear area.

8. a. No orders to retreat were issued on any day, since a retreat was not intended and, also, was impossible, since the troops committed in the battlefield had been almost entirely destroyed. Those people who were still alive rallied in the rear strong points and artillery positions or with the trains elements.

   b. Losses due to U. S. tanks or light weapons began when the U. S. tanks rolled over the destroyed front line and launched [their] attack in the depth of the battlefield. The strong points of the artillery and *Flak* positions suffered losses as a result of tank and machine gun fire. The II *Abteilung* (self-propelled) of [*Panzer-*] *Artl. Rgt.* [*Artillerie-Regiment* ] 130, which held out to the last near St. Gilles, was, for the most part, destroyed by U. S. armour in close combat.

(The staff of the *Panzer Lehr* [*Division*] was, however, committed as infantry in the Soulles sector east of Pont Brocard and almost totally wiped out by tank fire.)

Troop elements of other divisions that were attached to the division (*Kampfgruppen* of the 275th and 363rd *Inf.* [*Infanterie*]-*Divisionen* and of *Fallschirmjäger-Regiment* 14) were nearly worthless troops that almost always fell back to the rear, even if there was no major attack. In the rear areas one ran into *Fallschirmjäger* of the 'famed' 5th *Fallschirmjäger-Division* strolling around everywhere.[32]

c. The sector of the *Panzer Lehr* [*Division*] was handled poorly by the [84th *Armee-*] *Korps* and *Armee* [ *Armeeoberkommando* 7]. Most of the arriving replacements were given to the 2nd *SS-Div.*[2nd *SS-Panzer-Division 'Das Reich'*]. (The *Armee* commander-in-chief [*Generaloberst* {*SS-Oberstgruppenführer und Generaloberst der Waffen-SS*} Paul Hausser] was an *SS*-officer).

It was believed that the *Panzer Lehr* [*Division*] was far stronger than it actually was and no notice was taken of the fact that the division had already fought against superior enemy forces in the English sector for over three weeks and also in the U. S. sector from 8 to 24 July, suffering substantial losses of its best personnel.

After the division's sector had quieted down somewhat since 17 July and the attack had shifted more to the St. Lô sector east of the Vire, the [higher] command believed that the offensive would not come in the sector of the *Panzer Lehr* [*Division*]. Therefore the division received almost nothing by way of supplies and reserves, and what little it did get came only after exerting intense pressure and a hard fight.

9. Supply shortages and other difficulties:

   a. Fuel supplies were adequate, since driving was limited.

32 Tr. note – I am mystified by Bayerlein's repeated sarcastic references to the 'famed' 5th *Fallschirmjäger Division*. The 5th *Fallschirmjäger-Division* was, according to Tessin, only activated in March of 1944. Ritgen, (pp. 155-6) states that it was still in its initial training, had good human material, but soon proved totally unfit for combat due to lack of the simplest technical prerequisites for effective command. Blumenson, in *Breakout and Pursuit* states (p.140) that it consisted of young troops under inexperienced commanders, that the division had been rated in June as suitable only for defensive mission and that there was debate at various echelons as to whether their training was sufficiently advanced for the unit to be committed in Normandy. Perrigault (p. 263) quotes *Oberleutnant* Ebner, who commanded the heavy (eighth) company of *Panzergrenadier-Lehr-Regiment* 902, as saying that none of the so-called *Fallschirmjäger* had any actual training for air-drop, and that their officers came from *Luftwaffe Flak* units or ground-personnel on air bases, thus with no infantry training or experience. Whence came Bayerlein's evident bitterness in referring to what was, apparently, merely another new, partially trained division that was not yet really fit for action remains a question.

b. Ammunition: The shortage was severe. It was almost impossible for the artillery to provide harassing fire. Final protective fire and fire-for-destruction was inadequate. The ammunition shortage was a result of:

1. In general, little ammunition was available, and

2. As a result of the situation in the air, the ammunition allotted had to be hauled from great distances with difficulty and, therefore, almost never arrived on time. (The ammunition dumps were south of Le Mans and east of Paris.)

c. Artillery: As a result of the poor opportunities for ground-observation and the lack of aerial artillery spotters, artillery fire could not be employed and carried out in a desirable fashion. [That resulted in] imprecise firing data, and, thus, excessive expenditure of ammunition with uncertain results.

d. The primary difficulty was the shortage of manpower. The broad division sector was inadequately manned. (Defense in Normandy required many men, as is always the case in broken terrain). There was an extreme shortage of infantry manning the depth of the position. Artillery and *Flak* positions had to serve as strong points to make up [for the shortage of infantry]. The area between the front line and the artillery positions was hardly held at all.

signed BAYERLEIN

# ETHINT 67 – ( )

15 AUG 45

**AN INTERVIEW WITH GENLT FRITZ BAYERLEIN**

**CRITIQUE OF NORMANDY BREAKTHROUGH PANZER LEHR DIV FROM ST LO TO THE RUHR**

**Office of the Chief of Military History**
**Department of the Army**
**Washington 25, DC**

EUCOM:HD:OHGB COPY 1

**Department of the Army**
**Historical Division**
**Washington 25. DC**

12 July 1949

Note to: ETHINT 67
By: Kenneth W. Hechler
Major, Infantry (Res)

This is not an oral interview, but rather is the translation of a series of answers to questions in German written by General Bayerlein. I saw the German manuscript before it was translated by Sergeant Kiralfy, but I have no idea where it is now located.

Most of these questions were submitted by members of the ETO Historical Section, then translated into German by Sergeant Kiralfy and presented to General Bayerlein. General Bayerlein had no German maps of documents to assist him, but he was given American maps and also was briefed on the details of American operations in Normandy. General Bayerlein himself asked to make a critique of the Normandy breakthrough. I believe that here the reader can detect something of General Bayerlein's general attitude of saying things which he believed might sound good to the Americans. However, despite this shortcoming, I believe that most of his manuscript can be trusted so far as its discussion of the tactical operations of Panzer Lehr Division is concerned, as well as his appraisal of the operations which he discusses.

This account was written while General Bayerlein was confined to the hospital at Bad Nauheim with heart trouble. He was able to sit up during the preparation of this manuscript, which took about four days to complete. He appeared to be extremely interested in the subject, and volunteered that he would like to prepare some sketches as well as text (these sketches are attached to the report).

If we cannot find the German original of this report, I strongly suggest that this report be rechecked with General Bayerlein for accuracy, and that his annotations on it be attached to the report. However, I would not want General Bayerlein to see my annotation which I am now writing which casts some reflection on his candor.

## ETHINT 67 – ( )

| | |
|---|---|
| Title: | Critique of Normandy Breakthrough: Pz Lehr Div From St Lo To The Ruhr |
| Source: | Genlt Bayerlein, Fritz |
| Position: | Cmdr, Pz Lehr Div |
| Date: | 15 Aug 45 |
| Place: | Bad Nauheim, Germany |
| Interviewer: | Unknown (probably Maj Kenneth W. Hechler) |

**Foreword**

This interview is one of a series conducted by the Historical Section, ETOUSA, and its successors. Unfortunately, only a typed record in English is available for editing. It is not known whether a record in German was made at the time of the interview, nor, if one was made, can the accuracy of the translation be determined. Therefore, no absolute guarantee can be given as to the authenticity and completeness of detail of this version of the interview. Only obvious errors in spelling, punctuation, and grammatical construction have been corrected. All parenthetical statements, except those of the interviewer and editor, which are identified as such, are as they appear in the available record.

The originals of the sketches referred to in this interview are included with Copy 1, while reproductions thereof are included with Copies 1, 2, and 3.

(signed)
LE ROY S. STANLEY
Capt Inf
Historical Editor
[illegible date stamp ending in 1948]

[Note: Editorial notes added by the editor of the present book are bracketed and identified as 'FPS Ed:']

## CRITIQUE OF NORMANDY BREAKTHROUGH: PZ LEHR DIV FROM ST LO TO THE RUHR

TABLE OF CONTENTS — PAGE



## ETHINT 67

### *I. Critique of the Normandy Breakthrough, Jul – Aug 44*

1. Introduction: My description and my critiques are based solely on my own experiences in battle and on the operations as I saw them and judged

them, without being acquainted with the actual Allied plans, preparations, orders, or measures. I am equally unaware who drew up the plan of operations and by whom it was executed. Whoever he was, I consider him one of the greatest generals in the history of warfare. My account of the battle and the criticisms I make are the reproduction of my personal conviction, and are not a deliberate attempt to concoct something particularly fine. The battle of annihilation in Normandy – the breakthrough at St Lo, resulting in the envelopment, encirclement, and annihilation of the German defenders (Fifth *Pz* and Seventh Armies) – appears to me to be the greatest strategic and tactical achievement of this war, as well as the most decisive.

2. The feint at Caen: The Allied Command succeeded in completely veiling from the German Supreme Command the preparations for the breakthrough attack west of St Lo. This was achieved by means of the strong attacks in the British sector around Caen in the first half of Jul 44. These resulted in diverting the attention of the German command toward Caen, so that the majority of the German forces were committed in that sector, including six 'elite' Panzer-Divisions, as compared with two at St Lô Besides this, the St Lô front was completely denuded of heavy weapons such as Tiger tanks, GHQ (Ed: probably Heeres) artillery, smoke guns (Ed: Nebelwerfers?)[33], and antiaircraft artillery. On top of these strategic measures for deception came a tactical one: the American attack on the city of St Lo shortly before the main offensive. All eyes in the German Seventh Army sector, therefore, were turned onto the area east of the Vire. Since, in addition, it is impossible to foresee where air forces will be sent into ac-

33 FPS Ed: *Nebelwerfer* were rocket launchers, not guns or mortars. Although laying smoke screens and delivering chemicals were among their capabilities, the abstention from use of poison gas in WWII led to the rapid development of high explosive projectiles. The primary mission of the *Nebelwerfer* batteries rapidly became delivering massive volumes of high explosive rounds with powerful blast effect or of incendiary-oil projectiles. Because the spin-stabilized rocket projectiles for the *15 cm NbWf 41* had the rocket motor in front, the high-explosive payload in the rear, and detonated when the nose struck the ground, the bursting point was elevated above the ground surface, giving a devastatingly effective fragmentation and blast effect. Salvoes from an entire battery of multiple-tube *Nebelwerfer* bursting over an area in rapid sequence gave waves of high and low pressure that, in the early Russian campaigns, resulted in discovery of many enemy dead with no visible signs of external injuries, their lungs apparently burst by the extreme pressure differential. 'Smoke guns' is a singularly poor rendering of *Nebelwerfer*. The name was taken over from the 10 cm *Nebelwerfer 35*, which was a true 'trench mortar' employed by the *Nebeltruppen* for laying smoke screens. After 1940 the *Nebel-Abteilungen* gradually converted from mortars (*Werfer*) to rocket launchers, such as the six-tube electrically ignited breech-loading rocket launcher, the 15 cm *Nebelwerfer 41*, which retained the 'smoke mortar' designation for reasons of deception. By the time of the Normandy Invasion the *Nebelwerfer* batteries ranged from the 15 cm six-tube *Nebelwerfer 15 cm-41* and five-tube *21 cm Nebelwerfer 42* to the 28/32 cm *Nebelwerfer 41* and 30 cm *schwere Wurfrahmen* 40.

tion, the big plans of the American command for operations west of St Lo remained completely camouflaged.[34]

3. The concentration of forces at the point of main effort: The breakthrough of the German system of defenses west of St Lo was attained by an extremely strong concentration of American ground and air forces in a very small space and on a scale never before experienced. The attack of the Flying Fortresses had a destructive and paralyzing effect on the German command and on the German troops. This advantage was rapidly and skillfully exploited by the American ground forces (tanks and infantry) which thrust forward into the depths of the enemy positions.

4. The creation of the pocket at Coutances: The line of attack was first directed against the area south of Coutances so that prior to the further thrust in depth into the Avranches region, all German forces north of the Soulle River were destroyed and no longer constituted a danger to the American thrust toward the south. All German forces engaged north of Coutances (three infantry divisions, one parachute division, and parts of an SS division) were annihilated with all their materiel and very heavy artillery. The way to Avranches thus lay open, and the seacoast was gained to protect the west flank. This was followed by the enlargement of the breakthrough area by attacks against Percy – Tessy and later on Vire, and the creation of a strong screen for the east flank against movements from the Villedieu – Mortain area. The channel for the movement of the enveloping forces, the Third US Army, was forced.

5. The daring drive through the corridor and the significance of the Caen – Falaise hinge for the envelopment operation: The dash of Patton's Army through the narrow corridor into the deep rear of an unfamiliar region belongs to the boldest ventures of the battle in France, and demonstrates in the best possible light the discipline, the aggressiveness, and the drive of the American armored force. Whereas the British had the mission of tying down the German forces near Caen and serving as the hinge of the envelopment operation as it struck out, the American armored divisions poured in a steady flood through the corridor, practically without being observed by the Germans – the fault of inadequate German aerial reconnaissance. The news that an American armored division was in Rennes had a shattering effect, like a bomb-burst, upon us. By the continuation of the American attack frontally against Vire, the organization of the German forces for a counterattack (2 and 116 Pz Divs, plus elements of 2 SS Pz and 17 SS Pz Gren Divs) was so harassed and exposed to such dangers that it was necessary to shift the attack force farther southward into the Mortain region. This further delayed the urgent rapid execution of this German counterattack to the coast, in order to sever the corridor. This contributed in large measure to the inability to execute the counterattack

34 Tr. note- See note above at question 125, ETHINT 66 regarding significant place that the capture of St. Lô held in American plans.

at all in the end, or to its being so delayed that it could no longer lead to any practical results, as Patton's Army had already passed through the corridor and could be supplied by air (or sea).

6. The classic US armored encirclement of German forces: During the passage through the corridor, Gen Patton's feint westward with a combat command toward Brittany and Brest misled the German command into the false view that Gen Patton would first capture Brittany. Appropriate steps to meet a possible eastward drive by Patton, therefore, were not taken by the German command; Patton's tanks then rolled eastward. As the American armor suddenly appeared in front of Vire, Mayenne, Laval, and Le Mans, the greatest astonishment and consternation reigned. They surrendered, in most cases, without firing a shot, and did not even have time to destroy the transportation facilities. The speed and daring of this advance to the east into unfamiliar territory is the best testimony to the skill of the American tank commanders.

7. No sooner had the German command recognized Gen Patton's advance, than a new surprise was sprung, that is, the wheeling around of part of his forces to create the smaller pocket around Argentan and Falaise. The bulk of the German armor on the Western Front was in danger of being cut off, encircled, and annihilated. This turned the attention of the German command toward Argentan, while, at the same time, strong elements of Patton's Army drove farther east to create the next and larger pocket on the Seine. Those forces which escaped from the Argentan pocket were to be destroyed in this one. Thus, the formation of two smaller pockets proves to have been part of a general plan. The 9 Pz Div, moving up from the south to take part in the counterattack against Avranches, was drawn into the whirlpool of the Third US Army, split up as it was engaged, and within three days was almost completely cut to pieces.

8. The German Supreme Command still clung to the Avranches attack plan and, for this purpose, dragged more forces into the pocket, instead of evacuating it. By the northward movement of forces of Patton's enveloping group during the operation, German forces were continually held down and prevented from withdrawing from the pocket forming along the Seine. In the meantime, Patton's armored spearheads reached the Seine south of Mantes-Gassicourt and, since the Seine bridges were destroyed and the ferries and collecting areas for the crossings were exposed to the fire of the Allied air forces, the second large pocket was closed.

9. The annihilation of Fifth Pz and Seventh Armies: Only remnants escaped from the Falaise pocket, and no substantial German unit came back across the Seine. The Fifth Pz and Seventh Armies were annihilated. No important force could be sent to me et the further American advance against the West Wall; Patton's Army drove irresistibly on to create the next pocket on the Somme and to reach the West Wall quickly. With this, the Normandy battle became one of the greatest battles of annihilation in history.

Even though the Allied air superiority had a big share in the success, the battle was a masterpiece, tactically and strategically, in planning and execution.

10. The effects of the breakthrough battle: The successful battle in Normandy prepared the basis for the still greater battle of annihilation which ensued from the American forward thrust through southern France. Toward the end of Aug 44, two powerful wedges drove through France, one from west to east and the other from south to north. On 10 Sep 44, these two wedges united and created an enormous pocket between the Loire and the Rhone-Saone. The German forces engaged in this area were cut off from their rear communications and the entire materiel and the bulk of the troops, so far as they were not able to escape through gaps and reach the West Wall, fell into Allied hands. With this, the battle in France became the greatest battle of annihilation of all times.[35]

11. Conclusion: A book appeared in Germany after World War I, entitled 'The Battle of Annihilation as Exemplified in the History of Warfare.' This book was prepared by an officer of the former German 'Great General Staff' ('Grosser Generalstab'). In this book, all battles in history which have the character of battles of annihilation are described as understood by the outstanding German Chiefs of General Staff, Moltke and Schliefen, beginning with Cannae and dealing with the battles of Frederick the Great and Napoleon and up to the World War I battles of Tannenberg and Rumania. None of the battles there described, not even the German battles of annihilation of the 1940 Blitzkrieg in France or in 1941 in Russia, can approach the battle of annihilation in France in 1944 in the magnitude of their planning, the logistics of their execution, the collaboration of sea, air and ground forces, the size of the theater, the strength of the combatants, the bulk of the booty, or the hordes of prison-

35 Tr. Note: Bearing in mind Major Hechler's repeated comments in his notes to the various interview with General Bayerlein, that the General had a tendency to include material he thought the Americans would like to read and 'that, after the war, the best way to get ahead in life was to ingratiate himself with the Americans', I offer the following figures for comparison: Excerpt from a *Tagesbefehl der Heeresgruppe Mitte for 5 August 1941,* 'With the destruction of the Russian divisions cut off near Smolensk the three-week battle at the Dnjepr and Düna and around Smolensk founds its conclusion in a brilliant new victory for German weapons and German devotion to duty. 309,000 prisoners were brought in and 3,205 tanks, 3,000 guns and 341 aircraft were captured or destroyed.' (quoted in Emde, *Die Nebelwerfer*, p.46. Ziemke quotes a similar figure of 'over 300,000' for the Smolensk pocket. (Ziemke and Bauer, p. 32). Similarly instructive comparisons might be made with a number of other battles on the Eastern Front. Ziemke and Bauer state that the Germans captured 665,000 prisoners when the Kiev Pocket was closed on 16 Sept 1941.(Ziemke and Bauer, *Moscow to Stalingrad* p 34. Hinze (*Der Zusammenbruch der Heeresgruppe Mitte*, p. 274) says that about 300,000 men were lost in the collapse of the German *Heeresgruppe Mitte*, of which about 130,000 of which were captured, shot or otherwise killed at the time of capture by the Russians in 1944.

ers. Its greatest importance, however, consists in its strategic effects, that is, that it laid the foundation for the subsequent final and complete annihilation of the greatest military state on earth.

This annihilation began with the most powerful and daring operation of the war – the breakthrough at St Lo.

## *II. Northern France Campaign*

12. Q: Describe in detail the movements of the German armored units after the breakthrough.

A: At the time of the breakthrough on 25 Jul 44, Pz Lehr Div and one SS Panzer-Division, composed of elements of 2 SS Pz and 17 SS Pz Gren Divs, were in the area of the penetration around St Lo. During the breakthrough battle, 2 and 116 Pz Divs were moved up to support Seventh Army. The 2 Pz Div moved from its commitment area south of Caumont into the area Torigny-sur-Vire – Tessy sur Vir[36] with the mission, 'to attack the enemy in the flank as he advances through Canisy.' The 116 Pz Div, not previously engaged, moved from the area east of the Seine into the Tessy sur Vire – Percy area. After 28 Jul 44, rear elements of Pz Lehr Div (eight Mark V tanks and elements of the Reconnaissance Battalion located near Villebaudon) were committed (at the Division's own initiative) on the Percy heights to repel the enemy attacking southward. On the left, they were flanked by remnants of the SS panzer division (Kfgr Wisliczeny) as far as Sourdeval (Ed: probably Sourdeval-les-Bois). The remnants of the infantry divisions encircled north of Coutances were committed north of Villedieu-les-Poeles. In addition, 9 Pz Div, completely recuperated and in fighting condition, was brought up from the territory south of the Loire. See Sketches 1 and 2 for further movements of the Pz Lehr combat command.

13. Q: What orders were issued with regard to retreat and counterattack?

A: No order to retreat was given, but, on 29 or 30 Jul 44, the first orders were received for the occupation of the line Percy – Sourdeval by LXXXIV Inf Corps and particularly by XLVII Pz Corps, to which all forces between Torigny-sur-Vire and the Sienne River were subordinated. The XLVII *Pz Korps*, at the same time, was to counterattack from the Tessy sur Vire – Torigny-sur-Vire area. It was ordered that the counterattack thrust deep into the flank of the American troops advancing from Canisy toward Percy, with the objective of winning ground south of Coutances and thereby releasing the encircled forces north of that town.

14. Q: Why did the first counterattack of 2 and 116 Pz Divs fail? How far did it progress?

A: I do not know how far 2 Pz Div advanced; I only know that it did not get very far. I attribute its poor success to the fact that it too was already a

36 FPS Ed: Tessy-sur-Vire.

worn-out division. It had been in bitter defensive action south of Caumont since 14 Jul 44, and had suffered greatly from an air attack near Torigny-sur-Vire.

The 116 Pz Div was a completely new division with no combat experience against British and American troops. I myself have shared their experience with air attacks and have seen how careless driving and inadequate cover and camouflage resulted in heavy losses. Because of these losses, its movement into the front was greatly delayed, and the various elements of the Division arrived in an irregular trickle. Losses were high even as they arrived, and the air attacks had serious effects on morale as well as materiel, for they preyed on the minds of the inexperienced troops. This effect was not lessened in the fighting, especially with the heavy and accurate American artillery fire aided by artillery spotters in the region around Villebaudon – Tessy sur Vire – Percy. As the Division attacked, I could see with my own eyes that the assault troops, after gaining about half a kilometre, were stopped dead in artillery and tank fire and could not advance any farther against the Americans. On orders from higher headquarters, elements of 116 *Pz Div* (one tank battalion and one armored infantry battalion) were moved into the area west of Villedieu-les-Poeles to counter the enemy advance toward the south. Under the circumstances, a continuation of the attack, much less success, was unthinkable.

15. Q: What was the plan and execution of the counterattack of 7 Aug 44 toward Avranches? Why was the second plan preferred to the first, that is, why did the attack take place through Mortain instead of through Vire?

A: Although the plans and execution of the counterattack against Avranches are not familiar to me in detail, I do know that the following units were to participate in this attack: 2 and 116 Pz Divs, one SS Panzer-Division (composed of 2 SS Pz and 17 SS Pz Gren Divs), heavy artillery, smoke guns[37], elements of the I SS Pz Corps from Caen, plus 9 Pz Div (completely reorganized and reequipped) from south of the Loire. This latter division had already been engaged east of Mayenne by Third US Army as it advanced toward the east, and had suffered heavy losses. Elements of I SS Pz Corps arrived very late due to air attacks.

The second plan was preferred for the following reasons:

a. The strong American attacks in the direction of Vire – Villedieu-les-Poeles endangered and threatened the north flank of the attack troops. This danger increased the more the attack was delayed. (Gen von Funck (Ed: Cmdr, XLVII Pz Corps) didn't dare make the counterattack with the forces on hand, and was waiting until the promised reinforcements arrived. He thereby lost valuable time, which had a fatal result on the issue of the attack.)

37 FPS Ed: *Nebelwerfer.* See earlier note. Emphatically **not** 'smoke guns'.

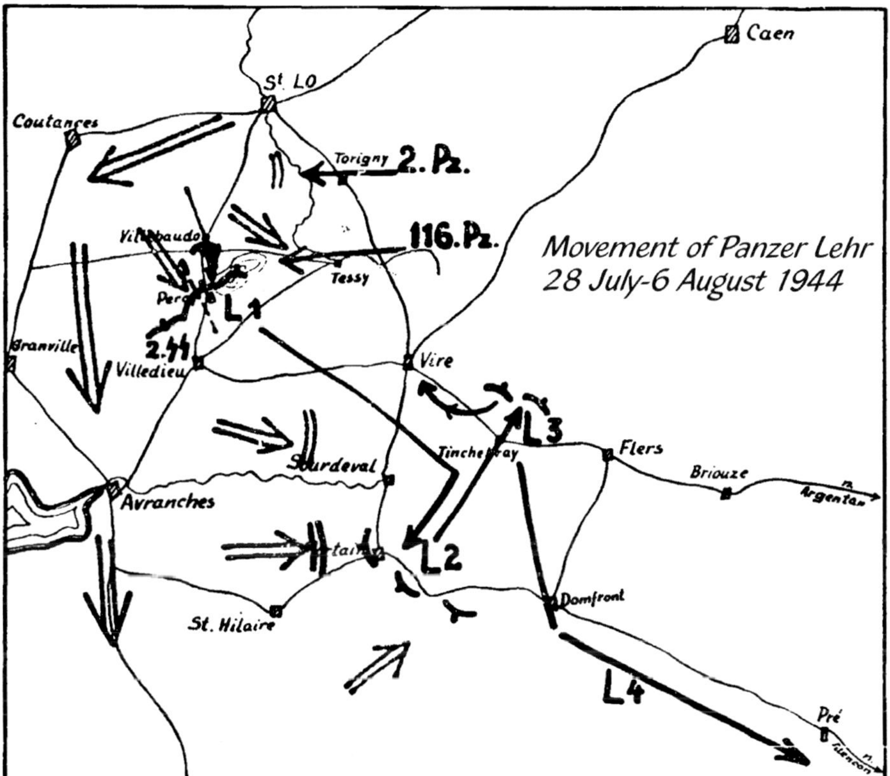


| L = | Panzer-Lehr |
|---|---|
| L 1 | 28 July-1 August 1944, under XLVII Panzer Corps. Defensive action near Villebaudon and then near Percy. |
| L 2 | 2-3 August 1944, under the XLVII Panzer Corps. Defensive action near and southeast of Mortain. |
| L 3 | 4-6 August 1944, under II Fallschirm Corps. Defensive action north-east of Tinchebray and counterattack against Vire. |
| L 4 | Beginning on the evening of 6 August 1944: movement into the area southwest of Alencon, leaving one Kampfgruppe with II Fallschirm Corps. |

ETHINT 67 Sketch 1: Movement of *Panzer-Lehr* 28 July-6 August 1944

b. The favorable terrain for an attack from the Mortain area. The right flank rested on the Le See River and this stream was not to be crossed in the course of the attack (in contrast to the case in an attack from Vire).

c. The shorter route to Avranches.

16. Q: What was the mission of 2 and 116 Pz Divs along the line Percy – Tessy sur Vire after the breakthrough?

A: An attack against the flank of the American forces advancing southward from the Canisy region, and gaining terrain around Coutances so as to release the encircled German forces north of there (mission of XLVII Pz Corps).

17. Q: On 1 Aug 44, Tessy sur Vire was taken by American forces. Was this a planned retreat or was it forced on the Germans?

A: I do not know exactly, but I think 116 Pz Div was forced to evacuate the village.

18. Q: Can you give any further details about the breakthrough, especially with respect to cooperation of armor and aircraft?

A: Further details are not familiar to me. Many divisional staffs and the remnants of forces of all kinds collected around the Villedieu-les-Poeles – Vire area, and many fled to the rear area supply echelons in the Domfront – Alencon- Argentan region. Very little of Seventh Army was left – just fragments. The only effective units were the newly arrived 2 and 116 Pz Divs and some heavy artillery and antiaircraft units.

I particularly noticed the cooperation of armor, especially tank spearheads, with the air force during the American advance, through the breakthrough point west of St Lo, for a breakthrough in depth. The tanks were guided by aircraft over the Soulles brook between Pont-Brocard and Soulles, where no resistance worthy of the name was developed. On 27 and 28 Jul 44, artillery fire ceased completely and was replaced by bombing and strafing attacks by the fighter-bombers supporting the attack. The fighter-bombers were in action over the main attack sector without a minute's interruption.

19. Q: Why was there such disorder in the German command and how was this given expression? What happened to Von Choltitz (Ed: Cmdr, LXXXIV Inf Corps)?

A: All communications were practically broken on 25, 26, 27, and 28 Jul 44. Messages and signal communications were replaced by motorcyclists, an expedient which, particularly because of the fighter-bomber patrolling of roads, was dangerous, insecure, and time-wasting. The command, therefore, was uninformed of the situation for a long time, both as to the location and the strength of the enemy forces. German aerial reconnaissance was impossible. For these reasons, hardly any orders were given, and even the ones that were given arrived at the front so late that the basis for the orders had become outmoded by the changed circumstances. Hence, the troops operated according to the situation they faced in their sectors and often without any orders.

Choltitz'z command post was overrun by American tanks on 27 and 28 Jul 44 and he lost so many vehicles and radio cars that the staff was also unable to operate on 28 and 29 Jul 44. Genlt von Choltitz was relieved as Cmdr, LXXXIV Inf Corps, at the end of Jul 44 (probably at the suggestion of the Seventh Army Commander, Ogrf Hausser) because of the St Lo catastrophe.

20. Q: Why did Von Kluge replace Von Rundstedt as C-in-C West on 28 Jun 44?

A: The relief of Von Rundstedt was due to (1) the surprisingly quick fall of Cherbourg, (2) the fact that no counterattack against the beachhead had been made and the beachhead now could not be reduced, and (3) Rundstedt, therefore, being considered too deficient in energy by OKW. Von Rundstedt had to be replaced by a man who was deemed especially energetic and aggressive and who had a good reputation in Hitler's Headquarters as a successful defensive fighter on the Eastern Front – this man was Genfldm von Kluge.

21. Q: What were the differences in command and general military theories between Von Kluge and Von Rundstedt?

A: Von Kluge played a more active and personal role and spent more time at the front checking on troop conditions; Rundstedt hardly ever did this. Although Von Kluge learned from experience how much more difficult and dangerous it was to drive around in the West than in the East, he also completely misappraised the leadership and fighting value of the British and Americans and, hence, made many blunders in his plans and in his demands on the combat troops. In particular, he never took into consideration the Allied air force in the Western theater.

22. Q: What is your personal opinion of Von Kluge?

A: My personal opinion of Von Kluge is that he was a good leader of troops, but was no armored general, and was a rather petty type of Junker. He was very much affected and shaken by his bad experiences on the Western Front. (I spoke to him shortly before his relief by Genfldm Model on 18 Aug 44, and again in his command post in La Roche Guyon.)

23. Q: What are the details of the conversation between Von Kluge and Model, and what are the reasons for Von Kluge's dismissal?

A: On 18 Aug 44, I was present at Von Kluge's command post when Model suddenly appeared and stated that he was to become A Gp B[38]

38 FPS Ed: *Heeresgrupe B.*

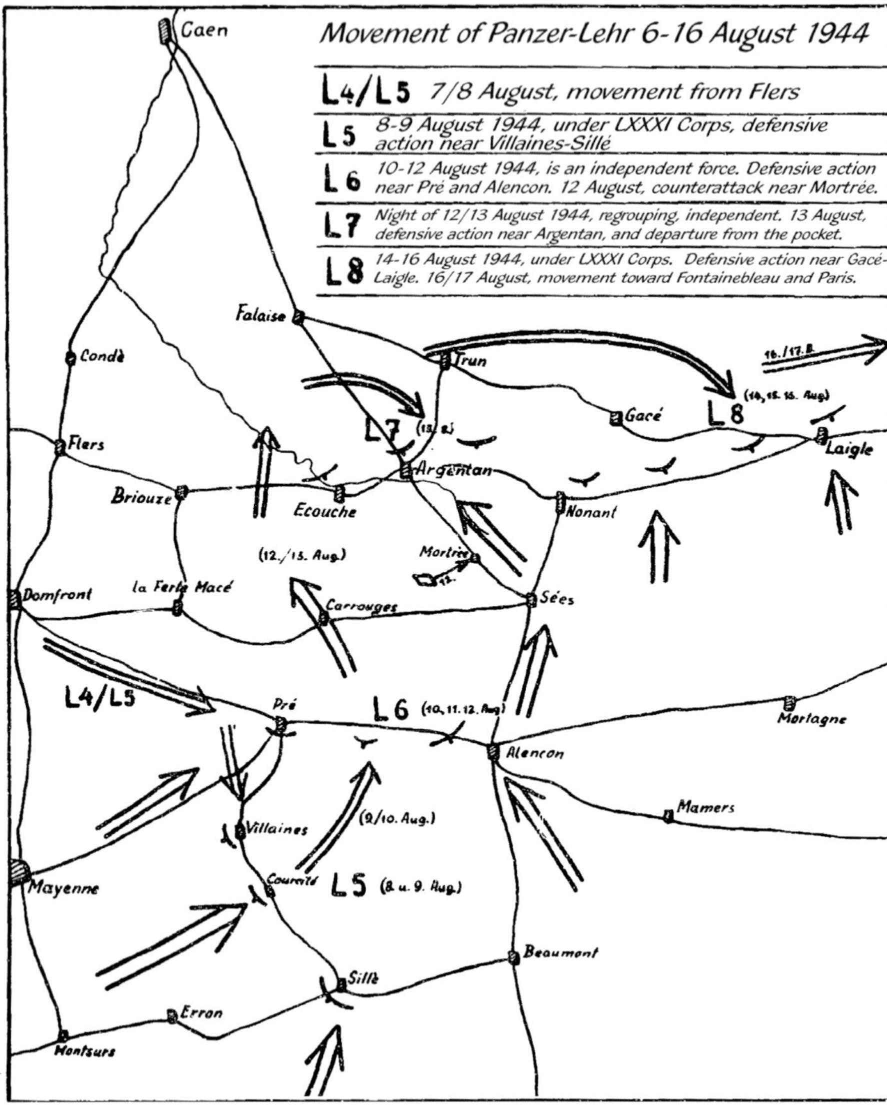


ETHINT 67 Sketch 2: Movement of *Panzer-Lehr* 6-16 August 1944

Commander and C-in-C West because Von Kluge was ill and must spare himself. Von Kluge was surprised, but realized that the real reasons for his dismissal were (1) the St Lo breakthrough, (2) his failure to launch a counterattack on Avranches, and (3) the reports he had sent to OKW on the state of affairs on the Invasion Front, which were true, but did not please OKW or Hitler.

Model was a special favorite of Hitler; he had often saved the day in the East. He was a very brutal, self-willed man, and he was devoted to Hitler. He had no experience in the West, and came to Normandy with completely false conceptions. He was unfamiliar with the Allied air force, and completely underestimated the leadership and combat value of the American forces. He characterized those of us who had already been on the Western Front for some time as cowards who were afraid of the incapable Americans and who had let themselves be bluffed by them.

24. Q: Can you give details about Stuelpnagel's (Ed: Gen Inf, Mil Cmdr of France) activities, his opinions, and his plans?

A: On 8 Feb 44, or thereabouts, I was in Paris with Gen von Stuelpnagel and his Chief of Staff, Obst iG[39] Kossmann, my best friend. I spoke about the Eastern Front, from which I had just arrived, of the bad conditions there, of the catastrophic fighting value of the German infantry divisions, and the bad leadership of OKW (Hitler). Von Stuelpnagel was very much interested. We conversed about the prospects for the impending invasion and found we agreed.

The next day, 9 Feb 44, I was invited to see Stuelpnagel alone in his office. In a completely private discussion, we agreed that the Supreme Command in Germany could not continue as it had, that Hitler would have to be removed as a prompt conclusion of peace was necessary, and that a personality had to be found to negotiate with Britain and America. Nothing was said of the preparations then already underway for the 20 Jul 44 Plot. In May 44, I spoke with Stuelpnagel again as I was returning from a visit with Genfldm Rommel, who had the same views as Gen Stuelpnagel.

On 20 Jul 44, as I was told, Gen von Stuelpnagel, acting in accord with the views expressed, had had the Gestapo, SD, and other leading people arrested. When the plot fell through, he was seriously wounded, in his flight, in a suicide attempt before his entourage. Long before 20 Jul 44, Von Stuelpnagel had worked up a lively secret activity in that direction. He was supported in this by his Chief of Staff, Obst Kossmann.

25. Q: What steps were taken to keep the Argentan – Falaise gap open?

A: In order to keep the Falaise gap open, it was necessary to protect at least the Orne sector near Argentan and the region north of Falaise, so as to be able to utilize the roads for an eastern retirement from the pocket. As plans for an attack on Avranches existed until 13 Aug 44, there were

39 FPS Ed: *iG* = *im Generalstab*, trained as a general staff officer.

troops available for the defense of Argentan. On 12 Aug 44, a combat command of Pz Lehr Div attacked the enemy in the Mortres neighborhood as he advanced from Sees toward Argentan. This attack succeeded in slightly delaying the advance. Elements of 116 Pz Div were employed near Argentan, while a combat command of Pz Lehr Div was somewhere east of these troops. The SS troops were substantially stronger near Falaise.

26. Q: Was it known that Third US Army would turn northward instead of continuing in the same direction?

    A: The turning was not anticipated, but was soon observed. It was a surprise anyway, and an unpleasant one in view of the plans we still had to make a counterattack on Avranches and the threatening danger of a pocket developing around Argentan – Falaise. There were no forces on hand to repel this envelopment, and it was difficult to extricate any, as all available forces were either pinned down or needed for the Avranches counterattack.

    Only weak rear units fought against the enveloping movement. The 9 Pz Div, which was moving up to participate in the counterattack on Avranches, was committed to try to stem it and was, to a large extent, mangled in the effort.

27. Q: After the loss of the Falaise pocket, what plans existed for retreat, particularly with respect to the crossing of the Seine?

    A: The bulk of the Fifth Pz and Seventh Armies were annihilated in the Falaise pocket. Remnants fled toward the Seine to save themselves, while others had already escaped on their own initiative prior to the closing of the pocket. Survivors of the higher staffs also fled, with no means of command or communication. No more orders were given nor could be given; even had any orders been issued, they could not have been executed.

    Ferry points for the Seine crossing were prepared and allotted to the divisions. This allocation was not observed, and everyone crossed the River wherever he felt like it. Most of the ferries were confiscated by the SS, who generally did not allow members of other units to use the ferries. Some effective elements and supply units escaped through the Mantes-Gassicourt gap up to 17 Aug 44, but in other respects, the retreat over the Seine, harassed by the Allied air forces, was a catastrophe.

28. Q: Where did Pz Lehr Div cross the Seine? How was the crossing effected, and how many men, tanks, and vehicles were able to cross?

    A: By 12 or 13 Aug 44, Pz Lehr Div had extricated itself from the Falaise pocket on its own initiative and had gone into action near Argentan and to the east. The rear elements, repair-tanks, half-tracks, artillery, antiaircraft artillery, crews without tanks, and armored infantry cadres were shipped back to Fontainebleau to recuperate.

On 16 Aug 44, the entire Division was ordered withdrawn from the front and rehabilitated. In compliance with this order part of the Division crossed the Seine near Fontainebleau, while another part, especially the troops still engaged in combat, proceeded trough Paris and Mantes-Gassicourt into the Senlis region (northeast of Paris) which had been designated as a rest area. (Model, however, rescinded this order because he was of the opinion that the Division could recuperate on the front, that is, in combat. He said, 'This would have been the case with me in the East.')

Into this rest area came approximately 5,000 men from rear and supply echelons, approximately 1,000 combat men (mainly convalescents from hospitals), approximately 20 tanks and tank destroyers still undergoing repairs, four batteries of artillery with approximately 10 guns, one and one-half batteries of antiaircraft artillery guns, about 100 half-tracks, and about 100 motor vehicles. (The half-tracks were never committed in combat as the Allied air superiority precluded their employment.)

29. Q: Which line did you establish and defend after crossing the Seine?

A: After crossing the Seine, Pz Lehr Div was in a rest area near Senlis and was subordinated to First Army. At this time, First Army had no usable combat troops, but only new replacements and some hurriedly organized units of stragglers and separated troops; Army Headquarters was the strongest unit. Pz Lehr Div received additional men through the arrival of four mobile battalions of former cavalrymen from Holland.

Pz Lehr Div was engaged at the following points: (a) the Aisne River, in the Rethal region, (2) Meuse River, in the Sedan region, (3) southwest of Neufchateau, in Belgium, (4) near Martelange, on the Luxembourg border, and (5) on the West Wall, southwest of Bitburg. Later, as LXXX Inf Corps reserve, Pz Lehr Div was withdrawn and committed against the penetration of American tank units in the Bettingen – Mettendorf – Kruechten – Mussbaum region. In this fighting, the Division succeeded in repelling the thrust through the West Wall, and in shooting up a large number of American tanks on or about 20 Sep 44.

30. Q: How was it that your intelligence service was poor and incapable of supplying usable material?

A: The material supplied by the German intelligence to the combat troops was very meager. In 1944, even before the Invasion, neither strategic nor tactical air reconnaissance was possible, and intelligence was limited to the data furnished by agents, whose reports were not always correct or reliable. Radio monitoring produced useful material. The combat troops had to get the best information themselves by evaluating the statements of prisoners; however, even those were scanty, as the British, and even more the American prisoners, hardly ever made any statements.

## *III. Pz Lehr Div Operations and Tactics in Lorraine*

[tr. note – See notes following interview MS- 901 regarding reconstitution of *Panzer Lehr Division* 130 following retreat to *Westwall* and its action in Lorraine.]

31. Q: When was the decision made to commit Pz Lehr Div near Sarre Union?

A:In Sep 44, Pz Lehr Div came into the Heilbronn area of Wuerttemberg for recuperation, and, in Oct 44, moved into the Paderborn – Detmold area of Westphalia (as part of Sixth Pz Army). Later, in Nov 44, the Division moved into the Hunsrueck region, near the Castellan – Morbach – Buechenbueren area (under Seventh Army). Because of these continual movements, very little recuperation was possible (damage to the railway system delayed delivery of the new materiel).

I feel that the plans for the Ardennes Offensive dictated the last movement into the Hunsrueck area, although we then knew nothing of these plans and did not suspect anything of the kind.

About 20 Nov 44, the US armored units broke into Alsace over the Saverne Rise. Pz Lehr Div, with its recuperation still incomplete, suddenly received orders on the evening of 21 Nov 44 to move as rapidly as possible into the area northeast of Saarguemines. At First Army Headquarters in St Ingbert, I received the following instructions: By the evening of 23 Nov 44, or the morning of 24 Nov 44 at the latest, attack over the line Saare Union – Waldhambach and then on the line Sarrebourg – Phalsbourg, with the objective of cutting the rear lines of communication of the American troops which have burst into the Rhine plain and annihilating them.

The Division was weak in tanks, having only one battalion and no tank destroyers. The Division had only two battalions of artillery, two regiments of armored infantry (incompletely equipped), a good reconnaissance battalion, a weak engineer battalion and one 88 mm antiaircraft battery. In addition to these forces, one volks artillery corps was attached to the Division. The movement up to the attack area was delayed by inadequate fuel supplies and the Division could only proceed to the attack at 1600 hours on 24 Nov 44. This was after a telegram had been received from OKW stating 'The fate of Alsace depends on you!' See sketch for course of the attack. (Ed: This sketch was not included in the available record.)

32. Q: What was the mission of Pz Lehr Div in the flank attack on 4 Armd Div (US)?

A: The Pz Lehr Div was to gain the Sarrebourg – Phalsbourg area as soon as possible. The attack began at 1600 on 24 Nov 44, with two combat commands being committed. Combat Command 1, composed of two battalions, 12 tanks, six antitank gun, and one artillery battalion, was to advance through Postdorf [Postroff], Baerendorf, and Rauweiler

[Rauwiller], and on to the Sarrebourg – Phalsbourg road. Combat Command 2, composed of two battalions, 15 tanks, and one artillery battalion, was to advance through Eizweiler [Eywiller] – Hirschland (Ed: Hirshlanden?) – Schalbach and on to Phalsbourg.

By the morning of 25 Nov 44, Combat Command 1 reached the village of Rauweiler and captured it by an enveloping attack against the surprised garrison. The attack of Combat Command 2 got nearly as far as Schalbach, but was driven back there by the strong garrison.

On 24 Nov 44, the attack of another enemy combat command via Mittersheim against the strongpoints of a volks grenadier division (Interviewer's note: 179?) was reported. Protective forces of Pz Lehr Div, composed of one armored infantry battalion, one engineer battalion, six antitank guns, and one battery of 105 mm guns, were in Wolfskirchen, Postdorf, and Baerendorf. (The antitank guns were almost always silenced once they had fired and disclosed their existence.)

In spite of the destroyed bridges, the enemy combat command crossed the Saar near Finstingen [Fénétrange] and, on the morning of 25 Nov 44, attacked the flank of Combat Command 1 near Baerendorf. Some 30 tanks accompanied the infantry, passing through Finstingen [Fénétrange] against Baerendorf. From very good and well covered (Ed: concealed?) positions, the artillery and most of the enemy tanks opened fire on the German strongpoints in Baerendorf, while several tanks, followed by infantry, rolled toward the village. Baerendorf was attacked on both sides in an enveloping movement. and the strongpoints on the eastern fringe were crushed. The tanks supported the attack in an exemplary manner. Early in the afternoon, the enemy pressed into Baerendorf, and bitter house-to-house fighting developed which lasted until evening. By evening, the village was in enemy possession. Nearly all of the German battalion was mangled, with only some 80 men escaping to the northeast in the darkness. The artillery battery lost all the guns except one, and every one of the antitank guns was destroyed. Because Baerendorf had been lost, it was now necessary to evacuate Rauweiler also. The attack of the American division was continued on 26 and 27 Nov 44, with the result that Wolfskirchen and Eyweiler were lost on 29 Nov 44 after a bitter fight.

33. Q: When did the Germans realize that 4 Armd Div (US) was engaged?

A: I did not know on 25 and 26 Nov that 4 Armd Div (US) was the one engaged; however, we knew it was a very good unit from its method of attack and the excellent use of its tanks. We first learned from a prisoner on 27 Nov 44 that it was the American 4 Armd Div.

34. Q: Why was Pz Lehr Div withdrawn before the attack had reached a decisive stage?

A: The Pz Lehr Div fought until 30 Nov 44 against continuous strong enemy attacks. Troops of three different US Divisions were identified opposite the Division. During the night of 30 Nov/ 1 Dec 44, Pz Lehr Div was unexpectedly withdrawn from the front and relieved by 11 Pz Div and elements of 25 Pz Gren Div. OB WEST pressed for an acceleration of the movement to the rear. I was told that the Division would be moved to the Eifel for a quick recuperation. The steps taken by me in removing the Division from the line and shipping it out were watched by agencies of OB WEST. The reasons for the quick removal were not known to me, but they must have been special ones. Only later, I learned that the rapid withdrawal was connected with the role of the Division in the Ardennes Offensive, and that after its recent mauling, recuperation of the Division would have to be performed with great speed in order to have the Division fit for use in time.

The fighting in the Saar had inflicted further heavy losses on the already weak Division. The tank destroyers of the Division were still with the 11 Pz Div, as the latter had become involved in combat with strong forces advancing againsts Rohrbach. I was still in the vicinity, and witnessed an outstanding tank attack (such as I have rarely seen) over ideal tank terrain in the area between Eichelbach and the old Maginot Line near Rohrbach. (Interviewer's note: The tank attack referred to was the 4 Armd Div attack in early Dec 44 against Singlingen, Biningen, and Rohrbach. Pz Lehr Divk which had held the line Dermingen – Vollerdingen – Domfessel – Lorentsen – Diemereingen on 30 Nov 44, had been relieved on that day by 11 Pz Div. That Division, however, did not take over the Pz Lehr Div line, but came in roughly on the line Saargemines – Achen – Biningen. Gen Bayerlein says that there were 11 battalions of German artillery opposing the 4 Armd Div (US) tank attack which he described. These were the three battalions (two light and one heavy artillery battalions, with one of the light artillery battalions being self-propelled) of 11 Pz Div, three battalions of 25 Pz Gren Div, and five battalions of 208 Volks Art Corps. The guns of these latter five battalions were of various calibers and ranged from 75 mm to 210 mm. The 208 Volks Art Corps had been attached to Pz Lehr Div for its attack of 25 Nov 44 and, on the relief of Pz Lehr Div, the Corps reverted to the control of 11 Pz Div. It was moved out of the area early in Dec 44 to take part in the Ardennes Offensive.) (Ed: The preceding 'Interviewer's Note' seems to have been the result of an interview with Gen Bayerlein on 26 Nov 45.)

35. Q: During the period from Nov to Dec 44, was 11 Pz Div in better condition that Pz Lehr Div? If so, why?

A: The 11 Pz Div was in considerably better condition. It had three tank battalions (two of its own and one from a disbanded panzer brigade), whereas Pz Lehr Div had only one tank battalion (the other was being reformed for use with the night vision (Sperber) instrument in the army training grounds at Fallingbostel on the Lueneburger Heide (Ed: a large flat area with little vegetation, in the Ulzen region). Particularly missed were the antitank men, many prime movers, guns, and weapons for the armored infantry. The 11 Pz Div, on the other hand, was completely equipped. As a front-line division, it got everything from the Center Armored Force Base (Panzer Stuetzpunkt Mitte) in Kaiserslautern, while Pz Lehr Div, when taken out of the line in Sep 44 for recuperation, had to leave behind all tanks, tank destroyers, guns, heavy weapons, and prime movers, as it was to receive new ones in the rest area. Only a fraction of these was received, however, as the Division was moved three times to different places in quick succession (Wuerttemberg, Westphalia, and Hunsrueck) and the equipment allotted to it arrived in only small quantities due to damaged railways and transportation difficulties. Pz Lehr Div had to go into combat in the Saar inadequately equipped and supplied, while 11 Pz Div was comparatively well equipped.

36. Q: Did the bad weather in Nov 44 help you in the defense? If so, why?

    A: The bad weather, almost incessant rain and frequent fog, was very favorable for the defense because (1) air attacks on artillery and tank positions were rare and troop movements were not harassed, (2) there were no enemy artillery observation planes, which meant less accurate enemy shooting, and (3) the swampy terrain was unfavorable for an attacker. In regard to this latter factor, the stream beds and river valleys were flooded and the soaked fields impeded or hampered the employment of armor. Attacks, therefore, in general were on the roads and paths or immediately adjoining them, or limited to ridges which made them easy to observe and be stemmed by the defenders.

37. Q: Did the muddy terrain in Lorraine cause you to employ fewer tanks?

    A: The muddy terrain in Lorraine (Saar) produced by the incessant rainfall, the flooded fields, and the river and brook valleys seriously limited the employment of tanks. Tanks, in combat forces, could be used in general only over a few less wet ridges or along roads of paths; however, all available tanks and tank destroyers of Pz Lehr Div were committed in the attacks of the 24, 25, and 26 Nov 44 and in the defense of 27–30 Nov 44.

38. Q: Are Mark IV and V tanks more or less maneuverable in muddy terrain than our Shermans?

    A: The Mark IV is the twin of the Sherman so far as maneuverability in muddy terrain is concerned. The Mark V, in view of its broad tracks, is superior to the Sherman.

39. Q: What were the general armored tactics in Lorraine, and how were they affected by weather, American attacks, and the availability of your tank reserves?

    A: The following principles were applied in the tank operations and engagements of Pz Lehr Div in attack and defense:

    a. Attack: On the strength of my experiences in the Battle of France, Jun 44 to Oct 44, a solid (Ed: mass?) tank attack of one or more battalions with the infantry riding on half-tracks, is no longer possible, in view of enemy air superiority. The fighter-bombers find tanks and half-tracks very vulnerable when they roll over the battlefield without cover or camouflage.

A solid tank attack is possible against an enemy equipped with antitank guns and dug-in tanks only if the attacker is in a position to hold down the enemy with artillery and bombers to the extent that the defensive weapons cannot be used. Should this be impossible or only possible to a certain extent, then the attacking tanks themselves must take over the task of holding down the enemy defensive weapons and destroying them. For this purpose, at least two-thirds of the attacking tanks must be used while the other one-third rolls on to attack the enemy positions. For the tanks used as a cover fire, the range of the cannon is very important. If the range is short, the tanks must drive in close to their targets in order to be able to fire effectively; if, however, the tank or tank destroyer is equipped with a long range weapon, it can go into position farther from its target. If the defending tanks have a greater range, it is dangerous for the tanks which attack or support the attack by fire, since they will be caught in the fire of the defending tanks at a time when they cannot effectively fight back.

The tank attacks of Pz Lehr Div, for these reasons, were generally in the form of attacks by several tank assault groups (Panzerkampftrupp), that is, several tanks forming a combat group with organically assigned infantry. (Since Normandy, the attacks launched had only limited objectives or were minor counterattacks against enemy penetrations.) Should weather conditions, the air situation, and the terrain occasionally and exceptionally permit the attack of one or several tank companies, the bulk of the tanks were engaged in support fire and in combating enemy defense weapons, while only a small number rolled on to the objective. A solid tank attack is possible against a weak and unprepared enemy, in pursuing fleeing troops, or after a breakthrough in depth. At this point, a smaller number of tanks are committed as cover fire while the bulk roll on into the enemy.

b. Defense: In defense, it is necessary to employ the tanks as armored antitank guns or armored machine guns as the backbone of a position. The infantry, in general, does not hold its positions without armored support. Tanks so committed, however, must be especially well camouflaged so as not to be observed by enemy fighter-bombers and artillery observation planes; otherwise they are lost. Additional tanks and tank destroyers, well covered and camouflaged, are to be deployed in depth on the battlefield at points where, by using their long barrels, they can fire on enemy tanks from the front or flanks. Several tank reserves (in the form of tank assault groups which include infantry) must be prepared and set up near the front so that they can be committed at once without having to move around and risk fighter-bomber observation. Owing to the enemy air superiority, our attacks could be executed only under bad weather conditions (rain or fog), at dusk (morning or evening), or at night (moonlight).

Regardless of the fact that bad weather permitted daylight attacks in the Saar, I launched mine in the dusk; all of them succeeded. Night attacks without moonlight are very difficult, particularly in the forests. They require an especially well trained and disciplined force. The night attacks in woods on moonless nights, which Pz Lehr Div was ordered to make, in most cases resulted in failure and huge German losses. The American attacks forced me to apply the principles of defense described above, especially in regard to the exploitation of the superior range of the cannon. The Division was quite successful in destroying American tanks (for example, Domfessel, forest of Armige?).

c. Briefly, tank tactics in the Saar can be summarized by saying that we launched no steamroller attacks, but rather attacks with numerous tank assault groups (each consisting of several tanks with organic infantry support). We committed many tanks for protective fire and to neutralize and destroy enemy defense weapons, while very few tanks rolled straight ahead. We attacked only at dusk or on moonlit nights and then only along straight roads or the like. In defense, we used many well covered and camouflaged tanks in the forward line as a backbone of the defense, and also as armored antitank guns or machine guns for the direct support of the defending infantry. We similarly used tanks in depth on the battlefield, so that by utilizing the long range of their cannon, we could fire frontally or laterally on enemy tanks at a great distance. We also held in readiness several tank assault groups just behind the forward line for immediate counterattack against enemy penetrations. In both attack and defense, we sought the best defilade (Hinterhangstellung), and the best cover and camouflage for our tanks. We exploited the superior range of the cannon, and sought tank-to-tank duels.

   These tactical principles for attack and defense were applied in Lorraine and, later, in the Ardennes Offensive.

d. Shortly after my commitment in the Saar, I was unexpectedly required by OKW to give an immediate report (not through channels) on tank duels and on panzer employment in attack and defense in the West. In this report, I described the principles given above, and said, among other things, 'The time is past for steamroller tank action in attacks against a defensively prepared enemy, occupying prepared positions (as Genobst Guderian always used to teach and still demands, and as they were applied in France and in 1941–42 against the Russians).' This principle applies to the Germans as a result of the air superiority of the enemy, his air-directed artillery, and his strong ground defense with prodigal employment of mines, and built-in antitank guns and tanks (the 'PAK front') (Ed: 'the antitank front'.)[40] It equally applies to the British and Americans as they do not always have good weather in

40 FPS Ed: The German term, *Pakfront*, refers to a carefully positioned and emplaced group of antitank guns (*Pak*) with infantry protection under unified fire-control, frequently in conjunction with carefully placed mine fields to channel the movement of approaching armour.

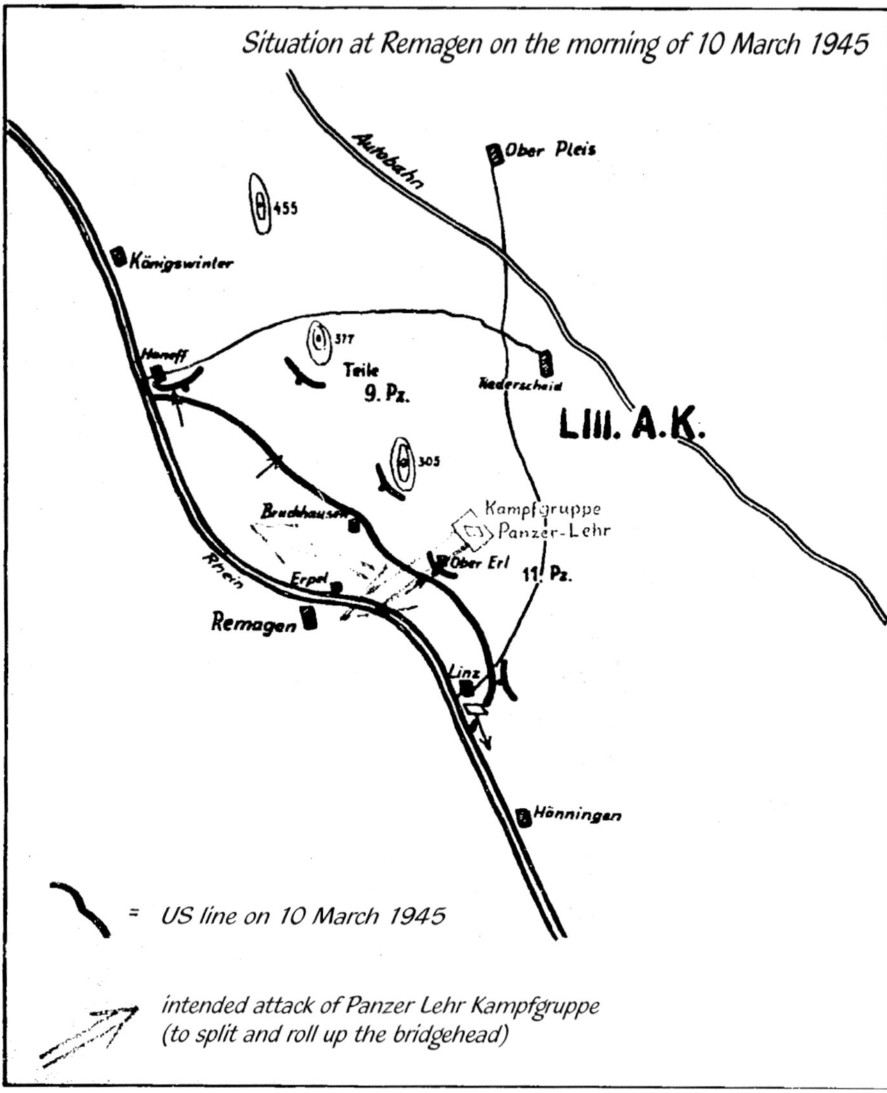


ETHINT 67 Sketch 3: Situation at Remagen on the morning of 10 March 1945

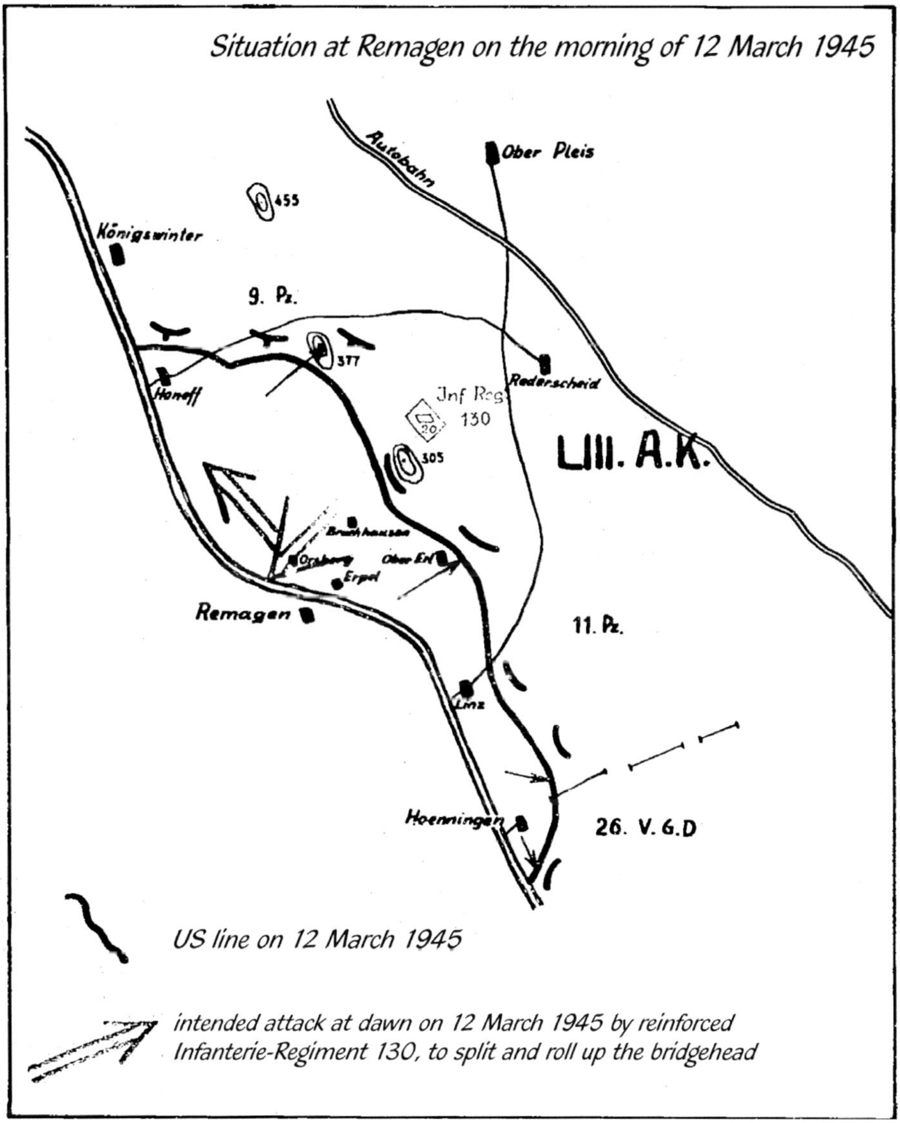


ETHINT 67 Sketch 4: Situation at Remagen on the morning of 12 March 1945

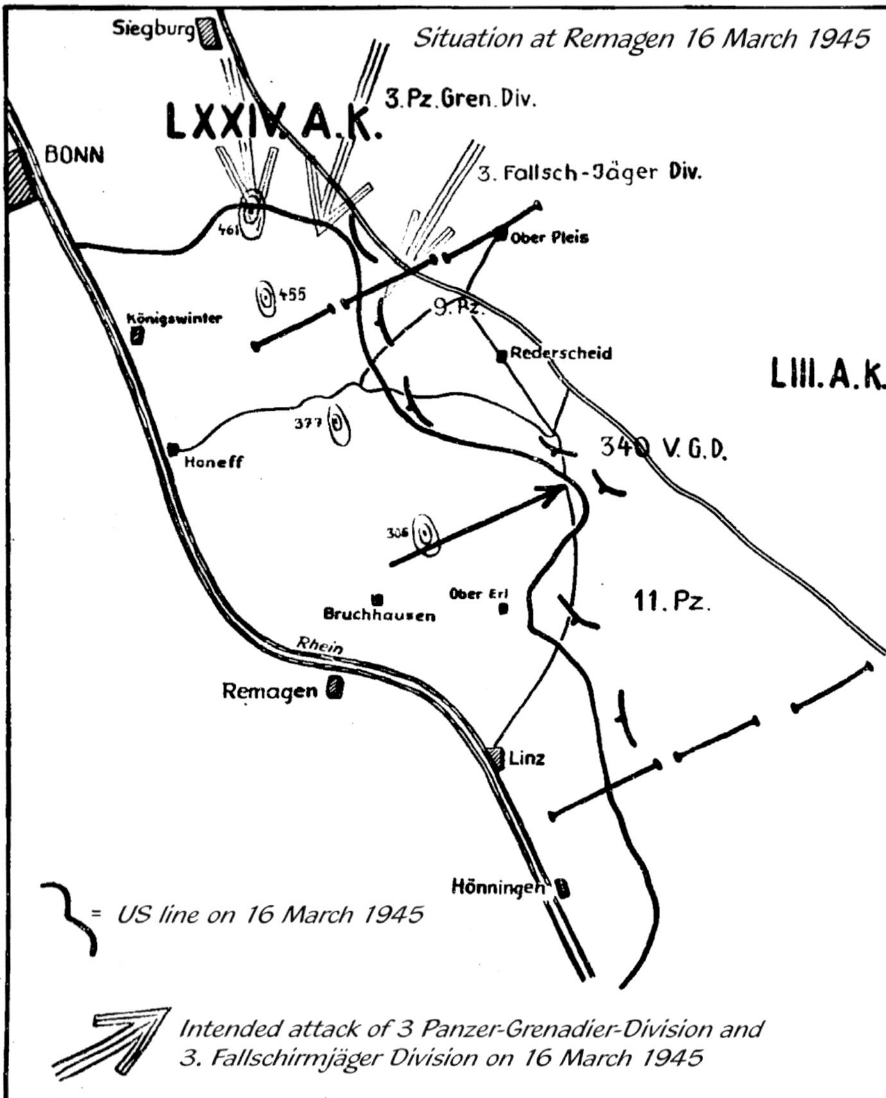


ETHINT 67 Sketch 5: Situation at Remagen 16 March 1945

which to employ their air forces in their attacks, and also because the German tank cannon (especially that of the Tiger tank) has a greater range.

## *IV. Remagen*

40. Q: Why was the Remagen Bridge not destroyed?

A: The chain of command in the 'Rhine Defense' was obscure, and no exact delimitation of sectors had been made. The 'Commander of the Rhine Defense' had only very few troops under his command and even these were poor. As fragments of the combat troops escaped over the River from the west, the confusion east of the River became still worse. No commander felt himself responsible for the sector including Remagen and the bridge. The antiaircraft and engineer troops at the bridge, not knowing whether it might still be needed for the retreating troops, did not decide to destroy the bridge quickly enough. As the Americans unexpectedly poured over the bridge, none of the remaining antiaircraft artillery troops got up sufficient courage to combat seriously the oncoming Americans, or even to destroy the bridge. The chief reason for the failure to destroy the bridge, however, is the faulty organization and leadership on the German side.

41. Q: To what extent did this failure effect the course of the war?

A: The American attack against Germany east of the Rhine was substantially accerlerated [*sic.*] by the rapid and unexpected seizure of the bridge and the subsequent prompt formation of a bridgehead.

The preparation for the systematic American attack across the Rhine and the attack itself would have consumed many days. During this time, it would have been possible to improve the organization of the German Rhine defense. An American attack against well prepared and well dug-in German defenders would have been much harder, produced many more casualties, and would have taken a long time. Through the collection of all movable forces by the German command at the bridgehead, other important points were made much easier for the Americans to reduce.

I estimate that the unexpected capture of the Remagen Bridge and the lightning-like exploitation of this success by the American command shortened the operations by about 14 days. In addition, the attack across the Rhine cost many less casualties than had a well organized defense been encountered.

42. Q: What plans existed for the liquidation of the bridgehead? Why were these plans a failure?

A: See Sketches 3, 4, and 5. On 9 Mar 45, I was unexpectedly entrusted with the command of the Remagen bridgehead and given instructions by Genfldm Model to reduce the bridgehead as soon as possible. To accomplish this mission, I received the folowing troops, elements of which were already on the way: 11 Pz Div, one combat command of 9 Pz Div, one combat command of Pz Lehr Div, and various heavy artillery battalions (Volksartilleriekorps).

Whereas 11 Pz Div and the combat command of 9 Pz Div were committed to block off the bridgehead, I intended to commit the combat command of Pz Lehr Div in an attack from Ober Erl, which we still held. This was the narrowest point of the bridgehead where a favorable ridge projected against the Remagen Bridge. The plan was to cut through the bridgehead and roll it back toward the northwest in the direction of Honnef.

Shortly before it was launched the attack was countermanded by Genfldm Model since, in the adjacent sector (LXVI Corps?), medium tanks had advanced from Linz toward Hoenningen against the unit on my left. It was feared that the Rhine defenses would be rolled back toward Neuwied. At this time, the combat command of Pz Lehr Div was pulled out of Ober Erl and committed in the Linz – Hoenningen region. The favorable and perhaps the only opportuntiy for a successful attack on the still weak bridgehead was thereby lost.

On 12 Mar 45, I intended to attack again with a newly arrived infantry regiment from Holland (130 Inf Regt). This regiment, very well equipped and well trained, was to be supported in its attack by 20 tanks and strong artillery and smoke guns.[41] The plan of attack called for an advance from the area around Hill 305 through Bruchhausen and the woods to Orsberg. This ws to be followed by rolling back the split bridgehead through a forwaard thrust to the northwest against Honnef or southward against Linz, depending on the situation.

The regiment was ready for the attack when Genfldm Model cancelled it. He wished to merge this good 130 Inf Regt with the recently arrived fragments of 340 Volks Gren Div. The Regiment was subordinated to this Division, and was committed defensively in the center of the sector. This second planned attack also might have had a chance of succeeding, with its abandonment, however, all prospects of reducing the bridgehead died.

OB WEST or OKW ordered an attack from the north on or after 16 Mar 45. This attack was to be launched from the Ober Pleis region west of the Autobahn and was to be executed by 3 Pz Gren Div and remnants of 3 FS Div. The former had been brought from Cologne for this purpose. When launched, however, the attack gained little ground and soon bogged down completely. The forces of 3 Pz Gren Div and the paratroopers were too weak and the American bridgehead had become too strong (and was composed of picked troops in the bargain).

Model's general idea was to wear down the Americans through a tough defense and cause gradual attritionof their forces, as well as eliminating the bridgehead through intensive use of artillery (for which the supply of

41 FPS Ed: *Nebelwerfer.*

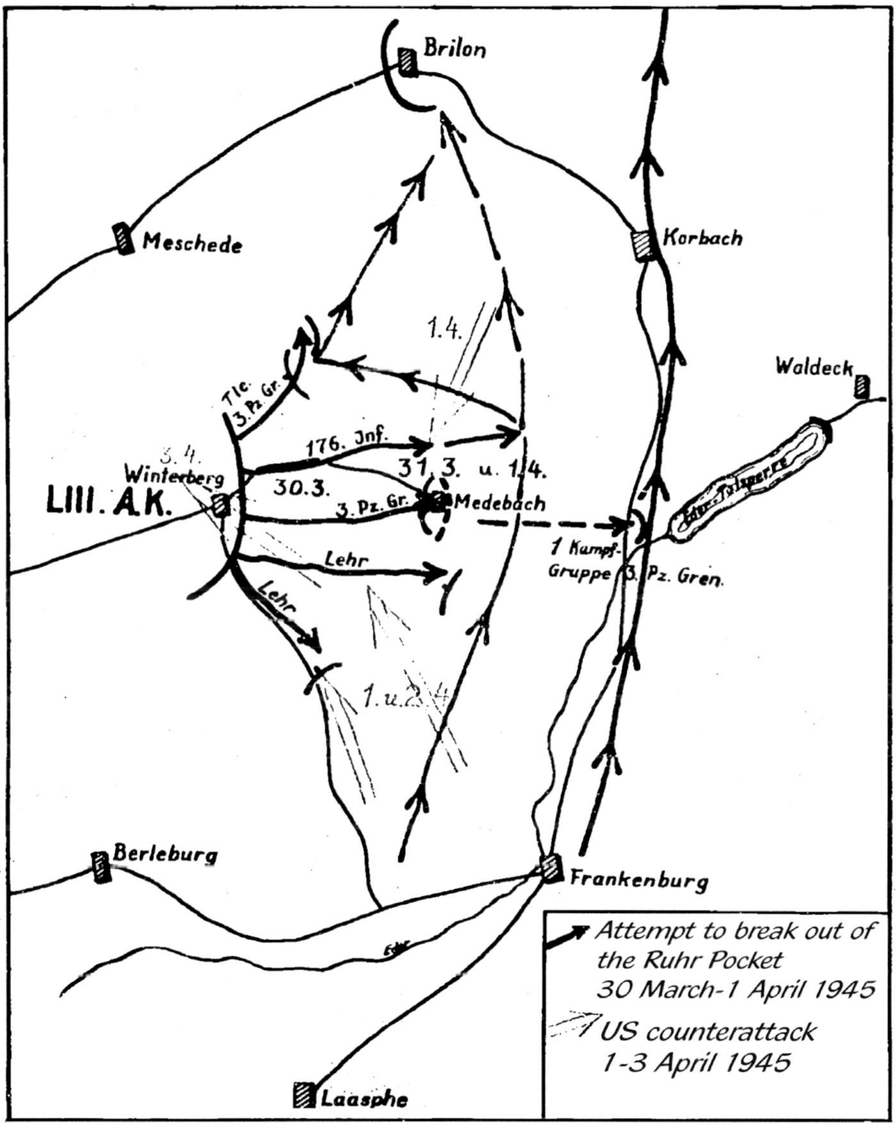


ETHINT 67 Sketch 6: Attempt to break out of the Ruhr Pocket 30 March-1 April 1945

ammunition had been hampered by the incessant air attacks) and smoke guns.[42] Divers and swimmers also were to be used to destroy the bridge, and the use of a V–2 against the bridgehead was planned. Instead of the American forces being the victims of attrition, however, the German forces became more and more mangled until the main attack of the American divisions on 23 Mar 45 (?) broke through the worn and exausted German defenders.

## V. *Ruhr Pocket*

43. Q: Did you yourself assume or foresee that we would form the Ruhr Pocket?

A: The deliberate creation of the Ruhr Pocket was neither suspected nor assumed by me. I held the view that the American attack spearhead would drive from Giessen and Marburg farther toward the east in order to gain the Weser and then the Elbe River line as fast as possible, and would pay little attention to the German forces located between the Americans and the British. I consider the encirclement of the Ruhr to eliminate a strong portion of the German Army from further participation in operations to be as good a measure as the formation of the smaller Argentan – Falaise pocket in Normandy, preceding the creation of the larger pocket on the Seine.

44. Q: What plans were forged in order to break out of the Ruhr Pocket?

A: See Sketch 6. On 29 or 30 Mar 45, the Ruhr Pocket was nearly closed; only a gap near Paderborn – Lippstadt was still open. On this day, I was called back from my front near Wissen – Siegburg, and ordered by Genfldm Model to take over the front near Winterberg (in the Rothaar Mountains).

Panzer Lehr and 3 Pz Gren Divs were to be brought under my command, immediately, as was 176 Inf Div (coming up from the Dortmund area) later. The 654 Tank Destroyer Bn and 512 Jagd Tiger Bn were to arrive later. Some heavy artillery batteries were also put under my command, as were the forces already committed in the Winterberg sector (only Volkssturm and fragments of Luftwaffe on foot).

My mission was to attack as soon as possible from Winterberg toward the Eder Dams to the east, in order to burst the threatening encirclement ring and cut across the roads leading north from the Frankenberg region toward Korbach and Brilon. As SS Div 'Westphalie' (Ed: actually an SS panzer replacement unit of brigade size) was to attack via Warburg from the outside, aand meet my attack.

On 30 Mar 45, I launched a night attack along the forest road with two weak combat commands (more had not arrived) and reached the area southwest and northwest of Medebach. Having received additional

42 FPS Ed: *Nebelwerfer.*

troops, I again attacked on 31 Mar 45 and 1 Apr 45 in three combat commands, took Medebach and, with one group, reached the road east of Medebach and Rheder and Hillershausen. Strong American counterattacks from the north and south against my flanks soon brought my advance to a stop and compelled me to retire toward Winterberg, which was taken by American troops on 3 Apr 45. I did not see any sign of the planned attack by the SS division.

Had these attacks been performed with stronger forces (which could have been pulled out from the Rhine and Sieg fronts and brought over in time), they could have been successful. With each succeeding day, the prospects for a successful breakout and a junction with the German forces coming from the east became smaller. By 5 Apr 45, the situation was hopeless.

Genfldm Model (or OB WEST or OKW) still planned an escape attempt and collaboration with the new Twelfth Army which was to come through Hannover. On 10 Apr 45, a breakout attack was to be staged from the Unna region toward the northeast. This attack, however, never took place as the troops needed for it were tied up at other points by the strong American attacks on the south rim of the pocket. It now was too late for a breakout. As the American attack toward the east was already 150 km on its way and was gaining steadily, any attempt to break out would have had no chance of success.

Alfred Zerbel

Koenigstein/Ts. 30. 5. 50

# MS # 901 [sic.]

### SUPPLEMENTARY QUESTIONS TO PREVIOUS QUESTIONNAIRE

### WITHDRAW[AL] FROM FRANCE

No headings for index.

[Translated by Frederick Steinhardt. Bracketed notes added by F. Steinhardt.

*Generalleutnant* Bayerlein Ober Ursel, 18 February 1946

## SUPPLEMENTARY QUESTIONS TO PREVIOUS QUESTIONNAIRE

### WITHDRAWAL FROM FRANCE

1.) [tr. note- the numbers here and below refer to the numbers of the questions Bayerlein was answering. The questions were not with the material.] After the St. Lô breakthrough the remnants of the *Panzer Lehr Division* were committed as follows:

a) From 28 July to 1 August: In the area north of Percy, under command of the 47th *Panzer-Korps*.

b) From 2 to 5 August: In the Mortain – Barenton area in defense, under command of the 47th *Panzer-Korps*.

c) From 6 to 12 August (elements only to 10 August) in the area east and southeast of Vire in defense and counterattack under command of the 2nd *Fallschirm-Korps* [parachute-corps].

As of 2 August the rear elements of the *Panzer-Lehr* [*Division*] were in the Alençon [corrected from Allencon] area. They consisted of: logistics troops; workshops; tank crews who were not in action as a result of lack of tanks; the *Feldersatzbataillon* [field replacement battalion] with some replacements from the homeland; and tanks and tank destroyers [*Panzerjäger*] that were being repaired. The remnants of *Panzergrenadier-Regt.* [*Regiment*] 902 joined these rear elements on 3 August for reconstitution.

All of these elements were committed on 8 August in defense against the advance of the U. S. 3rd Army east from Mayenne, under command of the 81st *Korps* in the Sillé [-le-Guillaume] area southwest of Alençon as *Kampfgruppe Panzer Lehr Division*.

Strength: Four *Panzergrenadier* companies, 15 tanks and tank-destroyers, one artillery *Abteilung*[equivalent to an artillery battalion] with two batteries (eight 10.5

cm guns). On 9 August the reconstituted *Pionier* [engineer] battalion joined [the *Kampfgruppe*].

Defensive positions from 9 to 12 August, as well as movements of the division during the nights of 12/13 and 13/14 August and the defensive positions on 13 and 14 August are shown in the sketch maps.

## COMBAT OPERATIONS

Sillé was finally lost on 9 August. The defense shifted to the commanding heights north of the built-up area which were held on 10 August. Enemy pressure, however, increased on both sides of the division against the 708th *Infanterie-Div.* [*Division*] via Villaines [-la-Juhel] and against the 9th *Panzer-Div.* [*Division*] via Fresnay sur Sarthe and against Alençon. North of Fresnay [-sur-Sarthe] the staff of the *Panzer Lehr* and 9th *Panzer-Divisionen* were attacked by surprise by U.S. tanks that had penetrated. Southwest of Alençon the staff of the 81st *Korps* was also surprised by the enemy and had to fall back.

During the night of 10/11 August, in the face of envelopment on both flanks, [*Kampfgruppe*] *Panzer Lehr* evacuated the position north of Sillé and fell back behind the Merderau [corrected from Menderau] [River] sector with no pressure from the enemy. On 10 August U. S. infantry had captured Villaines and Averton. The infantry regiment of the 708th *Infanterie Division* that had been committed there was attached to the *Panzer Lehr* [*Division*].

On 11 August the main enemy pressure was directed via Villaines against Pré en Pail. There was no strong attack elsewhere on the front held by *Panzer Lehr*. On 11 August strong enemy pressure against Alençon and westward led to the evacuation of Alençon on 11 August and, on 12 August, to a thrust via Sees – Mortree toward Argentan.

On 12 August *Panzer Lehr* held the line Pré en Pail — Ormain — Denis sur Sarthon. The *Panzer Lehr* division reserve (consisting of the *Pionier* battalion and eight tanks) attacked the flank of the enemy [forces] that had advanced via Mortréee on Argentan and brought them to a halt..

The 9th *Panzer-Division* – separated by the command in three separate groups that were committed individually –was completely split up and no longer had any effectiveness in combat.

In the evening of 12 August *Panzer Lehr* turned over its Pré en Pail — St. Denis [sur Sarthon] sector to the 708th *Infanterie Division*, leaving a weak battalion of *PanzerGren. Regt.* [*Panzergrenadier-Regiment*] 902 and six tanks, as well as one battery of artillery, in this sector.

During the night of 12/13 August the division was withdrawn and set in march via Ecouché – Putanges [-Pont Écrepin] to the area east of Argentan to join with the 116th *Panzer-Div.* [*Division*] in fending off the enemy advance on Trun.

In the morning of 13 August the first elements of the division occupied a defensive position near St. Leonhard [Le Bourg St. Léonard] and near Nouant le Pin [ Nonant le Pin ]. That put the division outside the Argentan – Falaise pocket that was forming.

On 11 August *Panzergrenadier-Regiment* 901, with ten tanks and one battery [of artillery], which had been committed with the 2nd *Fallschirm Korps* in defense and attack near Vire since 6 August, was returned to the division and set in march to the refitting area near Fontainebleau. The combat effectiveness of the regiment was extremely limited. The regiment was again committed in defense near Gacé and fought until 15 August against enemy forces attacking from the south.

On 17 August the division was withdrawn for reconstitution to the Senlis area and had to leave behind with the 81st *Korps* a *Kampfgruppe* in the strength of approximately one battalion of *Panzergrenadiere*, one *Pionier* company and ten tanks, along with one battery [of artillery].

2.) Strength of the Replacements in the Senlis Area. – Strength of the Division

| | |
|---|---|
| Replacements: | *Panzergrenadiere*: 2000 men, organized in four mobile battalions [*schnelle Abteilungen*], which came from Holland.<br>Tanks: 12 *Panzer IV* and *V*. [tr. note- *Panzer V*= *Panther*]<br>Guns: 6–10.5 cm howitzers. |

Combat Strength in the Senlis Area after Incorporation of Replacements:

| | |
|---|---|
| *Panzergrenadier-Regiment* 901: | About 800 men, armoured, on *SPW*, inadequately armed. |
| *Panzergrenadier-Regiment* 902: | About 300 men, on trucks, inadequately armed. |
| *Aufklärungs Abteilung* [*Panzer-Aufklärungs-Lehr Abteilung* 130] reconnaissance battalion]: | About 150 men, eight armoured cars. |
| *Panzer Regiment:* | About 20 *Panzer IV* and *V*. |
| *Panzerjäger Abteilung* [tank-destroyer battalion]: | Five *Panzerjäger*. The remaining personnel were assigned to tank-killer squads equipped with *Panzerfäuste*. |
| *Artillerie Regiment*: | Two batteries with five 10 cm guns each, One battery with three 15 cm guns. |
| *Flak Abteilung* [anti-aircraft artillery battalion]: | Not ready for action. |
| *Pionier Bataillon*: | About 150 men. |

The division thus had approximately one-quarter of its T/O (table of organization) strength in *Panzergrenadiere* and in artillery, only one-eighth of its T/O strength in tanks and tank-destroyers. [*Panzerjäger*].

43 Tr. note: *Schützenpanzerwagen*. Lightly armoured half-track troop-carriers, open on top.

44 Tr. note: The *Panzerfaust* was a recoil-less disposable light-weight one-man antitank weapon firing a large hollow-charge grenade. Later models increased the range from 30 to 100 meters, the armour penetration from 140 mm at 30° to 200 mm at 30°. A portion of the gases from the propellant charge in the disposable firing tube vented to the rear to eliminate recoil. These made conspicuous the position of the operator and created a danger zone behind the weapon.

The rear area elements in the Soissons area were at approximately two-thirds strength in personnel but with only about half of their motor-vehicles ready for service.

Question No. 3 cannot be answered precisely since I left the division on about 23 August due to wounds. Until about 8 September the division was led by the commander of the *Panzer Regiment*, *Oberst* Gerhardt and, until the end of September, by the commander of *PanzergrenadierRegiment* 901, *Oberst Freiherr*[Baron] von Hausser [*Fhr.* von Hauser, see Ritgen, *PANZER LEHR DIVISION*, *Stellenbesetzung der Truppenteile*, p. 322.]. These officers are in a position to make exact statements of combat operations.

[signed] Bayerlein

# NOTES ON THE PERIOD FROM RECONSTITUTION OF *PANZER LEHR DIVISION* 130 AFTER THE RETREAT TO THE *WESTWALL* THROUGH TO ITS INVOLVEMENT IN THE LORRAINE CAMPAIGN

## RECONSTITUTION OF *PANZER LEHR DIVISION* 130 AFTER RETREAT TO THE *WESTWALL*

As noted above, *Panzer Lehr Division* 130 had lost most of its combat troops and nearly all of its equipment by the time its fragments made their separate ways back to the *Westwall*. The first area assigned for reconstitution, the Mayen–Brohl area in the Rhineland, about 30 kilometres west of Koblenz and the Rhine, was unsuitable. It lacked training areas and was too close to the front. The consequent constant exposure to aerial attack would preclude training. In response to protests from the Division, a new reconstitution area was assigned east of the Rhine River, in Swabia.

On 6 September the Division reported that it needed an entire new *Panzergrenadier* regiment, since *Panzergrenadier-Lehr-Regiment* 902 had simply ceased to exist. Specific needs for personnel and materiel would follow upon its arrival at the new reconstitution site, but, as ordered by *Heeresgruppe* B, essentially all armored vehicles and heavy weapons, including prime movers, had been turned over to other divisions when *Panzer Lehr* departed the front. The Division reported a desperate need for 400 vehicles.

*Panzer Lehr Division* 130 was to be reconstituted as a standard '*Panzer-Division 44*'. Germany's desperate situation could no longer provide the materiel for reconstitution as a 'special division'. Henceforth, *Panzergrenadier-Lehr-Regiment* 901 would only have its staff and first battalion mounted on *SPW*, the rest would receive unarmed Steyr 1500 wheeled troop-carriers.

As for tanks, the battalion that had been in training as *Panzer-Lehr-Regiment* 130's first battalion never got to the Division. Instead, at the completion of its training in July it was sent to *Panzer-Bataillon* 113 and wiped out in the attack at Lunéville (on the Meurthe River, southeast of Nancy). Hopes that the I./ *Panzer-Regiment* 6 would again replace the Division's missing first battalion were dashed, when that battalion was returned to its parent 3rd *Panzer Division* effective 1 October. The Division thus ended up with only a single armoured battalion, the II./*Panzer-Lehr-Regiment* 130.

On 8 September 1944 *Generalleutnant* Bayerlein, having recovered from his wounds, resumed command of the Division.

On 10 September individual elements of the Division left for the reconstitution area in Swabia. *Kampfgruppe von Hauser*, however, remained in action for weeks at the *Westwall* and never did get to join the Division for reconstitution in Swabia. Beautiful weather in a beautiful area, far from the front, healed morale and discipline regained its former high level. Fuel shortage, however, detracted from vehicle training.

On 15 September, based on the recommendation of the *General der Panzertruppen West, Oberbefehlshaber West* gave priority for materiel, particularly tanks, prime-movers and heavy equipment, to *Panzer Lehr Division* 130 and the 21st *Panzer Division.* That same day *Panzer Lehr Division* 130 was attached to *Panzer-Armeeoberkommando* 6 (*Oberstgruppenführer und Generaloberst der Waffen-SS* Dietrich), which had been specified as the staff to direct reconstitution of all *Panzer* divisions that had been withdrawn for refitting.

*Generalleutnant* Bayerlein's 1 October report to *Generalinspekteur der Panzertruppen* Guderian indicated, in part, that the Division was still short 2500 men from its new (*Panzer-Division* 44) T/O strength of 14,000, only partially offset by the arrival of 299 replacements and the return of 47 convalescents. As for materiel (probably not including *Kampfgruppe von Hauser*), the Division did not have a single *Panther* or *Panzer* IV tank. It had 22 *SPW* serviceable, 20 more under repair. The artillery situation was grim, with two anti-tank guns and three artillery pieces.

Particularly critical was the shortage of experienced non-commissioned officers, which, in turn, seriously interfered with the training of the men. In mid-October the Division was transferred to continue reconstitution in Westphalia, in the Paderborn and Detmold area, where there was fear of an Allied airborne landing. The Division still had not received any armour or other heavy equipment.

At long last, *Kampfgruppe von Hauser* rejoined its parent division.

Finally, at the end of October, replacement equipment began to arrive. The II./*Panzer-Lehr-Regiment* 130 received 16 *Panther* and 24 *Panzer* IV tanks. It now consisted of two companies of *Panther* and two companies of *Panzer* IV. Back on 1 June 1944 the Division had two tank battalions, one with 86 *Panther* (*Panzer* V) and the other with 97 *Panzer* IV. Shortage of fuel prevented adequate training with tanks or other motor vehicles.

There were still no *Panzerjäger* (tank destroyers), and the artillery regiment was lacking guns or prime-movers for two of its *Abteilungen.* Instead of its projected 3.7 cm *Flak-Panzer* IV self-propelled anti-aircraft units, *Heeres-Flak-Abteilung* received 37 mm towed anti-aircraft guns, but no prime-movers to tow them.

Instead of the minimum of 400 trucks that the Division had requested as 'desperately needed', the Division was allotted 102 from a factory in Cologne. When Allied bombers knocked out the factory no alternative source was provided. The poor condition of the vehicles required ceaseless attention from the repair echelons.

As of 1 November, the last monthly report prior to going back into action, in spite of having received 1,363 replacements, the Division was still short 1,183 men. It now had operational 28 *Panzer* IV and 18 *Panzer* V. 50 *SPW* were in service, 29 undergoing repairs. As for transport, it had 10 Ford *Maultier* (half-tracked lorries), 216 all-terrain lorries, 34 of which were in the shops, and 686 open trucks, of which 122 were being repaired. There were 38 prime-movers, of which 14 were undergoing repairs. The Division now had six heavy infantry guns (regimental), 13 anti-tank guns and 15 howitzers.

Thus, the Division had only one, instead of two, tank battalions, was still devoid of *Panzerjäger* (tank destroyers), two of its artillery *Abteilungen* were entirely lacking in guns or prime-movers, the *Flak* battalion had none of its intended *Flak-Panzer* and nothing with which to tow the anti-aircraft guns that it had been given. The list of deficiencies went on at length. *Generalleutnant* Bayerlein's 1 November report concluded by saying the Division had 30% mobility and was, for the time being, unfit for either attack or defence. (Perrigault, pp. 327–8)

On 11 November *Panzer Lehr Division* 130 was ordered to the Hunsrück in Lorraine.

Dispersal of the elements of the Division, which were billeted in villages on both sides of the Hunsrück ridge road, interfered with further training and communication. Despite all these handicaps the Division prepared to go into action.

## *PANZER LEHR DIVISION* 130 IN LORRAINE

Prior to the Normandy Invasion, the SHAEF Planning Staff recommended that, after a lodgement area had been captured on the continent, the eastward advance was to be conducted on a broad front along two mutually supporting axes. The main emphasis was to be toward the northeast, 'with the object of striking directly at the Ruhr by the route north of the Ardennes'. The 'subsidiary axis' was to be south of the Ardennes, toward Metz and the Saar. (Cole, *The Lorraine Campaign*, pp. 8–9)

After its dramatic exploitation of the American breakthrough in Operation 'Cobra', Patton's American Third Army had pursued the German forces across northern France along that 'subsidiary axis' in one of the most spectacularly successful campaigns in military history, only to be brought up short of the German border by logistical problems.

The Allies were advancing on a vast front extending from the First Canadian Army on the Channel Coast to Patton's American Third Army, which, in addition to advancing toward Metz and Nancy, the Saar industrial region and the southern route into Germany via Metz – Saarbrücken – Frankfurt, screened the southern flank of the Allied armies in northern France along the Loire River.

With supplies still coming all the way from Normandy, there were not enough to support 'everyone, everywhere'. The Supreme Commander, General Eisenhower, gave priority to the northern thrust toward the Ruhr industrial area by Montgomery's British 21st Army Group, supported on its southern flank by Hodges' American First Army. Hodges' two northernmost corps were to support the British 21st Army Group in its drive toward the Rhine, the Ruhr industrial region and the heart of Germany.

On 2 September General Eisenhower, in a meeting of Bradley, Hodges, Patton and Major General Hoyt Vandenburg, commanding the Ninth Air Force, stated that, 'as soon as the First Army forces had completed the mover to the north [to trap retreating German forces in the vicinity of Mons, in conjunction withy Montgomery's forces], both the First and Third Armies would remain 'generally static' until sufficient gasoline and other supplies could be accumulated 'to permit the Third Army and the V Corps of the First Army to move to the Siegfried Line (West Wall) ... ' (Cole, *The Lorraine Campaign*, p. 13.) Bradley then gave Patton a future axis of advance that would take the Third Army across the Rhine in the Mannheim – Frankfurt sector. Patton then telephoned Third Army headquarters that, except for cavalry reconnaissance, the army was to hold at the Meuse.

Regardless of the order, although the American Third Army had achieved bridgeheads across the Meuse River and its cavalry had scouted to the Moselle River, the gasoline shortage had already halted the advance at the borders of Lorraine and would continue to keep Patton's army virtually immobilized from 1 to 5 September. By 10 September Patton's American Third Army would be past the period of critical fuel shortage.

On 4 September General Eisenhower, in a letter to the Allied commanders, while maintaining priority for the northern assault on the Ruhr by Montgomery's 21st Army Group, supported by Hodges' American First Army, assigned Patton's Third Army the mission: 'to occupy the sector of the [*Westwall*] covering the Saar and then to seize Frankfurt.' The following day Eisenhower dictated an office memorandum stating, ' ... I now deem it important, while supporting the advance on eastward through Belgium, to get Patton moving once again..' (Cole, *Lorraine Campaign*, pp. 53- 54)

While *Panzer Lehr Division* 130 worked at integrating and training its new replacements and fretted at the delays and insufficiencies in replacing equipment and weapons that had been lost or turned over to other units when it was withdrawn from combat, General Patton's American Third Army was finally moving again. The stage was now set for *Panzer Lehr Division* 130's next involvement, which would come as Patton's American Third Army, having crossed the Moselle and advanced through Lorraine, crossed the Sarre River and advanced toward Germany's vital Saar industrial region. At the same time the left wing of General Patch's American Seventh Army, which had landed on France's Mediterranean coast, also crossed the Saar as part of its Vosges Mountains campaign. (Note-Whether a place name includes 'Sarre' or 'Saar' varies depending on whether the map was of French or German origin, since both claimed this hotly-contested region.)

General Manton Eddy's American XII Corps of Patton's Third Army approached the Saar River. On November 23 CCB of the American 4th Armored Division captured Fénétrange, on the west bank of the Saar. The 25th Cavalry Reconnaissance Squadron then turned south along the river and crossed at Bettborn, about six kilometres south of Fénétrange. It then met patrols of the 44th Infantry Division of XV Corps, of the American Seventh Army.

On 13 November General Patch's Seventh Army had launched its XV Corps in a major drive to reach and cross the Vosges Mountains in the vicinity of the Saverne Gap. On 21 November XV Corps broke through the weak boundary between the German 1st *Armee* and 19th *Armee* and on 23 November connection was lost between the two armies. Reports of General Patton's American Third Army's XII Corps advance toward Saar-Union increased the urgency for counteraction.

There were no reserves or reinforcements available even to *OB West* (*Oberbefehlshaber West*). The only way to counter this threat was to call on *OKW's* reserves, which included *Panzer Lehr Division* 130.

Although the Division did not suspect it, *Panzer Lehr Division* 130 had already been earmarked and set aside for Hitler's planned Ardennes Offensive. Despite strict *OKW* orders that the Division was not to be employed for any reason prior to that offensive, when the American Third Army's XII Corps broke through the German Saar front north of Saar-Union, *Panzer Lehr Division* 130 was alerted at 1500 hours on November 21. Within an hour the *Oberkommando der Wehrmacht* released the Division to the 1st *Armee*, attaching it to XIII *SS-Armee Korps*..

The Division was ordered to proceed to the Saar-Alben area, ten kilometres south of Sarreguemines, launch an attack in the morning of 23 November against the flank of the American forces that were advancing eastward towards Strasbourg and annihilate them. The Division loaded fuel and ammunition and mounted up in haste. Since the 21 *Panzerjäger* for the tank-destroyer battalion had not yet arrived, *Panzer Lehr Division* 130 moved out with no more armour than its single tank battalion, II./*Panzer-Lehr-Regiment* 130.

Due to the danger from aerial attacks, the Division rolled by night and lay concealed during the day. The first night of marching revealed weaknesses in both training and materiel, Twelve of the precious few tanks dropping out with mechanical problems that ranged from electrical problems to engine and transmission weaknesses. There were instances of apparent sabotage by foreign workers in the plants where they were manufactured.

After a second night's march at a reduced pace, 'to spare the equipment' (Ritgen, p. 210), the Division finally reached Saar-Union by noon of 23 November. A collapsed bridge prevented the arrival of some elements of *Panzergrenadiere* and fuel vehicles. The commander of *Heeresgruppe* G, *General der Panzertruppen* Balck had made it clear in his order of the evening of 21 November that 'the fate of Alsace depended on an early start of the attack with concentrated forces in a ruthless thrust to the assigned objectives', so the attack could not wait.

*Generalleutnant* Bayerlein makes it apparent in the above interview that the attack was launched with little information and no reconnaissance. He did not realize that he was attacking an entire corps, or the fact that advance elements of the American 106th Cavalry Group were already in Weyer, nor the weakness of the defending 361st *Volksgrenadier Division*.

*Generalleutnant* Bayerlein organized the attacking force in two *Kampfgruppen* advancing south on parallel roads. The stronger eastern group, *Kampfgruppe von Hauser*, comprised of *Panzerkampfgruppe von Ritgen* (II./*Panzer-Lehr-Regiment* 130 [-]), and I./ *Panzergrenadier-Lehr-Regiment* 901, was to advance on the axis Eschweiler – Eywiller–Hirschland. The weaker western *Kampfgruppe von Poschinger* (*Panzergrenadier-Lehr-Regiment* 902) was to advance via Bärendorf – Rauwiller. Their first objective was the Rauwiller – Schalbach line. According to Cole (*The Lorraine Campaign*, p.466), Bayerlein 'intended that the two columns would continue south to Hazelbourg, at the edge of the Vosges, and then turn north to free the [German] troops around Phalsbourg.'

The German attack fell on the American Thanksgiving Day, as the troops were preparing for a traditional turkey dinner. *Kampfgruppe von Hauser* captured Eywiller and Eschweiler by 1900 hours. *Kampfgruppe von Poschinger* overcame strong opposition in taking Postroff and Bärendorf. As the German forces awaited the arrival of their supply columns a new order from *General* Balck directed that the attack be resumed and carried on through the night.

Accordingly, the armored columns moved out again with nearly empty fuel tanks at 2300 hours on 23 November. At about 0400 hours on 24 November *Kampfgruppe von Poschinger* drove the American cavalry out of Hirschland. Shortly thereafter Rauwiller also fell into German hands.

Before Weyer, however, the German advance was brought to a halt under heavy fire from American armour and artillery.

On 24 November leading elements of *Kampfgruppe von Poschinger*, the western column, fought their way into Rauwiller, cleaned up the American resistance and sent approximately 200 prisoners to the rear. Those prisoners, however, were later freed in Bärendorf. Fighting for Rauwiller continued throughout the day with men of the American 4th Armored Division who made their way into Rauwiller during the morning. At 2200 hours orders arrived for the German evacuation of Rauwiller, the last elements of II./ *Panzergrenadier-Lehr-Regiment* 902 pulling out at 2300 hours.

On 24 November two new factors impacted *Panzer Lehr Division* 130's position. General Eisenhower visited XV Corps headquarters in Sarrebourg and, after studying the Seventh Army situation, redirected XV Corps advance from directly eastward to northward astride the Vosges Mountains, permitting an offensive by that corps in the Sarrebourg sector.

More directly, CCB (Combat Command B) of the American XII Corps' 4th Armored Division crossed the Saar River, threatening the flank of the *Panzer Lehr Kampfgruppen*.. Task Force Churchill crossed at Rommelfing, just south of Fénétrange, Task Force Jaques at Gosselming.

The northern column of CCB, Task Force Churchill moved with little opposition to take a blocking position on high ground west of Postroff. The First *Batterie* of the I./ *Panzer-Artillerie-Regiment* 130 was shot to pieces in Postroff while changing firing positions, losing six guns, half the firepower of the *Abteilung*. CCB's southern column, Task Force Jaques (pronounced 'Jakes'), overcame brief, but spirited opposition by elements of the 361st *Volksgrenadier Division* at Kirrberg, then headed north to reach the main road at Bärendorf, striking into *Kampfgruppe von Poschinger's* western flank.

Covered by fire from tanks and assault guns, CCB's 53rd Armored Infantry Battalion waded an icy stream and took the high ground around Bärendorf. Then, in house-to-house fighting, it forced the I./*Panzergrenadier-Regiment* 902 out of the village. Although Bayerlein reported heavy losses in the defence of Bärendorf, the American forces felt their opponents offered light resistance, evidence of the inexperience of *Panzer Lehr's* recent replacements, most of whom were experiencing their first combat.

*Kampfgruppe von Hauser*, the eastern column, continued its attack southward in the early morning of 25 November while *Kampfgruppe von Poschinger* attempted an attack toward the American crossing site at Fénétrange. Its initial pre-dawn attack on Bärendorf from the north and east met strong opposition. Both sides lost heavily in a day of intense fighting that ended with the Germans retreating, leaving the American 53rd Armored Infantry Battalion of the 4th Armored Division's CCB holding the town.

While *Kampfgruppe von Poschinger* fought in vain to recapture Bärendorf, the eastern column, *Kampfgruppe von Hauser*, ran into the 2nd Battalion of the American 114th Infantry Regiment (44th Infantry Division) and the American 106th Cavalry Group before Schalbach. Initial uncertainty about the whereabouts of the American 4th Armored Division delayed the onset of American artillery fire, but thereafter it so shattered the German attacks that *Kampfgruppe von Hauser* fell back on Hirschland after losing heavily, leaving Schalbach in American hands.

The size and strength of the American forces ended German hopes for their destruction. In the evening of 25 November, *Generalleutnant* Bayerlein ordered the *Panzer Lehr Kampfgruppen* to fall back and take up defensive positions along the Wolfskirchen – Eywiller – Durstel road. *General* Balck ordered termination of the attack and reorganization of the German 1st *Armee* to defend the general line Richerling – Saar-Union – Wingen. *Panzer Lehr Division* 130 was to secure the construction of the new line of defence and be withdrawn, effective 28 November, into *Heeresgruppe G* reserve.

The American 4th Armored Division attacked Wolfskirchen on 26 November. By the time it again attacked with air support on 27 November, *Panzer Lehr's* forces had already been relieved by the 25th *Panzergrenadier Division*, which had to give up the town after concentric attacks.

*Kampfgruppe von Hauser's Panzergrenadier-Lehr-Regiment* 901 held out in Eschweiler against heavy attacks by Task Force Jaques until the American force captured Gungweiler, about a mile southeast of Eschweiler, rendering Eschweiler untenable.

At Durstel *Kampfgruppe von Hauser* was able to repulse all attacks of the American 4th Armored Division's CCA on 27 November, in large part thanks to the belated arrival of *Panzerjäger-Lehr-Abteilung* 130. Two days after the Division left Hunsrück for Saar-Alben, its tank-destroyer battalion finally received its promised 21 *Panzerjäger* IV with the new and more powerful 75 mm *Kanone L/70*. Without waiting to adjust and inspect the new tank-destroyers, the *Abteilung* hastened after its parent Division. Necessary adjusting and test-firing was conducted *en route*, during a march-pause on the edge of the Baumholder Troop-Training Ground. *Panzerjäger-Lehr-Abteilung* 130 proved what it could do in combat, despite lack of conversion-training in the new weapons system.

It cost three days of hard fighting for the American forces to force *Panzer Lehr Division* 130 off the heights east of the Saar-Union – Drulingen road and attain their jump-off positions for attacking Saar-Union, by which time, again, *Panzer Lehr Division* 130 had been relieved by the 25th *Panzergrenadier Division.*

Despite its ordered withdrawal from action, the German 1st *Armee* situation prevented release of the Division. Elements of the Division were sucked into the battle for Saar-Union on 1 December and again on 2 December.

On 3 December elements of *Panzergrenadier-Lehr-Regiment* 901 were committed at Ratzwiller. That evening the I./*Panzergrenadier-Lehr-Regiment* 902 was assigned to defend Domfessel, where, the next day, 4 December, the Americans cut off and broke into the town, forcing the remaining 140 men of the battalion to surrender.

Also on 4 December, a completely unexpected order arrived for the Division to prepare immediately to load up and head north. The American advance on 6 December threatened the railroad and the Division's entrainment, but the last trains carrying *Panzer Lehr Division* 130 rolled out on 9 December, just a bare week before the start of the great Ardennes Offensive, in which *Panzer Lehr Division* 130 was to play an important role.

*General der Panzertruppen* Hermann Balck, commander of *Heeresgruppe G* during *Panzer-Lehr's* commitment to the Saar, late 1944. (Bundesarchiv 101I-732-0118-03)

# PART II

## *PANZER LEHR DIVISION* 130 IN THE ARDENNES OFFENSIVE

# TO BASTOGNE

This brief account of *Panzer Lehr Division* 130's involvement in the Ardennes Campaign focuses entirely on *Panzer Lehr's* immediate participation as part of the German XLVII *Panzer Korps*. Contrary to plans, *Panzer Lehr Division* 130 was, in part, drawn into the initial battle to gain crossings over the Clerf (Clerve) River. Originally, the Division was to move fast and either take Bastogne in a *coup de main* or, that failing, bypass Bastogne to the south and race for the Meuse River crossings near Dinant, leaving capture of Bastogne to the 26th *Volksgrenadier Division*. However, the Division was drawn into the attempt to capture Bastogne and, when extricated from that involvement and freed to move on to the Meuse, it had to leave its most powerful battle-group, *Kampfgruppe* 901, at Bastogne with the 26th *Volksgrenadier Division*.

Unless the reader is fully familiar with the Ardennes Offensive or, as it is frequently known in America, the Battle of the Bulge, it is highly recommended that he refer to a good history such as Charles B. MacDonald's excellent *A Time For Trumpets*, or Cole's official United States Army Historical Series volume, *The Ardennes, Battle of the Bulge*, which still remains indispensable, and highly readable. Peter Elstob's *Hitler's Last Offensive*, though first published in 1971, is still highly useful, being extremely clear and comprehensible in presenting and relating the military events. *Panzer Lehr Division* 130 fought as part of the XLVII *Panzer Korps*, the southern of the two *Korps* in von Manteuffel's 5th *Panzer Armee*.

As noted above, despite strict orders that, unknown to the Division, *Panzer Lehr Division* 130 was not to be committed in any action because it was being reconstituted for the *Führer's* top-secret Ardennes Offensive, *Die Wacht am Rhein*, later renamed *Herbstnebel*, the American thrust into the Saar required employment of the Division there. While the Division was still involved in hard fighting in the Saar as a result of that commitment, a completely unexpected order arrived on 4 December 1944 for the Division to prepare immediately to load up and head north. Although the American advance on 6 December threatened the railway and the Division's entrainment, the last trains carrying *Panzer Lehr Division* 130 rolled out on 9 December, just a week before the start of the great Ardennes Offensive, in which *Panzer Lehr Division* 130 was to play an important role.

Commitment in the Saar had interrupted the Division's reconstitution for the impending Ardennes offensive. Hard fighting had taken its toll in casualties to both manpower and equipment. *Generalleutnant* Bayerlein's 3 December report (Ritgen, *Die Geschichte der Panzer Lehr Division*, p.215.) on its condition noted that:

> *1. State of training:*
>
> Inadequate replacement of non-commissioned officers has fallen far short of restoring those lost on the Invasion Front, most seriously impacting the combat effectiveness of the infantry. Constant relocations and commitment has interfered with training of the non-commissioned officers. The new replacements are not up to the demands of difficult offensive and defensive combat. Fuel shortage has resulted in poorly trained drivers for armour and motor-vehicles which, in turn, has

led to substantial losses of vehicles. 90% of the two *Panzer* IV companies that have only recently been converted to *Panther* tanks are not ready for action.

*2. Particular problems:*

The Division went back into action before completion of its reconstitution and reorganization. Accordingly, only half of its combat effectiveness was available during the decisive period.

*Heeres-Flak-Abteilung* 311 had only four 8.8 cm anti-aircraft guns and two 2cm single-barrel guns serviceable.

*Panzer-Artillerie-Regiment* 130 went into action with only five light and six heavy guns. That amounted to one mixed *Abteilung* instead of the three allotted.

Out of the 500 tons [lorry-transport capacity] allotted to the Division's supply commander [*Kodina*] only 120 tons are serviceable, since 25% of the vehicles assigned in Action-X are not usable and, in some cases with serious mechanical problems, are in the repair shops. It is impossible to transport the initial ammunition allotment.

Shipments of replacement parts for armoured vehicles and communications equipment still have not arrived. 95% of the *Panzer* V [*Panther*] are immobilized by lack of replacement parts.

Troop morale: is good.

Level of mobility: 100%

Combat capability: The Division is conditionally ready for attack.

After the battering it took in the Saar, the Division assembled from 10 – 12 December near Cochem on the Mosel River, about 50 kilometres southwest of Koblenz, where it took on about 600 replacement *Panzergrenadiere*, along with guns, armour and other materiel.

According to the 12 December status report (Perrigault, *op.cit.*, p. 348) out of its T/O strengthy of 34 *Panzer* V, the Division had 29, of which 23 were ready for action. Out of 34 *Panzer* IV, the Division had 34, 30 ready for action. The T/O called for 21 *Sturmgeschütze*. 15 were on hand, 14 in service. Of the 13 heavy anti-tank guns called for, only three were present, all serviceable. 12 light howitzers were allotted, but only five of the seven on hand were ready for employment. The T/O called for 16 heavy howitzers. Nine of the 12 on hand were ready for use.

According to Ritgen (p. 218) the *Sturmgeschütze* listed above were actually *Panzerjäger* 40 (self-propelled anti-tank guns) of the Division's *Panzerjäger-Lehr-Abteilung* 130. Perrigault (*op.cit.* p.348) says that *Panzerjäger-Abteilung* 130 amounted to two companies equipped with *Jagdpanther* with 8.8 cm *Pak* 43/3 [*Jagdpanzer* V *'Jagdpanther'* with *8.8 cm Pak* 43/3 L/71 *(Sd. Kfz.* 173s)], and an unarmoured company of towed anti-tank guns. Since the Division was still without its I. *Abteilung* of *Panzer-Lehr-Regiment* 130, *schwere Panzerjäger Abteilung* 559 was attached effective 11 December but did not arrive until after Christmas, and was withdrawn 21 January 1945. Ritgen (p.218) states that *schwere Panzerjäger Abteilung* 559 had 'a few *Jagdpanther*'. *Sturmgeschütz Brigade* 243 was also supposed to join the Division from 11 to 30 December.

The Division remained weak in artillery. *Panzer-Artillerie-Regiment* 130 was reduced to two *Abteilungen*, the II. *Abteilung,* mixed, with three batteries and the III. *Abteilung* with two heavy batteries. Due to lack of prime movers, the III. *Abteilung* was not able to join *Kampfgruppe von Hauser* until shortly after Christmas.

*General der Panzertruppen* Hasso von Manteuffel, commander of 5 *Panzer Armee* during the Ardennes offensive. *Panzer Lehr Division* 130 fought as part of the XLVII *Panzer Korps*, the southern of the two *Korps* in von Manteuffel's 5th *Panzer Armee*. Photo of Manteuffel taken earlier in 1944, during fighting in the Baltic states. (Bundesarchiv 101I-732-0132-43A)

Perrigault (p. 348) indicates that the Division was weak in *SPW* (lightly armoured half-tracks for the infantry) and entirely lacking in infantry guns for the cannon companies of the *Panzergrenadier* regiments.

Bayerlein discusses the levels to which this reconstitution restored the Division to its T/O strength in his answers to questions 6, 7 and 8 in MS # A–941.

*Generalfeldmarschall* Model's *Heeresgruppe B* would direct three armies in the offensive. *Panzer Lehr Division* 130 was attached to XLVII *Panzer Korps* in *General* von Manteuffel's 5th *Panzer Armee*. *Oberstgruppenführer und Generaloberst der Waffen-SS* Dietrich's 6th *Panzer Armee*[1] was to launch the main thrust toward Antwerp from a front extending from Monshchau in the north part-way into the Losheim Gap. *General der Panzertruppen* von Manteuffel's adjoining 5th *Panzer Armee,* was to launch its attack on a front extending from just south of Heckhuscheid south to approximately half-way between Gemünd and Stolzembourg. It was to take St. Vith and Bastogne, cross the Meuse River upstream from its bend at Namur and wheel northwest, bypassing Brussels and covering Dietrich's southern flank. *General der Panzertruppen* von Brandenburger's 7th *Armee*, with no armoured divisions, was, in turn, to attack on both sides of Echternach and build a solid southern shoulder for the German offensive.

*Panzer Lehr Division* 130, held in 5th *Panzer Armee* reserve by *General der Panzertruppen* von Manteuffel, would be attached to *General der Panzertruppen Freiherr* von Lüttwitz's XLVII *Panzer Korps*, the southernmost corps of the 5th *Panzer Armee*. XLVII *Panzer Korps* was to cross the Our River in the vicinity of Dasburg and Gemünd, its sector bounded by the villages of Dahnen in the north and Stolzembourg in the south, gain the commanding ridge that the Americans called 'Skyline Drive', advance west via Clerf (Clervaux), capture Bastogne and, deeply echelonned to the left and rear, dash for the Meuse upstream from (south of) Namur. XLVII *Korps* was to seize the Meuse crossings near Namur and drive on through Brussels to Antwerp. For such a drive to succeed it would be necessary to avoid frontal attacks on strongly held American positions and to leave protection of 5th *Panzer Armee's* southern flank to the echelonned advance of the *Korps* own forces and to the infantry divisions of *General der Panzertruppen* von Brandenburger's 7th *Armee* to the south. Facing XLVII *Panzer Korps* was the110th Infantry Regiment of the 28th Infantry Division of the American VIII Army Corps.

XLVII *Panzer Korps* consisted of the 2nd *Panzer-Division*, commanded by *Oberst* von Lauchert and the 26th *Volksgrenadier Division* under *Generalmajor* Kokott. *Panzer Lehr Division* 130, under *Generalleutnant* Bayerlein, was in *Armee* reserve, to be committed as soon as the 26th *Volksgrenadier Division* had a bridge in place and had built a bridgehead.

*Panzer Lehr Division* 130 was ordered to standby to support the 26th *Volksgrenadier Division* in securing the crossings over the Our River at Gemünd and over the Clerf River at Drauffeld., *Panzer Lehr Division* 130 was then to

1 Though frequently referred to as 6th *SS-Panzer Armee* before its official designation as such, Dietrich's 6th *Panzer Armee* was not officially designated 6th *SS-Panzer Armee* until it became officially a part of the *Waffen-SS* in April 1945 with its move to Hungary.

advance from the bridgeheads to Bastogne and, later, to the Meuse River near Dinant. Bastogne was to be taken in a *coup de main*. If strong enemy resistance developed, Bastogne was to be bypassed to the south and then taken by the 26th *Volksgrenadier Division*.

Helmut Ritgen (p. 220) describes the terrain in which *Panzer Lehr Division* 130 was to fight:

> The terrain in which the *Panzer Lehr Division* was to attack and, later, defend, was characterized by the frequent alternation between deeply incised, winding mountain valleys and broad plateaus with extensive forests. The approach march along the sinuous, steep and narrow mountain roads of the Eifel (the rugged extension of the Ardennes across the Our River in Germany) had placed heavy demands on drivers and vehicles, even in dry weather. The American front line ran along the ridge-road, N 7, just behind the steep-walled valley of the Our River, which was swollen by high water. Only a few, barely-improved, narrow byways, impassable to armour, snaked their way up the slope. The ridge-road offered good fields of observation and fire to its possessor. Beyond [the ridge] the valleys of the Clerf and Wiltz [rivers] were shallower, easier to traverse. Thence westward forested hilly terrain rose to the divide between the Moselle and Meuse [rivers]. [The terrain was] then transformed into an extensive depression, favorable for armour, which extended to the Meuse [river]. This depression was interrupted by the still-shallow valleys of the Ourthe, l'Homme and Lesse [rivers], significant obstacles in their lower courses. The grain of the terrain and, thus, the good highways, ran from northeast to southwest, lacking good east-west roads. The other roads and byways were narrow and unsuitable for heavy traffic. Possession of the few major highway-nodal-points – Bastogne in the sector of the *Panzer Lehr Division* – was vital for the movement and supply of armoured formations.

The American 28th Infantry Division, facing the German 7th *Armee's* LXXXV *Korps* and von Manteuffel's 5th *Panzer Armee's* XLVII *Panzer Korps* and LVIII *Panzer Korps* had been moved to the relatively inactive Ardennes front after suffering heavy losses in the bloody Hürtgen Forest fighting. Opposing von Lüttwitz's XLVII *Panzer Korps,* that division's 110th Infantry Regiment was thinly stretched, defending a fifteen mile front. During the daytime, squad-sized outposts watched near the river, while, at night, patrols roved through the mile or so of open country cut by draws between the ridge-road and the river. Rifle-companies garrisoned villages astride or near the ridge-line on the five roads leading up from the river. The village of Marnach controlled the road through Clerf (Clervaux) to Bastogne, and Hosingen, the road through Drauffelt to Bastogne via Eschweiler, Ober- and Nieder-Wampach, Benonchamps, Mageret and Neffe. Clerf and Drauffelt were vital crossing points over the Clerf (Clerve) River. Due to the extent of the regiment's sector, its supporting artillery had to be positioned unusually close to the front in order to be able to cover all of the regiment's positions.

The veteran 26th *Volksgrenadier Division*, under *Majorgeneral* Heinz Kokott, was responsible for establishing crossings over the Our and opening the way for the 2nd *Panzer Division,* under *Oberst* Meinrad von Lauchert and then *Panzer Lehr Division* 130. The American positions in the villages of Marnach and Hosingen were to come under direct attack, to open the two roads leading west to Bastogne, while the remaining German troops infiltrated through the gaps between the other American positions.

*Major* Gerd Born-Fallois, commander of *Panzer-Aufklärungs-Lehr-Abteilung* 130 and, during the Ardennes Offensive, *Kampfgruppe Fallois*, often referred to as 'The Advance Detachment'. (Bundesarchiv 146-2007-0146)

*Generalleutnant* Bayerlein organized his division for the attack with:[2]

Advance Detachment, *Kampfgruppe von Fallois*:
Under the commander of *Panzer-Aufklärungs-Lehr-Abteilung* 130, [*Major* von Born-Fallois]:
*Panzer-Aufklärungs-Lehr-Abteilung* 130
8./*Panzer-Lehr-Regiment* 130 (15 *Panzer* IV)
3./*Panzerjäger-Lehr-Regiment* 130, 4./*Panzer-Artillerie-Regiment* 130 (4 light howitzers), one *Panzer Pionier* company.

*Kampfgruppe* 901: under the commander of *Panzergrenadier-Regiment* 901, [*Oberst Freiherr* von Hauser]
*Panzergrenadier-Lehr-Regiment* 901, 6./*Panzer-Lehr-Regiment* 130 (*Panzer* IV), II./*Panzer-Artillerie-Regiment* 130 (–), *Sturmgeschütz Brugade* 243.

*Kampfgruppe* 902: under the commander of *Panzergrenadier-Lehr-Regiment* 902, [*Oberstleutnant Ritter* von Poschinger]
*Panzergrenadier-Lehr-Regiment* 902, II./*Panzer-Lehr-Regiment* 130 (–) (2 *Panther* companies [under *Major* Ritgen]), I./*Panzer-Artillerie-Regiment* 130

Division Reserve: *Panzerjäger-Lehr-Abteilung* 130 (–), *Divisions Begleitkompanie* (escort company)

The Advance Detachment was initially to support the 26th *Volksgrenadier Division*. After bridgeheads were built across the Our and Clerf Rivers, it was then to advance as rapidly as possible toward Bastogne, capture it, if possible, in a *Coup de main* and then continue on toward Dinant.

*Kampfgruppen* 901 and 902 were to follow the Advance Detachment over the Gemünd bridge and standby to attack Bastogne.

Panzer Artillerie Regiment 130 was, initially, to go into position east of the Our [river] so as to be able to support the attack of the 26th *Volksgrenadier Division* with fire on identified enemy strongpoints, then, when ordered, to follow the *Panzer Lehr Division.*

*Panzer-Pionier-Bataillon* 130 had to build two 60 ton military bridges (*B-Gerät*) over the Irsenbach, one kilometre northeast of Gemünd and over the Our. Later it was to follow the Division as ordered.

On 16 December, 1944, *Panzer Lehr Division* 130 stood by in the Waxweiler–Mauel–Rollersdorf–Krautscheid area awaiting the building of the bridgeheads. As originally planned, the Division was not to become involved in fighting before its departure from the bridgeheads.

The offensive opened, in the XLVII *Panzer Korps* sector at 0530 hrs of a morning that started with chilly mist and fog. Although greatly outnumbered, the American troops fought stubbornly, denying the 2nd *Panzer Division* the vital road through Marnach and the 26th *Volksgrenadier Division* the critical route through Hosingen. Many of the infiltrating German elements were tied down in bitter combat around isolated strongpoints that proved impossible to bypass. Except for a few *Flak* wagons that joined the attack on Wahlhausen after dark,

2 Ritgen, p. 221

heavy weapons to support the attacking German troops did not get into action in the XLVII *Panzer Korps* sector on 16 December.

Though unhampered by American interference, the strong current of the swollen river and difficult access for heavy equipment down the steep and winding roads descending the valley walls set the German pioneers behind schedule in constructing their bridges. The first tanks of the 2nd *Panzer Division* rolled across the Dasburg bridge by 1600 hours. The bridge at Gemünd did not open until late evening. Even after the bridge at Gemünd was completed, felled trees and two giant explosion-craters greatly on the western side of the river delayed progress to Walhausen on the road to Hosingen.

Continuing American control of Hosingen denied the Advance Detachment the road to Drauffeld. The main body of *Panzer Lehr Division* 130 remained stuck in the bridgehead on 16 December.

On 17 December the Division moved forward to the Our River under rain clouds that prevented American air attacks. Due to continuing difficulties at the Gemünd bridgehead, *Panzer Lehr's Kampfgruppe* 902 was diverted to the 2nd *Panzer Division's* Dasburg bridgehead, where it crossed the Our River and, at 1830 hours, reported that it was refuelling at Marnach.

The bitter battle for 'Skyline Drive', the ridge-road positions controlling the roads leading west to Bastogne, continued, upsetting the German schedule and putting *Panzer Lehr Division* 130 a full day behind in its movements. The American garrison in Holsingen, which did not fall until the morning of 18 December, blocked the Advance Detachment's progress toward the Clerf crossing at Drauffeld.

In the adjoining 7th *Armee* sector, *Fallschirmjäger-Regiment* 54 of the 5th *Fallschirmjäger-Division* were reported to have captured Kautenbach, opening another crossing over the Clerf River. Thereupon XLVII *Panzer Korps* ordered the Advance Detachment of *Panzer Lehr Division* 130 to advance via Holzthum and Consthum to the Kautenbach crossing rather than via Drauffeld. The Advance Detachment ran into stiff American resistance at Holzthum. *Fusilier-Regiment* 39 of the 26th *Voksgrenadier-Regiment* fought into the evening when, at last, the American defenders surrendered after exhausting their ammunition. According to von Manteuffel, the 5th *Flaschirmjäger Division* was still fighting for the Kautenbach crossing over the Clerf River on 18 December. (*ibid.* p. 106). Cole reports in the U. S Army official history that the 14th *Fallschirmjäger-Regiment* captured the Kautenbach Crossing on 17 December. (Cole, *op.cit.* p. 222.)

Disturbed by the continued American possession of Hosingen and Holzthum, *General der Panzertruppen* von Lüttwitz, contrary to the original plan whereby no elements of *Panzer Lehr Division* 130 were to be committed prior to its movement out of the bridgeheads toward Bastogne, committed *Generalleutnant* Bayerlein's Advance Detachment to assist the 26th *Volksgrenadier Division* in the fighting at Holzthum.

Bayerlein states (MSA# A–942) that 'on 17 December … the U.S. Garrison still held out in Hosingen. In the meantime strong elements of the 26th *Volksgrenadier-Division* infiltrated through the woods southwest of Hosingen toward Drauffeld. At this point XLVII *Panzer Korps* ordered the withdrawal of *Panzeraufklärungs-Lehr-Abteilung* 130 [from the fighting] near Holzthum in order to be able to commit it immediately to the west in accord with the original intention after the capture of Drauffeld.' Von Manteuffel explains that the Division was ordered by XLVII *Panzer-Korps* to exchange *Panzergrenadier-Lehr-Regiment* 901 for *Panzeraufklärungs-Lehr-Abteilung* 130 in its attachment to the 26th *Volksgrenadier Division Kampfgruppe Kaufmann* so that the corps could have the reconnaissance battalion at its disposal to commit, as orignaly planned, by way of Eschweiler and Derenbach against Bastogne. (Hasso von Manteuffel in *Hitler's Ardennes Offensive*, edited by Danny S. Parker, p. 104.) Since the fighting for the crossing over the Clerf River east of Alscheid and the *Panzergrenadier-Lehr-Regiment* 901's attachment to *Kampfgruppe Kaufmann* was not over until midnight of 17/18 December, *Kampfgruppe* 901 was separated from the main body of *Panzer-Lehr-Division* 901 and would not be available to the Division for some time.

Bayerlein discusses at length the fragmentation of the Division due to premature commitment of *Panzeraufklärungs-Lehr-Abteilung* 130 in his answers to question 1 in MS # A–942.

After the fall of Holzthum, in the evening of 17 December, *Kampdfgruppe* 902 resumed its march to the Kautenbach crossing. However, the *Kampfgruppe* again ran up against strong American resistance in the next village, Consthum. As Bayerlein continued, in the above cited interview, 'Accordingly, by order of the [47th *Panzer*] *Korps, Panzergrenadier-Lehr-Regiment* 901 was employed for the capture of Consthum.' Thus, the Division's strongest *Kampfgruppe* was tied down in hard fighting at Consthum, which did not fall until the middle of the following day.

Hosingen finally fell in the morning of 18 December. Since, by the end of 17 December, the 26th *Volksgrenadier Division* had already captured the bridge over the Clerf River at Drauffeld, another between Drauffeld and Wilwerwiltz and a third at Wilwerwiltz, the way was, at last, open for the *Volksgrenadiers* and *Panzer Lehr Division* 130 to begin their belated part in the dash for Bastogne.

However, the Germans had also learned, on 17 December, from an intercepted radio message, that the Allied command had alerted two American airborne divisions for fast movement to the battle area. Lüttwitz reasoned, from his map, that the two divisions, the 82nd and 101st Airborne, would be sent to Bastogne (S.L.A. Marshall, *Bastogne, The First Eight Days*, p. 178.) Thus, the delay won by the stubborn American defence of the positions on the ridge-road, N 7, had gained critical time for the Allies. Bastogne was now to be the prize in a desperate race. The 2nd *Panzer Division* was to bypass it to the north while *Panzer Lehr Division* 130 and the 26th *Volksgrenadier Division* advanced directly on Bastogne. At risk for the Germans was, not only Bastogne and its critical road junctions, but the entire hope for reaching the Meuse River.

However, as noted above, the Division was already fragmented, its Advance Detachment and *Kampfgruppe* 901 involved in action that prevented commitment of the Division as a unified force in the advance on Bastogne. *Kampfgruppe* 901 was advancing from the Gemünd bridge via Walhausen, Holzthum and Consthum to the Clerf crossing at Kautenbach. *Kampfgruppe* 902 had been diverted northward into the 2nd *Panzer Division* sector to cross the Our River at Dasburg, then through Munshausen to the Clerf crossing at Drauffeld. After being pulled out of the fighting at Consthum, the Advance Detachment was turned north, advancing via Bockholtz to rejoin the advance route through Drauffeld. *Panzer-Aufklärungs-Lehr-Abteilung* 130 crossed the bridgehead line west of Drauffeld at about 0900 hours on 18 December, advancing westward toward Eschweiler, followed by *Kampfgruppe* 902. American artillery and mortar fire delayed the climb out of the Clerf River valley.

At this point *Kampfgruppe* 901 was still engaged in hard fighting at Consthum, which was not overcome until afternoon. Lack of cooperation between the 5th *Fallschirmjäger Division*, attacking from the south, and *Kampfgruppe* 901 resulted in failure to take Wiltz.

At the fork of the road about two kilometres east of Eschweiler the Advance Detachment turned south toward Erpeldange while *Kampfgruppe* 902 continued on the serpentine road to Eschweiler, which was in German hands by 1400 hours. As the American garrison attempted to break out of Eschweiler to the south they ran afoul of the armour of *Panzer Lehr's* Advance Detachment near Erpeldange. *Panzeraufklärungs-Lehr-Abteilung* 130 captured eight half-tracks and four tank-destroyers. Both the Advance Detachment and *Kampfgruppe* 902 then converged on Derenbach, *Kampfgruppe* 902 arriving first because the Advance Detachment was delayed by the enemy at Erpeldange.

The advance guard of *Kampfgruppe* 902, II./*Panzer-Lehr-Regiment* 130, continued westward from Derenbach in the darkness. Tank gunfire resounded and the night sky lit up with heavy firing and the flare of burning vehicles reflected on the low clouds to the north. *Panzer Lehr's* concerned troops could not know that they were distant witnesses of the battle between the 2nd *Panzer Division's Panzer-Regiment* 3 and Task Force Harper, at the Fe'itsch road junction on Highway N 12 near Allerborn, just nine miles from Bastogne. This was one of two blocking positions set up by CCR (Combat Command, Reserve) of the American 9th Armored Division on the main paved road system approaching Bastogne from St. Vith. That well-paved highway, N 12, was also joined, about half-way between Trois Vierges and Allerborn, by the paved highway that led from the Dasburg crossing over the Our River through Marnach and Clerf, which was also an important crossing over the Clerf River.

At about 1900 hours on 18 December the leading elements of *Kampfgruppe* 902 reached Nieder-Wampach without enemy contact. There they refuelled, but had only enough to half-fill the tanks.

A message from the *Korps* stated, erroneously, that Bastogne was a major American fuel depot with millions of gallons of gasoline, and urged *Panzer Lehr* to take it as soon as possible.

Orders arriving for 19 December directed *Panzer Lehr Division* 130 to advance on Bastogne from the east across the Magéret–Wardin line and, if possible, that same day to push on through to the west. The 26th *Volksgrenadier Division* on the Division's right was to advance through the Bois Jaques with the objective of entering Bastogne from the north.

Von Lüttwitz expressed concern about mud and recommended that *Panzer Lehr* advance on Bastogne via the more distant but solid road through Bras. Belgian civilians assured *Generalleutnant* Bayerlein that the shorter and more direct side road through Benonchamps to Magéret was feasible for armour and would meet his needs. 'It looks bad but will get better and better.' (S. L. A. Marshall, *op.cit.* p. 182).

In the event, the road turned out to be bad and it got worse and worse. Nevertheless, there was no enemy resistance and Bayerlein's force crossed the Luxembourg – Belgium border at about midnight and reached Benonchamps by 0100 hours, the main road at Magéret at 0200 hours on 19 December, 1944. An American medical clearing station was captured in Magéret and secured for treatment of casualties from both sides.

Although *Kampfgruppe* 902 was commanded by *Oberst* von Poschinger, *Generalleutnant* Bayerlein rode in one of the lead tanks and personally directed the *Kampfgruppe*.

In Magéret a Belgian civilian warned Bayerlein that an American armoured force with fifty tanks and forty other armoured vehicles, commanded by an American major general had passed through Magéret only two hours earlier. (See the extensive note regarding this incident attached to Bayerlein's answer to question 17 in MS #A–941.) The greatly exaggerated force referred to was, in fact, Captain Willis B. Ryerson's detachment from Combat Command B of the American 10th Armored Division. At this point Bayerlein seems to have taken counsel of his fears and become increasingly concerned about the American armour behind him on the Longvilly Road between his force and the main body of the German forces.

Bayerlein set up a small roadblock in Magéret consisting of three tanks, some infantry and mines to cover his rear. At 0400 hours the German force in Magéret began to draw moderate fire from the nearby terrain. Balancing the need for haste and that for strength, Bayerlein decided to hold up in Magéret until 0530 hours to allow *Kampfgruppe* 902 to close up. At about 0530 hours Bayerlein started moving his armour out along the road toward Neffe, drawing considerable fire from the high ground on the right.

Shortly before 0600 hours, in dense fog, the leading elements, a reconnaissance probe, of Bayerlein's Advance Detachment consisting of a couple of tanks and two platoons of infantry entered Neffe and ran into a roadblock that Team Cherry had set up with the 3rd Tank Battalion's Reconnaissance Platoon. The Germans claimed two American tanks knocked out near the chapel and several wheeled vehicles captured.

Near the railway station the lead tank, and then a second tank, of the 5. *Kompanie / Panzer-Lehr-Regiment* 130 blew up on mines. While the remaining mines were being cleared, the *Panzergrenadiere* searched the houses in the village and an infantry company proceeded south of the railroad tracks toward the Neffe Chateau. At 0800 hours the infantry reported that Neffe and the chateau were free of Americans, an error which would exact a heavy price.

The advance on the road resumed at 0550 hours and reached Neffe Station at 0700 hours.

S.L.A. Marshall, famous for his development of post-battle interviews as a means of reconstructing complex military events, personally interviewed the principal German officers involved in the advance on Bastogne, *Generalleutnant* Bayerlein, who commanded the *Panzer Lehr Division, General der Panzertruppen* von Lüttwitz of the XLVII *Panzer Korps* and *Majorgeneral* Kokott, commander of the 26th *Volksgrenadier Division*. In the final chapter of his study, *Bastogne, The First Eight Days* he analyzes the German experience:

> At 0700 the head of the armor reached the Neffe station and there it paused for almost an hour – an interlude that cost Bayerlein his one chance to strike Bastogne before Colonel Ewell [commander of the American 101st Airborne Division's 501st Parachute Infantry Regiment which was moving into position as *Kampfgruppe* 902 approached] could get started. All of the dash had gone out of the man by this time. There was no good tactical reason for the pause. But his own doubt about the situation stayed him.

As Bayerlein's *Kampfgruppe* resumed its advance it was hit by American fire. A leading German tank fired its machine gun. Nobody knew which fired first. Colonel Ewell interpreted the encounter as being with a German roadblock. Both sides recoiled. This small encounter had great consequences. The German infantry stopped moving and the tanks would not advance without infantry protection. For an hour the German drive ceased, and that was sufficient time for the American 101st Airborne's supporting artillery to go into action against the German Neffe position.

There, too, Bayerlein's apparent depressed condition played a part. In the fog, with no observation, the airborne's glider-transportable short 105 mm gun sounded like a tank main-gun. Bayerlein decided he was up against armour.

The original meeting engagement with Colonel Ewell's force had been with the 1st Battalion of his 501st Parachute Infantry Regiment. When his men hit the dirt in the face of the German fire, Colonel Ewell deployed his 1st Battalion on the gently rising ground to his left (north). He then sent his 2nd Battalion into Bizory, on the crest of the gentle hill to his left. Hopes of flanking the German position in Neffe by a drive from Bizory into Magéret proved vain when the 2nd Battalion ran into a German position of the 26th *Volksgrenadier Division* on the crest of the high ground, Hill 510, between Magéret and Neffe.

Colonel Cherry, whose American 10th Armored Division Combat Command B's team had set up the roadblock where the leading German tank had blown up on a mine, established his headquarters in the chateau south of Neffe. The platoon manning Team Cherry's roadblock had been hit hard and forced back at 0600 hours by fire from German tanks and infantry coming from the east, leaving the roadblock unmanned, as Bayerlein's force found it. Colonel Cherry and his headquarters personnel valiantly defended the stoutly built chateau throughout the day of 19 December. Despite a blazing roof and other fires set by German shells, he hung on until darkness fell, when he led his men out of Neffe to the American lines in the adjoining village of Mont. Cherry reported that he had been burned out, not driven out, and that he was 'moving', not withdrawing.

Here again, courageous action by a small American force had great effects. Bayerlein felt himself in danger of being enveloped. As he felt out the situation on his right (north), he ran into Ewell's 2nd Battalion. Apparently he was greatly impressed by the sound of Colonel Cherry's defence of the chateau on his left. When he returned to Magéret he found American armour attacking the little roadblock he had left there. He was unaware that the armour in question consisted of elements of the American 9th Armored Division's Combat Command Reserve (CCR) force withdrawing from its Longvilly roadblock.

After destruction of the two 9th Armored Division CCR roadblocks at the Fe'itsch junction and near Allerborm, what was left of its Taskforce Harper and remnants of Task Force Rose headed west toward Longvilly where CCR's headquarters had been set up. After the arrival of the 10th Armored Division Combat Command B's (CCB) Team Cherry at Longvilly, a little before midnight, Colonel Gilbreth, commanding the 9th Armored Division CCR forces, ordered them to start withdrawing via Magéret. When it became apparent that the movement was becoming disorderly, Colonel Gilbreth ordered it held up until morning light.

When Colonel Cherry learned of *Panzer Lehr's* roadblock between his headquarters and the team's roadblock, he ordered Captain Ryerson, in command of the roadblock, to send a patrol back to Magéret and open the road. However, the patrol, consisting of two squads in a half-track, found the German force, which they estimated at three tanks and about a company of infantry, far beyond their capabilities.

As the 9th Armored Division's CCR started its withdrawal from Longvilly, the *Panzer Lehr* roadblock knocked out the lead vehicles, blocking its escape route. The Longvilly – Magéret road quickly became packed with a confused mass of American vehicles, unable to move. When it became apparent that *Panzer Lehr* was present in force behind the American roadblock, Team Cherry directed the main body of its force to also withdraw toward Bastogne behind a covering force under Lieutenant Hyduke.

By now the American armour on the Longvilly road had come to the attention of *General* von Lüttwitz, commander of the German XLVII *Panzer Korps*, *Generalleutnant* Bayerlein and his *Panzer Lehr Division* force and *Oberst* von Lauchert and the 2nd *Panzer Division*. Each decided separately that the American force posed a threat, and each, on his own, took action to eliminate the threat.

First to take effect were five or six 8.8 cm guns that *Oberst* von Lauchert had set up to counter American fire that hit his 2nd *Panzer Division* as it turned north at the intersection just east of the American roadblock. With no knowledge of the 2nd *Panzer Division* action, *Generalleutnant* Bayerlein ordered his *Panzer Lehr Division* force to attack eastward from Benonchamps through the woods toward Longvilly with two companies of infantry and 20 tank-destroyers. Unaware of both *Oberst* Lauchert's and *Generalleutnant* Bayerlein's action, *General* Lüttwitz, commander of the XLVII *Panzer Korps* met the commander of the 26th *Volksgrenadier-Division's* 77th *Volksgrenadier Regiment*, which was moving between Ober- and Nieder-Wampach, and directed him to gather all artillery and heavy weapons in the general area and attack Longvilly from the southeast. The *Panzer Lehr* and 77th *Volksgrenadier Regiment* attacks happened to strike the American force simultaneously, with terrible effect. In addition to destroying much of the armour in the congested section of road, the action diverted some of *Panzer Lehr's* force and attention from pushing on toward Bastogne. During this time Bayerlein's force was also fighting in Neffe, attacking Colonel Cherry's valiant defenders of his chateau headquarters, and discovering organized opposition to its north, in and east of Bizory.

Bayerlein was slightly wounded by a shell-fragment during the fighting in Neffe.

Bayerlein's force had captured an American hospital in Magéret. According to Ritgen (*op.cit.* p. 226), the general went to the American hospital for treatment and returned shortly thereafter. According to S.L.A. Marshall (*op.cit.* p. 185), when

Bayerlein asked one of the nurses to look after his wounded, he apparently was distracted by the nurse, whom he noted was 'young, blond and beautiful.' Liddell Hart (*History of the Second World War*, footnote p. 651) quotes ' ... a spearhead commander [Bayerlein] confessed to me in later discussion that at this vital moment he dallied with a young American nurse, 'blonde and beautiful', who held him spellbound in a village his troops had overrun. Battles are not always decided in the way that the military textbooks teach!' Jacques Nobécourt repeats this assertion (Nobécourt, *Le Dernier Coup de Dés de Hitler*, p. 295 of Éditions Encontre edition). Helmut Ritgen emphatically denies this allegation, saying (Ritgen, *op.cit.* p. 312), 'Anyone who knew *General* Bayerlein knows how nonsensical the assertion is that a beautiful American nurse turned his head.' However, since both S.L.A. Marshall and Liddell Hart, two highly respected and trusted historians, personally interviewed Bayerlein, the incident seems likely. Charles B. Macdonald, who authored several volumes of the massive United States Army official history of the war in the European Theater of Operations, before writing, in retirement, his own history of the Ardennes Campaign, *A Time for Trumpets*, included this incident, saying, 'Through much of December 19, [Bayerlein] 'dallied' with the nurse, who 'held him spellbound.'' (MacDonald, *A Time for Trumpets*, p. 295).

The Advance Detachment (*Kampfgruppe von Fallois*) was committed against Wardin – Marvie to get at Bastogne from the south and to counter envelopment of Bayerlein's force from that direction. However, at 1300 hours, as its advance elements entered Wardin from the east, with armoured and artillery support, they became involved in a meeting engagement with I ('Item') Company of the American 501st Airborne Infantry Regiment. In bitter house-to-house fighting the American paratroopers were forced back out of Wardin by evening, but the German Advanced Detachment was too exhausted to continue to Marvie.

Colonel Ewell, commander of the American 501st Airborne Infantry Regiment, recognized that his forces had reached the limit of their advance and obtained permission to fall back and establish a defensive position on the high ground extending southwest from Bizory. That defensive position held, essentially, for the remainder of the fighting around Bastogne. Bayerlein's *Panzer Lehr Division* would make no further progress toward capturing Bastogne, but would, on 22 December, leave *Kampfgruppe* 901 to assist the 26th *Volksgrenadier Division* in its attempt to take Bastogne, while the main body of *Panzer Lehr Division* 130 resumed the advance toward the Meuse crossings near Dinant.

In the afternoon of 19 December *General der Panzertruppen* Lüttwitz appeared at the *Panzer Lehr Division* command post in Nieder-Wampach. *Generalleutnant* Bayerlein urged the immediate capture of Bastogne, employing all forces of the XLVII *Panzer Korps*. He stressed three reasons: The advance to the Meuse and beyond required control of Bastogne as a critical transportation hub for its logistical support; furthermore, unless eliminated, the presence of strong allied forces in Bastogne would be like a festering ulcer in the German rear. Also, unless eliminated, strong German forces required for the advance to the Meuse and beyond would remain behind, tied up reducing Bastogne.

As of that time, all of the forces of the XLVII *Panzer Korps* were in favourable locations to attack Bastogne. The 2nd *Panzer Division* was advancing westward just north of Bastogne, but still available if it turned south. The 26th

*Volksgrenadier Division* was north and east of Bastogne, attacking Foy and Bizory, with *Panzer Lehr Division* 130 adjoining to its south. In the 7th *Armee* sector, the 5th *Fallschirmjäger Division* had just reported the capture of Wiltz.

However, despite the apparent agreement of *General* Lüttwitz and similar views expressed by the commanders of the other divisions, von Lüttwitz, commanding XLVII *Korps*, ended up having to bow to the view taken by *General* von Manteuffel, commanding the 5th *Panzer Armee*, that such a diversion of all the *Korps*' forces would endanger the offensive thrust to the Meuse.

Accordingly, XLVII *Panzer Korps* ordered for 20 December:

– The 2nd *Panzer Division* is to take Noville [directly north of Bastogne] and immediately advance west.

– The 26th *Volksgrenadier Division* is to continue its attack from the positions attained on 19 December and, after reaching the Noville – Bastogne road, force its way into Bastogne from the north.

– The *Panzer Lehr Division* is to capture Bastogne by attacking it from the east from the positions attained on 19 December. However, if enemy resistance proves too strong, then [the Division] is … while pinning [the enemy] … to proceed with its main body to the south in order to [resume the] advance to the west.

During the night of 19/20 December *Kampfgruppe* 902 attempted another attack on Bastogne near Neffe and Mont but heavy American artillery fire scuttled the effort. A reinforced *Panzergrendier* company briefly penetrated Marvie at daybreak but was then thrown out. Additional attacks on Marvie in conjunction with attacks by the 26th *Volksgrenadier Division* on 20 December were no more successful.

On 20 December *Grenadier-Regimenter* 77 and 78 of the 26th *Volksgrenadier Division* were temporarily attached to *Panzer Lehr Division* 130. The 26th *Volksgrenadier Division* was to attack Bastogne with its reinforced *Füsilier Regiment* 39, attacking via Lutrebois and Remoifosse, then north from the Assenois sector into Bastogne. *Panzer Lehr Division* 130 was to attack Bastonge from the east. *Panzer Lehr* launched its attack with the attached *Grenadier Regimenter* 77 and 78 at 1100 east of the Foy – Bizory Road while the Division's own forces attacked from Neffe toward Mont and from Bras via Wardin to Marvie. Strong American resistance held *Grenadier Regimenter* 77 and 78 close to the Foy – Bizory road. The Division's attack from Neffe to Mont got nowhere. Wardin fell but the Americans held Marvie fast.

On 21 December XLVII *Panzer Korps* ordered *Panzer Lehr Division* 130 to leave *Kampfgruppe* 901 (*von Hauser*) In its positions southeast of Bastogne, turn over the Neffe sector to the 26th *Volksgrenadier Division* and resume the westward advance past the south side of Bastogne.

Bayerlein, in the interview recorded in MS # A–941 repeatedly emphasized that, 'One of the greatest mistakes was that, after the failure of the *coup de main*, Bastogne was not captured by concentration of all [available] forces. If that had been done then the attack would have succeeded.' (MS # A–941, question 11 h. See also discussion for 22 December in MS # A–942.).

# *KAMPFGRUPPE* 901 AT BASTOGNE

*Kampfgruppe* 901, consisting of *Panzergrenadier-Lehr-Regiment* 901, 6./ *Panzer-Lehr-Regiment* 130, III./ *Panzer-Artillerie-Regiment* 130 and probably *Sturmgeschützbrigade* 243 was attached to the 26 th *Volksgrenadier-Division* for the battle of Bastogne effective 22 December 1944 to 6 January 1945. Its initial sector extended from a bridge across a stream southeast of Mont via Marvie and Remoifosse to a rural road from Salvacourt to Bastogne.

On 22 December *Kampfgruppe* 901 supported the 26th *Volksgrenadier's* 39th *Infanterie Regiment* in its attack on Villeraux (Villeroux?) with an armoured group that advanced from the area south of Remoifosse to the Hazy woods. Assenois was cleared of American forces in the evening and Senonchamps captured, narrowing the ring around Bastogne. However, American forces of Patton's 3rd Army were already exerting pressure from the south.

A reconnaissance patrol from the American 4th Armored Division of the American III Corps drove through the 5th *Fallschirmjäger Divisionis* screen of the westward advancing *Panzer Lehr* forces, setting several German vehicles on fire at an intersection three kilometres northwest of Remichampagne.

On 23 December, the 26th *Volksgrenadier Division* continued to attack. The attached *Kampfgruppe* 902 prepared for an evening assault on Marvie. During the day, American forces took Chaumont, to the south, endangering the 26th *Volksgrenadier Division* command post in Hompré. *Generalmajor* Kokott commandeered 'four heavy tanks', presumably *Panthers* of the II./ *Panzer-Lehr-Regiment* 130 *en route* from the workshop to the front, and put together a *Kampfgruppe* which succeeded in repulsing the American forces.

Somewhat delayed, *Kampfgruppe* 901's attack northward on the Arlon–Bastogne highway took a large part of Marvie in extremely heavy fighting. The fighting continued throughout the night. The next day, both sides claimed that they were holding Marvie. In fact, the Americans still held houses in the northern fringe, the Germans the southern portion.

On 24 December *Kampfgruppe* 901 held the positions it had achieved, while securing the Bastogne–Arlon highway to the south with tanks, mines and other obstacles. 5th *Panzerarmee* informed the *Generalmajor* Kokott that, in addition to the 26th *Volksgrenadier Division*, he would have the use of the 15th *Panzergrenadier-Division* (which, in the event, turned out to be reduced to the use of merely one *Kampfgruppe* of about one-and-one half battalions of infantry and 20 tanks, the remainder being needed to help the 2nd *Panzer Division* at the 'thin end' of the wedge driving toward Dinant and the Meuse) to mount a major attack on Bastogne on 25 December.

On 25 December the action at Bastogne shifted to the northwest sector, with a major German attack between the Marche road and Champs. The attack got off to a promising start, as German tanks with infantry broke through the American lines in two locations, but the American lines closed tightly behind them, sealing off the penetration, the infantry separated from the tanks or swept from the tanks they were riding on by intense machine gun and rifle fire. All the German tanks were destroyed and the penetrating forces eliminated, with little information on their fate reaching German lines.

On 26 December, while *Kampfgruppe* 901 held its positions astride the Bastogne–Arlon highway, facing south, the American relief force linked up with the defenders of Bastogne. In the evening of 29 December, as command of the sector south of the Wiltz River passed to the XXXIX *Panzer Korps*, *Kampfgruppe* 901 was attached to the 167th *Volksgrenadier Division*. In an attempt to support a vain attack by the new *Korps* via Lutrebois to sever the newly opened supply route, the *Panzer Lehr Panzer* company was badly battered.

The American relief of Bastogne also cut the supply routes for the main body of *Panzer Lehr Division* 130, which had advanced toward Rochefort. Henceforth, logistical support for all German forces west of Bastogne was via a single road upon which Allied air concentrated its fury.

On 2 January the Americans attacked on a broad front in the Neffe area, entering Wardin, Neffe and Magéret, only to be forced back again by German counterattacks in a snowstorm on 3 January. *Kampfgruppe* 901's sector then quieted down until, on 6 January, the *Kampfgruppe,* now mere remnants, a few officers, about 100 men and five Panzer IV, was ordered, after its relief, to return to its parent division. After two nights march, it rejoined *Panzer Lehr Division* 130 on 8 January.

# THE MAIN BODY OF *PANZER LEHR DIVISION* 130 RESUMES THE WESTWARD MOVEMENT TOWARD THE MEUSE CROSSINGS

On 21 December the 2nd *Panzer Division* captured the bridge over the Ourthe River at Ortheuville. Although the 26th *Volksgrenadier Division* relieved *Kampfgrruppe* 902 near Neffe, fuel shortage allowed only the Advance Detachment (*Kampfgruppe von Fallois*), along with *Panzer-Pionier-Bataillon* 130 and *Sturmgeschützbrigade* 243 to resume the westward advance.

Initially following *Aufklärungsabteilung* 26 to Hompré, the Advance Detachment turned westward there, making contact with the enemy near Tillet and Moircy, capturing an American supply column with 60 – 80 lorries and, in the evening, encircling the American 58th Field Artillery Battalion near Tillet.

After supporting the defenders at Longvilly, eight self-propelled howitzers of the 58th Armored Field Artillery Battalion had withdrawn to a new position near Tillet. When the American artillery battalion was cut off by the *Panzer Lehr* reconnaissance battalion in the afternoon of 21 December, the drivers and gunners dug a circle of foxholes around their guns and vehicles. Thwarted in an initial attempt to breakout, as ordered, during the night, the battalion returned to its position and fought valiantly throughout the day of 21 December with their guns and from their foxholes. By the end of 22 December only one of the eight self-propelled howitzers was still in firing condition when the battalion's commander, Colonel

Paton, ordered destruction of all equipment and for the men to break out. Shielded by trees and moving in small groups through the falling snow, most of the American battalion made it back to VIII Corps lines.

On 22 December, leaving *Kampfgruppe* 901 behind at Bastogne, the main body of *Panzer Lehr Division* 130 moved out toward St. Hubert and, more distant, the Meuse River. The lead elements of *Kampfgruppe* 902 crossed the main Bastogne – Arlon road at noon. Overcoming light opposition, the Division made rapid progress via Morhet–Remagne–Moircy–Hatrival. Despite breaks in the clouds and clear intervals the column proceeded without attack from the air.

Fuel shortages began to interfere as the first tank ran dry west of Moircy, already having to draw on the spare gas cans carried by the wheeled Steyr troop-carriers. The hope for captured fuel in St. Hubert proved illusory.

Forced to wait for fuel to arrive, the Division made a delayed start from St. Hubert in the morning of 23 December. The Division advanced on Rochefort by two routes, the Advance Detachment (reinforced *Aufklärungs-Lehr-Abteilung* 130 under *Major* von Born-Fallois) moving via Masbourg–Fourrieres (Forrières), *Kampfgruppe* 902 via Grupont–Wavreilles (Wavreille). *Generalleutnant* Bayerlein rode with the Advance Detachment.

As early as 23 December reconnaissance patrols reported an increasing American presence on the Division's south flank. Also, the 5th *Fallschirmjäger Division*, shielding to the south, was under mounting pressure as Patton's relief force battled toward Bastogne and, at the same time, ruptured *Panzer Lehr Division* 130's supply lines. The relief force linked up with the Bastogne defenders on 26 December.

By nightfall the leading company reached the hills south of Rochefort. Patrols sent to Rochefort reported that the town was undefended. Apparently the patrols did not enter the town.

The report was incorrect. The first of the divisions being assembled for the American General 'Lightning Joe' Collins' VII Corps, which was to attack the flank of the advancing German forces from the north, was the American 84th Infantry Division, whose leading elements arrived in Marche two hours before midnight in the night of 20/21 December. The main body of the division was still coming out of the line near Geilenkirchen and would arrive within the next 24 hours.

One of the ubiquitous small forces of American engineers that so often played crucial local roles in the Ardennes battle delayed the 2nd *Panzer Division* in its capture intact of the Bailey Bridge over the Ourthe River at Ortheuville. Capture of the bridge was not followed by a renewed advance, however, for the 2nd *Panzer Division* then had to wait for fuel to arrive. Its tanks had run dry. This delay on 21 and 22 December allowed the American 84th Infantry Division to reach Marche. A small detachment of the American 51st Engineer Combat Battalion manned a small roadblock at a crossroads just three miles from the Ortheuville bridge named Barrière de Champlon. During the extra time provided by the delay they felled trees to strengthen the block and blew a large crater in the road.

When enough fuel had arrived to enable the 2nd *Panzer Division's Aufklärungsabteilung* to resume its advance by nightfall of 22 December, the light tanks and armored cars of the reconnaissance battalion bypassed the roadblock using trails through the woods. However, when the main body of the 2nd *Panzer Division* finally got moving on 23 December its heavier vehicles had to wait an additional four hours while pioneers constructed a bypass around the crater.

Upon arriving in Marche, where he set up his headquarters in the late afternoon of 21 December, the commander of the 84th Infantry Division, General Bolling, learned that elements of the German 116th *Panzer Division* had already attacked the bridge over the Ourthe River at Hotton. By midnight of 21/22 December General Bolling had the entire 84th Infantry Division and attached 771st Tank Battalion assembled and deploying along a line of defense.

Realizing that his division's assembly position was endangered by the German advance he immediately committed his 334th Infantry Regiment in front of the Hotton – Marche highway, with the 335th defending in front of the town of Marche, its line refused to protect the division's open southern flank. Colonel Fraser, commanding the 51st Engineers Combat Battalion, requested aid from the 84th Infantry Division for his detachment that was defending the Hotton bridge. However, when the troops that Bolling sent from his 334th Infantry Regiment arrived at the Hotton bridge, they found that the detachment of the 51st Engineers Combat Battalion that had been guarding that bridge, aided by a few men of the arriving 3rd Armored Division, had halted the enemy and saved the bridge in a praiseworthy feat of arms.

Marche was as critical a transportation hub as Bastogne, astride two important paved highways, the main road north to Liège and the main road, N 4, to the Meuse crossing at Namur with an offshoot to Dinant. *General* von Manteuffel needed Highway N 4 as a first-class highway leading through easy tank-country directly to the Meuse at Namur for his 5th *Panzerarmee's* advance. The 2nd *Panzer Division* was advancing toward Marche. *Panzer Lehr Division* 130 was advancing via lesser roads that converged via Rochefort, seven miles southwest of Marche, on Namur from southeast of Highway N 4. Rochefort was on the Liège – Sedan highway. Secondary hard-surface roads led west, north and southwest from Rochefort, offering another, though less favorable, route to the Dinant crossing of the Meuse by way of Ciergnon and Celles.

At noon on 22 December an order arrived from the American XVIII Airborne Corps, (General Collins' VII Corps had not yet assumed command) instructing General Bolling to block all roads east, southeast and south of Rochefort until the American 3rd Armored Division could extend its flank to that area.

The 2nd *Panzer Division's* delay allowed General Bolling to send a rifle company to Rochefort, followed later by a motorized infantry battalion, the 335th Infantry Regiment's 3rd Battalion (minus two companies, one left in Hargimont, where it had run into German forces *en route* to Rochefort, and another sent on past Rochefort to scout villages further south)), and for a task force of the American 3rd Armored Division's Combat Command A to arrive, strengthening General Bolling's force.

During the day of 22 December General Collins and some of the corps troops of the VII Corps arrived in the new corps area southwest of Liège.

As *Kampfgruppe* 902 approached Rochefort, the 335th Infantry Regiment's 3rd Battalion had, in addition two platoons of 57 mm antitank guns from the regimental anti-tank company, a platoon of the 309th Engineer Combat Battalion, a platoon of the 638th Tank Destroyer Battalion and a platoon of the 29th Infantry Regiment that had been defending the cable-communications repeater station at nearby Jemelles.

Based on the erroneous report that Rochefort was undefended, Bayerlein, who was personally supervising *Panzer Lehr's* attack, allowed the *Kampfgruppe* to approach Rochefort through a defile between two commanding hills, without first securing the hills.

Heavy fire halted the attack at its onset. *Generalleutnant* Bayerlein immediately ordered a withdrawal, sent a platoon of tanks around behind the town to cut it off and prepared his forces for a deliberate midnight assault.

Rochefort was large enough so that the American force could not prevent the Germans from entering it. After a night of house-to-house fighting, the American forces were ordered to withdraw, having achieved the desired delay. The closely-engaged men of the battalion had difficulty disengaging, but most succeeded eventually in making their way back to Marche by circuitous routes.

After taking Rochefort, there was nothing left between *Panzer Lehr Division* 130 and the Meuse but another battalion of the 84th Infantry Division, which was ordered to withdraw from its position in the valley of the Lesse River during the night. However, while sending reconnaissance patrols to check out the Lesse River valley, *Generalleutnant* Bayerlein chose to delay again in Rochefort to give his exhausted troops a chance to rest and enjoy the special rations that had arrived for Christmas.

On 23 December skies cleared over the Ardennes and Allies air joined the battle in full force, flying over 7,000 sorties in the next four days.

*General* von Lüttwitz and *General* von Manteuffel met on the night of 23 December and agreed that the Americans now held Marche in strength, eliminating Highway N 4 as a feasible route to the Meuse at Namur. Since the 2nd *Panzer Division* had already bypassed Marche to the south, and *Panzer Lehr Division* 130 could now reach the valley of the Lesse River via Rochefort, the 5th *Panzer Armee* would now have to use that less favourable route from Rochefort to the Meuse at Dinant, a distance of only 14 miles.

However, the two *Panzer* divisions were now at the thin end of a long wedge with both flanks seriously exposed to the gathering American forces. Both divisions had already started shedding elements as they advanced to cover their flanks. German hopes rested on the possible arrival of the 9th *Panzer Division* sometime in the next day or two, as well as some part of the 15th *Panzergrenadier Division*, which had already been, in part, committed at Bastogne. If the 116th *Panzer Division* succeeded in cutting and crossing the Marche–Hotton highway east of Marche and then Highway N 4, that would also prevent the Americans from concentrating their forces against the German spearhead. In the event, hard fighting and massive artillery support thwarted the German attempt to cross the Hotton – Marche highway and, in so doing, also scuttled the attempt to cover the vulnerable north flank of the 2nd *Panzer Division*.

Henceforth, *Panzer Lehr's* actions can only be understood in relation to those of the 2nd *Panzer Division* as the Division's drive to the Meuse was transformed into a last-ditch effort to save the cut-off elements of its desperate partner in the XLVII *Panzer Korps*.

The reconnaissance *Abteilung* and the leading *Kampfgruppe* of the 2nd *Panzer Division*, consisting of one *Abteilung* of the division's 3rd *Panzer Regiment* with about 40 *Panther* tanks, 25 self-propelled guns – most of the division's artillery – and *Panzergrenadiers* of the division's 304th *Infanterie Regiment* in half-tracked *SPW's,* bypassed Marche to the south and advanced through Humaine and Buissonville westward toward Dinant on the Meuse. The remainder of the 2nd *Panzer Division* was stretched all to way back to south of Marche with the dual missions of continuing the westward advance and of protecting XLVII *Panzer Korps* northern flank. Leading elements of the *Aufklärungsabteilung* reached Celles, only six miles from Dinant and the Meuse crossing, before daylight on 24 December.

At just about that time Combat Command B of the powerful American 2nd Armored Division began to arrive in Ciney, about six miles northeast of Celles. In the meanwhile, one of the two task forces of the 2nd Armored Division's Combat Command A, under orders to reach Rochefort, passed through Buissonville after the passage of the 2nd *Panzer Division* force, the remainder of CCA joining its advance on parallel roads. A long German column approaching Buissonville was shot to pieces.

Nearby the 24th Cavalry Reconnaissance Squadron of the 4th Cavalry Group moved into Humain. With Buissonville and Humain in American hands, the 2nd *Panzer Division* route of advance was blocked, the *Aufklärungsabteilung* and leading *Kampfgruppe* cut off. The only route left for the German advance was the highway through Rochefort up the valley of the Lesse River, the road in front of the *Panzer Lehr Division*.

In the meanwhile, the 2nd *Panzer Division Aufklärungsabteilung* resumed its advance. The *Kampfgruppe* following it, however, was forced to halt in the village of Conjoux, two miles back from Celles and wait for fuel, its tanks almost dry.

After losing one tank to a mine at Celles, the German reconnaissance battalion then ran into five British Sherman tanks of the 3rd Royal Tank Regiment, which was defending the west bank of the Meuse at Dinant. Losing two vehicles to British fire and running out of petrol, the reconnaissance battalion went for cover among the houses of the nearby village of Foy-Notre Dame, only three miles from the Meuse. A single German tank, knocked out in the garden of the curé of the village of Foy -Notre Dame, marked the western limit of the German armoured advance. That was the closest any significant German force got to the Meuse crossings. *General* Model ordered the men of the *Aufklärungsabteilung* to leave their immobilized vehicles and continue to the Meuse on foot. That order was ignored.

At this point the main body of the German 2nd *Panzer Division* was blocked in its advance, its *Aufklärungsabteilung* and leading *Kampfgruppe* separated and cut off by strong American forces. Also, good flying weather exposed the 2nd *Panzer Division*, especially its leading elements that had been cut off and its supply columns, to savage and relentless aerial attack.

General Ernest Harmon, commanding the American 2nd Armored Division requested permission to attack the vulnerable German 2nd *Panzer Division*.

Field Marshal Montgomery was concerned about a possible major German attack. He felt that the enemy had the forces for another major breakout. Accordingly, in the afternoon of 24 December, he released General Collins from his mission to attack and authorized him to withdraw his forces, if necessary, to a line from Hotton northwest to the Meuse River at Andenne, twelve miles downstream (north) of the bend at Namur. General Collins, however, was only 'authorized', not ordered, to withdraw his forces. He also had been given unrestricted use of all his divisions. Having secured written orders to cover himself against recriminations, he gave General Harmon the go-ahead to attack.

The Germans were not yet aware of the arrival of the American 2nd Armored Division. Still hoping to attain the goal of the Meuse River, early on Christmas Day *General* von Lüttwitz, commanding the XLVII *Panzer Korps* ordered *Panzer Lehr Division* 130 to recapture Humain and Buissonville, reopening the 2nd *Panzer Divisions's* line of communications and best route to the Meuse while the main body of the 2nd *Panzer Division* forced its way through to its cut-off elements.

All this was part of a larger plan to revive the offensive toward th Meuse. The 6th *Panzer Armee* was to rapidly advance its II *SS-Panzer Korps* to take over the fighting east of the Ourthe River on the right. The 116th *Panzer Division* of 5th *Panzer Armee's* LVIII *Panzer Korps* was, after taking Vendenne and Marche, to move north to take Baillonville and then wheel left, advancing through Pessoux to Ciney, covering the 2nd *Panzer Division's* right flank and giving breadth to the drive on the Meuse. The 9th *Panzer Division* was, on its arrival, to move in on *Panzer Lehr's* right. In the event, none of the elements of this plan materialized.

On 25 December the American 2nd Armored Division launched its attack on the German 2nd *Panzer Division*, a two-pronged envelopment to destroy the German forces believed to be in the Celles area. The day was clear and the attack received some of the best tactical air support ever seen in the war. The 2nd Armored Division's Combat Command B constituted two task forces that attacked southwest from Ciney, converging on Celles where they enveloped *Kampfgruppe von Cochenhausen* (reinforced *Panzergrenadier-Regiment* 304). By day's end there was little left of the *Kampfgruppe*. At the same time the 2nd Armored Division's 82nd Reconnaissance Battalion, supported to its right by the British 29th Tank Brigade, attacked *Kampfgruppe von Böhm*, (the *Aufklärungsabteilung* and part of the division's artillery), destroying it with the help of close air support. Farther east, the 2nd Armored Division's Combat Command A advanced south, cutting the 2nd *Panzer Division* axis of advance near Buissonville and Humain.

As ordered, *Kampfgruppe* 902 (*von Poschinger*) set out at midnight of 25/26 December for Humain, the Advance Detachment (*Kampfgruppe von Fallois*) for Buissonville. *Kampfgruppe* 902 drove the American 24th Cavalry Squadron out of Humain, but the Advance Detachment ran into the American 2nd Armored Division's CCA which stopped it cold before Buissonville. Highway N 4 remained blocked, the 2nd *Panzer Division Aufklärungsabteilung* and forward regimental *Kampfgruppe* cut off from each other and from outside aid as they were annihilated by the American 2nd Armored Division and Allied air forces.

During the night of 25/26 December *Panzeraufklärungs-Lehr-Abteilung* 130 (Advance Detachment) was relieved in Humain by a *Kampfgruppe* from the 9th *Panzer Division* and returned to the Division at Rochefort.

On 26 December further German attempts by the 9th *Panzer Division Kampfgruppe* and by the remainder of the 2nd *Panzer Division* to break through to the cut-off elements of the 2nd *Panzer Division* failed. When the cut-off elements, bereft of fuel, finally received belated permission to withdraw, abandoning all their equipment, about 600 men made it back the following night to their own lines in Rochefort.

That marked the end of the German advance. The defunct *Panther* in the garden of the curé in Foy–Notre Dame was the western-most German tank, the last flotsam cast up at the high-water mark. Charles B. MacDonald put it very well when he said (p.604, *A Time for Trumpets*), ' … the Germans in front of the Meuse on Christmas Day and the next day suffered 'one of the most serious things that can possibly happen to one in battle' – as Tweedledee explained to Alice – getting one's head cut off.' Hitler still refused to admit that his forces could not reach the Meuse, but he placed immediate priority on the elimination of Bastogne. *General* von Manteuffel tacitly shifted his emphasis from continuing the drive for the Meuse to capturing Bastogne. Suddenly *Panzer Lehr Division* 130 and the truncated 2nd *Panzer Division* were out of the limelight. The 2nd *Panzer Division* was pulled back through Rochefort. *Panzer Lehr Division* 130 was shifted southeast to Remagne, five miles northwest of the Neufchâteau – Bastogne Highway where, no longer strong enough to attack, it would stubbornly hold a sector of the front while others struck the left flank of the corridor linking Bastogne with Patton's Third Army to the south.

# RETREAT FROM THE ARDENNES

After an exceedingly brief reorganization, on 27 December XLVII *Panzer Korps* ordered *Panzer Lehr Division* 130 to the Mirwart – Rondu sector, Mirwart being a little less than five miles northwest of St. Hubert, Rondu about seven miles southeast of St. Hubert. The Division thus defended approximately twelve miles of front. Under constant enemy pressure, both on the ground and from the air, the Division held this sector defending the southwest flank of the German salient with no more than minor losses of terrain until the start of the general retreat on 10 January. Comprehension of the *Panzer Lehr* role requires understanding of the initial stages of the southern arm of the American attempt to cut off the German salient and of the German attempt to renew the ring around and eliminate the American forces at Bastogne.

*Panzeraufklärungs-Lehr-Abteilung* 130 collected its forces near Wavreille, then blocked the Lesse River sector, destroying bridges, felling trees across the road and laying mines, before falling back behind the l'Homme River, with strongpoints in Mirwart and Arville. *Panzeraufklärungs-Lehr-Abteilung* 130 established its command post in Arville.

Adjoining to the left, division pioneers obstructed Arville, Hatrival and Vesqueville and mined the river-bed in front of *Kampfgruppe von Poschinger's* sector. At this point *Kampfgruppe von Poschinger*, with its command post in St. Hubert, consisted of the II./*Panzergrenadier-Lehr-Regiment* 902 (*Bataillon Böhm*), *Panzer-Pionier-Bataillon* 130 and *schwere Panzerjäger-Abteilung* 559. Remember, in reading the names of these units that all had been reduced to mere shadows of their full establishments.

On the Division's extreme left, *Kampfgruppe Neumann*, consisting of the I./ *Panzergrenadier-Lehr-Regiment* 902 and two *Panther* companies, defended the Moircy–Remagne sector. *Panzer -Artillerie-Regiment* 130 supported the sector with two of its own *Abteilungen* (battalions), a *Volks-Artillerie-Korps*, a 21 cm *Mörser* (heavy howitzer) battery and *Heeres-Flak-Abteilung* 311. *Generalleutnant* Bayerlein set up his headquarters in a château near Lavacherie, about seven miles northwest of St. Hubert.

*Panzer-Lehr-Regiment* 130 faced no more than local reconnaissance by the British 6th Airborne Division, reinforced with the 29th Armoured Brigade of the British 11th Armoured Division.

*Kampfgruppe von Poschinger* resolutely held its sector against constant attacks by the American 87th Infantry Division from 28 December until the general retreat on 11 January.

The only enemy penetration came in *Kampfgruppe Neumann's* sector, where, on 28 December, the American 28th Cavalry Squadron forced the advance outposts from Freux and Rondu back to Moircy and Remagne in the start of an attempt to cut the St. Hubert–Morhet road in the opening move of the American offensive described below.

In the evening of 28 December General Eisenhower released the 87th Infantry Division and 11th Armored Division from SHAEF reserve to Bradley's 12th Army Group. Bradley, in turn, then released them to Patton's Third Army, with the reservation that they must be attached to the American VIII Corps.

The Allied plans now called for Middleton's VIII Corps, which was facing *Panzer Lehr Division* 130, the remnants of the 26th *Volksgrenadier Division* and the battered *Kampfgruppe of* the 15th Panzergrenadier-Division and the 3rd *Panzergrenadier-Division*, to open the attack northward from the Bastogne area, its first objective the high ground and road hub south of Houffalize. Milliken's III Corps would then join the action from its positions east of Bastogne on 31 December, driving toward St. Vith. From the northern side of the German salient, Collins VII Corps and the Ridgeway's XVIII Airborne Corps were to attack south on 3 January toward Houffalize and St. Vith, respectively, thus linking up with the drive from the south.

This attack coincided with an attack ordered by von Manteuffel. Manteuffel's plan called for an attack in three phases: first, to re-establish the ring around Bastogne; second to force the American forces back to the south; and, third, with the help of reinforcements then *en route,* to annihilate the American force in Bastogne.

The new XXXIX *Panzer Korps* under *Generalleutnant* Karl Decker was brought in from *OKW* reserve to handle the attack on Bastogne. Over *General* von Lüttwitz'z protests, XXXIX *Panzer Korps* was attached to von Lüttwitz's own XLVII *Panzer Korps.* Von Lüttwitz now commanded *Armeeabteilung von Lüttwitz*, consisting of those two corps.[3] XXXIX *Panzer Korps* would attack from east to west via Lutrebois toward Assenois with the remnants of the 1st *SS-Panzer Division* '*Leibstandarte SS Adolf Hitler*', now reduced to a *Kampfgruppe*, the 167th

3 Sometimes incorrectly referred to as *Armeegruppe Lüttwitz*. An *Armeeabteilung* consists of two or more *Korps*, but less than an *Armee*. An *Armeegruppe* consists of two or more *Armeen*, but less than a *Heeresgruppe*.

*Volksgrenadier Division* and the 14th *Fallschirmjäger Regiment.* The *Führer-Begleit-Brigade* would spearhead XLVII *Panzer Korps*'s attack from the west via Sibret to meet the XXXIX *Panzer Korps* thrust at Assenois.

In the XLVII *Panzer Korps* attack the 3rd *Panzergrenadier Division* would advance south through the Bois de Fragotte, between Chenogne and Senonchamps, echeloned to the right of the *Führer-Begleit-Brigade*, and swing southeast to take Villeroux. Attached to the 3rd *Panzergrenadier Division* the *Führer-Begleit-Brigade* would capture Sibret and the combined force then move against Assenois and Hompré, linking up with the XXXIX *Panzer Korps* force and closing the ring again around Bastogne.

The remnants of the 26th *Volksgrenadier Division* and a *Kampfgruppe* from the 15th *Panzergrenadier Division* were to screen to the north and west of Bastogne while what was left of *Panzer Lehr Division* 130 firmly defended its sector on the *Korps* far right. The 26th *Volksgrenadier* and 15th *Panzergrenadier Divisions* had both lost heavily in their unsuccessful Christmas Day attack on the northwest part of the American 101st Airborne Division sector at Bastogne.

Before the opening of the two opposed offensives, on 29 December, CCA of the American 9th Armored Division was continuing the attack it had launched on 27 December north toward Sibret along the left flank of the 4th Armored Division to open the Neufchâteau – Bastogne highway and establish a line of departure for the new offensive. Its Task Force Karsteter unwittingly approached and endangered the assembly position of the *Führer-Begleit-Brigade.* Later Task Force Karsteter came under heavy fire and suffered heavy losses when it ran into the main body of the 3rd *Panzergrenadier Division.*

Then, on 30 December, the two opposing attacks were launched. Aside from a few minor meeting engagements (minor, that is, from the American viewpoint) between the margins of the American 11th Armored Division's CCB and the *Führer-Begleit-Brigade,* most of the American attack by the 87th Infantry and 11th Armored Division, advancing north to the left of the 9th Armored Division, struck the German sector held by *Panzer Lehr Division* 130 and the 26th *Volksgrenadier Divison.* With the exception of the penetration described below, *Panzer Lehr's* staunchly defended line held with no significant changes, as did the positions of the 26th *Volksgrenadier Division* and 15th *Panzergrenadier Kampfgruppe.*

Shelled heavily in its assembly position in the Bois de Fragotte by 4th Armored Division artillery and facing severe cross-fire from the 9th Armored Division's CCA tanks in Villeroux, the 3rd *Panzergrenadier Division* took little action on 30 December.

The *Führer-Begleit-Brigade* formed two forces, one consisting of a battalion of *Panzergrenadiere*, which was to force an opening into Sibret, the other consisting of its armour with another battalion of *Panzergrenadiere* riding the tanks. The armoured force would wait in Chenogne and then advance on a parallel route through Flohimont and enter Sibret from the west.

Starting out in dense ground fog the *Führer-Begleit Panzergrenadier Bataillon* made initial progress, pushing back the American Task Force Collins of CCA of the 9th Armored Division toward Sibret. However, the German battalion commander was killed, the advance slowed down and the fog lifted to reveal about 30 American tanks of CCB of the 11th Armored Division.

Though *Oberst* Remer, commanding the *Führer-Begleit-Brigade*, chose not to engage the American armour to his west, since his mission was to attack to the east, his outpost line to the west became involved and, as the action developed, more of his force was sucked in. The day passed and, by evening of 30 December, the *Führer-Begleit-Brigade* had accomplished little of note.

On 30 December CCA of the American 11th Armored Division and the 87th Infantry Division advanced via Rondu toward Remagne and via Freux toward Moircy. As the 11th Armored Division CCA's 63rd Armored Infantry Battalion reached the crest of the Ridge north of Rondu *Kampfgruppe Neumann's* fire swept them from the ridge. Despite extremely heavy American artillery fire, *Kampfgruppe Neumann* held resolutely. The American infantry lost heavily.

On the left wing of the American VIII Corps advance, the 87th Infantry Division committed two regiments, the 345th Infantry Regiment on the right to capture Pironpré, the 346th Infantry Regiment on the left to block the roads leading south from St. Hubert.

The American 345th Infantry Regiment on the right had an easy start, *Panzer Lehr's* former roadblock detachments on its route apparently having been called in. However, the regiment ran into the first outpost within sight of Moircy. Heavy fire came in about 500 yards short of Moircy. By 1400 hours, after a series of costly, short rushes, the two companies reached the edge of Moircy after losing most of their officers and many enlisted men. The battalion's reserve company was sent to circle west of the village and take the adjoining hamlet of Jenneville. A hot reception claimed heavy casualties, but the company reached the edge of Jenneville. By then, however, Moircy was in American hands and the reserve company was recalled. *Kampfgruppe Neumann's* counterattack came in at about 0300 hours on 31 December. After a night of hard fighting that was costly to both sides *Kampfgruppe Neumann* received permission on 31 December to evacuate Moircy, but continued to hold the St. Hubert – Morhet road. *Kampfgruppe Neumann* suffered heavy losses.

The Americans shifted unit boundaries to leave *Panzer Lehr's* position to the 87th Infantry Division and allow the 11th Armored Division's CCA to join with its CCB east of the Bois de Haies.

In the afternoon of 31 December the American 87th Infantry Division's 345th Infantry Regiment captured Remagne. Lack of adequate German forces precluded counterattack. By that point the 345th Regiment had sustained many casualties and was replaced by the newly-arrived 347th Infantry Regiment.

The XXXIX *Panzer Korps* assault to cut the Bastogne corridor failed in the east, with the capture of just two villages, Lutrebois and Villers-la-Bonne-Eau, which, with the total failure of the XLVII *Panzer Korps* attack from the west, put 'paid' to the German hopes of eliminating Bastogne.

Hitler, however, still insisted on another attempt, which would take place on 4 January. That attack, however, which would be conducted by the 1st *SS-Panzer Korps* would come in astride the Bastogne– Houffalize highway and would not involve *Panzer Lehr Division* 130. XLVII *Panzer Korps* was simply expected to hold in place.

The new year came in with snow, sleet and bitter cold. The 87th Infantry Division's 347th Infantry Regiment advanced through drifted snow from

Remagne and Moircy to cut the Bastogne – St. Hubert highway and capture Amberloup.

During the day the American 1st Battalion with armoured support fought its way through deep snow into the woods. While daylight held enemy reaction was limited to small arms and occasional bursts of artillery fire. When night fell, however, German tanks struck and drove the American 1st Battalion back toward Remagne.

In the meanwhile 347th Infantry's 3rd Battalion advanced north from Moircy toward Pironpré, taking the village of Jenneville that had cost its sister battalion so heavily two days earlier. However, as the battalion continued north from Jenneville heavy fire from a few German tanks that were carefully concealed in lumber piles around the local sawmill halted the American attack for the night.

On 2 January the two American battalions renewed their attack, steering well clear of the Pironpré hornet's nest. Despite repeated American attacks, Pironpré remained in German hands until the general retreat on 11 January. The American's took Gerimont, to the east and Bonnerue, to the west, cutting the St. Hubert–Morhet road. Gerimont remained American, but a German counterattack reclaimed Bonnerue. The American 87th Infantry Division committed its third Battalion to clean up and close the dangerous gap that had developed between its two attacking forces. Concerned, *Generalleutnant* Bayerlein committed *Kampfgruppe von Poschinger* in a counterattack that regained Bonnerue, as noted above. Lengthy and intense forest fighting against the skillfully infiltrating American troops held them to a line generally about one kilometre north of the St. Hubert – Bastogne road until the 11 January general retreat.

In a curious find, the Germans discovered a cache of artillery ammunition left over either from the 1940 advance or the 1944 retreat. Some rounds had suffered moisture damage, but many were still usable. The find of usable German propellant cartridges allowed the German artillery to fire captured American 105 mm shells back at the Americans from German pieces..

On 3 January the great American offensive of the First Army from the north and northwest and the Third Army from the south opened in a heavy snowstorm with falling temperatures. *Panzer Lehr Division* 130 was spared the initial assaults, but became involved in the general retreat.

Hotly contested, Bonnerue changed hands several times on 8 and 9 January. What was left of *Panzergrenadier-Lehr-Regiment* 901 finally returned from east of Bastogne to its parent division on 9 January and launched a carefully prepared and well supported counterattack, retaking Bonnerue and capturing 80 prisoners.

To the west Allied attacks forced the German front back. Rochefort was lost. After the loss of Rochefort and under tremendous Allied pressure on the entire salient, Hitler agreed to a phased withdrawal. He also withdrew the 6th *SS-Panzer Armee,* as the former 6th *Panzer Armee* was now designated for commitment in Hungary to protect Germany's last available source of petroleum.

The German front was pulled back to the line Mirwart–Bure–Wavreille–Hargimont–Charneux. Savage winter weather with bone-chilling cold, heavy snowstorms and ice-bound roads grounded Allied air and hindered pursuit. As the German phased withdrawal developed, *Panzer Lehr Division* 130's position holding the line west of Bastogne was transformed into *Panzer Lehr* serving as rear-guard.

For the time being,, *Panzer Lehr Division* 130, now rear-guard, had to hold at what had become the western apex of the German salient. On 8 January Hitler authorized withdrawal to the Dochamps (15 kilometres east of Hotton)–Longchamps (6 kilometres north of Bastogne) line. '*Unternehmen Veilchen*' ('Operation Violet') was to start with withdrawal of the units adjoining the Division to the right, the remnants of the 2nd *Panzer Division* and the 9th *Panzer Division*. The evacuation of St. Hubert, originally planned for the following night was postponed 24 hours, presumably due to fuel shortages and/or traffic conditions. St. Hubert was, in the event, evacuated during the night of 11/12 January.

The German perception was that the Allies were hesitant in following their withdrawal, due, in part, to mining and obstruction by German pioneers, the snow and ice conditions delaying removal of the blocks, to some extent due to the grounding of all air support, and, in part to lack of flexibility and initiative on the allied side,, what the Germans called '*schematisch*' tactics. However, Allied artillery harassing fire on villages, intersections and other sensitive points was considered extremely unpleasant.

The withdrawal continued according to plan.

On 13 January *Panzer Lehr Division* 130 constituted the right flank rear-guard of the XLVII *Panzer Korps*, adjoined on the right by the badly battered 116th *Panzer Division*. In the evening of 13 January *Panzer Lehr* was ordered to dispatch a *Kampfgruppe* to link up with the 116th *Panzer Division* on its right. *Kampfgruppe von Poschinger* accordingly moved to Nadrin, approximately eight kilometres east of la Roche, but was unable to make contact with the 116th *Panzer Division* in the dark. South of the Ourthe River, *Kampfgruppe von Hauser* fell back to the line Thimont–Cens.

On 14 January superior enemy forces attacked the *Panzergrenadiers* north of the Ourthe both from the north and northeast. By afternoon both Nadrin and Filly were lost. The fords over the Ourthe were effectively blocked by crippled vehicles. The *Panzergrenadiers* were able to mine the streets and, at the last moment, blow the bridges across the Ourthe River, thereby blocking immediate pursuit. However, many of their own men were trapped on the north side of the icy river and captured. South of the Ourthe River, Warempage and Nisramont fell to the Allies.

Throughout the retreat, highways were jammed with unbroken streams of vehicles, all types and units mixed in a desperate attempt to reach the crossings over the Our to Germany. Special detachments spread sand on the icy roads. All available officers worked at traffic control, attempting to get damaged or disabled vehicles out of the road.

During the night of 14/15 January the new German front line was set at Achouffe–Bonnerue–Mabompré, almost directly north and a trifle east of Bastogne. As American forces forced back the fought-out remnants of the 116th *Panzer Division*, *Panzeraufklärungs-Lehr-Abteilung* 130 prepared to backstop the 116th *Panzer Division* by defending the northern approach to Houffalize in Mont, which had to be evacuated in the afternoon.

*Panzer Lehr Division* 130 had contact with the 26th *Volksgrenadier Division* in Mabompré, to the south. When a combat-group of the American 11th Armored Division advanced straddling the Bertogne–Houffalize road to Mabompré *Panzergrenadier-Lehr-Regiment* 901 was able to destroy the bridge so that the American tanks could not cross, but was forced to fall back to the north. When American forces occupied the woods northeast of Mabompré, *Kampfgruppe von Hauser* was forced to fall back to the hills south of Houffalize. A counterattack by the 26th *Volksgrenadier-Division* recaptured Mabompré but resulted in the loss of the remaining six *Jagdpanther* of *schwere Panzerjäger-Abteilung* 559. The newly-employed proximity fuses gave devastating air-bursts as American artillery harassing fire mounted throughout the sector.

The situation had deteriorated to the point where Houffalize had to be evacuated. *Panzer Lehr Division* 130 fell back to a position behind Houffalize during the night of 15/16 January and held that position through 16 January. That night the Division prepared a fall-back position in the in Cetturu – Tavigny, which it fell back to on 18 January.

Under cover of a blinding snowstorm on 19 January withdrawal continued without enemy interference to the railroad line west of the Luxembourg border. During the night of 19/20 January 1945 *Panzer Lehr's* rear-guards passed through the new Biwisch–Asselborn defensive line that was held by the 26th *Volksgrenadier Division* and 15th *Panzergrenadier-Division*.

*Panzer Lehr Division* 130 had acquitted itself admirably as a fighting rear-guard during the German retreat from the Ardennes, but received no rest. General Patton had, from the very start of the German Ardennes Offensive, pushed for bold thrusts to slash through the German salient at the very base. The sparse road network south of the strong American defensive position on the Elsenborn Ridge, which had provided a firm shoulder against the northern flank of the German thrust, precluded a northern thrust from there. For a variety of reasons, the Allies chose what *General* von Rundstedt termed the 'small solution', paired thrusts aimed at Houffalize and St. Vith, approximately half-way up the German salient. No significant German forces were cut off. Now, after those two arms of the pincers had linked up at Houffalize, Patton finally launched an attack where he would have chosen to do so much earlier.

On 18 January two American infantry divisions crossed the Sûre (Sauer) River by surprise, a regiment of the 4th Infantry Division close to the German border at the junction of the Sauer and Our Rivers, two regiments of the 5th Infantry Division on either side of Diekirch. The 5th Infantry Division advanced north up 'Skyline Drive', seriously endangering the vital German crossings of the Our River at Vianden and Gemünd, threatening to cut off the three divisions of the LIII *Armee Korps*.

The German 7th *Armee* committed a *Volksgrenadier Division* on the ridge road. On 19 January *Generalfeldmarschall* Model immediately ordered to the 7th *Armee,* first a *Kampfgruppe*, then the entire remnants of *Panzer Lehr Division* 130 along with the XLVII *Panzer Korps* command and the 2nd *Panzer Division* remnants to establish a blocking position athwart the ridge west of Vianden to secure the retreat of the LIII *Koprs* from the Ardennes.

Heavy snow on 19 January intervened in all planned movements, but by the morning of 20 January *Kampfgruppe von Poschinger* was in position south and southwest of Hoscheid with the 9th *Volksgrenadier Division* on its right. Hoscheid was on Skyline Drive where the secondary road from Wiltz via the Wiltz River crossing at Kautenbach to the Vianden and Gemünd crossings over the Our to Germany crossed the ridge road.. If the American forces continued north on the highway through Hoscheid they could completely cut off the remaining German forces from the Our crossings.

American artillery was now within range and pounded the retreating LIII *Korps* as its crowded columns wound their tortuous way down ice-bound roads into the deep Our valley, across the bridges and up the German side of the valley.

On 21 January, after a heavy artillery preparation, the American 5th Infantry Division attacked Hoscheid. The initial assault was repulsed, but skies cleared the next day and American air and artillery joined the fray. *Kampfgruppe von Hauser* was shifted to the right to assist, but on 25 January Hoscheid fell. *Panzer Lehr Division* 130 was forced back to Walhausen as the last of the LIII *Korps* flowed back over the Clerf and Our Rivers. On 26 January 1945 *Panzer Lehr's* rear-guard received permission to fall back across the Our, ending the Division's involvement in the Ardennes offensive.

[Following (MS#A–941) translated by Frederick Steinhardt, except for the covering letter by Kenneth W. Hechler]

# MS # A–941

## PANZER LEHR DIVISION (1 DECEMBER 1944–26 JANUARY 1945) (ARDENNES)

### DEPARTMENT OF THE ARMY HISTORICAL DIVISION WASHINGTON 25, D. C.

12 July 1949

Note to: MS #A–941
By: Kenneth W. Hechler
Major, Infantry (Res)

This is one of the many reports which was prepared by General Bayerlein while he was assisting the Historical Section. This particular report was written while General Bayerlein was confined to the hospital in Bad Nauheim with heart trouble. He was allowed to get up and to write at a table in order to prepare this report. I urged him to include as many illustrative sketches as possible in order to support the text of his report.

Although General Bayerlein was very eager to supply a complete account of his operations, along with a critical analysis of the tactics of the Panzer Lehr Div, I have a feeling from talking with him and from reading his reports that often he would include material which he felt the Americans would like to read. This was part and parcel of General Bayerlein's general philosophy that after the war the best way to get ahead in life was to ingratiate himself with the Americans. It was this attitude which caused General Bayerlein to be held in considerable contempt by some of his German general associates.

Aside from General Bayerlein's specific comments on American units and American fighting power, however, I believe that he was accurate in his discussion of the general tactics, plans, and movements of his division. He was extremely enthusiastic about preparing the answers to the questions which we presented to him, and I know from reports I received from the hospital that he worked long and hard in order to complete the details of his manuscript and to prepare the necessary supporting sketches.

Alfred Zerbel — Koenigstein, 15 June 1950

### INDEX FOR MS # A 941 (PANZER LEHR DIV, 1 DEC 44 – 26 JAN 45)

[Translated by Frederick Steinhardt]

(signed)
(Alfred Zerbel)

BAYERLEIN Bad Nauheim. 2. XX. 45[4]

4 Tr note: Date appears to be given as '2.XX.45'. Since German practice is to give day-month-year that does not make sense as written and I am hesitant to twist it into American reading of month-day-year and call it Feb 20 45.

## PANZER LEHR DIVISION
## 1 Dec 44–25 Jan 45
### translated by Frederick Steinhardt

**MS # A–941**

***(Panzer Lehr Division, 1 Dec 44–26 Jan 45)***

[Note- this section was translated from the original German by Frederick Steinhardt who was also responsible for the bracketed editorial notes.]

Questions 1–18

1. When did you first hear of the planned Ardennes Offensive?

I first learned of the planned offensive and the participation of the *Panzer Lehr* [*Division*] on 8 (or 10) December 1944 in conjunction with a map exercise in the headquarters of the 47th *Panzer Korps* in Kyllburg (Eifel). The first part of the attack (to the Maas [as the Meuse is called in Holland] between Namur and Dinant) was worked over in this map exercise.

Attending were: *General* von Manteuffel, *General* Krueger of the 58th *Panzer Korps*, the commanders of the *Panzer Lehr*, 2nd *Panzer* [*Oberst* Meinrad von Lauchert] and 26th *Volksgrenadier Divisionen* [*Oberst* Heinz Kokott].

It was already evident that something special was planned in the West, without knowing exactly what it would be. In November the *Panzer Lehr Division* was being reconstituted in Westphalia under control of the 6th *SS-Panzer Armee*. [Although often referred to as 6th *SS Panzer Armee*, the official designation at that time was 6th *Panzer Armee*. The *'SS'* was not added until the spring of 1945. After *Panzer Lehr Division's* nearly complete destruction under the carpet-bombing accompanying Operation Cobra in the American breakthrough in Normandy, as noted earlier, the division's remnants became part of a composite division, with all of six tanks, that halted the American advance in the Eifel in September, suffering additional painful losses. It was then in the process of reconstitution in preparation for the *Führer's* Ardennes Offensive, which meant that it could not be committed in action before that offensive without express permission from the *Führer*. Despite that express order, von Rundstedt alerted the Division for action against Patton's army in the Lorraine, official release of the Division following a day later. Yet again, the division was badly battered, requiring a near miracle of last-minute re-reconstitution to put it sufficiently in shape in a two-week period to participate in the Ardennes Offensive (after Elstob, *Hitler's Last Offensive*. pp. 56–7)]. On 9 November all of the divisions of that army were shifted 'by surprise' to the west bank of the Rhine, indeed, to approximately the area from which they later launched the attack. There were rumours of an intended attack in and south of the Aachen area. Sepp Dietrich's Army was supposed to play the leading role in that [operation].

The *Panzer Lehr Division* was withdrawn from the 6th *SS*-[*Panzer*] *Armee* and was assigned to the 58th *Panzer Korps*. The billeting area was east of Castellaun, in Hunsrück. The division was, however, 'by surprise', committed in the Saar area. [see note following interview MS # A- 901 on '*Panzer Lehr Division* 130 in Lorraine', regarding Saar action.]

On 1 December, after heavy fighting and substantial losses – again 'by surprise' – [the division] was withdrawn for 'rapid refitting' in the Cochem area (on the Mosel [Moselle] River). A 'Special Commission' of *OB West* supervised the rapid withdrawal from the fighting and quick transport away. Therefore there must have been something special planned for the division, since the pressure for extreme haste was suspicious. Nobody could imagine that it had to do with imminent action, since the division was scarcely fit for action. Thus it was all the more surprising when the division received orders to take part in an offensive.

2. Measures to insure secrecy:

The regimental commanders were not informed of the intention to attack and the plan of attack until just three days before the start of the attack (thus on 12 or 13 December.) Until then, all (orders and measures taken) had to be camouflaged as, for example, a 'map exercise' for a counterattack or as orders in the event of a counterattack against an enemy attack or penetration.

There was no concealing the numerous rail transports (of troops and materiel) in the Mosel River Valley and in the Eifel, which clearly indicated intentions to concentrate troops and attack. Maps could only be issued just before the start of the attack.

3. Date of orientation.

a. The Chief of Staff or Operations Officer (*Ia*) participated in a *Korps* map exercise on 8 or 10 December, whereby he was orientated. In addition, the division's commander of artillery and the combat engineers [*Pioniere*] [received orientation] because they had to make vital preparations (concentration of the artillery at the West Wall and preparation for constructing bridges near Gemünd and Eisenbach).

   The *Ib* (logistics) had already been briefed before 10 December by his logistics authorities (corps, army [*Armee*]) since major, time-consuming work was necessary in the logistical area.

b. The other staff officers of the Division were briefed, according to need, between 10 and 13 December.

c. Commanders of regiments and commanders of independent battalions (*Abteilungen*) [were briefed] on 12 December.

d. Commanders of battalions were briefed on 13 and 14 December, prior to the advance, in the assembly areas (some company commanders likewise, as required).

e. & f. Noncommissioned officers and enlisted men: [were briefed] in the evening of 15 December or in the morning of 16 December with the announcement of the appeals by Model and Rundstedt. [*'Soldiers of the Western Front!* Your hour of greatness has arrived! Powerful assault armies are today attacking the Anglo- Americans. I need say no more. You all feel it: *We are staking everything on this!* Bear within you the holy obligation to give your all and achieve the superhuman for *our Fatherland and our Führer!* The Commander in Chief, West, signed von Rundstedt, *Generalfeldmarschall.*'. MacDonald (pp.189–90), quotes endorsements to von Rundstedt's order by Field Marshal Model and General von Manteufel: '*Model*: We will not disappoint the Führer and the Fatherland who created the sword of retribution. Forward in the spirit of Leuthen! *Von Manteuffel*: Forward, march, march! In remembrance of our dead comrades, and therefore on their order, and in remembrance of the tradition of our proud Wehrmacht!']

4. a. How did lack of instruction interfere with the preparations?

That did not cause problems. All preparations of the Division, regiments and battalions went smoothly. The troops were always prepared in advance for anything (practiced by the many 'surprise' commitments) and came directly from the fighting in the Saar region. The command personnel were always particularly well trained and prepared for anything.

b. Effect of the moment of surprise and maintenance of secrecy?

The enemy in *Panzer Lehr's* sector seemed locally surprised, or he would have shifted his defense to the Our [River]-sector and would have been able to cause extreme difficulty and heavy losses to the Germans crossing there. Thus, [in the event], the crossing and bridge-construction were not interfered with at all. The enemy reserves were not yet there for a counterattack on the first and second days of the attack, so that the attack was able to rapidly advance over the Clerf [Clerve River] and into the Bastogne area.

5. Where was *Panzer Lehr* reconstituted?

In the Cochem (Mosel) Lutzerath–Mayen (Eifel) starting 8 December. Thus the Division had only six days to refit and re-equip itself.

6. Reserves (allocations) in manpower, armour, guns and special weapons?

The following replacements were assigned by 15 December:

a. Manpower: 600, but almost all without weapons (more men arrived later during the offensive), about 250 returning convalescents.

b. Tanks and tank destroyers [*Panzerjäger*]: 40 from the armour support facility at Mayen (later another 15 tank destroyers).

c. Guns: 18 (8.8, 10.5 and 15 cm) – Almost all, however, lacking prime movers.

d. Special weapons: (Mortars, machine guns and machine pistols) only isolated allocations, so that one entire battalion had no mortars and only a few machine guns.

The Division had only one *Panzer-Abteilung* [tank battalion] with three companies, each with 14 tanks. The other *Panzer Abteilung* of the *Panzer Regiment* was being activated anew in Fallingbostel (Luneburger Heide) and being equipped with '*Sperber Gerät*' [infra-red aiming devices, sights and IR illumination devices].

7. Actual strength as a percent of authorized strength.

| | |
|---|---|
| Manpower: | 60% fighting strength. |
| Tanks and tank destroyers: | 40% (one *Abteilung* missing). |
| Guns: | 60%. |
| Other weapons: | 40%. |

8. What special weapons were received?

   In place of the missing *Panzer Abteilung* the Division received:

   a. Schwere Panzerjäger-Abteilung 539 (*Jagdpanther*). 30% equipped at the start of the attack (additional allotments of tank destroyers later).

   b. Sturmgeschütz-Abteilung 243, 70% equipped.

   c. *Nebelwerfer* and heavy artillery were not received by the Division. Those were attached directly to the corps and primarily supported the first attack over the Our [River].

9. Fuel?

   a. Promised: 5 units [*Verbrauchssätze*]. (at one *Verbrauchssätz* per 100 km) = 500 km.

      Received: 2–1/2 units = 250 km.

      However, in the difficult terrain of the Eifel and northern Luxembourg, with the miserable roads and unfavorable weather conditions, one could only count on 2½ units = 100 km.

   b. Road priority for fuel vehicles: Basic right-of-way and right to pass (special permit on the windshield.).

      Rotary-traffic or one-way traffic. One way traffic for specified time periods.

   c. Fuel supply for armour.

      Special columns or vehicles with particularly effective column- and vehicle commanders.

   d. Captured fuel and other captured matériel.

      I did not allow myself to rely on captured fuel, though I did hope for it, particularly in Bastogne, St. Hubert and Rochefort.

Booty was, however, vanishingly scant during the entire offensive: only a few fuel lorries. [There was] some captured by draining the tanks of captured or damaged (or destroyed) enemy tanks and motor vehicles, for example: approximately 15 cubic meters [ = 3962 US gal or 3300 Imperial gal] east of Bastogne near Longwilly [Longvilly].

Other booty:

a) Near Magret and Longwilly [Longvilly]: 14 armoured cars, 23 tanks (Sherman), 15 guns (self-propelled), 30 jeeps, 25 lorries (all undamaged!).

b) Near Carimont and Tillet (east of St. Hubert) 53 lorries, 15 jeeps (all undamaged!).

c) In Rochefort. 15 jeeps, 18 lorries. (All undamaged!)

d) North of St. Hubert. American and German ammunition (particularly 10.5 cm) in large quantities. A great deal of ammunition had been expended near St. Hubert and Rochefort and, given the miserable logistics situation, [the captured ammunition] was a great help.

e) In all the Division captured and placed in service approximately 120 undamaged jeeps and over 150 intact lorries.

10. Discussions and conferences before and during the offensive.

a. Map exercise and first discussion of the operation on 8 (or 10) December at 47th *Panzer Korps* in Kyllburg.

Main question: Preparation of the attack on the first day of the attack: artillery support; fire plan, artillery preparation or not. Missions of the 26th *V.G.D.* [*Volksgrenadier-Division*] in building bridgeheads over the Our and Clerf. Mission of the Panzer-Divisions.

Advance detachment.

Question of Bastogne: *Coup de main*? Or, in the event of strong opposition – should it be taken or bypassed and only observed or guarded. Later capture by rear elements.

b. Discussion in *Führerhauptquartier* [*Führer* headquarters] in Ziegenberg near Bad Nauheim.

Present: Commanders of the *Heeresgruppe*, the armies, corps and divisions. Hitler presented the plan of the offensive, its significance for the future conduct of the war and its political significance (Canada and the U.S. A.).

Plan of Operations in detail: Advance via Liège–Namur on Antwerp. *Schwerpunkt* [point of main effort] with the 6th *SS-Panzer-Armee*.

Encirclement of the 21st Army Group and its destruction. For this purpose the 5th *Panzer-Armee*: via Bastogne–Laroche to Namur–Dinant (later Antwerp), 6th *Armee* to Liège.

Extreme demands on officers and troops, since success of the offensive is decisive to the outcome of the war.

c. Discussion at *Panzer Lehr* by division commander on 13 December at Maeden east of Cochem (Mosel) regarding the Division's plan of attack in detail.

d. Discussion at 47th *Panzer Korps* on 15 December, 1600 hours, in Rickuscheid (north of Neuerburg). Brief final instructions and encouragement (all commanders of divisions, regiments and independent battalions present.)

e. Second discussion at *Panzer Lehr* on 15 December, 1900 hours, at Seffern command post (north of Bittburg [Bitburg]. Commanders of regiments and independent battalions present. Course of the attack (ultimate) and individual or special instructions (pioneers, the *Ala* [*Aufklärungs-Lehr Abteilung, Panzeraufklärungs-Lehr-Abteilung* 130 – the Division's reconnaissance battalion] advance-detachment, sequence in crossing the Our near Gemünd and elements [crossing at] Dasburg – (in 2nd *Panzer* [*Division*] sector)).

f. 19 December. Discussion with the Commander in Chief of the 47th *Panzer Korps* von Lüttwitz at the Division command post at Nieder Wampach. Question whether Bastogne is to be taken in the event that the *coup de main* fails and a second attack is also repulsed. I had the impression ' that Bastogne would have to be attacked employing all the available forces of the 47th [*Panzer*] *Korps* (*Panzer Lehr* [Division], 2nd *Panzer* [Division] and 26th *Volksgrenadier*-Division.) One cannot dare to bypass it and, judging from my experiences on 18 and 19 December, employment of weak *Korps* forces will prove unsuccessful, since Bastogne appears to be held by extremely good troops. In any case, however, Bastogne has to be taken by us soon, before our attack can be resumed past it to the west. Bastogne is vital for us as a transportation hub. Without Bastogne, the base for our continued attack is to narrow and that is a serious danger.

   After lengthy discussion in the course of which Lüttwitz endorsed my views my proposal – to attack with the concentrated forces of the entire 47th [*Panzer*] *Korps* – was rejected, probably under instructions from higher levels. There – as I heard – people were convinced that Bastogne was a "trivial problem", which should not be permitted to interfere with the rapid progress of the offensive.

g. Renewed discussion with General von Lüttwitz in the morning of 20 December along the same lines as that of 19 December and subsequent orders that elements of the Division (*Aufklärungs-Lehr-Abteilung* [130]) and *Pionier-Bataillon* [130]) be sent ahead toward St. Hubert. Discussion regarding the" Surrender Demand to the garrison of Bastogne" that had been conceived by von Manteuffel and Lüttwitz. [tr. Note- General von Manteuffel emphatically denied knowledge of or complicity in the transmission of what he considered to be a ridiculous and counter-productive surrender demand, since he knew that the German forces could not in any way carry out the threats contained therein.] The [Surrender Demand] was transmitted by a parliamentary (Adjutant of the *Panzer Lehr* [Division] on 12 December.

h. Discussion with General von Manteuffel on 22 December regarding the marche from Bastogne to St. Hubert near Morhet.

   The advance of *Panzer Lehr* was too slow. Sepp Dietrich was making very good progress. He was already before Liège. What it came down to was that *Panzer Lehr* was to take St. Hubert as quickly as possible and then advance via Rochefort to Dinant.

   Sufficient fuel arrived.

i. Discussion with *General* von Lüttwitz on 24 December, in the evening, by telephone.

   'The – 'courageous'- 2nd *Panzer-Division* is facing destruction east of Dinant. It has been cut off.

   Immediate help from *Panzer Lehr* is necessary. Mission: Thrust forward this very night on Humain

   and Buisonville [Buissonville](north of Rochefort) to fight free the supply road of the division'.

   I proposed to advance along the Lesse [River] via Ciergnon to Custinne, since this area (Ciergnon) was already held by my armoured patrols and [that way] we would get to the encircled elements of the [2nd *Panzer*] division more rapidly. [My proposal] was turned down.

k. [German practice does not include 'j' in such lists] On 27 December consultation with *General* von Lüttwitz at the Division command post in St. Hubert. The attack to the north across the Maas was, for the time being, to be discontinued. What it came down to was holding at the limit of the present advance and, first, to attack and capture Bastogne with all means. For this purpose strong elements of Sepp Dietrich's army [6th *Panzer Armee*] would be committed there. *Panzer-Grenadier-Regiment* 901 of the *Panzer Lehr* [*Division*] (reinforced with additional armour and one artillery *Abteilung*) would have to remain at Bastogne and take part in the attack. It would be attached to the 39th *Panzer Korps*.

l. Between 27 December and 5 January only trivial discussions took place, since the Division had only defensive assignments in the St. Hubert area and the [47th *Panzer*] *Korps* (and the [5th Panzer] Armee) were primarily concerned with the Bastogne area.

m. Discussion with *General* von Lüttwitz at the *Panzer Lehr* command post north of Lawacherie [Lavacherie] on 7 January 1945: The St. Hubert area was to be held to the last. Therefore '*Kampfkommandanten*' were to be appointed and made responsible for

   1 St Hubert,

2. Champlon (highway intersection),

3. Pirompre [Pirompré, Pironpré] (southeast of St. Hubert).

[note- The *Kampfkommandant* was responsible for the defense of the stipulated locality and was given special powers, and responsibilities. One of his special powers was that he could commandeer any troops coming within the boundaries of his jurisdiction.]

n. Since I, myself always commanded in the very front line, my discussions within the division were limited to individual instructions and orders on the spot with the commanders of those particular assault or defense groups.

11. Reasons for the initial success of the offensive.

a. Surprise of the enemy with respect to area and time of the attack.

b. Good training and spirit of attack of the *Panzer* troops, despite inadequate equipment and constant, nearly unbroken commitment in combat and despite the many failures and the miserable command at the top in recent years.

The German troops preferred attack over defense, so long as the attack received some sort of support from heavy weapons.

c. Absence of the enemy airforce in the first days.

Reasons for the failure of the offensive.

a. Incorrect initial commitment of the forces. The left (enveloping) wing should have been stronger than the right. The strength of the enemy was on the [German] right (at and south of Aachen) and that was where he also had mobile reserves available for a counter-stroke. One needs, however, to put one's strength where the enemy is weak, therefore on the German left wing.

The German command did not keep out any reserves to be committed during the course of the battle where the advance was going well.

b. Insufficient forces for the wide-ranging operation (Maas [River] and then Antwerp).

c. Lack of any adequate forces to protect the long southern flank (west flank)! The worst division in the entire *Heeresgruppe*, the 5th *Fallschirm Division* was employed for that purpose.

d. Employment of fought-out and miserably equipped divisions.

e. Amateurish [*dilettantenhafte*] preparation, particularly with respect to logistical support, which was totally inadequate and was, in part, based on the hope of capturing matériel. [The reason I included the bracketed *dilettantenhafte* is that, in the literature written by former German officers, the term *Dilettante*, and its adjective, is frequently employed specifically in reference to Hitler's personal intervention in matters requiring professional military training and experience, so that its use here is a pointed, if barely veiled, reference to the *Führer's* baneful influence.]

f. Miserable terrain for concentration and assembly areas. Miserably difficult road conditions were equally unfavorable for fighting troops and logistical support. During periods of favorable flying weather the bottlenecks in the Eifel and northern Luxembourg were catastrophic. Therefore little armour got into action and the attacks and defense could not be supported with sufficient ammunition.

g. The artillery preparation of the first attack across the Our [River] was wasted because the troops were too far away and were unable to take advantage of it. That led to delays resulting from the opposition on the St. Vieth [St. Vith] – Diekirch road and at the Clerf [River] sector. The result of these delays was failure to get to Bastogne in time to be able to take it by a *coup de main*.

h. Bastogne. One of the greatest mistakes was that, after the failure of the '*coup de main*', Bastogne was not captured by concentration of all [available] forces. If that had been done then the attack would have succeeded.

   Leaving that transportation center to the enemy made the basis for the advance to the Maas too narrow. Bastogne absorbed and later tied down so many forces that the offensive could no longer really be carried out. It posed a continual threat to the flank with the danger of being cut off if Bastogne was relieved and the enemy utilized this base for his attack to cut off the German salient.

12. Plans to advance to the south to roll up the U.S. 3rd Army.

    I never heard of any such.

13. When was it clear that attaining the original objectives was impossible?

    a. In general: I was skeptical from the beginning and felt that this offensive with its far-reaching objectives could not succeed. I do not say this just with the benefit of hindsight. I expressed this opinion at the time to my chief of staff and others who were quite close to me and whom I trusted absolutely; not, however, before my subordinate commanders, since I did not want to cripple their aggressive spirit. I persuaded myself that the attack would succeed in order to give my measures and orders the requisite conviction, even though I was convinced the offensive would fail. I viewed the offensive as the final convulsions ('*dernier cri*') of the collapsing *Wehrmacht* and its supreme command before its end, which had been clear to me since December 1942 (after the U.S. landing in North Africa). If, therefore, something could still be attempted, then it was this offensive.

b. When was it clear to me that the objective of the offensive was unattainable?

Within the context of the offensive in my own thinking (without regard to the general [answer] to 'a.' [above]), it was totally clear to me on 25 December that this was over, after the 6th *SS Panzer Army*, despite its outstanding [level of] equipment, could no longer advance; as the attacks of the 116th and 9th *Panzer* [*Divisionen*] failed; the main body of the 2nd *Panzer* [*Division*] was cut off and destroyed; and, finally, my own attack near Buisonville [Buissonville] and Humain failed, Bastogne could not be taken and the strong threat to the German southern flank by the U.S. 3rd Army became evident.

c. When did it become clear that the retreat was necessary?

Actually it was already clear on 25 December, since no additional German forces followed.

Quite definitely, however, on 2 January 1945. It seemed to me that the only correct [course] would be an immediate and rapid withdrawal to the Westwall out of the sack that was developing toward the west. After the attack on Bastogne everything continued to go wrong and the linkup of the garrison with the U.S. 3rd Army was complete. With that, the basis for the 5th and 6th German Armies was too narrow and the corridor to the elements that were fighting far to the west was too tight. The danger of being cut off became ever greater and it was only a question of time. The continued holding of the salient was insanity. In addition then came the effect of the enemy airforce on the narrow corridor and the exposure of the logistic support on the few, narrow roads. Any waiting and holding the salient meant daily additional losses to the troops in men and matériel that bore no relationship to the operational significance for the German command. This significance (utility) consisted in tying up strong enemy forces to prevent them from attacking at another location on the Western Front. (Anyhow, this was [what was] later given out by *O. K. W.* as the sense and purpose of the Ardennes Offensive.) As then stated, apparently, *O. K. W.* had never intended Antwerp [as an objective], but merely wanted to bind enemy forces and prevent them from attacking in the Saar region and near Aachen.

d. Discussions with higher levels of command in this situation.

On about 6 or 7 January with *General* von Lüttwitz in this regard (as described above under c.) This discussion, however, was senseless and pointless, since all orders came 'from above' and the viewpoint of the troops was never listened to or heeded, for we were always pessimists and 'negative' in our attitude.

14. Did the U.S. forces react more rapidly than expected and how?

Yes, they reacted essentially more rapidly that expected. Specifically:

1. The first surprise for the Germans was the rapid occupation and strong defense of Bastogne and the courageous steadfastness of the 101st Airborne. The rapid bringing up of armoured forces in the area east of Bastogne to offensive defense against the German attack (U.S. 9th Armoured Division).

2. The second surprise was the rapid reorientation of the U.S. 3rd Army against the German southern flank. By 21 December the situation on the flank was already such that the route of advance to St. Hubert near Remichampagne and Moircy could only be used under fire from enemy tanks or armoured cars.

15. Importance of the capture of Bastogne and orders to that effect?

Already in the preparatory discussions and the map exercise one of the primary questions was whether Bastogne really would have to be captured or not, [and, if so,] whether by *coup de main* or, if that failed, in a systematic attack (at that time general preference was for the *coup de main*). When the *coup de main* miscarried on 17/18 December, the question arose anew as to whether there should be a systematic attack or whether it should be bypassed and kept 'under observation'. My opinion at that time was that it should be attacked by concentrating all the available forces of the 47th [*Panzer*] *Korps*. That, however, did not take place. Isolated attacks were ordered that dissipated [the available forces]. One part of the troops had to attack, another portion hurried on to the west. These measures resulted in no attack in sufficient strength. Then it was attempted with the demand for surrender, whose text was written by von Manteuffel and Lüttwitz. [Von Manteuffel, however, states that: 'This was done without my approval. I regarded it as a pointless action, since in the event of the enemy's refusal to surrender, there was nothing we could do to enforce our wishes. Our artillery did not even have sufficient ammunition for a heavy bombardment of the town.'(Von Manteuffel, 'The Ardennes', in *The Fatal Decisions: Six Decisive Battle of the Second World War from the Viewpoint of the Vanquished*, Michael Joseph, London 1956, p.245). According to C. B. MacDonald, (p. 522), ' When General von Manteuffel learned of it he was furious, for, quite clearly he lacked sufficient artillery to make good on the threat.'] Finally the half of *Panzer Lehr* [*Division* that had been left at Bastogne] was taken away and the already-weakened 26th *Volksgrenadier-Division* was supposed to capture the fortress alone. Hence all local attacks failed. Thus precious time was lost. Bastogne was constantly reinforced and the relief army (U.S. 3rd Army) kept drawing nearer.

The rapid conquest of Bastogne was particularly vital for the following reasons:

1. The outstanding highway center was indispensable for the offensive to the Maas. Without Bastogne there were insufficient roads (north of Bastogne, in general, there was no road that side of Houffalize that was really good for use in winter, and most were not trafficable as the result of constant aerial attacks and destruction).

*General der Panzertruppen* Hasso von Manteuffel, with whom Bayerlein had a strained relationship. (Bundesarchiv 146-1976-143-21)

2. Bastogne was always an arrow in the flesh of the German troops. The corridor to the west was thus, without Bastogne, extremely constricted and the basis for carrying the attack onward to the west was too narrow.

3. Bastogne constituted a standing threat to the German attack. Strong forces therefore had to be left there to screen it that were then lacking from the force advancing toward the Maas.

4. In the event that the U.S. flank attack by the 3rd Army from the south could not be contained, then, after its relief by the U.S. 3rd Army, Bastogne would form the best jump-off point for the U.S. counter-offensive to cut off the German salient (or the German troops attacking to the west).

5. Bastogne was particularly indispensable as a logistical transportation nodal point and rear area center for the German logistical system after Houffalize mostly dropped out.

   A glance at the map suffices even for one without military training to recognize that Bastogne was indispensable for the offensive. The German command had not seen that or failed to act accordingly.

Orders for the attack on Bastogne:

1. 15 December. Basic order for the '*coup de main*' capture of Bastogne as part of the offensive.

2. 18 December. Order from the 47th *Panzer Korps* for the 'systematic' attack by *Panzer Lehr* [*Division*] against Bastogne on 19 December.

3. 19 December. New order from 47th [*Panzer*] *Korps* for the 'systematic' attack from the east by *Kampfgruppe Panzer Lehr* and a *Kampfgruppe* of the 26th *Volksgrenadier-Division*, as well as [an attack] from the southeast by a *Kampfgruppe* of *Panzer Lehr* on 20 December.

   (All attacks miscarried.)

   Then *Panzer Lehr* moved off to the west and left *Panzergrenadier-Regiment* 901 (with two *Panzer* companies and one artillery *Abteilung* [battalion]) near Bastogne for further attacks, which, however, are not known to me in detail.

16. Methods of collecting intelligence before the Ardennes Offensive.

    Intelligence was collected through:

    1. Ground reconnaissance.

    2. Secret agents,

       who moved back and forth across the border (front lines) (Luxembourgers or Germans).

3. Radio (listening) reconnaissance.

In any case, it was known to us that the U.S. 87th (?) Infantry Division was in the area of the 26th *Volksgrenadier-Division*; that it was in the process of 'refitting' after it had been employed near Aachen and suffered heavy losses there. [The U.S. 28th Infantry Division was in position facing the 26th *Volksgrenadier-Division* after losing over 5000 men in the bloody Hürtgen Forest fighting.(MacDonald, pp. 83–4.)] Nothing was known regarding reserves (armoured divisions) behind the front.

The extent to which civilians (Luxembourgers, Belgians) were used to gain intelligence I do not know. During the offensive a Belgian gave me very good, clear and even knowledgeable information in Magret [Magéret](east of Bastogne) regarding the movement and concentration of a combat command of the U.S. 9th Armoured Division. [*General* Bayerlein might have been less enthusiastic about the information provided by that 'helpful' Belgian if he had known all the facts. Below Bayerlein says that the Belgian told him of a U.S. task force with 50 Sherman tanks, 25 guns and another 40–50 armored vehicles and that there was a U.S. general in Magéret. Based on that information, Bayerlein, who had only a weak *Kampfgruppe* and the *Panzeraufklärungs-Lehr-Abteilung* 130, but still no artillery, which was, as usual, delayed, decided to wait until 0530 hours for *Kampfgruppe Panzergrenadier-Lehr-Regiment* 902 to close up. According to Cole's official history, *The Ardennes, Battle of the Bulge*, the force in question was actually 'Team Cherry', the leading team in CCB (Combat Command B) of the U.S. 10th Armored Division column. According to Charles B. MacDonald, in *A Time for Trumpets*, p. 290, 'Team Cherry had, in fact, not forty tanks – as the Belgian had told Bayerlein – but only seventeen mediums, ten lights, and no artillery ... [Nor, for that matter, was there an American General in Magéret]. The word of the American force made Bayerlein cautious and delayed even a probe toward Bastogne for six hours and a genuine attack considerably longer than that'. That was at a time when every hour's delay was precious, as the American 101st Airborne and 10th Armored Divisions desperately sought to get to Bastogne before Bayerlein's *Panzer Lehr Division* and the 26th *Volksgrenadier-Division*.]

17. Effect of the U.S. Air Force on the course of the offensive?

The U.S. Air Force acted primarily against the logistical traffic in the Eifel, then in North Luxembourg and Belgium, particularly the numerous bottlenecks, difficult roads and passages through built-up areas. The attacks were particularly concentrated on the area around Bastogne. The German logistical support was thereby seriously affected. Losses (especially in fuel, motor-lorries and ammunition) were extremely serious.

The front-troops were conspicuously rarely attacked in comparison with previous commitments. The air-directed (artillery spotter planes) artillery was – as always – particularly unpleasant.

In summary, I can say:

The U.S. Air Force did not have any essential influence on the failure of the offensive.

The main share [of the responsibility of the failure of the offensive] was due to the U.S. ground troops, particularly the courageous and tough defense of Bastogne, later (but to a far lesser degree, [the defense] of Rochefort) the strong defense before the front of the 6th *SS-[Panzer] Armee* and the fresh engagement of the *Kampfgruppe* of the 2nd *Panzer-Division*. [' *... und das frische Zufassen gegen die Kampfgruppe der 2. Panzer-Division.*' C. B. MacDonald, (*A Time for Trumpets*, p. 500) notes, regarding the action at Noville, north of Bastogne, in which Team Desobry, one of the teams of the 10th Armored Division's CCB, suffered heavy losses, that: 'Team Desobry had nevertheless imposed telling losses on the 2d Panzer-Division, at least thirty tanks and perhaps as many as six hundred to eight hundred men. Ironically, while fighting in defense of Bastogne, Team Desobry had made its greatest contribution in delaying the Panzer-Division's drive for the Meuse River by at least forty-eight hours – two days that were to have a telling effect.']

An extremely substantial share [of the responsibility] goes to the U.S. command, which, with great flexibility, rapidly made the correct tactical decisions and, just as quickly, took all countermeasures and carried them out with great energy and skill.

18. Description of the movements and actions of *Panzer Lehr* to the end of the offensive.

(Nine sketch maps)

Overview of the entire course of the operation, 16 – 26 December.

(Before the fighting retreat)

(For fighting retreat, [see] Map 8).

Map 1

(16 December)

(Map 2) Attack of the 26th *Volksgrenadier-Division* in the front in the Eisenbach – Gemünd sector.

Mission: Building bridgeheads, first over the Our [River] near Gemünd (bridges) in the line Hosingen – Wahlhausen, then over the Clerf (Clerve) [River] near Drauffeld [Drauffelt].

After building the bridgeheads: Attack of *Panzer Lehr* through the Drauffeld bridgehead against Bastogne.

Support of the first attack of the 26th *Volksgrenadier-Division* and [*Panzer*] *Lehr* and additional reinforcing artillery and *Nebelwerfer* of the *Korps*. The strong employment of artillery, however, amounted to nought because it could not be utilized by the infantry of the 26th *Volksgrenadier-Division*, which was too far distant. Building of bridges by the *Pionier Lehr Bataillon* [*Panzer-Pionier Bataillon* 130] of the *Panzer Lehr Division*.

In the event: Wahlhausen was captured. The attack on Hosingen failed.

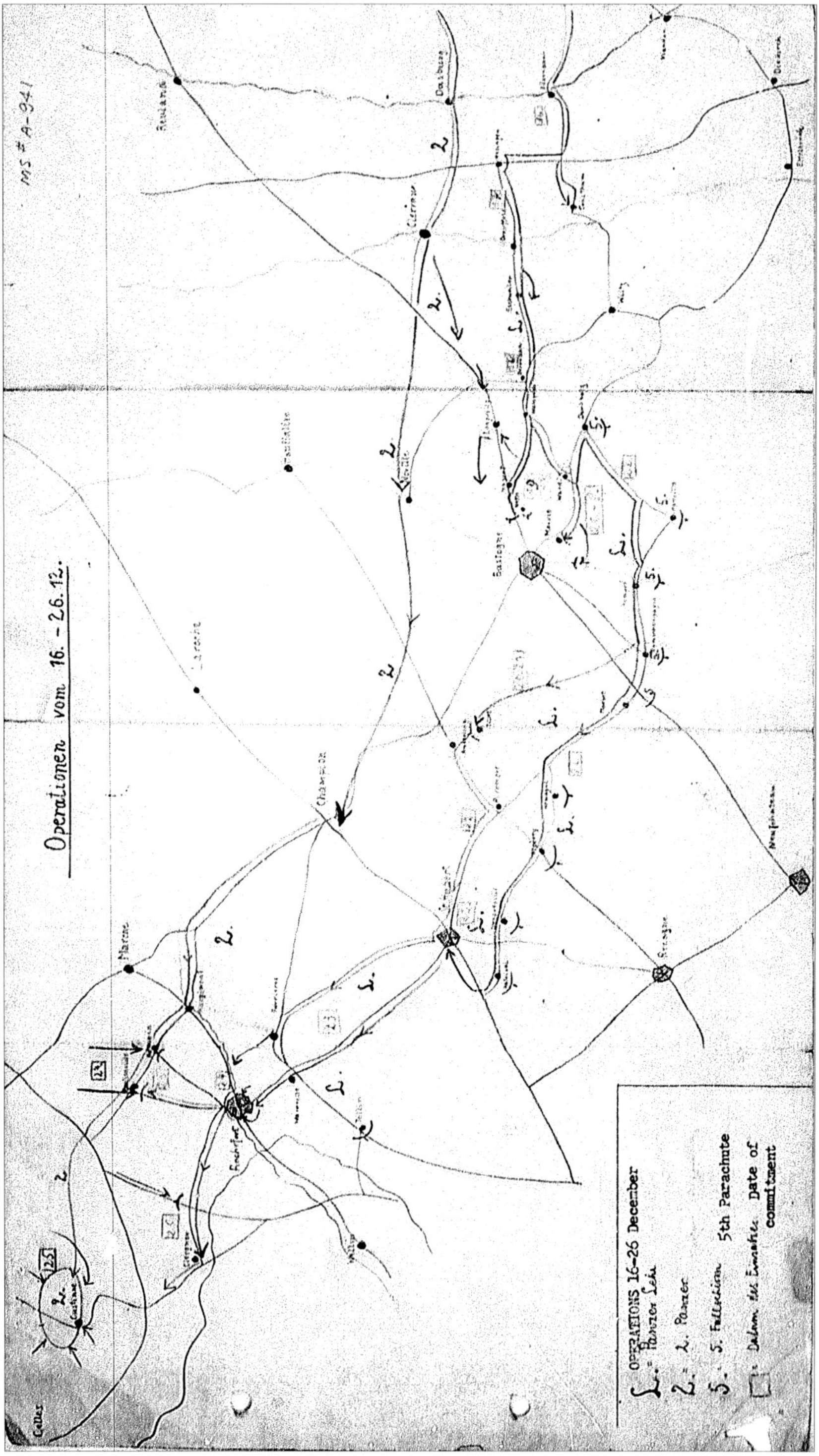


A-941 Map 1: Operations 16-26 December 1944

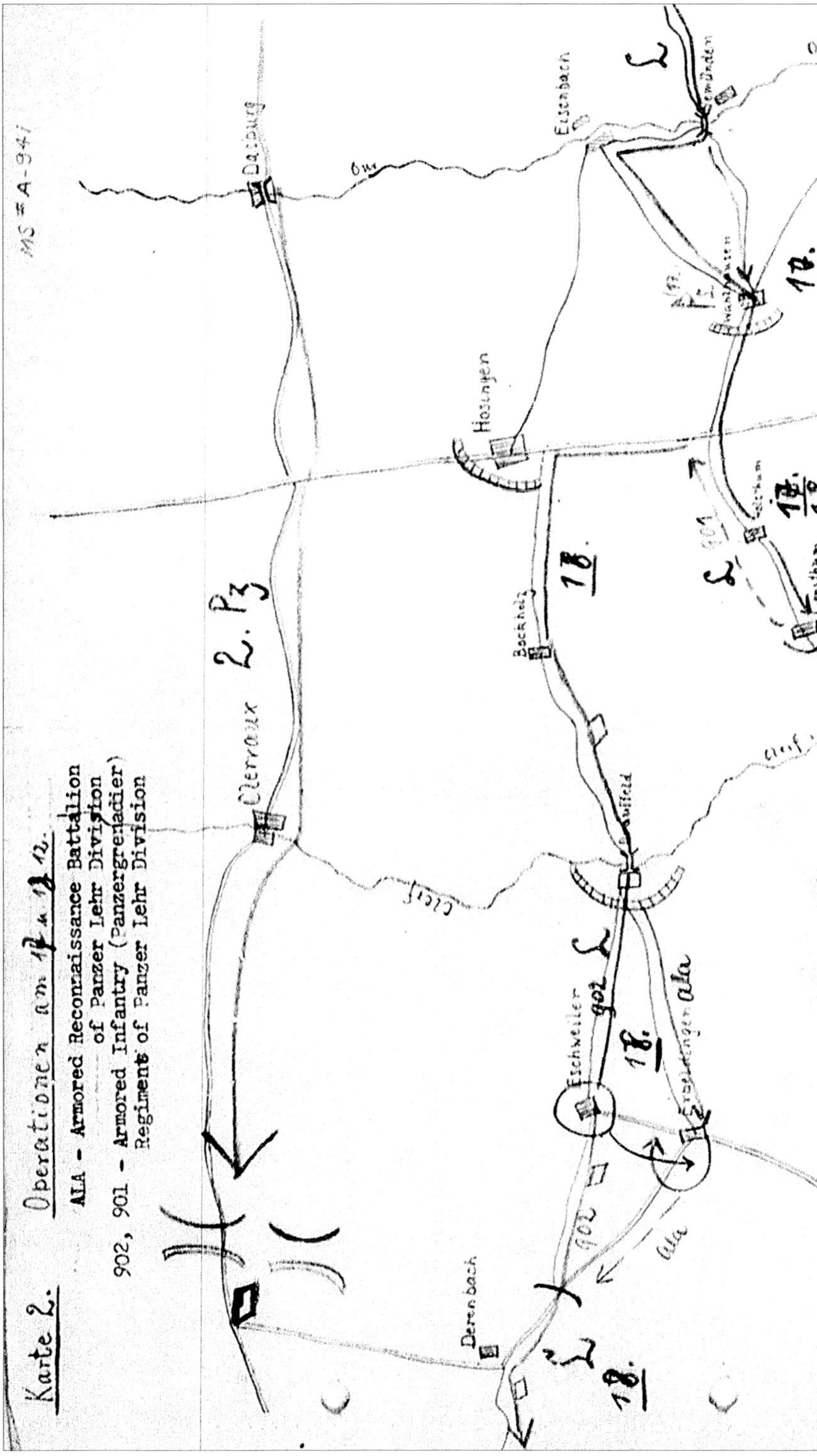


A-941 Map 2: Operations 17-18 December 1944

Elements of the *Panzer Lehr Division* were brought up and the *Ala* ([Panzer-] *Aufklärungs-Lehr-Abteilung* [130]) already had to be committed in support of the 26th *Volksgrenadier-Division*. It was committed, reinforced with one *Panzer* company and one battery of 10.5 cm guns, at the Wahlhausen Kolonie and at Holzthum.

During the night of 16/17 [December] *Panzergrenadier-*[*Lehr-*] *Regiment* 901 was brought up since the attack on Consthum failed and was committed there. *Panzeraufklärungs-Lehr-Abteilung* 130 was withdrawn so that it could be committed in the advance on Bastogne for its capture in a *coup de main*. *Panzergrenadier-Lehr-Regiment* 902 was brought forward in the sector of the 2nd *Panzer* [*Division*] over the bridges at Dasburg.

(17 December)

Fighting of *Kampfgruppe Panzer Grenadier Regiment* 901 near Consthum, which was taken in the afternoon. Attack of *Panzeraufklärungs-Lehr-Abteilung* 130 on Erpeldingen,

(Map 2)

*Kampfgruppe Panzer Grenadier Regiment* 902 via Drauffeld (on the Clerf [River. Drauffelt was the site of a bridge that was captured intact.] to Eschweiler, Derenbach, Nieder Wampach. In Eschweiler there was resistance, which was quickly broken. Erpeldingen was taken by *Panzeraufklärungs-Lehr-Abteilung* 130.

During the further advance the 2nd *Panzer Division* (on the right) was engaged in heavy armoured combat north of Derenbach. Four kilometres distant, *Kampfgruppe Panzergrenadier-Regiment* 902 (reinforced with one *Panzer* company and one battery (10.5 cm)) passed by, headed west toward Bastogne, its guns directed to the north, without being noticed. The Division Commander was at the point. At 2000 hours Nieder Wampach was reached without opposition.

(Map 3)

Decisions were necessary there regarding the advance on Bastogne: Either via Benonchamps Magret [Magéret] or via Wardin, Marvie.

Since reconnaissance indicated that the route via Benonchamps was usable, that was the direction chosen.

2300 hours, Benonchamps, no opposition.

Magret [Magéret] 2400 hours. The place appeared unoccupied (but has, however, actually held by U.S. Troops). A Belgian reported [see editor's note above] that, two hours earlier, a U.S. task force of 50 tanks (Sherman), 25 guns (cannon, self-propelled mounts) and an additional 40–50 armoured vehicles had passed through Magret [Magéret] headed east to Longwilly [Longvilly]. There was [said to be] a U.S. general in Magret [Magéret].

Thereupon the road to Longwilly was blocked and held with tanks. Mines were laid. There was ongoing motor-vehicle traffic headed east from Bastogne. The vehicles were intercepted. That developed into a night-fight in and around Magret [Magéret]. Magret {Magéret] was mopped up by 0300 hours.

(18 December)

With that the presence of German troops near Bastogne became evident and the surprise assault on the city moot. Nevertheless, it was decided that *Kampfgruppe Panzergrenadier-Lehr-Regiment* 902 would attack in the faint light of early dawn of 18 December.

[At] 0600 hours [the attack was] launched. Resistance near Neffe. Neffe was taken by 0900 hours. The attack carried to 2 kilometres east of Bastogne. There the attack was halted in the face of strong enemy resistance.

By noon the enemy received reinforcement. [The enemy began] envelopment via Bizory and from Longwilly, as well as in the south via Wardin – Marzy [presumably Marvie]– Bras, which was exceedingly unpleasant for *Panzergrenadier-Lehr-Regiment* 902. The only narrow corridor still open to the rear was through Benonchamps.

In the meantime artillery and tank destroyers [*Panzerjäger*] had closed up to *Kampfgruppe Panzergrenadier-Lehr-Regiment* 901. This *Kampfgruppe* [now] attacked north from the Benonchamps area against the hills southwest of Longwilly. *Panzeraufklärungs-Lehr-Abteilung* 130 screened to the south toward Wardin – Bras. The attack by *Kampfgruppe Panzergrenadier-Lehr-Regiment* 901 was successful. The Combat Command of the U.S. 9th Armored Division at Longwilly Longvilly was[with respect to] matériel, almost completely destroyed. Fourteen armoured cars, 23 tanks (Sherman), 15 self-propelled guns, 30 jeeps and 25 lorries were captured, undamaged. All other vehicles and armour were destroyed.

The destruction of this [Combat Command] can be attributed to the fortunate circumstance that, at the same time, a *Kampfgruppe* of the 2nd *Panzer Division* joined the battle from the east, and the artillery of the 26th *Volksgrenadier-Division* could also be employed. This success eliminated the danger of envelopment of *Kampfgruppe Panzergrenadier-Lehr-Regiment* 902.

(19 December)

In the morning *Kampfgruppe Panzergrenadier-Lehr-Regiment* 902 made a new attack on Bastogne from Neffe, which miscarried. An attack by one of the infantry regiments of the 26th *Volksgrenadier-Division* that was attached to the *PanzerLehr Division* via Longwilly – village south of Michamps succeeded and thrust forward as far as Bizory, which, however, could not be taken.

The enemy artillery fire steadily increased.

*Kampfgruppe Panzeraufklärungs-Lehr-Abteilung* 130 took Wardin.

*Kampfgruppe Panzergrenadier-Lehr-Regiment* 902 was committed via Bras against Marvie.

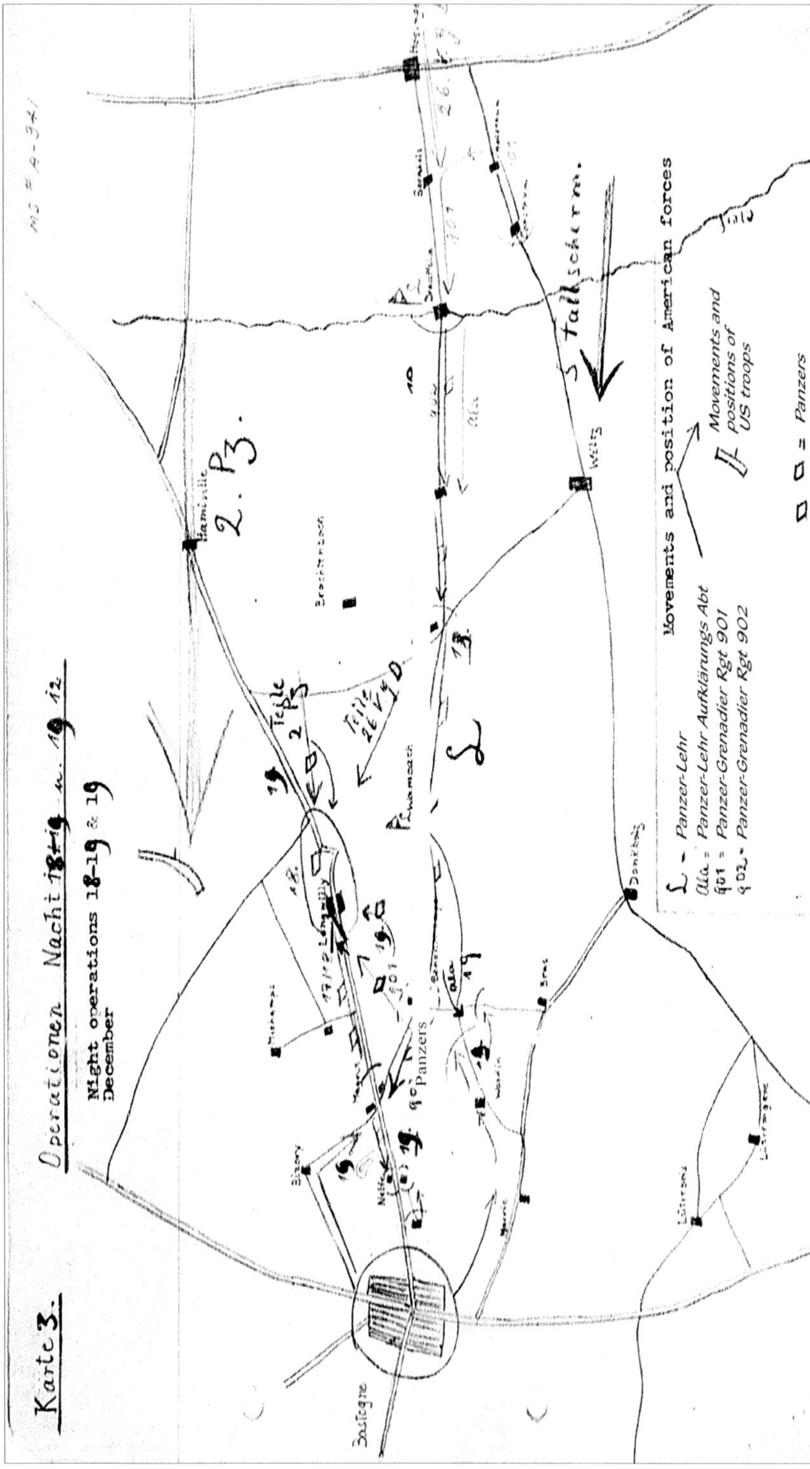


A-941 Map 3: Operations during the night of 18-19 and 19 December 1944

(20 December)

(Map 4)

In the morning a new attack by *Kampfgruppe Panzergrenadier-Lehr-Regiment* 902 and one regiment of the 26th *Volksgrenadier-Division* from the east on Bastogne failed with heavy losses.

An attack by *Kampfgruppe Panzergrenadier-Lehr-Regiment* 901 on Marvie miscarried. On the other hand, Lutrebois was captured and the main road west of [Lutrebois] was reached and blocked.

Elements of the 26th *Volksgrenadier-Division*. sent to the area of and north of Libret to cut off Bastogne on the west. *Panzeraufklärungs-Lehr-Abteilung* 130 and pioneer battalion [*Panzer-Pionier-Bataillon* 130] of the *Panzer Lehr Division* were set in march via Libret for the continued advance to the West in the Amberloup area.

(21 December)

The 26th *Volksgrenadier-Division* fought near Bizory to no avail. A last attack of *Kampfgruppe Panzergrenadier-Lehr-Regiment* 902 via Neffe also miscarried. The regiment was withdrawn in the evening – relieved by elements of the 26th *V.G.D.* – and set in march via Donkholz [Doncols]to the west.

(22 December)

*Kampfgruppe Panzergrenadier-Lehr-Regiment* 902 advanced via Remichampagne – Morhet.

(Map 5)

*Kampfgruppe Panzergrenadier-Lehr-Regiment* 901 (with two *Panzer* companies and one artillery *Abteilung*) remained committed southeast of Bastogne and was attached to the 26th *V.G.D.*.

The advance of *Kampfgruppe Panzergrenadier-Lehr-Regiment* 902 was disturbed by enemy tank fire from the south near Remichampagne and Morhet. Resistance near Remagne, which was quickly broken, gave way to a smooth advance via Moircy – Vesqueville – Hatrival to St. Hubert, which was occupied at 0200 hours on 23 December without resistance. *Panzeraufklärungs-Lehr-Abteilung* 130 and *Panzer-Pionier-Bataillon* 130 fought near Gerimont and Tillet with good success. Several enemy supply columns were captured with numerous lorries and jeeps.

(23 December)

1600 hours, advance continued from St. Hubert to Rochefort.

(Map 6)

*Kampfgruppe Panzeraufklärungs-Lehr-Abteilung* 130 via Maburg [Masbourg] – Forriers [Fourrieres].

*Kampfgruppe Panzergrenadier-Lehr-Regiment* 902 via Grapont [Grupont] [–] Wavreille[s].

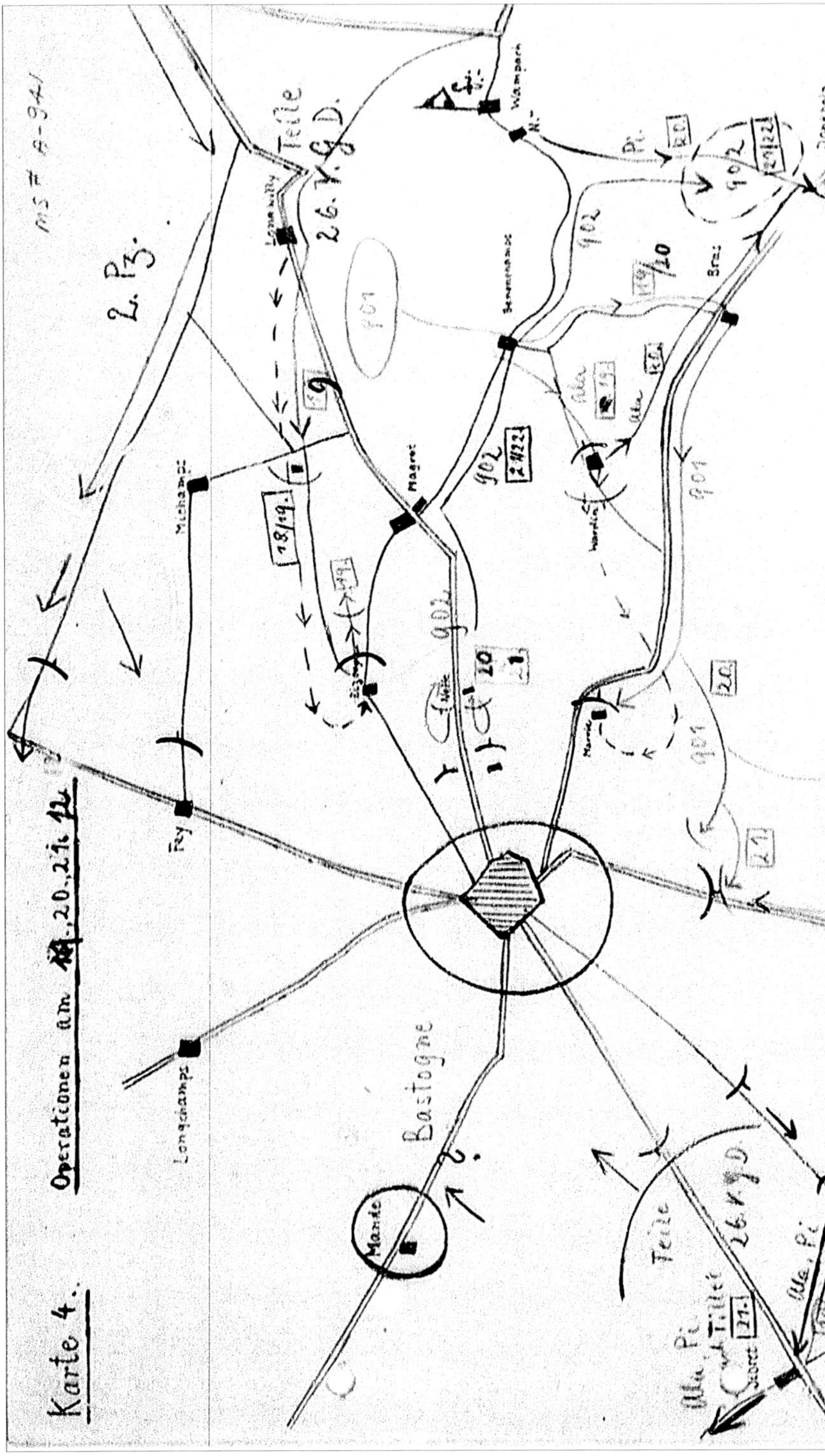


A-941 Map 4: Operations 19-21 December 1944

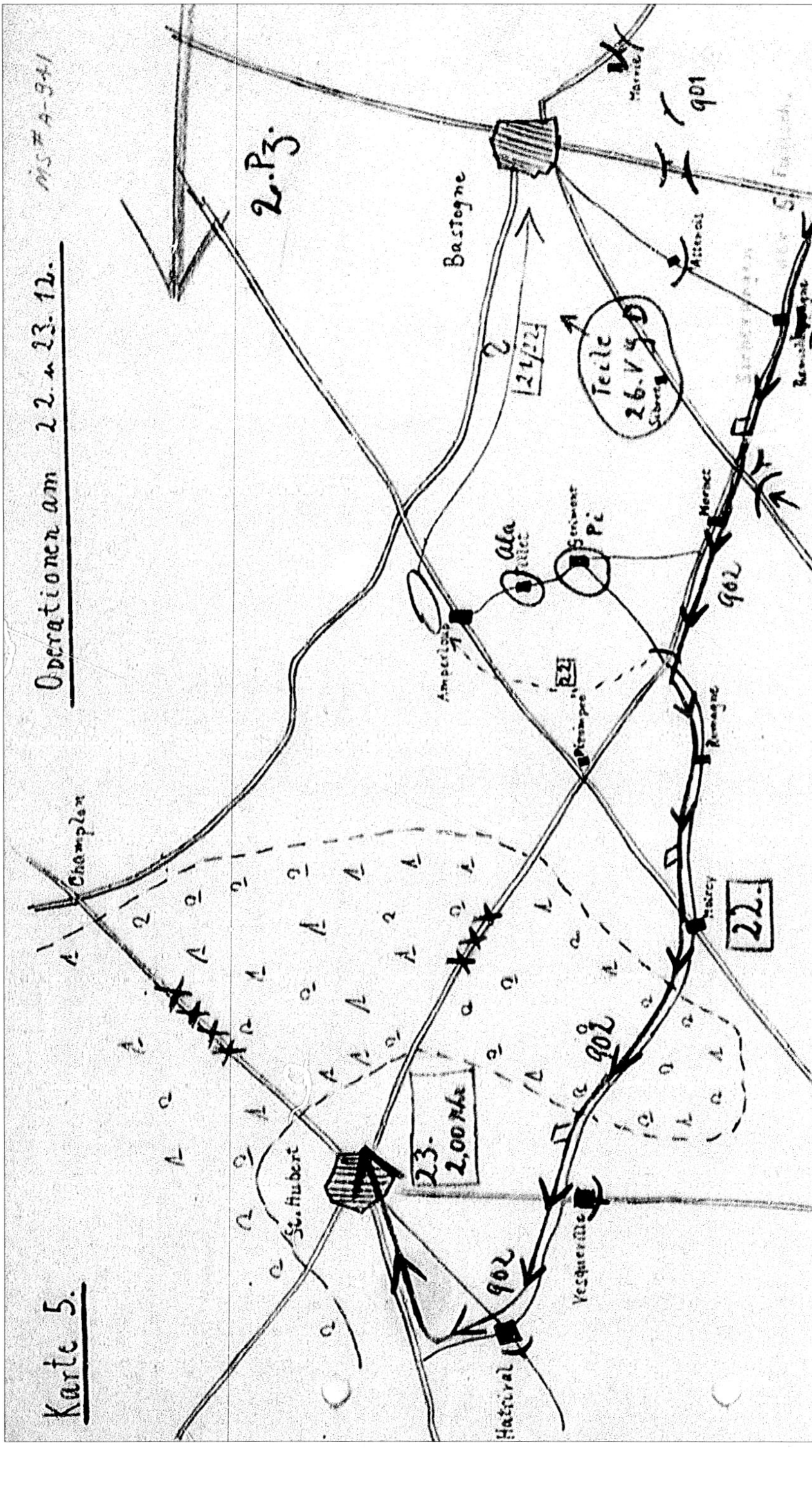


A-941 Map 5: Operations 22-23 December 1944

Patrols [from *Kampfgrupppe Panzeraufklärungs-Lehr-Abteilung* 130] reported Rochefort free of enemy at 1800 hours (that was not consistent [with the facts]).

The attack on Rochefort from the south ground to a halt at a roadblock. At the same time strong sudden artillery concentrations from the hills on both sides of the roadblock caused German losses. At about midnight *Kampfgruppe Panzergrenadier-Lehr-Regiment* 902 broke into the town with an enveloping attack.

Strong resistance in the center of the town. Substantial German losses.

(24 December)

The fighting in the inner-town lasted into the afternoon. Then the town was mopped up. The northern bridge was destroyed. A ford was mined, but a good road-bridge remained at the east edge, usable for heavy loads. It was immediately occupied. A bridgehead was built. The enemy was not pursued to the north as a result of exhaustion of and heavy losses among the German assault troops.

In the evening came a [47th *Panzer*] *Korps* order: Attack Humain and Buisonville [Buissonville] to free the encircled *Kampfgruppe* of the 2nd *Panzer Division* by clearing its supply route.

2200 hours, attack:

With one Kampfgruppe of *Kampfgruppe Panzergrenadier-Lehr-Regiment* 902 on Humain,

*Kampfgruppe Panzeraufklärungs-Lehr-Abteilung* 130 on Buisonville [Buissonville].

Another weak *Kampfgruppe of Kampfgruppe Panzergrenadier-Lehr-Regiment* 902 advanced on Ciergnon.

[note-The *Kampfgruppe* terminology needs clarification. *Kampfgruppe Panzergrenadier-Lehr-Regiment* 902 refers to the reinforced regimental combat team of *Panzergrenadier-Lehr-Regiment* 902 and attached armour, II./*Panzer-Lehr-Regiment 130 (-)* (2 *Panther* companies); artillery, I./*Panzer-Artillerie-Regiment* 130; tank destroyers, *Panzerjäger-Lehr-Abteilung* 130 and *Divisionsbegleit* [*begleit*=escort]-*Kompanie*. In order to relate Bayerlein's account to Ritgen's history of the *Panzer Lehr Division* and other German accounts, one must know that *Kampfgruppe Panzergrenadier-Lehr-Regiment* 902, which Bayerlein regularly refers to as either *Kampfgruppe* 902, or just, 902, was also commonly referred to as *Kampfgruppe von Poschinger*, after its current commander, *Oberstleutnant Ritter* von Poschinger. That *Kampfgruppe* could, in turn, create smaller *Kampfgruppen* for specific tasks out of its own forces. What Bayerlein refers to as *Kampfgruppe* 901 was also referred to as *Kampfgruppe von Hauser*, for its commander, *Oberst Freiherr* von Hauser, and, in similar fashion, what Bayerlein refers to as *Kampfgruppe Ala* [*Panzeraufklärungs-Lehr-Abteilung* 130] was also referred to as *Kampfgruppe*

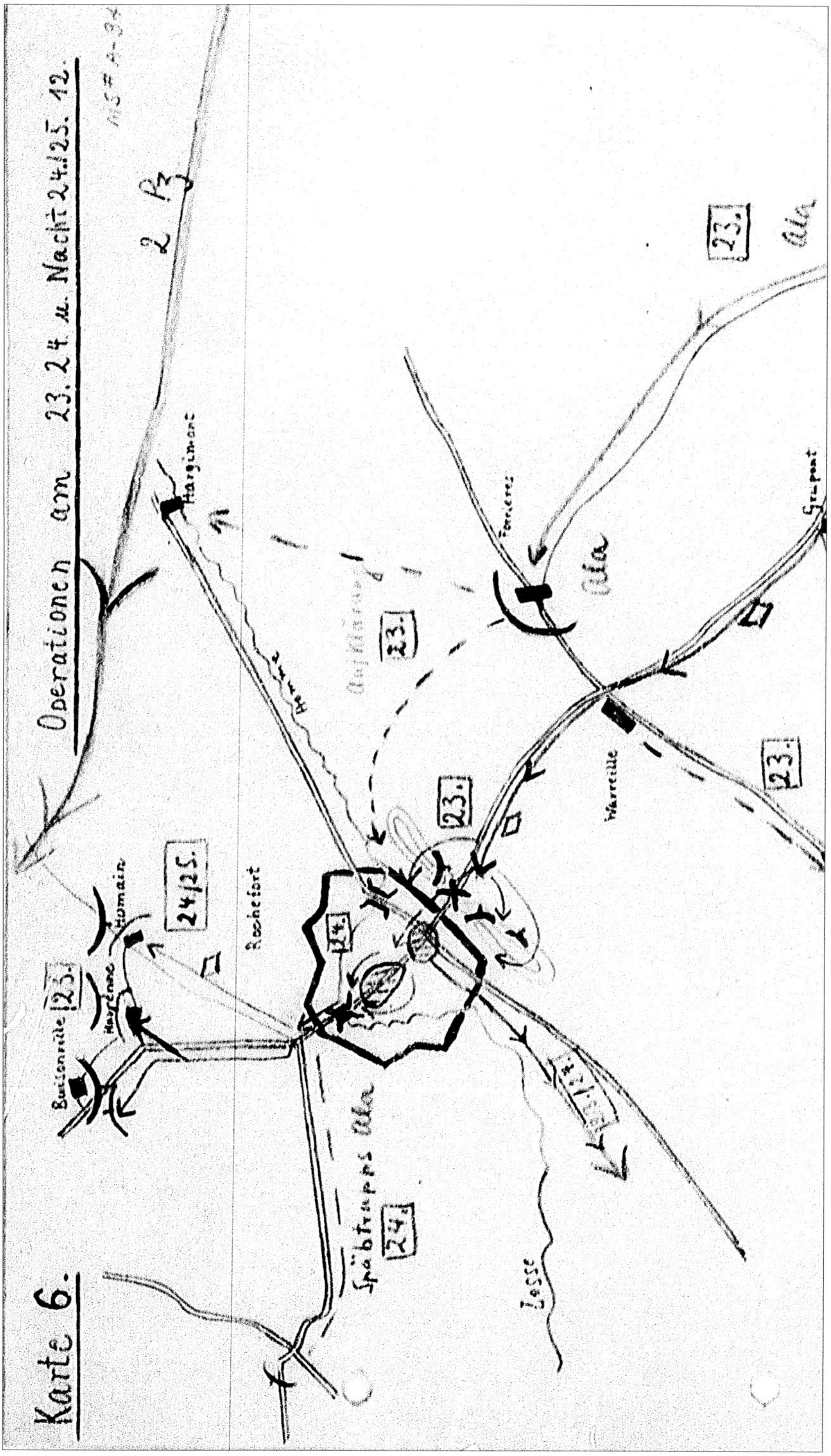


A-941 Map 6: Operations 23-24 and night of 24-25 December 1944

*von Fallois,* after *Major* von Fallois, its commander. Standard German practice was to name *Kampfgruppen* after their commanding officer.]

Flank security:

by [Heeres] *Flak Abteilung* [311] near Remagne and Moircy,

by *Panzer-Pionier- Bataillon* 130 south of St. Hubert near Vesquville [Vesqueville] and Hatrival,

by elements of *Kampfgruppe Panzergrenadier-Lehr-Regiment* 902 near Tellin.

Reconnaissance by *Panzeraufklärungs-Lehr-Abteilung* 130 in the area east of Beauraing.

(25 December)

0900 hours Humain taken by *Kampfgruppe Panzergrenadier-Lehr-Regiment* 902,

(Map 6)

Havrenne was captured by *Panzeraufklärungs-Lehr-Abteilung* 130. The attack on Buisonville [Buissonville] was unsuccessful.

Air attack at about noon and heavy, air-directed artillery fire against *Panzeraufklärungs-Lehr-Abteilung* 130 south of Buisonville [Buissonville].

The evening mission was evacuation of Humain. *Panzeraufklärungs-Lehr-Abteilung* 130 fell back from Havrenne and south of Buisonville [Buissonville] after substantial losses at the Rochefort bridgehead position.

Elements of the 2nd *Panzer Division* advanced via Ciergnon toward Custinne, but were unable to free the encircled *Kampfgruppe*. That was nearly totally wiped out. Only a few people escaped. [According to Ritgen's history of the *Panzer Lehr Division*, the immobilized *Kampfgruppe* of the 2nd *Panzer-Division* that was encircled near Celles and Foy-Notre-Dame had to leave behind all of its matériel, but 600 men reached German lines in Rochefort the night after the failed relief attacks by *Kampfgruppen* of the 9th and 2nd *Panzer Divisionen* on 26 December.]

Night of 25/26 [December]. Defensive position around Rochefort – Ciergnon.

With that the offensive was concluded.

(26 December)

Defensive fighting on the entire Division front and on the flanks near Tellin, Hatrival, Moircy and Remagne.

(Map 6)

Defensive fighting on the entire front.

(Map 7)

For the first time English forces were identified near Tellin.

(28 – 29 [December])

Defensive fighting. *Schwerpunkt* near Remagne and Moircy. A *Kampfgruppe* of *Kampfgruppe Panzergrenadier-Lehr-Regiment*] 902 was committed there. (*Kampfgruppe Panzergrenadier-Lehr-Regiment* 901 was still tied up at Bastogne.)

(30 December)

Remagne lost; the rest of the front held.

(31 December)

Moircy lost. Successful defence near Vesqueville and Hatrival.

(Map 7)

Turned over the Tellin sector to the 2nd *Panzer Division.*

*Organization of the Panzer Lehr Division* for defense:

Avenne [Awenne]–Arville sector :

*Panzeraufklärungs-Lehr-Abteilung* 130,

St. Hubert sector: (Vesqueville, Hatrival):

*Kampfgruppe Panzergrenadier-Regiment* 902 (with tank-destroyers [*Panzer-Jägern*],

Forest sector (northeast of Vesqueville):

Pioneer battalion [*Panzer-Pionier-Bataillon* 130],

Pirompré [Pironpré] sector: *Kampfgruppe Panzergrenadier-Lehr-Regiment* 901 (with tanks).

Adjoining on left: 2nd *Panzer Division.*

(1 – 6 January)

Successful defense near St. Hubert. Heavy defensive fighting at the Pirompré [Pironpré] road junction, which always remained in German hands.

(Map 7)

U.S. penetration into the forest between Bonnerne [Bonnerue] and Vesqueville. Heavy forest fighting.

(7 January)

*Kampfkommandanten* were appointed for St. Hubert (*Kampfgruppe Panzergrenadier-Lehr-Regiment* 902), Champlon (Panzeraufklärungs-Lehr-Abteilung 130), Pirompré [Pironpré] (*Kampfgruppe Panzergrenadier-Lehr-Regiment* 902). These places were to be held to the last.

(8–9 January)

Successful defense near St. Hubert and Pirompré. [Pironpré]

(10 January)

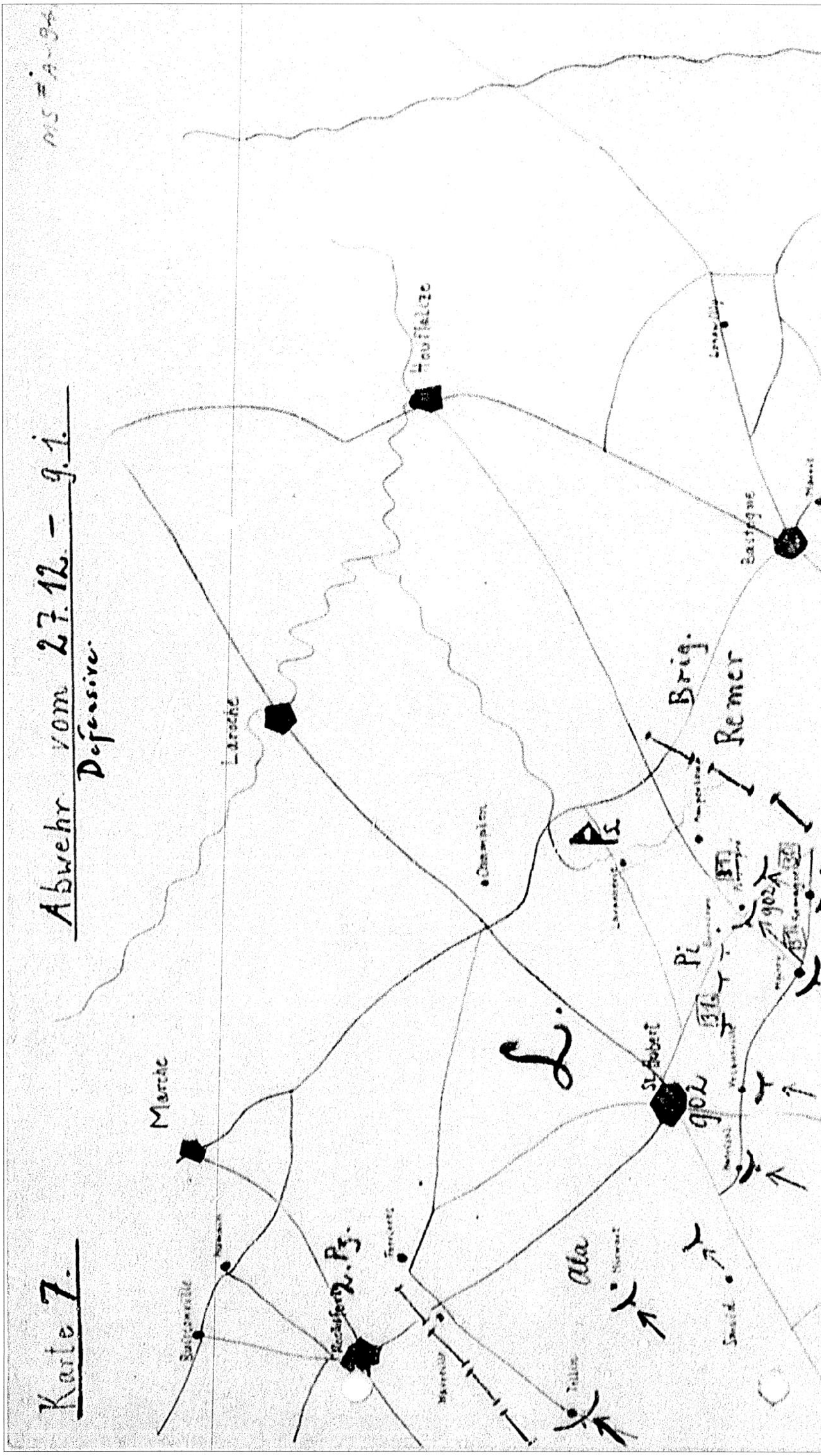


A-941 Map 7: Defensive operations 27 December 1944-9 January 1945

Bonnerne [Bonnerue} lost, Pirompré [Pironpré] held.

Remnants of *Panzergrenadier-Lehr-Regiment* 901 (about 150 men, 5 tanks and one battery [of artillery]) returned from the Bastogne area and, after an absence of 18 days, were re-attached to the Division.

(11 January)

Counterattack on Bonnerne [Bonnerue], which was recaptured (80 prisoners).

(Map 8)

(11/12 January)

Fall back to the line Amberloup – Lavacherie – Champlon.

(12/13 January)

Fall back to the line Hives – Erneuville – Cens.

(13/14 January)

Fall back to the line Nadrin – Nisramont – Warempage.

(14/15 January)

Area Aschouffe [Achouffe] – Bonnerne [Bonnerue] (west of Houffalize) – Mapombrè [Mabompré]. *Kampfkommandant* appointed in Houffalize to defend the town 'to the last'.

Collapse of the front of the 116th *Panzer-Division* north of Houffalize.

(15 January)

Strong U.S. attack via Mapombrè [Mabompré] on Houffalize destroyed all German forces southwest of the city and broke into the city.

(15/16 January)

Fall back in the line Cetturu – Tavigny – Buret. Adjoining on the left was the 26th *Volksgrenadier-Division*, on the right, the remnants of the 116th *Panzer Division.*

(16/17 January)

Fall back to the Belgium – Luxemburg border position.

(17 January)

Hold the border position.

(18 January)

Hold the border position.

*Panzergrenadier-Lehr-Regiment* 902 was withdrawn for commitment in the Diekirch sector.

(18/19 January)

Fall back to the Biwisch – Asselborn area.

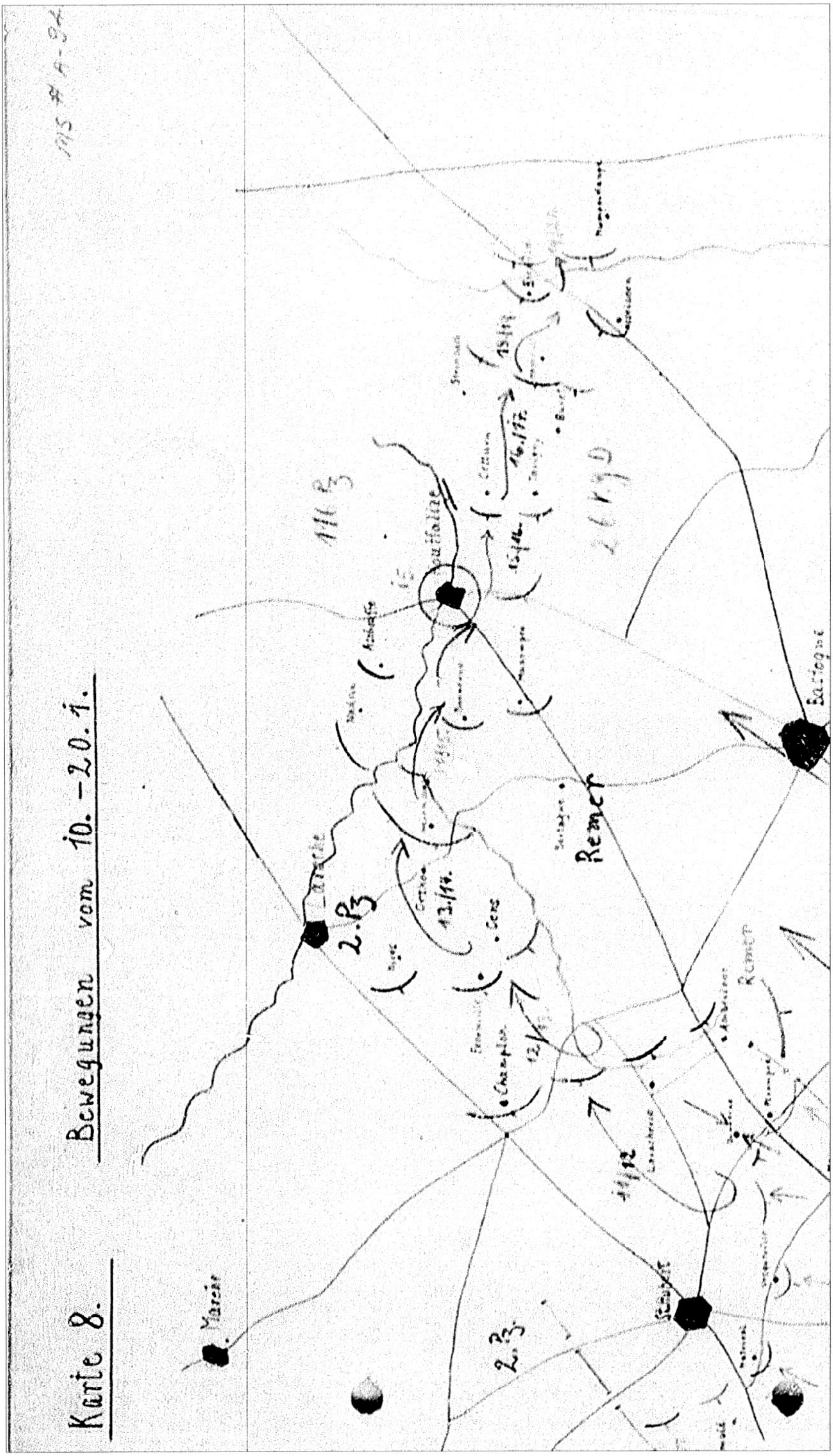


A-941 Map 8: Movements 10-20 January 1945

(19 January)

Hold this line.

(19/20 [January])

Fall back to the Clerf sector near Humperdange [Hupperdange].

(Map 9)

*Kampfgruppe Panzergrenadier-Lehr-Regiment* 902 defended south of Hoscheid against strong enemy attacks.

(20/21 January)

Withdraw all elements of the Division to new employment west of Vianden.

(21 January)

Hoscheid lost after hard fighting.

(22–24 January)

Commitment of *Kampfgruppen Panzergrenadier-Lehr-Regimenter* 901 and 902 north of Hoscheid – Wahlhausen.

(25/26 January and 26/27 January)

Withdrawal of the Division to the area south of Neuerburg for reconstitution.

Combat strength on 27 January:

400 *Panzergrenadiere*

Five tanks, seven *Panzerjäger* [tank destroyers] ready for service. Nine guns (artillery and *Flak*). Logistics troops, columns, *Feldersatz-Bataillon* [field-replacement battalion], tank crews without tanks amounting to a total of about 5000 men.

Tactics employed.

a. Attack: Rapid, bold advances with small *Kampfgruppen*. *'Panzerkampftrupp'* – tactics. (Several tanks and riflemen closely linked). In attacks against a weaker enemy: tanks forward.

Every attack otherwise escorted and protected by armour. Take advantage of the superior range of the main-gun (*Panzer V* [*Panther*]). (This gave particularly good results in the fight for Longwilly [Longvilly] on 18 December).

Almost all attacks were in the evening- or morning- twilight. [There were] also night-attacks along roads and byways. No use of *S.P.W.* [*Schützenpanzerwagen*, lightly armoured half-track troop carriers] in 'systematic' attacks. The backbone of the defensive front was the tank or tank-destroyer. The *Grenadiere* grouped themselves around these. ((The best defensive success near Pirompré [Pironpré], southeast of St. Hubert, was by tanks that were well camouflaged in wood piles and employed as armoured antitank guns or armoured machine guns. The U.S. attack near Pirompré [Pironpré] was held off for twelve days with limited [German] forces).

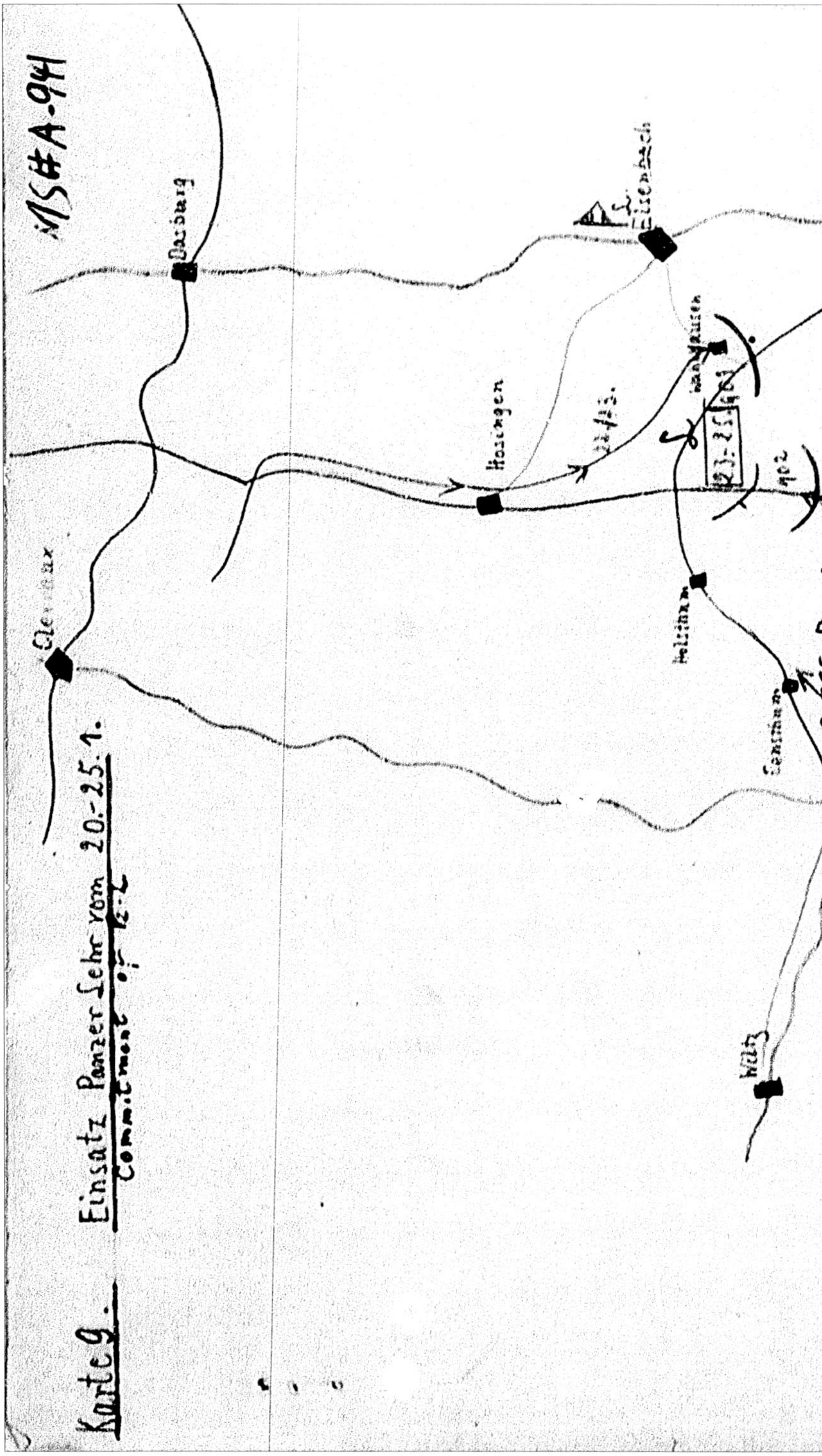


A-941 Map 9: Actions of *Panzer-Lehr* 20-25 January 1945

Small reserves for immediate counterattacks against enemy penetrations.

Utilization of the superior range of the tank-main-guns.

(Special:)

Manifold employment of the *'Panzerfaust'* in forest fighting and fighting in built up areas against nests, bunkers, cellars and houses. Very good effect (also against dug-in enemy).

Estimation of U.S. losses.

Noteworthy losses: East of Bastogne, material destruction of an entire combat command of the U.S. 9th Armored Division.

(Captured or destroyed 50–60 tanks (Sherman), 40 half-tracks, 25 self-propelled guns, 22 armored cars. 40 lorries and 30 automobiles (jeeps)).

Other major losses near Neffe and Marvie resulting from German artillery fire and in house-to-house fighting in Rochefort. Particularly heavy losses in the attack on Moircy and Piromprè [Pironpré] (southeast of St. Hubert) from German artillery and tank fire. (U.S. 87th or 78th Infantry Division). [Actually, it was the U.S. 84th Infantry Division that had built up a garrison in Rochefort. Despite the intense fighting in Rochefort, Cole, in the U.S. Army Official History of the battle, (*The Ardennes, Battle of the Bulge*, p. 439–40) states, 'The defense of Rochefort had not been too costly: fifteen wounded men, under the care of a volunteer medic, were left in the town and another twenty-five were killed or captured. But the *Panzer Lehr* commander, who had fought in both engagements, would later rate the American defense in Rochefort as comparable in courage and in significance to that at Bastogne.'] Otherwise [American] losses cannot be estimated in anything approaching detail. I believe, however, that they were not particularly high.

Evaluation of the performance of the *Panzer Lehr Division*:

In general and in summary it can be stated that the *Panzer Lehr* [*Division*] performed very well in the Ardennes offensive, despite its deficient outfitting with equipment, its fought out condition, the logistical difficulties and the fragmented commitment that was ordered by higher command with:

a. one *Kampfgruppe* [*Kampfgruppe Panzergrenadier-Lehr-Regiment*] 901 at Bastogne,

b. one *Kampfgruppe* (pioneers and *Flak*) defending 40 kilometres of flanks,

c. one *Kampfgruppe* [*Kampfgruppe Panzergrenadier-Lehr-Regiment* ] 902 attacking vie St. Hubert, Rochefort, Humain and Ciergnon.

Signed BAYERLEIN
formerly *Generalleutnant*

# MS # A–942

## PANZER LEHR DIVISION, 15 – 22 DECEMBER 1944

**INDEX FOR**
**MS # A 942**
***PANZER LEHR DIVISION,* 15 – 22 DECEMBER 1944**

Translated by Frederick Steinhardt. Notes in square brackets also by Frederick Steinhardt.

(Signed) Alfred Zerbel (Alfred Zerbel)

**Index for MS # A 942**



Fritz BAYERLEIN
Oberursal, 1 March 1946
former Commander, *Panzer Lehr Division*

# *PANZER LEHR DIVISION*, 15–22 DECEMBER, 1944
# MS # A–942

1. Employment of the *Panzer Lehr* [*Division*] during the first days of the Ardennes Offensive.

During the night of 15/16 December the *Panzer-Pionier-Bataillon* [130] of the *Panzer Lehr Division* prepared bridges for the Irsen Stream (one kilometre northwest of Gemünd) and the Our River and built them in the morning of the 16th. These bridges could be used during the morning of 16 [December] by the 26th *V.G.D.* [*Volksgrenadier-Division*].

The entire artillery of the *Panzer Lehr Division* was already committed on 14 December for the battle for the Our and Clerf [Clerve River] crossings by the 26th *Volksgrenadier-Division*

The reconnaissance battalion of the *Panzer Lehr Division* (*ALA*) [*Panzeraufklärungs-Lehr-Abteilung* 130] was attached to the 26th *Volksgrenadier-Division* on 16 December and initially received the following mission from the [47th *Panzer*] *Korps*: After building the bridgeheads over the Our near Gemünd and the Clerf near Drauffeld [Drauffelt], to immediately advance to Bastogne to capture the town in a *coup de main* and then immediately resume the advance to Dinant. Route of march via Eschweiler–Derenbach and then either via Nieder Wampach or Doncols–Bras to Bastogne. For this *Panzeraufklrungs-Lehr-Abteilung* 130, consisting of one armoured car company, two *Panzergrenadier* companies and one heavy company, was reinforced with one *Panzer* company (15 *Panzer IV*), one *Pionier* company and one battery of artillery (10.5 cm).

The main body of the *Panzer Lehr* Division, likewise, after building the bridgehead of the 26th *Volksgrenadier-Division* near Drauffeld and the 2nd *Pz. Div.* [*Panzer Division*] near Clervaux [both bridgeheads over the Clerf River. The town of Clervaux is also referred to as Clerf in Cole's official U.S. Army history of the battle and various German accounts.], was to advance via Bastogne to Dinant. Accordingly

*Panzergrenadier-[Lehr] Regiment* 901 with one *Panzer Abteilung* [battalion] and one artillery *Abteilung* [battalion] was to [cross] over the bridge at Gemünd behind the 26th *Volksgrenadier-Division.*

*Panzergrenadier-Lehr-Regiment* 902 with one *Panzer Abteilung* and one artillery *Abteilung* [was to advance] via Dasburg – Marnach behind the 2nd *Pz. Div.* [2nd *Panzer-Division* ], then also via Eschweiler.

Events, however, proved otherwise: The stubborn resistance put up by the U.S. troops in Hosingen and in Holzthum against the 26th *Volksgrenadier-Division* caused the 47th *Panzer Korps* to commit *Panzeraufklärungs-Lehr-Abteilung* 130 in the fighting around Holzthum. With that, the original basic principle (no premature employment of the motorized elements] was already violated. On 17 December, too, the U.S. garrison still held out in Hosingen. In the meantime strong elements of the 26th *Volksgrenadier-Division* infiltrated through the woods southwest of Hosingen toward Drauffeld. At this point the 47th *Panzer Korps* ordered the withdrawal of *Panzeraufklärungs-Lehr-Abteilung* 130 near Holzthum in order to be able to commit it immediately to the west in accord with the original intention after the capture of Drauffeld. Accordingly, by order of the [47th *Panzer*]

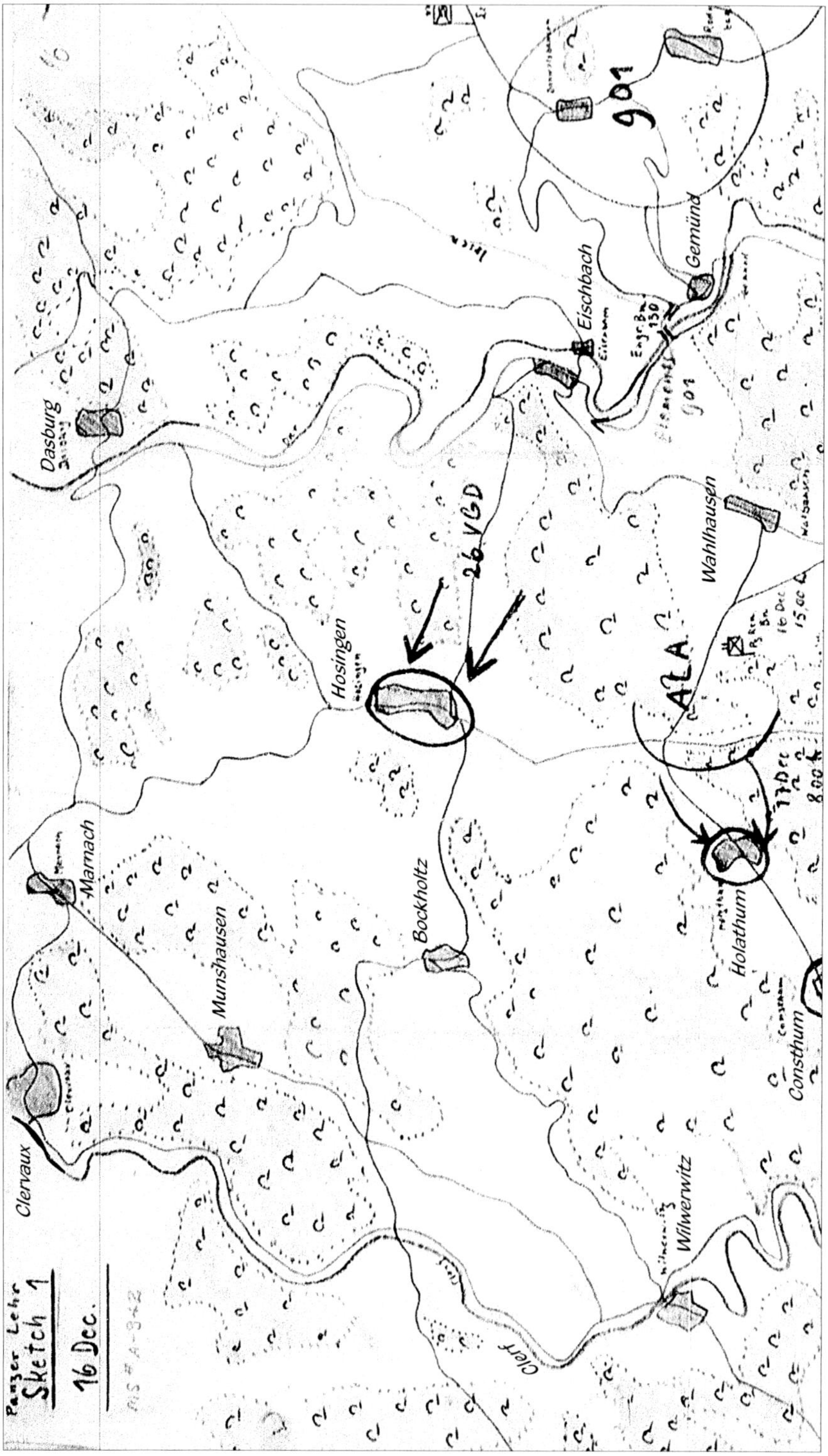


A-942 Sketch 1: *Panzer-Lehr* 16 December 1944

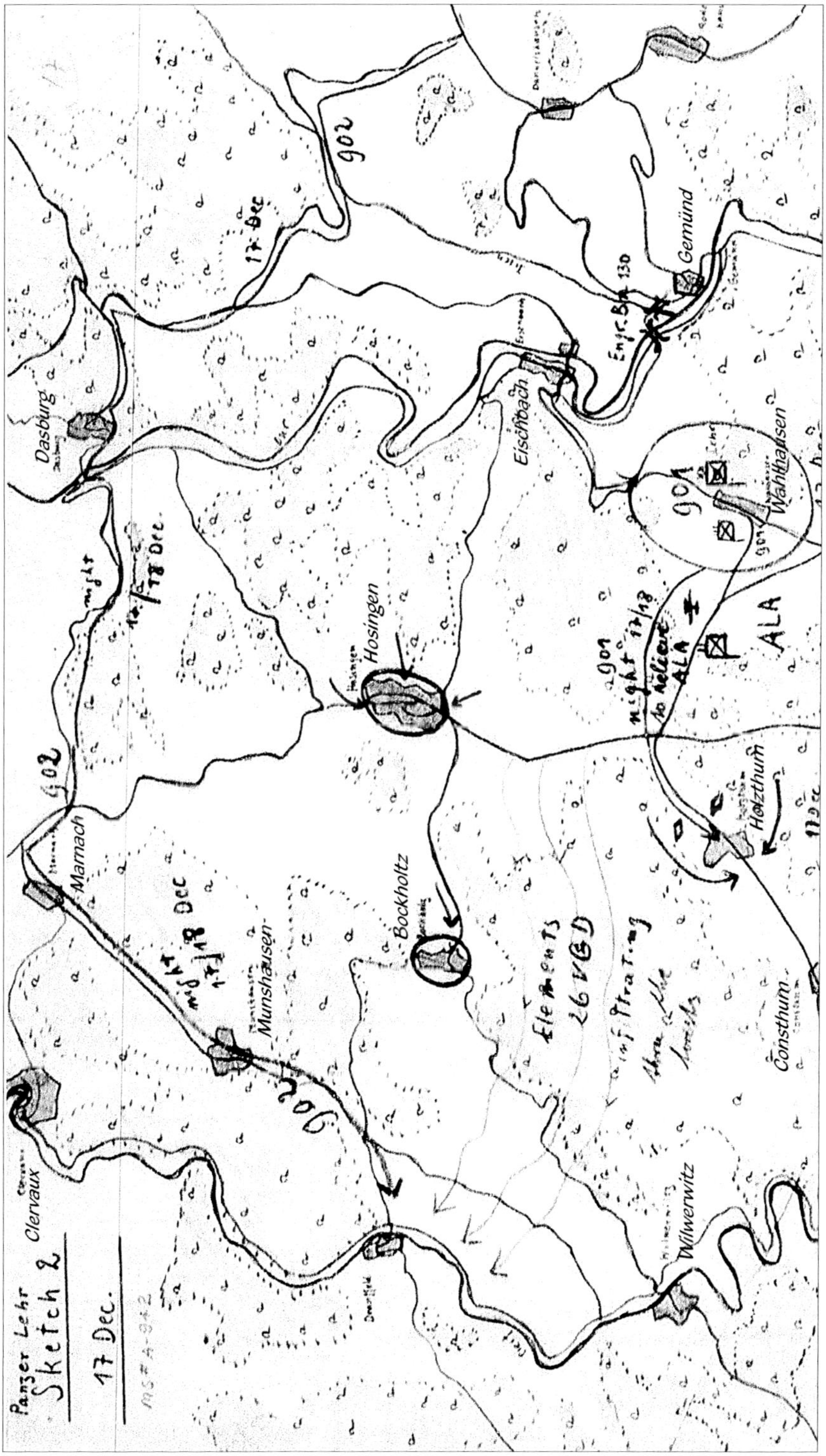


A-942 Sketch 2: *Panzer-Lehr* 17 December 1944

*Korps*, *Panzergrenadier-Lehr-Regiment* 901 was employed for the capture of Consthum.

Hosingen, which had continued to be courageously defended, was finally taken in the morning of 18 December. The lengthy resistance at Hosingen delayed the entire advance of the 26th *Volksgrenadier-Division* and, thereby, that of the *Panzer Lehr Division* for 1 ½ days. The command had assumed that the *Panzer Lehr Division* would already have been advancing via Drauffeld by the evening of the 16th. In my opinion, the following moments were already decisive for the unfavorable development of the offensive:

1. Premature commitment of *Panzeraufklärungs-Lehr-Abteilung* 130 and *Panzergrenadier-Lehr-Regiment* 901 in costly fighting. As a result, *Panzergrenadier-Lehr-Regiment* 901 was not available later at the proper time near Bastogne.

2. Lengthy holdout of the U.S. troops in Hosingen, which was not attacked with sufficient energy by the 26th *Volksgrenadier-Division* on the 16th. That, in turn, meant that the *Panzer Lehr Division* was too late in crossing the bridge at Drauffeld and, thus, too late in [arriving in] the Bastogne area. That was decisive for the fighting around Bastogne, where hours were critical. When the leading elements of the *Panzer Lehr Division* arrived at Bastogne they were not strong enough to break the enemy resistance which had just grown stronger.

3. The rapid reaction of the supreme U.S. command to the surprising German attack by throwing all mobile elements in to delay the German advance, which cost the Germans precious time.

In the morning of 18 December the Drauffeld bridgehead was built. While *Panzergrenadier-Lehr-Regiment* 901was still fighting near Consthum, *Panzergrenadier-Lehr-Regiment* 902 advanced via Dasburg – Marnach – Munshaussen [Munshausen] [to be] committed near Drauffeld, *Panzeraufklärungs-Lehr-Abteilung* 130, likewise, [advancing] via Bockholtz. At about 0900 hours *Panzeraufklärungs-Lehr-Abteilung* 130 crossed the bridgehead line west of Drauffeld and advanced on Eschweiler. *Panzergrenadier-Lehr-Regiment* 902 followed it. During the advance the Drauffeld – Eschweiler valley-road was under unpleasant harassing fire by enemy artillery and mortars from the vicinity of Knaphoscheid and Eschweiler. At the fork in the road two kilometres east of Eschweiler *Panzeraufklärungs-Lehr-Abteilung* 130 turned off to the south to continue its advance via Erpeldange while *Panzergrenadier-Lehr-Regiment* 902 attacked along the serpentine road to Eschweiler. At about 1200 hours the garrison of the town fell back to the outh before the attack and was engaged by the armour of *Panzeraufklärungs-Lehr-Abteilung* 130 on the road between Eschweiler and the fork in the road two kilometres north of Erpeldange. Eight U.S. armoured cars were set afire by gunfire and a number of prisoners captured. *Panzeraufklärungs-Lehr-Abteilung* 130 then thrust on through Erpeldange toward Derenbach. *Kampfgruppe Panzergrenadier-Lehr-Regiment* 902 continued from Eschweiler toward Derenbach with an initial strength of four companies and about 15 tanks. The Division Commander placed himself at the head of this *Kampfgruppe*. At the road fork three kilometres southeast of Derenbach at 1500 hours there was a fight with U.S. tanks that were behind a roadblock consisting of felled trees. While advancing further south of Derenbach – Schimpach [Schimpach is about 2 km due west of Derenbach] one could observe an intense armoured combat in the area of and north of Brachtenbach (2nd *Panzer Division* against a combat command of the U.S. 9th Armored Division [Task Force Harper of CCR, 9th Armored Division, commanded by Lt. Col. Ralph S. Harper was the southern of the two strong roadblock positions that General Middleton ordered Combat Command R to set up on the main paved road to Bastogne 'without delay'. Task Force Harper consisted of the 2nd Tank Battalion (-) and two companies of the 52nd Armored Infantry Battalion. *Panzergrenadiere* started the action in the late afternoon. *Panzer IVs* and *Panthers* of the 2nd *Panzer Divison's Panzerregiment* 3, equipped with the new infrared sighting devices, wiped out most of Task Force Harper after dark. [MacDonald, p. 287, Ritgen, p. 224, Cole, pp. 294–296].). With main-guns pointed north, the *Panzer Lehr* tanks drove several kilometres in the dusk past the site of that imposing spectacle, which received a fantastic touch from the tracer rounds of the tanks. The enemy did not notice us and we reached Nieder Wampach, unharmed, at 1800 hours.

Decision to attack Bastogne

The question was which route to choose, either via Senonchamps [Benonchamps]– Mageret or via Bras – Marvie! The [47th *Panzer*] *Korps* recommended, but did not order, the southern [choice, Bras – Marvie, a wider road].

Our own reconnaissance and statements by local inhabitants indicated that the route via Senonchamps [Benonchamps] was usable. [In this passage Bayerlein repeatedly says Senonchamps when referring to Benonchamps. The real Senonchamps is west of Bayogne. Although Bayerlein's writing, in labeling his own hand-drawn maps that accompany this paper, is somewhat illegible, the first letter of the name of the village in question is clearly 'B', not 'S'. Equally clearly, it is at the location of the real Benonchamps.] In addition, it was the shorter route and the enemy was unlikely to think that the Germans would come on this byway (This turned out to be true). For these reasons I decided to choose it. However, as the night progressed the route grew worse and worse, since it had no surface (non-metalled) and the incessant rainfall had softened it. Thus the main body of the Division was delayed several hours in following. (I have described the choice of the route exactly, because time played a decisive role in the first days of the battle for Bastogne and because the Commanding General of the 47th *Panzer Korps* [*General der Panzertruppe* Heinrich *Freiherr* von Lüttwitz], with the advantage of hindsight, now is of the opinion that utilization of this route so delayed the *Panzer Lehr Division* that the U.S. 101st Airborne arrived 1 – 2 hours ahead of the leading elements of the *Panzer Lehr Division*. In my opinion, however, the fault for the delay is with the 26th *Volksgrenadier-Division* because it took too long capturing the bridgeheads and with the 47th *Panzer Korps* because, contrary to all intentions, it had already committed elements of the *Panzer Lehr Division* east of the Clerf [River] and, indeed, in completely fragmented fashion, so that the *Panzer Lehr Division* could not be in the Bastogne area in time in sufficient strength.)

18 December, 2100 hours: Departure of *Kampfgruppe* [*Panzergrenadier-Lehr-Regiment* ] 902 from Nieder Wampach.

Strength : One battalion *Panzergrenadiere,* 12 tanks, one battery artillery. The *Kampfgruppe* proceeded, unnoticed and without enemy contact, via Senonchamps [Benonchamps] to Margeret [Magéret]. A Belgian civilian informed us that, two hours earlier, a U.S. task force consisting of about 40 tanks and many other armoured and unarmoured motor vehicles, as well as artillery, had driven through Margeret toward Longvilly. [see note above to question 16 on collecting intelligence in MS # A–941 regarding the discrepancy between this civilian's statement and the reality. Bayerlein's account varies slightly in different documents. In his brief earlier mention regarding map 3 in MS #A–941, he said, ' A Belgian reported that, two hours earlier, a U.S. task force of 50 tanks (Sherman), 25 guns (cannon, self-propelled mounts) and an additional 40–50 armoured vehicles had passed through Magret [Magéret] headed east to Longwilly. There was [said to be] a U.S. general in Magret.' What matters is that, based on this incorrect intelligence, Bayerlein made a critical decision that delayed the arrival of the *Panzer Lehr Division* at Bastogne at a time when a few hours might have made possible taking Bastogne in a successful *coup de main* before the arrival of the U.S. 101st Airborne Division and the leading combat elements of the U.S. 10th Armored Division.]

Therefore I immediately blocked the road at the northeast exit from Margeret [Magéret] with mines and tanks. I, myself, was in Margeret. Individual U.S. tanks and vehicles continued to arrive from Bastogne, since nobody yet knew that German troops were already in Margeret. However, it was also not yet known to us that there were U.S. troops occupying Margeret. It was only while we were searching the village that a firefight developed. The [village] was mopped up by daybreak. A U.S. field hospital in Bois St. Lambert was left in operation and cared for American and German wounded.

After several U.S. tanks that were returning from Longvilly on the road had been knocked out, the advance was resumed toward Bastogne at 0600 hours. In the dim light of early morning I, myself, saw how the U.S. troops were organized for defense on the ridge southwest of Margeret [Magéret]. After elimination of a roadblock at the Neffe strongpoint at 0700 hours, the village of Neffe was taken in an enveloping attack from the south at 0800 hours. The further advance against Mont was repulsed. U.S. resistance mounted steadily. Reconnaissance indicated that the villages of Bizory and Marvie were held by the enemy and U.S. patrols were also reported in Wardin. Ever strengthening enemy pressure made itself evident from the north via Arloncourt and the woods west of Longvilly. Accordingly, at about noon, those elements of *Panzergrenadier-Lehr-Regiment* 901 that had arrived were committed from Senonchamps [Benonchamps] toward the north to eliminate the impending envelopment of *Kampfgruppe Panzergrenadier-Lehr-Regiment* 901.

(During the night of 18/19 December *Panzergrenadier-Lehr-Regitment* 901 was relieved near Consthum after it had succeeded in capturing the village on the 18th. The regiment had arrived near Senonchamps [Benonchamps] by 1000 hours with one battalion and the *Panzerjäger-* [tank destroyer] *Abteilung* (20 *Panzerjäger IV lang)* and one artillery *Abteilung* with two batteries.)

The woods were mopped up by 1400 hours and the *Panzerjäger* achieved a great success in that, in cooperation with elements of the 26th *Volksgrenadier-Division,* a large number of U.S. tanks and armored vehicles were knocked out between Longvilly and Arloncourt. They completed cutting off the combat command of

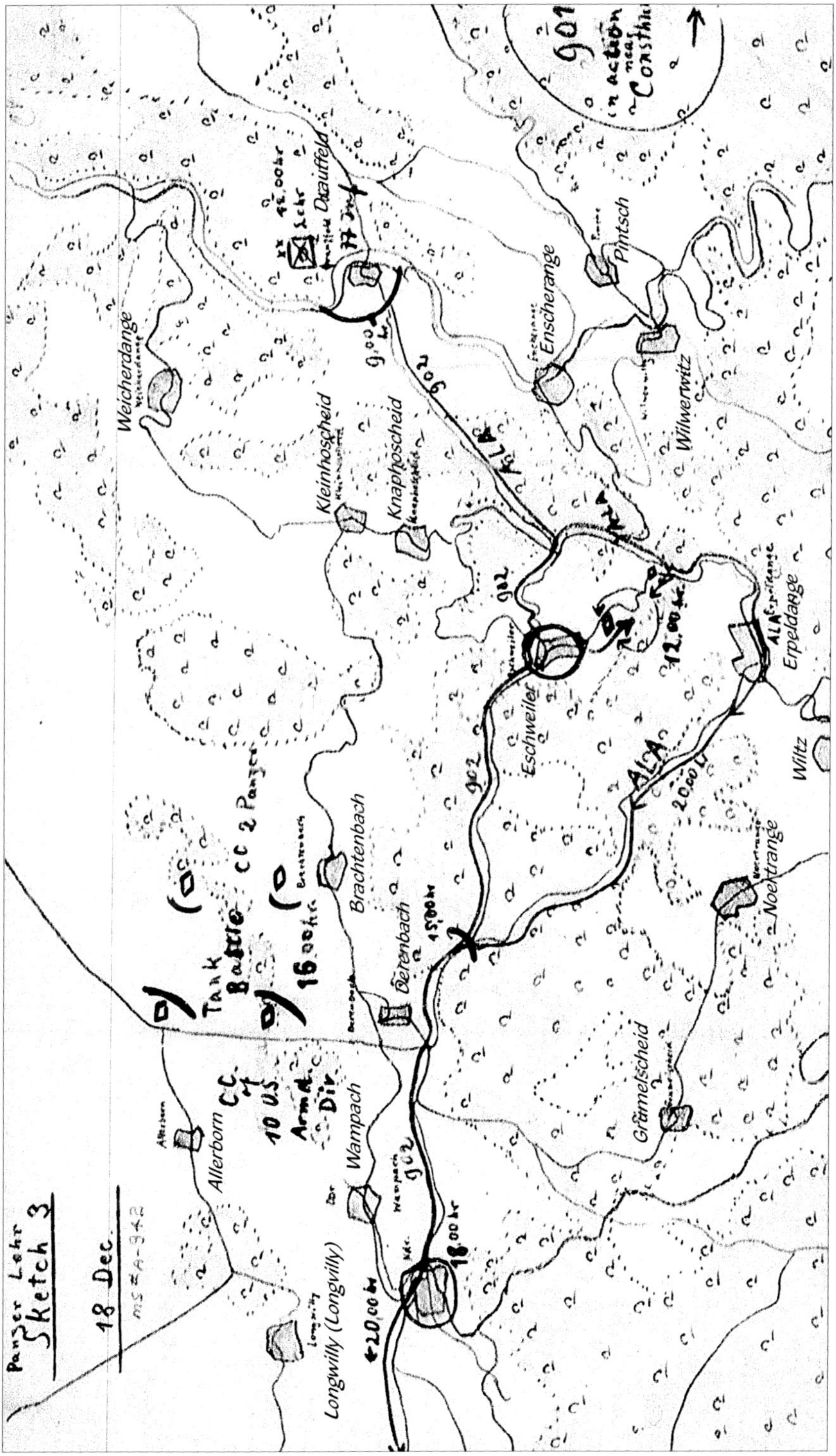


A-942 Sketch 3: *Panzer-Lehr* 18 December 1944

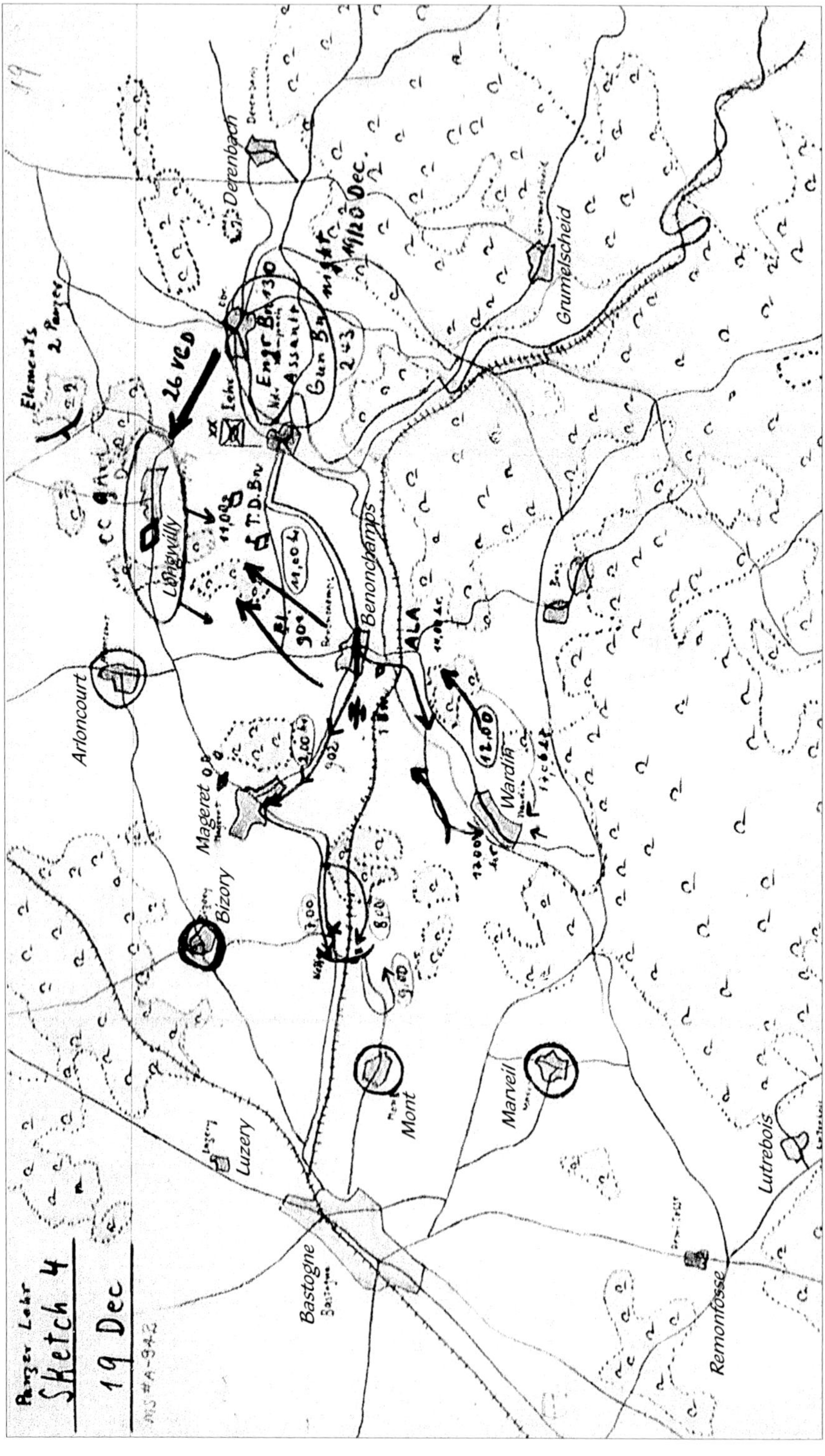


A-942 Sketch 4: *Panzer-Lehr* 19 December 1944

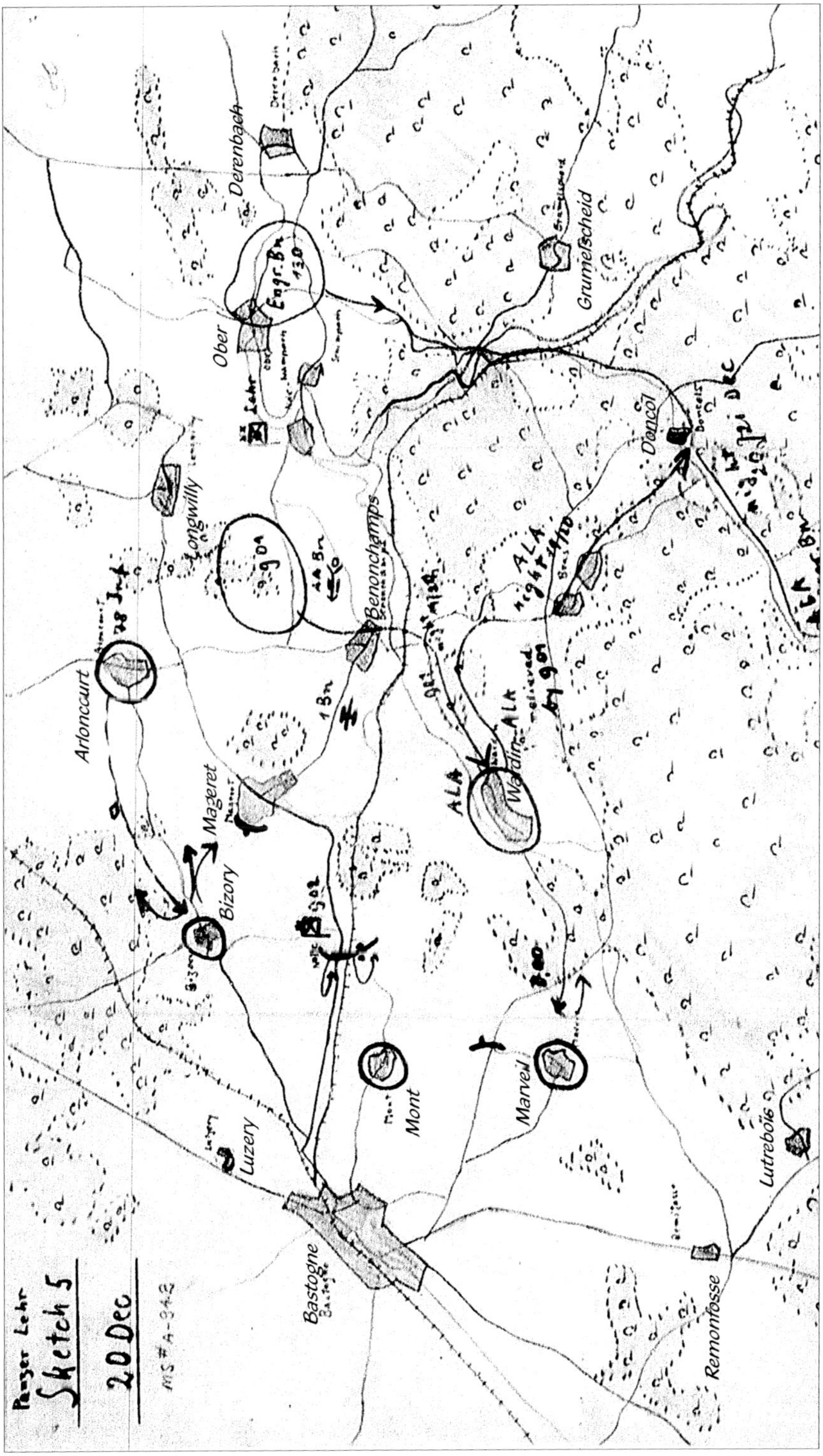


A-942 Sketch 5: *Panzer-Lehr* 20 December 1944

the U.S. 10th Armored Division from the west and played an essential part in its destruction. ['Team Cherry [of the 10th Armored Division's CCB] and the 9th Armored Division's CCR paid dearly along the Mageret-Longvilly road. The effect, when combined with earlier losses [stands by Task Force Rose and Task Force Harper of the 9th Armored Division's CCR at nearby road junctions] was that [9th AD's] CCR had virtually ceased to exist ... Team Cherry [from 10th AD's CCB] lost 175 officers and men – a fourth of the command – 7 light and 10 medium tanks and 17 half tracks. (MacDonald, p. 296.]

In the morning of 19 [December] *Panzeraufklärungs-Lehr-Abteilung* 130 was committed in an attack on Wardin to eliminate the impending envelopment of *Kampfgruppe Panzergrenadier-Lehr-Regiment* 902 from the south. Wardin was captured in the evening. However, the continued attack on Marvie on 20 [December] failed. In the meantime additional artillery and the *Flak Abteilung* [*Heeres Flak Abteilung* 311] closed up from the rear. They were committed near Senonchamps [Benonchamps].

Elements of the *Pionier* battalion [*Panzer-Pionier-Bataillon* 130] – relieved at the Gemünd bridge – and elements of *Sturmgeschütz-Abteilung* 245 also arrived and were held available in Ober Wampach.

On 20 December *Infanterie-Regiment* 78 of the 26th *Volksgrenadier-Division* was attached to the *Panzer Lehr Division* to carry out an attack on Luzery via Bizory. Eight *Panzerjäger* [tank destroyers] were attached to the regiment for that [attack]. The attack of *Infanterie-Regiment* 78 came to a halt before Bizory. Also, the attack by *Panzergrenadier-Lehr-Regiment* 902 in the evening of 20 [December] via Neffe along the road to Bastogne was repulsed with heavy losses. The resistance and the combat strength of the enemy had substantially strengthened in this sector and artillery fire had significantly increased.

*Panzergrenadier-Lehr-Regiment* 901, reinforced with one company of tanks and an artillery *Abteilung,* was committed to attack Marvie via Bras. By [47th Panzer] *Korps* order *Panzeraufklärungs-Lehr-Abteilung* 130 was withdrawn during the night of 20/21 [December] from Wardin in order to push on past Bastogne to the south with the *Pionier* battalion [*Panzer-Pionier-Bataillon* 130] toward St. Hubert. During the night this *Kampfgruppe* advanced via Lutremange–Hompré–Sibret to the Gerimont–Tillet area.

21 December: In the evening of the 21st *Panzergrenadier-Lehr-Regiment* 902 made another attempt to attack Bastogne from Neffe, which, however, again miscarried. The attack by the two infantry regiments of the 26th *Volksgrenadier-Division* on Bastogne's eastern front also essentially failed.

The front of *Panzergrenadier-Lehr-Regiment* 902 was extended to the Bastogne–Arlon (Remifosse) road. The attack of the other elements of *Panzergrenadier-Lehr-Regiment* 901 on Marvie miscarried.

During the night of 21/22 [December] *Panzergrenadier-Lehr-Regiment* 902 was relieved near Neffe by *Infanterie-Regiment* 78 of the 26th *Volksgrenadier-Division*. The *Panzer Lehr Division* was assigned the mission of advancing with all elements on St. Hubert.

*Panzergrenadier-Lehr-Regiment* 901, reinforced with 15 tanks and one artillery *Abteilung*, was to remain in the Marvie–Remifosse area. It was attached to the 26th *Volksgrenadier-Division*. With that the Division lost its most valuable and combat-

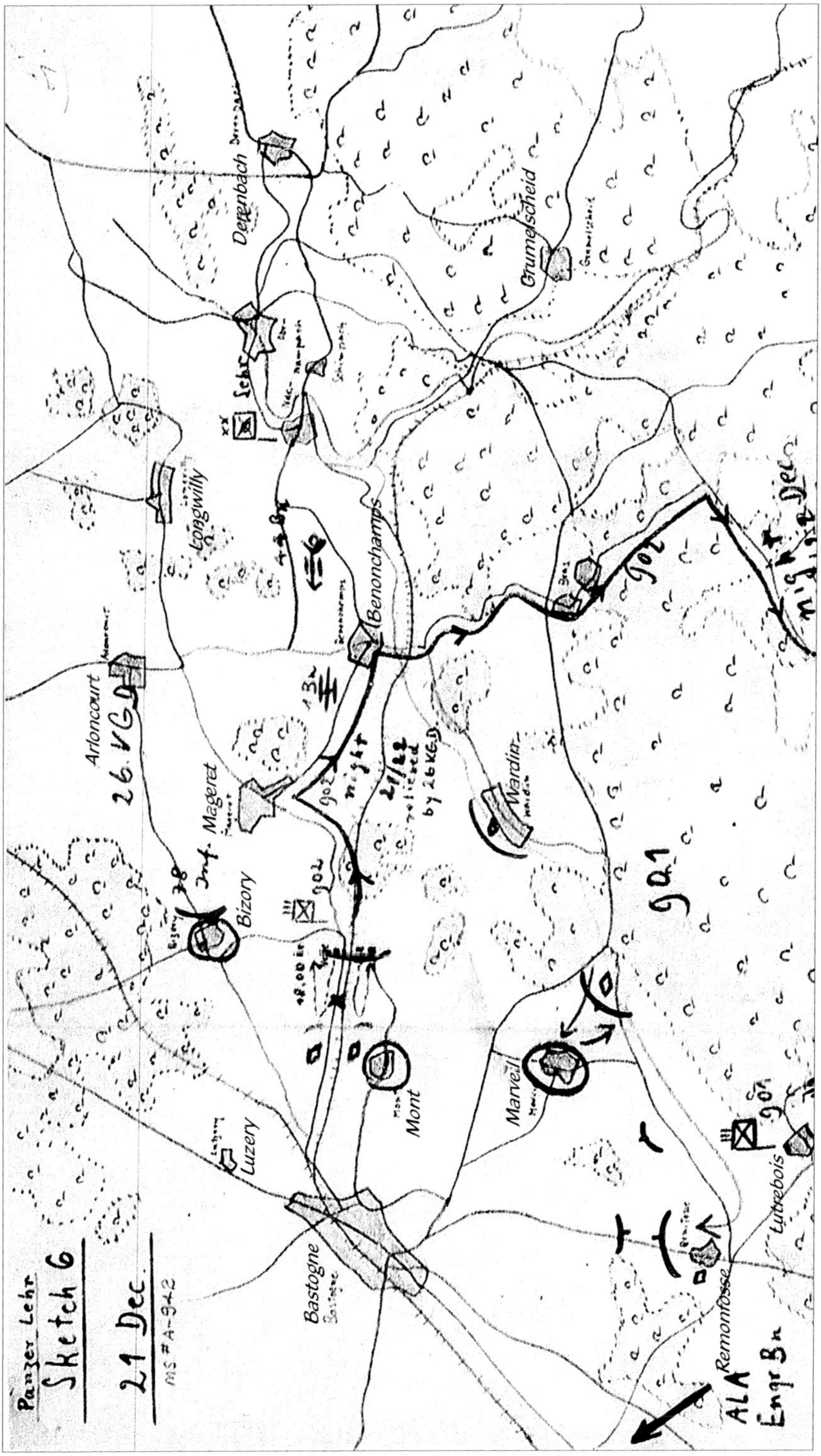


A-942 Sketch 6: *Panzer-Lehr* 21 December 1944

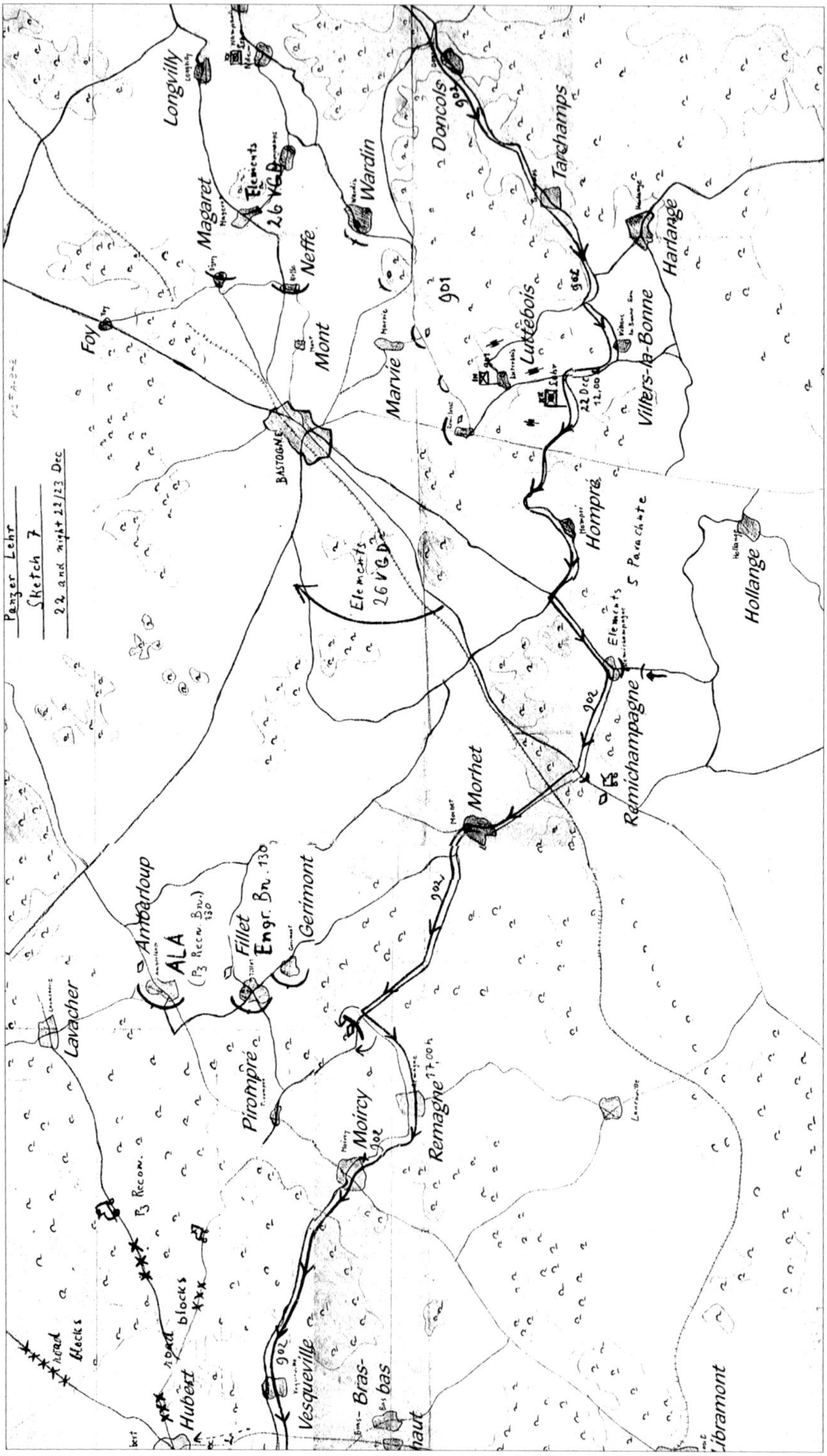


A-942 Sketch 7: *Panzer-Lehr* 22 December and night of 22/23 December 1944 (series)

worthy element. That regiment remained in the Bastogne sector outside of the Division's formations until 7 January 1945.

On 21 December *Panzeraufklärungs-Lehr-Abteilung* 130 and the *Pionier* battalion reached the Amberloup–Tillet–Gerimont area and, after a short fight, captured a large enemy supply column, including, undamaged, 60 lorries and 32 jeeps. The main roads to St. Hubert from the east and northeast were reported to be effectively blocked.

On 22 December at 1200 hours *Kampfgruppe* 902 (one battalion, ten tanks and the main body of *Sturmgeschützabteilung* 245 – about 20 *Sturmgeschütze*; one artillery *Abteilung* – the second battalion of [*Panzergrenadier-Lehr-Regiment*] 902 followed later) set out from Hompre [Hompré] to St. Hubert via REMICHAMPAGNE–MORHET–REMAGNE–MORCY [Moircy]–VESQUEVILLE–HATRIVAL. With that the battle for Bastogne ended for the main body of *Panzer Lehr* (except *Panzergrenadier-Lehr-Regiment* 901, reinforced with artillery and armour.)

In an examination of the battle for Bastogne from 19–21 December it must be said that the command by the 47th *Panzer Korps* was neither energetic or unified enough. The forces of the three divisions that were committed at Bastogne were fragmented instead of being employed as a concentrated force in an attack on Bastogne with all the massed forces of the 47th *Panzer Korps*. After the so-called *coup de main* (capture by surprise) of Bastogne had failed, since the German forces arrived too late, meaning after significant U.S. forces had concentrated there, the concentrated attack was all the more necessary and would have assuredly attained the objective. In particular, it was a grievous mistake to commit the elements of *Panzer Lehr* separately before Bastogne, after the Division had already been uselessly committed and split up in the early days of the offensive.

A further mistake was to leave the mobile elements of *Panzer Lehr* tied down in the stabilized front before Bastogne (Neffe, Marvie, Remichampagne) and to send the immobile, slow elements of the 26th *Volksgrenadier Division* marching on foot for an enveloping attack in the area west of Bastogne.

All of that resulted in the fact that a proper attack on Bastogne never came, nor could come.

Signed BAYERLEIN

# MS # B 049

## ARDENNES – PANZER-LEHR DIVISION, DESCRIPTION OF COMBAT OPERATIONS FROM 12 TO 20 JANUARY 1945 (WITHDRAWAL FROM THE ARDENNES)

Alfred Zerbel
Koenigstein, 8 August 1950

**ARDENNES – *Panzer Lehr Division***

**Description of Combat Operations from 12 to 20 January, 1945**

**(Withdrawal from the Ardennes)**

**No Index**

[Translated by Frederick Steinhardt. Bracketed notes inserted by F. Steinhardt. Publishers' note – original maps so poor they were not able to be reproduced with any clarity.]

MS # B–049
Bayerlein, Fritz
Oberursel
Former Commanding Officer of the *Panzer Lehr Division*
25 April 46

**ARDENNES – *PANZER LEHR DIVISION***
**DESCRIPTION OF THE ENGAGEMENT FROM 12–20 JANUARY 1945 (WITHDRAWAL FROM THE ARDENNES)**

MS # B–049

**ARDENNES – *PANZER-LEHR DIVISION***
**Description of Combat Operations, 12–20 January 1945**
**(Withdrawal from the Ardennes)**

During the night of 11/12 January, as ordered, the *Panzer-Lehr Div.* [*Division*] fell back from the St. Hubert area to the line Champlon – Ortheuville – Lavacherie – Sprimont (red line on the sketch-map). The Roads and byways in the approaches to this position were mined and blocked with felled trees.

On 12 January an enemy combat team, avoiding the Champlon – road junction strong point, advanced toward Journal and Champlon and penetrated the division's lines. Artillery fire from the north progressively increased and was extremely unpleasant since all road junctions and bottlenecks, bridges and built-up areas were under nearly constant harassing fire. In the southern sector Amperloup [Amberloup] was held by the enemy. However, no further attack ensued. In the sector adjoining *Pz.* [*Panzer*] *Lehr* (*Brigade Rehmer* [The *Führer Begleit Brigade*, commanded by *Oberst* Otto Rehmer]) an enemy combat team advanced from Tillet to Sprimont. Our own line held everywhere that day.

During the night of 12/13 January, as ordered, [the Division] fell back to the line Lavaux–Beaulieu–Cens–Wyompont. The 2nd *Panzer-Div.* [*Division*] and *Brigade Remer* were withdrawn as army [*Armee*] reserves. Adjoining the division on the right was the 116th *Panzer-Div.* [*Division*[, on the left, the 26th *Volks Gren. Div.* [*Volksgrenadier Division*].

On 13 January enemy pressure was only felt on the Division's right wing around Hives – Lavaux. In the afternoon of that day and during the night of 13/14 January the Division fell back behind the southern Ourthe [river] sector. Since the 116th *Panzer-Division* was extremely weak at this point and the enemy exerted heavy pressure north of the Ourthe against Nadrin, the Division had to take over the Nadrin – Filly sector. Retreat across the Ourthe sector was extremely difficult since no bridges, only fords, were available, and [the fords] were blocked by damaged tanks and wrecked vehicles. Furthermore, enemy patrols infiltrating the Ourthe river valley interfered with the withdrawal.

The development and course of the fighting north of the Ourthe around Nadrin and Houffalize has already been thoroughly described in another report.

No enemy pressure was felt south of the Ourthe, so positions could be held there on 14 January. However, the enemy pressed hard against the 26th *V.G.D.* [*Volksgrenadier Division*]. Therefore, during the night of 14/15 [January] the Division was forced to fall back behind the Suhet stream sector and to Houffalize.

On 15 January a strong enemy armoured group broke into the Division's defensive position from the southwest between Mapombré [Mabompré] and Houffalize. I watched this superbly conducted armoured attack myself, from my command post in Alhoumont. The attack achieved complete success. The last six *Panzerjäger* [tank destroyers] of *Jäger-Abteilung* 539 were destroyed and a weak battalion wiped out in the woods west of Neuf Moulins. That opened the road to Houffalize, although the town and the high ground immediately to its south could still be held [by our forces].

Remarks: I am in disagreement with *General* Kokott [*Generalmajor* Heinz Kokott, commanding the adjoining 26th *Volksgrenadier Division*], who believes that this attack was not carried out on 15, but on 16 January. I, however, was only in Alhoumont on 15 January, where I watched the attack personally with my *Ia* [operations] officer and admired its execution. On 16 January I was already at the Bernistap command post (10 km farther east). Thus I must stick to my opinion that the attack took place on the fifteenth.

During the night of 15/16 January *Panzer Lehr* shifted its position behind the Ourthe – Cowan stream sector. Only weak patrols remained in Houffalize.

During the morning of 16 January U.S. troops entered Houffalize from the north. There were no attacks on 16 January against the main front of the Division at the Cowan stream, so this line could also be held on 17 January. That day the enemy's northern and southern groups linked up in Houffalize. As a result of strong enemy pressure on its neighbours to the north and south, the division had to fall back during the night of 17/18 January to the line Bourjeussel–Cetturu–Tavigny–Boeur. Enemy pressure then let up completely on the *Panzer Lehr* front. However, since strong enemy attacks continued on the adjoining units, during the night of 17/18 January, as ordered, the Division fell back to the railroad position west of the Steinbach–Buret line.

There were no more enemy attacks in the Division's sector. In the context of the general withdrawal of the army [*Armee*] the Division was pulled back during the night of 19/20 January to the Bassballin–Troisvierges–Cassel line. After one regiment had already been withdrawn on 19 January to be committed north of Diekirch, the entire Division was transferred to the Hoscheid area (west of Vianden) during the night of 21/22 January for employment in defense against the enemy's envelopment movement north of Diekirch.

Signed BAYERLEIN

# MS # A–943

## ADDITIONAL QUESTIONS ON THE ARDENNES OFFENSIVE

MS # A–943 16 June 1950

ADDITIONAL QUESTIONS ON ARDENNES OFFENSIVE 6 pp in German

Alfred Zerbel
Koenigstein, 16 June 1950

**INDEX FOR**
**MS# A 943.**

**ADDITIONAL QUESTIONS ON THE ARDENNES OFFENSIVE**

Translated by Frederick Steinhardt. Notes in square brackets by Frederick Steinhardt.

Zerbel (Alfred Zerbel)



*MS # A – 943*
Generalleutnant Bayerlein
Oberursel, 22 February 1946
former Commander, *Panzer Lehr Division*

## Additional Questions on the Ardennes Offensive

Short description of how the pressure of the American and British forces developed west and south of the *Panzer lehr* [*Division*] line from 22 December to 10 January.

1. On 21 December *Kampfgruppe Panzer Lehr*, led by the Division Commander, started its advance on St. Hubert in the morning. Route of advance: Lutremange – Homre [Hompré] – Remichampagne – Morhet – Remagne –

Moircy – Vesqueville – Hatrival – St. Hubert. On this day enemy reconnaissance forces had already advanced to Remichampagne and the highway intersection ten kilometres northeast of Vaux-le-Rosieres [Vaux-les-Rosières]. Elements of the 5th *Fallschirm[jäger] Division* fell back before this reconnaissance to the southern edge of Remichampagne and the highway intersection. The intersection was under constant direct fire from enemy armoured cars and tanks. This threat to the flank was extremely unpleasant for movements on the highway. Aside from limited resistance northeast of Remagne and near Moircy, the *Panzer Lehr* advance went smoothly.

2. At noon and in the afternoon of 22 December *Kampfgruppe Panzer Lehr* moved out from St. Hubert toward Rochefort in two groups: One via Massbourg [Masbourg]–Forrieres [Forrières] and the other via Grupont – Wavreilles [Wavreille]. This gave rise to skirmishes with enemy reconnaissance forces near Bure and Tellin which, however, were forced back over the Lesse [river]. The Lesse bridges at Han-sur-Lesse, Bellvaux [Belvaux] and Resteigne were held by weak elements of *Panzer Lehr* and armoured reconnaissance was advanced via Willen to the southwest. Other than enemy reconnaissance, there was, for the time being, no enemy pressure on this sector of the front.

   On 23 December German reconnaissance in two of the usual motor vehicles to Libramont via Bras Haute–Serpont (returning via Seviecourt) reported that Libramont was strongly held. One German vehicle was, thereby, knocked out and destroyed by U.S. outposts north of Libramont.

3. On 24 December pressure from enemy infantry and armour was already developing against Remagne and Moircy. Both locations were held by *Flak Abteilungen* which were employed as infantry, anti-tank defense and artillery. Everywhere the enemy thrusts were repulsed.

4. On 24 December Rochefort was captured by *Panzer Lehr* and, during the night of 24/25 December, the attack continued north against Humain, Havrenne and Buissonville in the attempt ordered by the 47th *Panzer Korps* to fight free the supply route for the elements of the 2nd *Panzer Division* that had already been cut off near Custinne. Humain and Havrenne were taken by noon on 25 December. The attack on Buissonville failed. Heavy enemy artillery fire – directed by artillery spotters – exacted serious losses from the reconnaissance *Abteilung* south of Buissonville.

   The enemy counterattack started in the afternoon of 25 December from Buissonville. On 26 December Humain was attacked concentrically by numerous tanks. The German lines had to be pulled back to the Rochefort bridgehead position. That opened the battle for Rochefort. *Panzer Lehr* turned over the Rochefort sector to the 9th *Panzer Division* on 26 December and, on 27 December, the Lesse sector to *Kampfgruppe Gutmann* of the 2nd *Panzer Division*. Following the loss of the Rochefort bridgehead the pressure increased greatly on Rochefort, until it had to be given up on 29 (?) December.

The only pressure on the Lesse sector came from enemy armoured reconnaissance forces. The German positions at Han sur Lesse – Tellin could still be held.

5. In the Mirwart–Smuid forest sector enemy reconnaissance forces already exerted pressure on 25 December. Smuid was evacuated under heavy enemy pressure on 26 or 27 December. The more favorable position on the east bank of the L'Homme stream were occupied after the approaches were heavily mined and blocked.

6. The St. Hubert sector was under constant attack starting on 28 December. The positions were held until the general retreat on 11 January in at-times heavy fighting by weak defending forces. All enemy attacks were repulsed and a very large number of enemy tanks were destroyed. In particular, all enemy attempts to break through to St. Hubert by concentric attacks through the woods on both sides of Hatrival and west of Vesqueville failed.

7. In the Moircy–Remagne sector pressure on the front increased starting 28 December after Freux and Rondu were taken by the enemy. On 28 December the enemy infiltrated the woods northwest of Moircy. That was extremely awkward for the weak infantry forces defending that sector, since forest-fighting particularly demands lots of infantry. The attack on Remagne began at the same time. On 29 December what were apparently fresh forces attacked Moircy concentrically from the east and west and took it, after locally fierce house-to-house fighting. A counterattack delivered during the night of 29/30 December by the sector-reserve, consisting of a company of *Panzergrenadiere* and six tanks regained possession of Moircy, bringing in prisoners from the U.S. 'Golden Acorn Division'. [The U.S. 87th Infantry Division was known as the 'Golden Acorn Division'. According to pp620 ff of Cole the 87th ID was working with 11th Armored Div when, ' … The expected German counterattack at Moircy came about three hours before midnight … '] The enemy finally captured Moircy on 31 December. Remagne, too, was lost on 31 December. Continuing his thrust past Moircy the enemy took Jenneville on 1 January.

   Enemy armored reconnaissance was already advancing along the Morhet – St. Hubert road on 29 December, but was repulsed at the fork in the road northeast of Remagne.

   On 31 December the St. Hubert–Remagne road was held at all points by German troops.

8. Now came the lengthy and exhausting struggle for the highway intersection at Pirompre [Pirompré], which was held by an incredibly small garrison of about 30 men and six tanks until 10 January against numerous, almost daily enemy attacks. The German defense was particularly well supported by the tanks, which were positioned, almost invisible, in the wood-piles of a sawmill at Pirompré. On 8 January Bonnerue was lost after numerous attacks. It was recaptured on 9 January by individual tanks and two *Panzergrenadier* compa-

nies of *Panzergrenadier-Regiment* 901, which had previously been committed at Bastogne and recently returned to the Division. One hundred members of the 'Golden Acorn Division' fell into German hands.

On 7 January the woodlots southwest of Tillet were lost, which meant that the forward line had to be pulled back to the Pirompré–Tillet road. The well positioned German *Panzerjäger* [tank destroyers] along the edge of the woods northwest of Tillet took a very successful and effective part in the fighting of their neighbours (*Brigade Ramer*) near Gerimont and Tillet. They were able to knock out several enemy tanks and exact heavy losses from the attacking infantry.

Bonnerue and Pirompré were evacuated according to plan as part of the general retreat on 11 January.

9. The unexpected enemy advance into the forest region between St. Hubert and Pirompré was extremely unpleasant. The last forces of the Division had to be committed to prevent and seal off the dangerous enemy infiltration and the resulting outflanking of the positions south of St. Hubert and near Pirompré. This forest fighting was particularly fierce and costly. Weak enemy forces had already crossed the St. Hubert–Pirompré road on 31 December. Scattered counterattacks were repulsed. The infiltration, however, continued. A counterattack on both 1 and 2 January by the reserve of *Kampfgruppe Poschinger* brought some relief and temporarily halted the enemy advance but did not put an end to the continued infiltration.

   The enemy penetration was finally blocked about one kilometre north of the highway, and this line was held until the general retreat on 11 January.

10. In the adjoining sector, the battle for Tillet began on 7 January and continued, surging back and forth in costly house-to-house fighting until 10 January, when the town was finally captured by U.S. troops (the 'Golden Acorn Division') after hard fighting. This fighting was effectively supported by *Panzerjäger* and artillery of *Panzer Lehr*.

# MS # A–944

## PANZER-LEHR DIVISION SITUATION MAPS (23 DECEMBER 1944–11 JANUARY 1945)

Maps redrawn from Bayerlein's sketchmaps of actions of the main body of *Panzer Lehr Division* 130 after moving west past Bastogne, 24 December through 11 January.

NOTES TO GO WITH MAPS: MS # A–944

[Tr. note – This list of legends and keys to symbols for the map was such a hodge-podge of German fragments and poor English 'equivalents' that it was impossible to accept as it was. Therefore I departed from my usual rigid adherence to whatever the original army translator had done and, instead, chose to make what alterations were needed so that it would make sense in supporting the sketch maps.]

[Tr. note – Bayerlein's somewhat illegible hand-drawn sketchmaps were traced and the information re-entered. The notes that follow are based on Bayerlein's notes and the accompanying English language explanations, but, in some cases, re-worded for clarity.]

**Maps for 23, 24, 25 December 1944:**

1. *Flak Abt.* 314

   23 Dec

   *Flak Abteilung* 9 (AA battalion) (2 8.8 cm batteries) committed as infantry, anti-tank guns and artillery from 23 Dec. 1600 hrs

2. Mot. Recce

   24/25

   Motorized reconnaissance toward Libramont on 24 and 25 Dec. reports Libramont occupied by U.S. Infantry.

3. Elements of *Panzer-Grenadier-Lehr-Regiment* 902 and *Panzer-Pionier-*

   *Bataillon* 130 @ 0400 hrs. Elements of *Panzergrenadier-Lehr-Regiment* 902 and *Panzer-Pionier-Bataillon* 130 from 23 Dec., 0400 hrs.

   'Pioneer work' – road blocks by felled trees and mining by pioneers.

   Xx – felled trees, roadblock.

4. Command Post of *Panzer Lehr Division* 130

   *ALA* 23 Dec 1200 hr

   *Panzeraufklärungs-Lehr-Abteilung* 130 with 8 tanks starts from St. Hubert for Forrières on 23 Dec. At 1200 hrs.

   *Pz. Gren.* 902

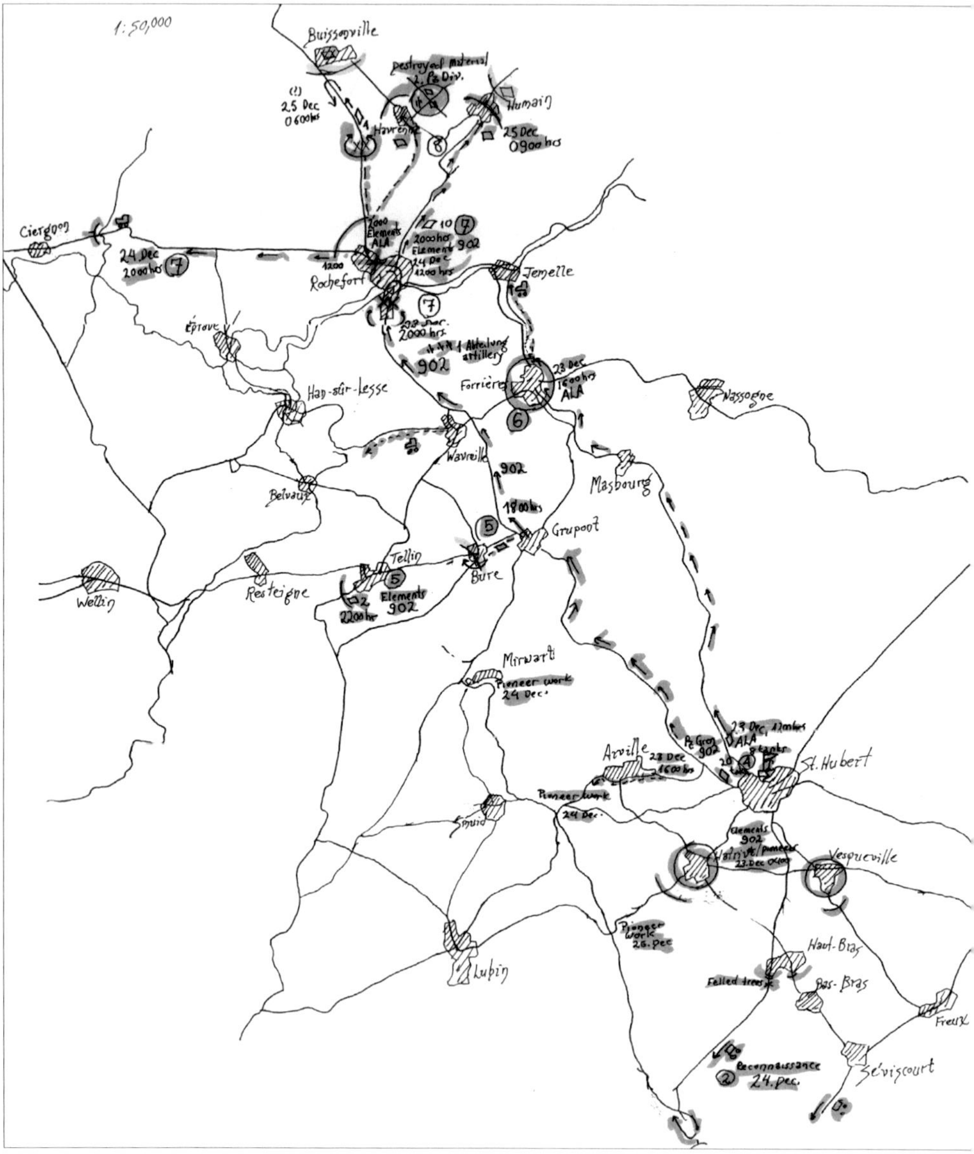


*Panzer-Lehr* 23–25 December 1944

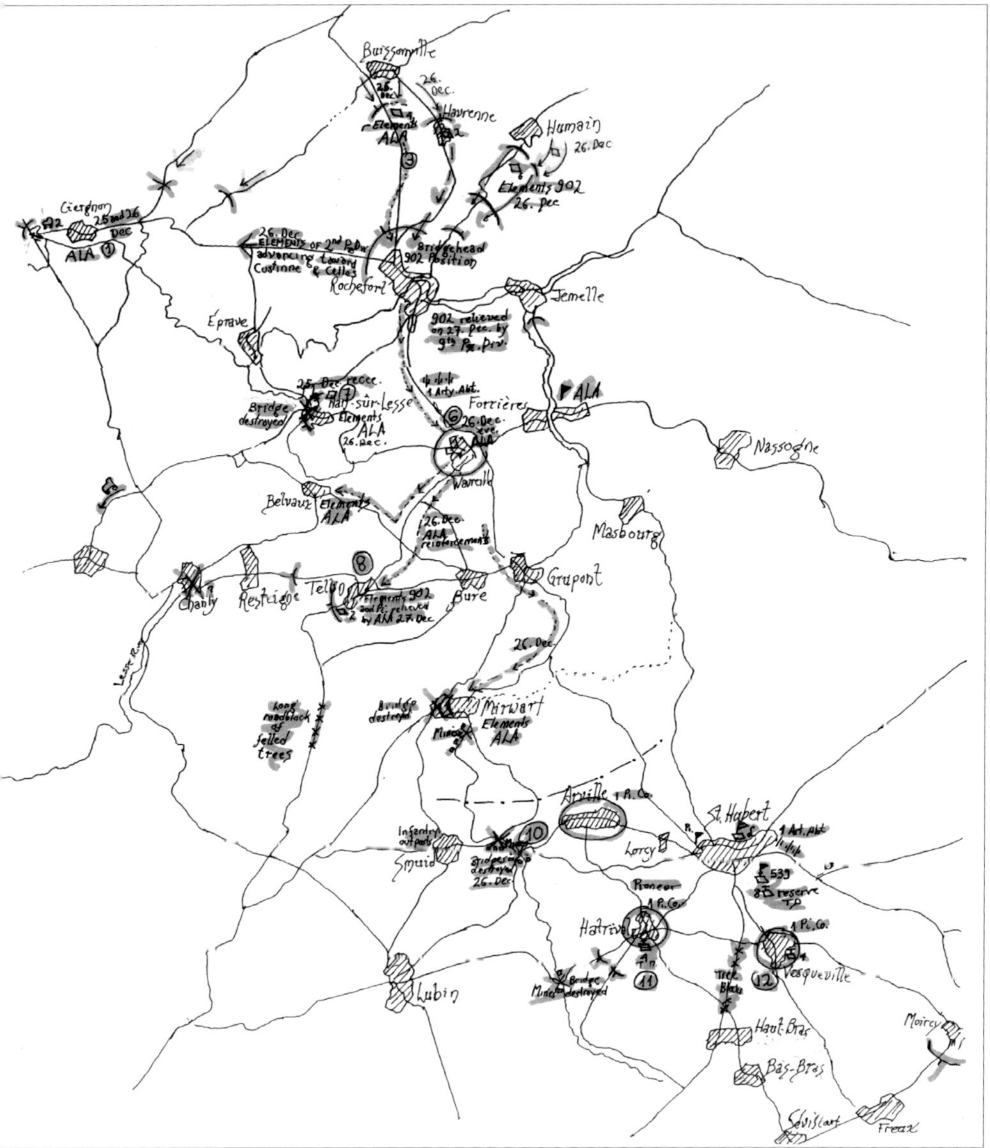


*Panzer-Lehr* 23–25 December 1944 (continuation)

*Panzer-Grenadier-Lehr-Regiment* 902 (with 20 tanks) stafts from St. Hubert for Rochefort on 23 Dec. At 1600 hrs.

(Arrow) Advancing

Pioneer work – pioneer works (road blocks and mining)

5. 902 1800 hrs

*Panzergrenadier-Lehr-Regiment* 902 passes Grupont for Rochefort. Elements (one platoon with two tanks) are committed towards Bure and Tellin. At Bure fight with U.S. Armored cars. Tellin taken at 2200 hrs.

6. *ALA* 23 Dec 1600 hrs

*Panzeraufklärungs-Lehr-Abteilung* 130 : armoured reconnaissance towards Jemelle, Rochefort and Han-sûr-Lesse.

7. 902 23 Dec. 2000 hrs

*Panzergrenaider-Lehr-Regiment* 902 – U.S. road blocks and the southern outskirts of Rochefort taken on 23 Dec at 2000 hrs. Night of 23/24 Dec, hard fighting in the center of Rochefort. Town taken at 1200 hrs. Rochefort cleaned up, bridgehead built. North bridge destroyed. East bridge not destroyed.

24 Dec at 1800 hrs *Panzeraufklärungs-Lehr-Abteilung* 130 moves toward Ciergnon. 2000 hrs elements of *Panzergrenadier-Lehr-Regiment* 902 with 10 tanks and elements of *Panzeraufklärungs-Lehr-Abteilung* 130 with 8 tanks attack towards Humain, Havrenne and Buissonville.

8. 25 Dec. 0900 hrs

Elements of *Panzergrenadier-Lehr-Regiment* 902 take Humain. Elements of *Panzeraufklärungs-Lehr-Abteilung* 130 take Havrenne. The attack towards Buissonville fails.

Xx – U.S. Roadblocks.

Destroyed material 2nd *Panzer-Division*

Destroyed material of 2nd *Panzer Division* (guns, tanks and armoured vehicles)

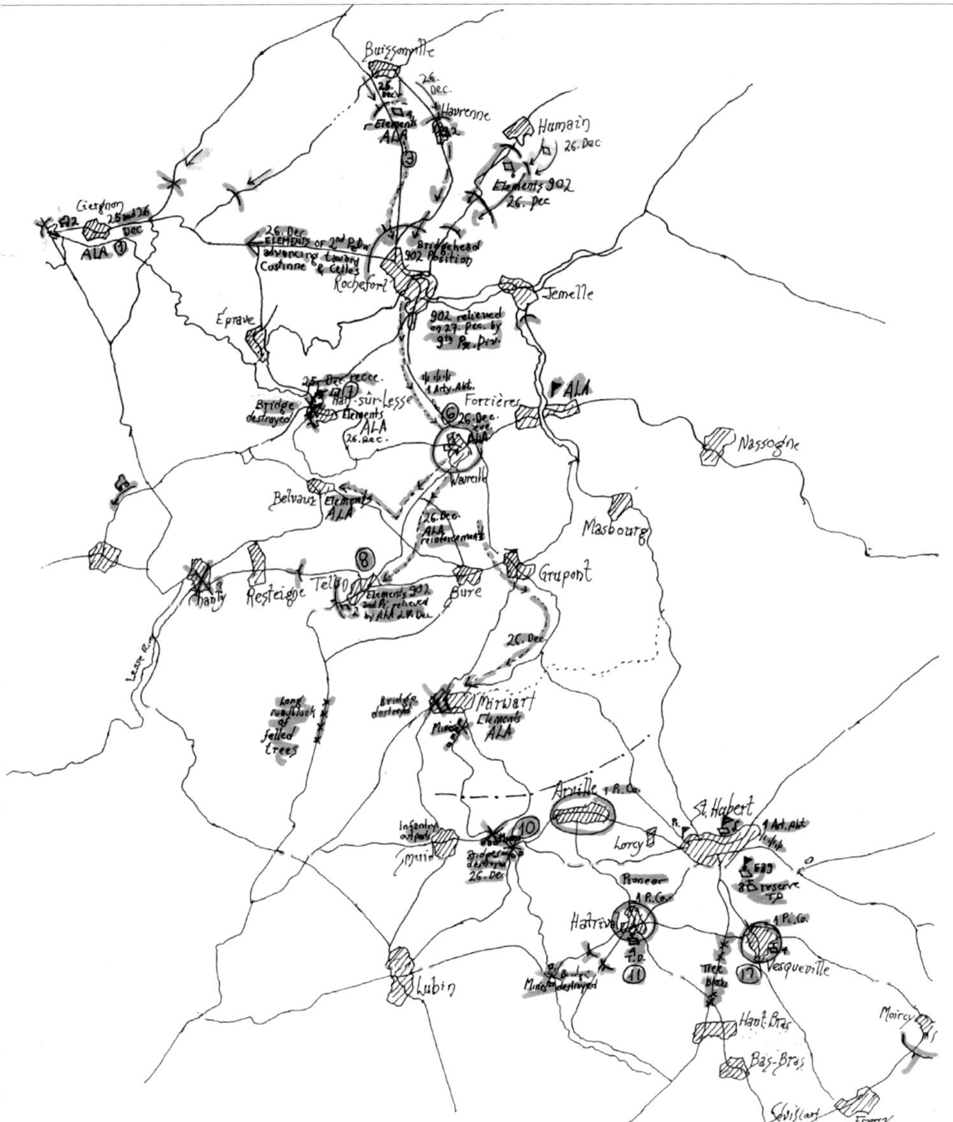


*Panzer-Lehr* 25–27 December 1944

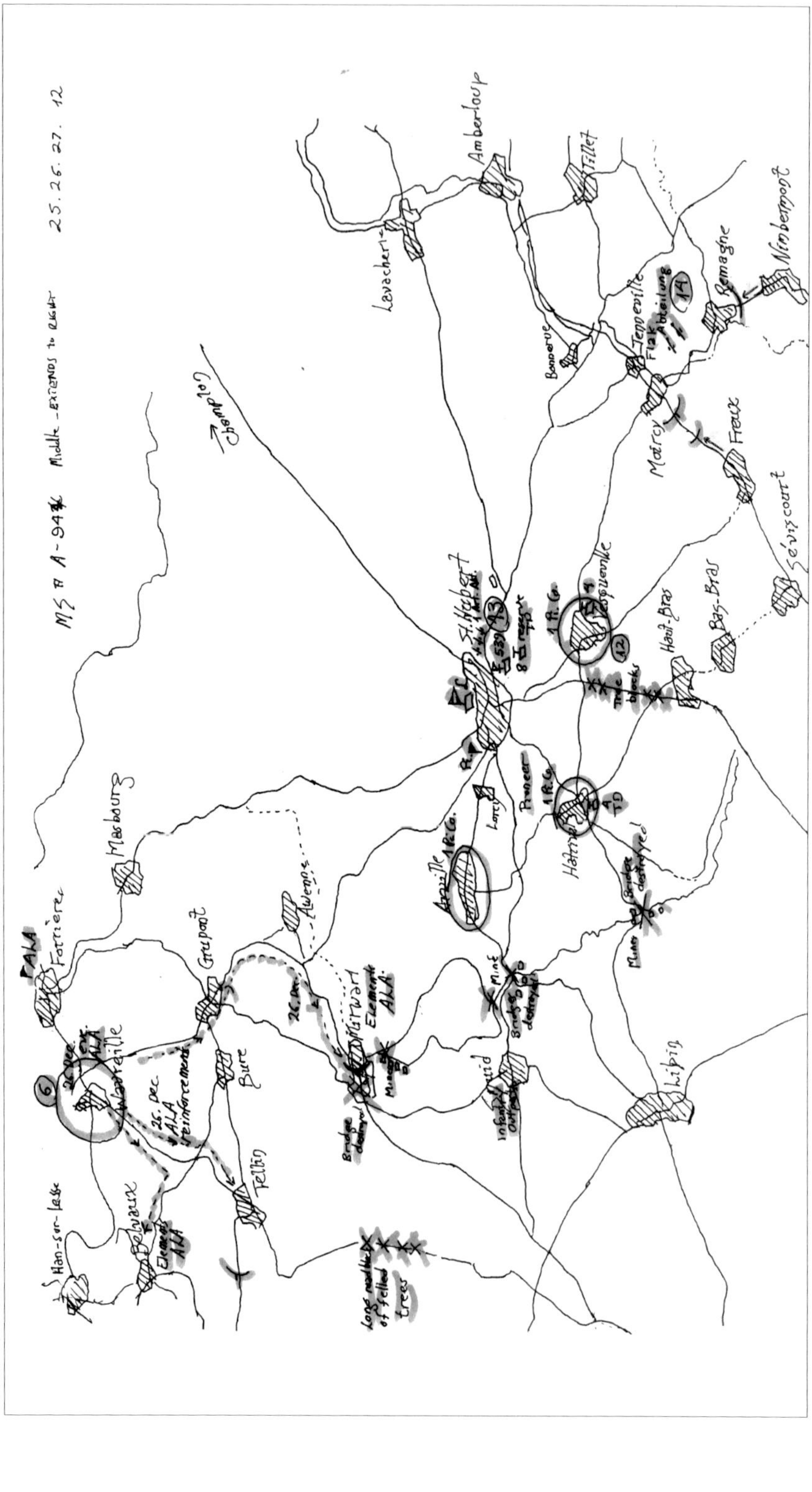


*Panzer-Lehr* 25–27 December 1944 (continuation)

**Maps for 25, 26 and 27 December:**

1. ALA 25 and 26 Dec.

   Combat team of *Aufklärungs-Lehr-Abteilung* 130 consisting of half a platoon, two armoured reconnaissance cars, one anti-tank gun on 25 and 26 December.

   (Arrow) Advancing U.S. Troops on 26th December.

   26 Dec.

2. Elements (infantry and tanks) of 2nd *Panzer Division* advance towards Custinne – Celles to relieve the combat command surrounded near Celles.

3. Elements ALA 25 Dec 26 Dec

   Elements of *Panzeraufkilärungs-Lehr-Abteilung* 130 (one company and six tanks) on 25 and 26 Dec. Strong counterattack from Buissonville. Elements of *ALA* fall back into the Rochefort Bridgehead in the afternoon of 26 December.

4. Elements 902 25. Dec, 26. Dec.

   Elements (two companies and six tanks) of *Panzergrenadier-Lehr-Regiment* 902 on 25 and 26 December. U.S. Counterattack from Humain against the right German flank. Elements of *Panzergrenadier-Lehr-Regiment* 902 withdraw into a position three kilometres north of Rochefort.

5. Bridgehead Position 902.

   Bridgehead position (two companies of *Panzergrenadier-Lehr-Regiment* 902).

   Command Post, *Panzergrenadier-Lehr-Regiment* 902

   902 relieved on 27 Dec. by 9th *PzDiv*

   Panzergrenadier-Lehr-Regiment 902 relieved by 9th *Panzer Division* on 27 December.

6. 1 Art. Abt. – One artillery *Abteilung*

   *ALA* 26 Dec. Evening

   *Panzeraufklärungs-Lehr-Abteilung* 130 concentrated at Wavreille in the evening of 26 December and committed as reinforcement for the positions at6 Han-sûr-Lesse, Belvaux, Tellin and Mirwart.

   ALA Command Post, *Panzeraufklärungs-Lehr-Abteilung* 130

7. 25 Dec, recce.

   25. December, armoured reconnaissance.

   26. Dec. Elements *ALA*

   Elements of *Panzeraufklärungs-Lehr-Abteilung* 130 on 26. December.

X – bridge destroyed

Elements of *Panzeraufklärungs-Lehr-Abteilung* 130 (anti-tank gun crew).

8. Tellin. Elements 902 and Pi. Relieved by *ALA* 27 Dec.

   Elements of *Panzergrenadier-Lehr-Regiment* 902 and *PanzerPionier-Bataillon* 130 relieved by elements of *Panzeraufklärungs-Abteilung* 130 on 27 December.

   X? Bridge at Ambly [although somewhat illegible, the original typed name was whited-out or erased and a hand-written 'Ambly' inserted. The actual location on the sketchmap is clearly at Chanly].

9. Mirwart Elements *ALA* 26/27 Dec. Elements of *Panzeraufklärungs-Lehr-Abteilung* 130, 26/27 December

   XXXX long roadblock with trees 26 Dec – Long roadblock of felled trees

   bridge destroyed x – Bridge destroyed

   mines – mines

   . ——. ——. — Boundary between *Panzeraufklärungs-Lehr-Abteilung* 130 and *Panzer-Pionier-Bataillon* 130

10. Arville 1 Pi. Co. One pioneer company with 1 antitank gun

    bridges destroyed 26 Dec – bridges destroyed 26 December.

    infantry outposts in Smuid – Infantry outposts in Smuid

11. Hatrival

    1 Pi. Co. 4 TD

    One pioneer company, 4 tank-destroyers (Mark V)

    Bridge destroyed X – Bridge destroyed

12. Vesqueville

    1 Pi. Co, 4 TD

    1 pioneer company, 4 tank-destroyers

    Tree blocks – Felled-tree roadblocks

    Haut Bras – outposts – outposts at Haut-Bras

13. St. Hubert

    *Panzer Lehr Division* 130 command post

    *Panzer-Pionier-Bataillon* 130 command post

    *schwere-Panzerjäger-Abteilung* 539 command post

    1 art. *Abt.* – one artillery *Abteilung*

    8 – eight tank-destroyers in reserve

14. *Flak Abteilung* – Antiaircraft *Abteilung*

Moircy and Remagne

*Flak* – Half an 8.8 cm *Flak* battery was committed at Moircy and half an 8.8 cm *Flak* battery at Remagne as anti-tank guns. One 8.8 cm *Flak* battery was committed as artillery.

[arrow] – U.S. Attacks.

**Maps for 28, 29. Dec.**

1. *Kampfgruppe Gutmann* 2nd *Panzer Division*

*Kampfgruppe Gutmann* of the 2nd *Panzer Division*

Command post of *Kampfgruppe Gutmann*

——————*xx*——————*xx*———- Boundary line between 2nd *Panzer Divsision* and *Panzer Lehr Division* 130

2. *ALA*

*Panzeraufklärungs-Lehr-Abteilung* 130

Mirwart and Arville

Each occupied by half a company of *Panzeraufklärungs-Lehr-Abteilung* 130 reinforced by anti-tank guns and tanks.

Smuid given up.

(Arrows) – Allied advances on Smuid and along road to Tellin, bypassing felled trees in roadblock.

Pioneer works in the valley of the stream.

3. *Kampfgruppe Poschinger*

One battalion *Panzergrenadier-Lehr-Regiment* 902 reinforced by tank-destroyers.

Hatrival: One company with 4 tank-destroyers. Outposts to the south. Enemy advancing from south and southwest on 28 December. Road from Haut-Bras blocked and occupied by tanks. Haut-Bras occupied by U.S. Troops.

Vesqueville: One company with four tanks. Ouposts to the southeast.

4. Forward command post of *Panzer Lehr Division* 130

Command post of *Kampfgruppe Poschinger* (*Panzergrenadier-Lehr-Regiment* 902)

Command post of *schwere Panzerjäger-Abteilung* 539.

*Panzer-Pionier-Bataillon* 130 as Division reserve. Elements carry out pioneer works.

8 tank-destroyers in reserve.

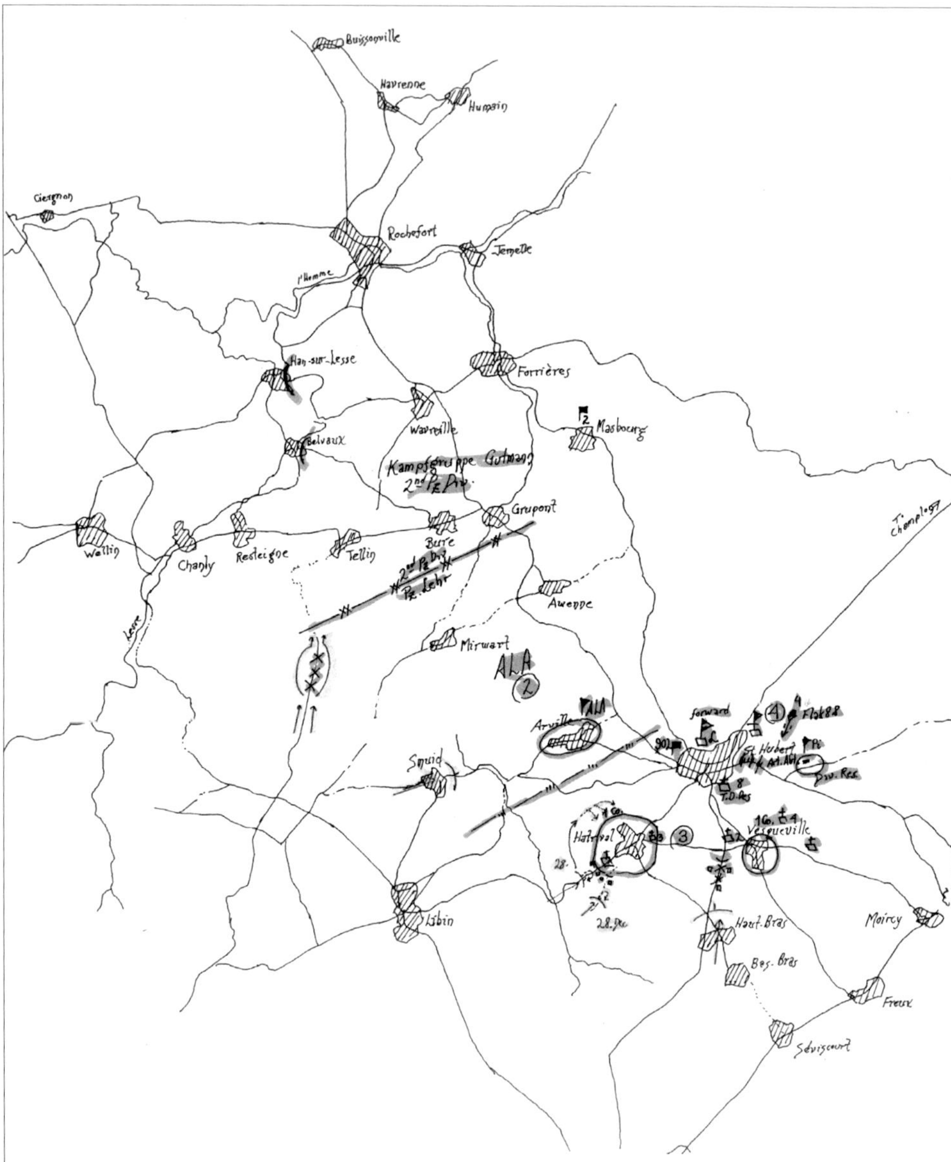


*Panzer-Lehr* 28–29 December 1944

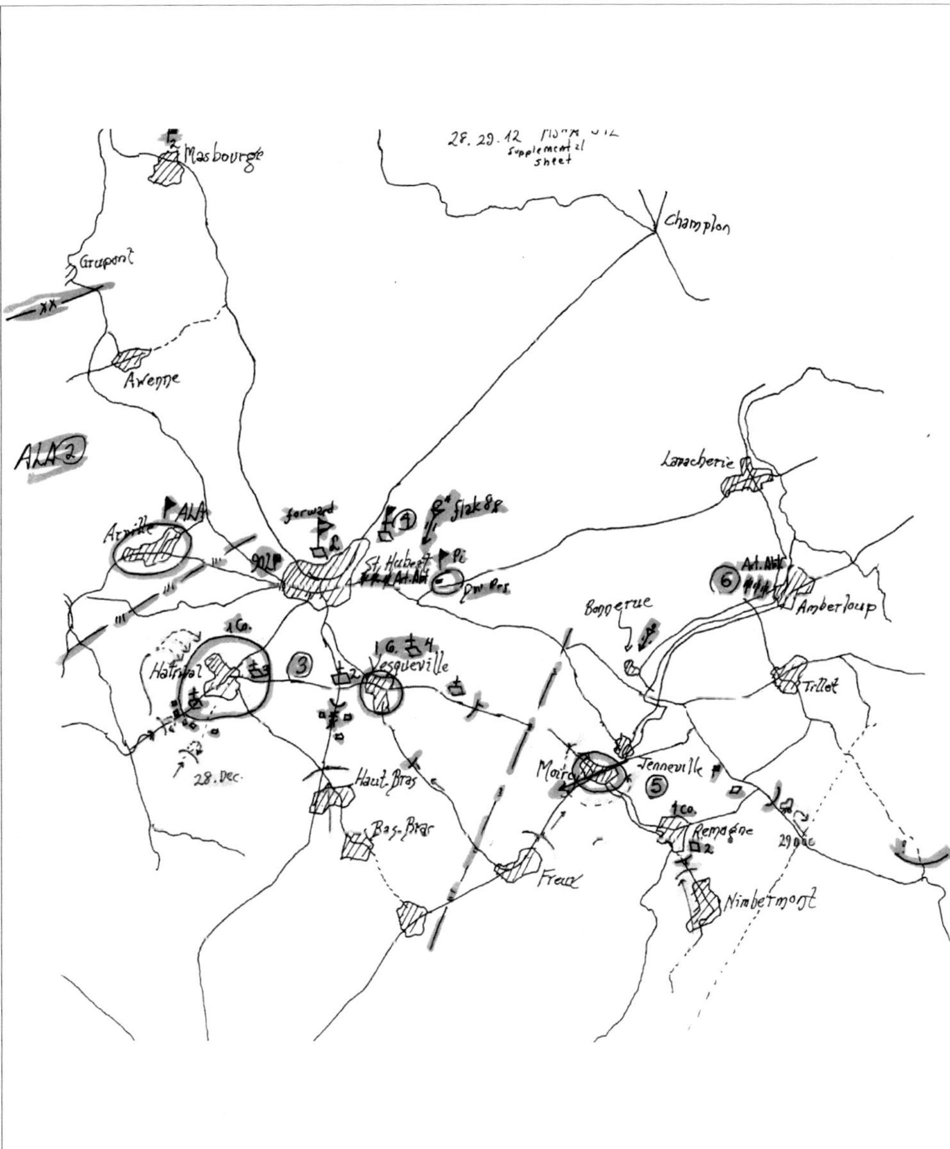


*Panzer-Lehr* 28–29 December 1944 (continuation)

One artillery *Abteilung* (three batteries)

Antiaircraft (*Flak*) battery. 4 8.8 cm guns employed as artillery.

5. *Kampfgruppe Neumann*

   One battalion *Panzergrenadier-Lehr-Regiment* 902 reinforced with tanks and [hand written] 9 [T?]D's.

   Moircy occupied by one company, three tanks

   U.S. Troops occupy the forests north of Freux on 28 December and take Moircy by enveloping attacks. German counterattack night of 29/30 recaptures Moircy.

   Remagne: Occupied by one company, several tanks.

   Reserve: Six tanks, one company located in the forest northeast of Remagne.

   U.S. Troops 26 Dec.

   U.S. Troops take the area south and southeast of Remagne. U.S. Armoured reconnaissance east of Remagne repelled.

6. One battery 8.8 cm *Flak* consisting of four guns.

   Artillery *Abteilung* (eight light, four heavy guns).

   Rear command post *Panzer Lehr Division* 130.

**Map 30, 31 December**

1. *Kampfgruppe Gutmann* 2nd *PzDiv* – *Kampfgruppe Gutmann,* 2nd *Panzer Division*

2. *ALA* *Panzeraufklärungs-Lehr-Abteilung* 130.

   Mirwart: Half platoon *Panzeraufklärungs-Lehr-Abteilung* 130, one anti-tank gun.

   Arville: Command post of *Panzeraufklärungs-Lehr-Abteilung* 130. Half a platoon, one anti-tank gun, two tanks.

3. *Kampfgruppe Poschinger*, one battalion of *Panzergrenadier-Lehr-Regiment* 902.

   Hatrival: One company *Panzergrenadier-Lehr-Regiment* 902, several tanks.

   U.S. Attacks were driven back on 30 and 31 December.

   Vesqueville: Half a company with several tanks located on both sides of the St. Hubert –Haut-Bras road. U.S. Attacks failed.

   In Vesqueville one company *Panzergrenadier-Lehr-Regiment* 902 with several tanks.

   U.S. Attacks repulsed on 30 and 31 Dec.

4. St. Hubert

*Panzer-Lehr* 30–31 December 1944

Forward command post of*Panzer Lehr Division* 130

Command post of *Kampfgruppe Poschinger*

Command Post of *schwere Panzerjäger Abteilung* 539.

Reserves of the *Kampfgruppe.*

Artillery *Abteilung* consisting of 12 guns.

One battery of 8.8 cm anti-aircrat guns committed as artillery.

5. Attacking U.S. Troops infiltrating into the forests between St. Hubert and Piromré

   [tr.note – these hooked arrows were not on the 30–31 Dec map, but on the 1 –11 Jan map ]

   Pioneer battalion

   *Pionier Bataillon* committed to prevent enemy from infiltrating

   Command post of *Panzerpionier-Bataillon* 130

6. *Kampfgruppe Neumann*

   Elements of *Panzergrenadier-Lehr-Regiment* 902.

   Moircy: Retaken by U.S. Troops on 31 December.

   Line occupied in the evening of 31 December.

   Remagne: taken by U.S. Troops on 30 December

   Command post of *Kampfgruppe Neumann.*

   ——— xx ——————- xx ——————— Boundary to *Brigade Remer*

   Presumed line of defense of *Brigade Remer*

7. Rear command post of *Panzer Lehr Division* 130

   One artillery *Abteilung*

   One anti-aircraft battery (four 8.8 cm guns) committed as artillery

**Map for 1 – 11 January 1945**

1. *ALA*

   *Panzeraufklärungs-Lehr-Abteilung* 130, unchanged.

2. *Kampfgruppe Poschinger*: drives back all attacks against Hatrival and Vesquevbill and holds its positions from 1 January to 11 January 1945.

3. St. Hubert

   Command post of *Kampfgruppe Poschinger*

   Reserve of *Kampfgruppe*

   Artillery *Abteilung*

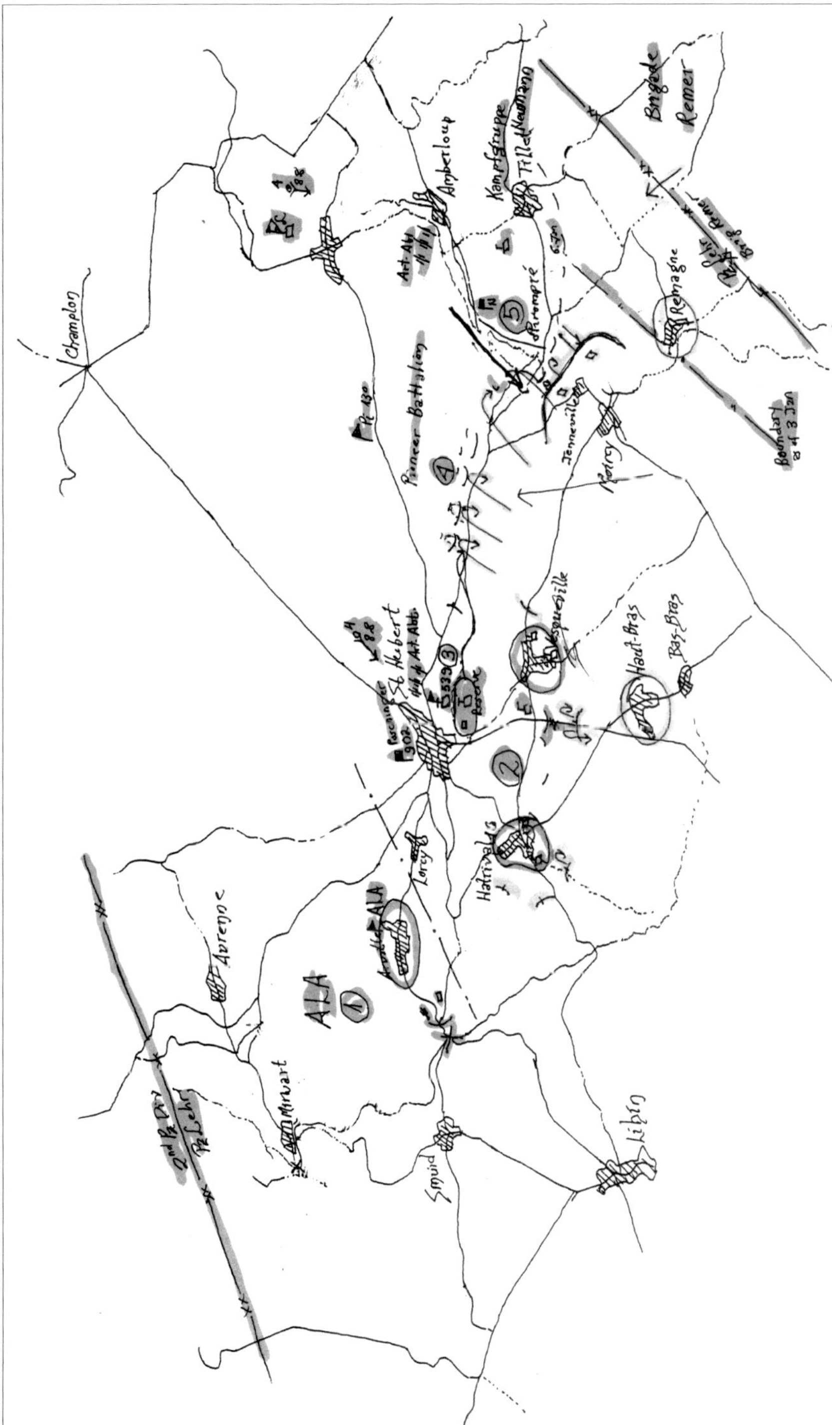


*Panzer-Lehr* 1–11 January 1945

4. Pioneer Battalion

*Panzer-Pionier-Bataillon* 130

U.S. Attacks stopped in hard forest-fighting north of the St. Hubert – Pirompré road from 1 to 1 to 11 January.

German counterattacks on 2 January 1945.

5. *Kampfgruppe Neumann*

Piompré – Bonnerue

All U.S. Attacks against Priompré were repulsed. Hard fighting continued from 1 to 11 January 1945. Priompré remained in German hands.

Bonnerue was lost [to U.S. Forces] on 10 January but was retaken in the morning of 11 January 1945.

Counterattack on 11 January

Command post of *Kampfgruppe Neumann*

————-xx ————-xx ———— Boundary between *Panzer Lehr Division* 130 and *Kampfgruppe Remer* effective 3 January 1945.

Alfred Z e r b e l Koenigstein 16 May 50

**INDEX FOR**
**MS # A 944.**

**(PZ LEHR DIV – SIT MAPS (23 DEC 44 – 11 JAN 45))**

**No keywords for index**

(Signature)
(Alfred Z e r b e l)

# MS # A 945 (16 June 1950)

## ADDITIONAL QUESTIONS ON ARDENNES OFFENSIVE

Alfred Zerbel
Königstein, 16 August 1950

**Index for**
**MS #A 945**

**ADDITIONAL QUESTIONS ON THE ARDENNES OFFENSIVE**

(Signed)
(Alfred Zerbel)

**Index for MS # A 945**



*Generalleutnant* Bayerlein
Oberursel, 23 February 1946
Former Commander, *Panzer Lehr DIvision*

## Additional Questions on the Ardennes Offensive

Translated by Frederick Steinhardt
MS # A–945

Additional Questions on the Ardennes Offensive

Description of operations from 11–20 January near Houffalize, which provides evidence of the development of American pressure from the north.

In the course of the major withdrawal from the St. Hubert area, which had been ordered from on high, the Division was committed in defense during the night of 13/14 January, with one *Kampfgruppe* (*Panzergrenadier-Lehr-Regiment* 901 [tr. -*Kampfgruppe von Hauser*]) in the Ortho area, and with the other (elements of *Panzergrenadier-Lehr-Regiment* 902 [tr.-*Kampfgruppe von Poschinger*]) with individual tanks and one battery of artillery north of the Ourthe [river] in the Nadrin – Filly area. Commitment north of the Ourthe was necessary because the 116th *Panzer Division* was so weak that it could not on its own hold its entire sector north of the Ourthe. When *Kampfgruppe* 902 arrived in the area of Nadrin there were no more elements of the 116th *Panzer Division* to be found there. It was known that the U.S. 84th Infantry Division was attacking in that sector. On 14 January *Kampfgruppe* 902 came under surprise attack, not only frontally, but by strong infantry and armoured forces [tr.–1st Battalion, U.S. Infantry Regiment 334] in an enveloping attack from the northeast, from the Nibrin [Wibrin?] area. The enveloping attack came because the 116th *Panzer Division* had already fallen back before the attack, thereby exposing the flank of *Kampfgruppe* 902. The enemy captured Nadrin by noon and Filly during the evening. *Kampfgruppe* 902 thereby lost a large number of personnel captured since they could no longer break out of the envelopment. In the evening of 14 January the stream sector near Aschouffe [Achouffe] was held by *Kampfgruppe* 902. *Panzeraufklärungs-Lehr-Abteilung* 130 (about 150 men with a few tanks) was shifted to the area north of Houffalize, but not yet committed, since it was the only available Division reserve.

On 15 January *Panzer Lehr* received orders to hold Houffalize at all costs. A *Kampfkommandant* [A *Kampfkommandant* was an officer specifically assigned to hold a specified location, with special powers to employ any and all troops within that location. He was not permitted to give up or evacuate the specified location unless ordered to do so.] was to be assigned and was, at all costs, to prevent the enemy from penetrating into Houffalize. Houffalize was not to be surrendered. The *Aufklärungs Abteilung* was thereby committed to immediate security of Houffalize, while elements of the 116th *Panzer Division* still held a large bridgehead near Taverneux. This bridgehead was eliminated on 15 January. Elements of *Panzeraufklärungs-Lehr-Abteilung* 130 held the heights directly west of the Ourthe, north and east of [the bridgehead]. The heights south of Houffalize were held by strong elements of *Panzer Lehr* (*Panzergrenadier-Lehr-Regiment* 901 with *Panzerjäger*) to prevent an enemy advance from Noville–Maprompré [Mabompré] and junction of the enemy northern and southern group in Houffalize. That day strong U.S. forces (infantry and armour) advanced in a fast-moving attack via Maprompre [Mabompré] – Wicourt, reaching the woods northeast of Maprompre [Mabompré] early in the afternoon.

At about noon on 16 January U.S. forces broke into Houffalize from the north. The southern attack made further progress in the morning hours, attaining the south edge of the city.

The U.S. northern and southern groups thereby joined up in Houffalize, establishing contact.

On 16 January the *Panzer Lehr* line ran along the Ourthe from Bourjeusel to the mouth of the Cowan Stream, then along that stream to the woods east of Neuf Moulin. Enemy pressure on the front let up markedly on 17 January.

Enemy units identified on the *Panzer Lehr* sector of the front in the Houffalize area were: North of the Ourthe: Elements of the U.S. 2nd Armored Division, the 84th Infantry Division; South of the Ourthe: Elements of the English 53rd Infantry Division, and, attacking Houffalize from the south, the U.S. 11th Armored Division.

See sketch maps for details and positions of *Panzer Lehr* during the period from 11 to 20 January.

Signed BAYERLEIN

# PART III

## *PANZER LEHR DIVISION* 130 AFTER ARDENNES, BEFORE REMAGEN

# MS # D–322

## EMPLOYMENT OF PANZER LEHR DIVISION IN THE SAAR SECTOR IN NOVEMBER 1944

[Editor's (FPS) note – this (MS # D–322) was translated by an Army Translator. The German original was not available so this is copied exactly. Any additions or comments by FPS are in brackets. Due to illegibility of some place names, reference was made to Helmut Ritgen, pp 204–212 in *Die Geschichte der Panzer-Lehr Division* and Map XXXIV and discussion in Cole, *The Lorraine Campaign*, pp.464 ff.]

### Employment of the PANZER-LEHR DIVISION in the SAAR Sector in November 1944

Around the 20 November strong US forces had advanced th rough the SAARBURG-PFALZBERG area to the VOSGES (SAVERNE Heights) in ALSACE.

The PANZER-LEHR DIVISION, at approximately 50% strength, was alerted on 22 Nov in the area CASTELLAN-BUECHENBEUREN-MOORBACH and moved to ST WENDEL-ST INGBERT with the mission of attacking from vic[inity] SAARUNION and clearing the area between SAARBURG And PFLAZBURG [Pfalzburg]. After this was accomplished the division would then attack the flanks of the advancing enemy force and cutting [*sic.*] it off from its rear communications and thus prepare the annihilation of the forces which had advanced into ALSACE.

For this mission the division was attached to the First Army.

The PANZER-LEHR Division arrived at 1600, 22 Nov in vic[inity] SAARUNION in two combat teams:

### Combat Team I

(902 PzGren Regt, light artillery battalion, 12 tanks [*Kampfgruppe v. Poschinger*]).

Mission to attack and take WOLFSKIRCHEN, POTSDORF, BAERENDORF [Bärendorf] and RAUWILLER [Rauviller on sketchmap] and advance to SAARBURG-PFLAZBURG [Pfalzburg] road.

### Combat Team II

(901 PzGren Regt, medium-artillery battalion, 20 tanks [*Kampfgruppe v. Hauser*])

Advance over EYWILLER, HIRSCHLAND [Hirschlanden on sketchmap], SCHALLBACH to PFALZBURG.

Combat Team I had on the 25th, after fighting in and around POTSDORF [ Postroff on Cole map and on sketchmap in Ritgen, but Porsthof in text of Ritgen, *Die Geschichte der Panzer Lehr Division*], and BAERENDORF, captured RAUWILLER. The latter was taken by envelopment from both sides and one enemy battalion captured.

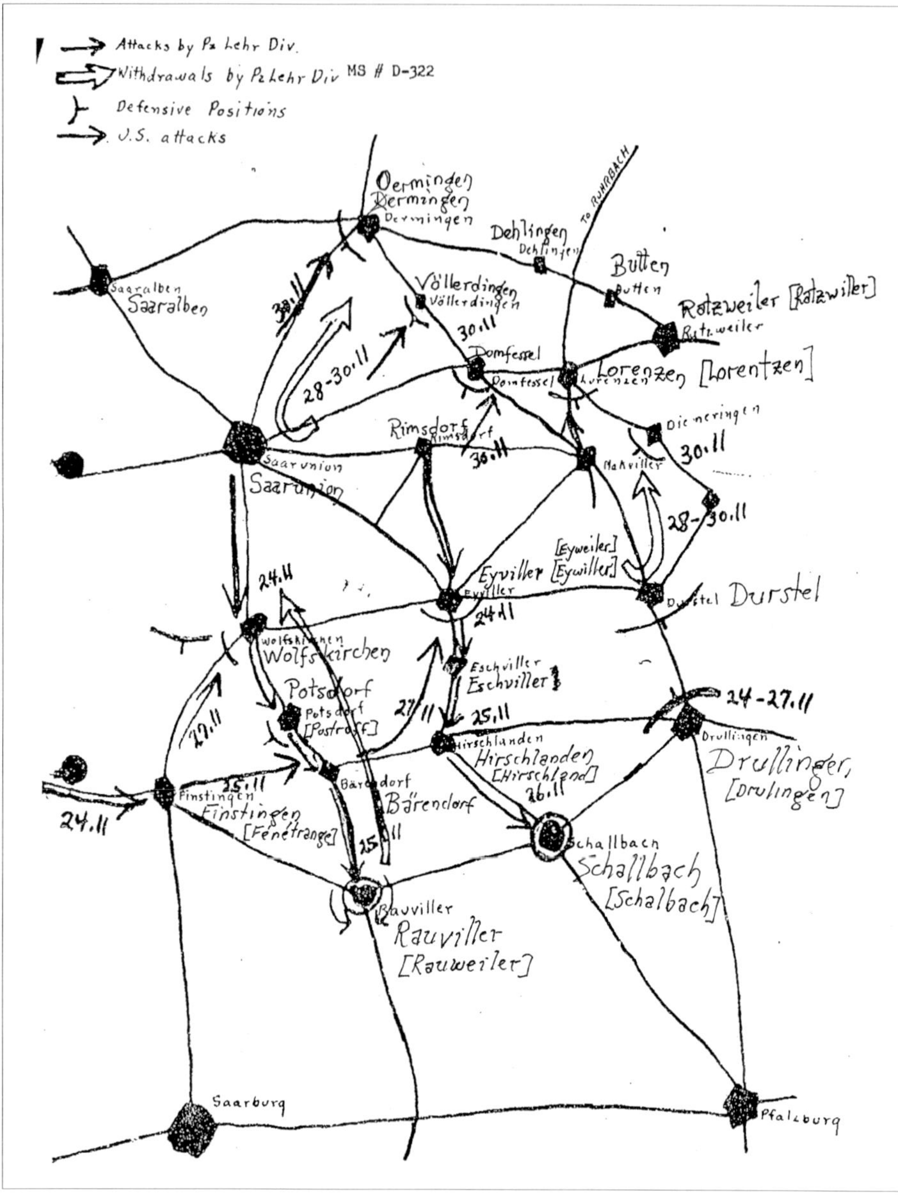


Attacks and withdrawal of *Panzer-Lehr* Division November 1944, Saar region. Note from editor - the map Bayerlein provided is clear enough on military annotations, but the place names are mostly illegible. I rewrote the names as written on the original map on the copy. Where the names on Bayerlein's sketchmap differed significantly from those on the maps in Ritgen's *Die Geschichte der Panzer-Lehr Division* (p. 209), Cole's *The Lorraine Campaign*, map XXXIV or, where neither of those included the location, the current Michelin map, I placed a more generally used name in brackets.

Combat Team II attacked and took Eschwiller [Eschviller on sketchmap] and HIRSCHLANDEN and advanced to the high ground near SCHALLBACH but could not take the town.

Already on 25 Nv [November] the enemy countermeasures could be felt.

1. From MITTERSHEIM a new US formation (4th Armd Div) advanced over FINSTINGEN [Fénétrange (?) on map in Cole, *The Lorraine Campaign*] and threatened the flank of the PZ-LEHR Div at BAERENDORF.

2. At DRULLINGEN [Drulingen] the enemy was reinforced.

3. In addition enemy attacks increased westward near SAARALBEN and eastward attacks were being launched in a northerly direction into the RHINE plain.

On 25 Nov BAERENDORF was lost.

On 26 Nov the attack (German) on SCHALLBACH failed.

Since the enemy attacks were increasing near DRULLINGEN the division was forced to withdraw in order to avoid double envelopment.

On 27 Nov the line WOLFSKIRCHEN-EYWILLER-DURSTEL was still being held. Prior to the attack of the US forces on the entire front on 28 Nov the division was fighting a delaying action along the line OERMINGEN [Dermingen?] –DOMFESSEL-LORENZEN-DIEMERINGEN and still held on 30 Nov. During the night of 30 Nov through 1 Dec the division was relieved by elements of the 11th PANZER Div and 35th PZ GREN Div and withdrawn from the front in order to be transferred to the EIFEL for participation in the ARDENNES offensive.

See attached sketch

BAYERLEIN
Formerly CG PZ LEHR Div

# *Panzer Lehr Division* on the Lower Rhine against Canadian Operation 'Veritable'

The context in which the *Panzer-Lehr-Division* was committed on the lower Rhine, as described in MS # B–768, was in defence against the Canadian Army's participation in Operation 'Veritable', aimed at destroying the German forces between the Maas and the Rhine. After the failure of the counterattack there described, the division was hastily moved to the Schiefbahn area to take part in the frantic efforts to halt Simpson's American Ninth Army's northeastward drive from the area northeast of Aachen in Operation 'Grenade', the southern arm of the 21st Army Group's pincers. This action is described below in MS # B–830.

After the conclusion of the German Ardennes Offensive, Eisenhower's plan, as Supreme Commander in Europe, for the final western offensive against Germany was to close up to the Rhine so as to be able to hold the west bank with minimal forces. Then a consecutive series of drives would unfold, from north to south, the *Schwerpunkt* with Montgomery's 21st Army Group in the north. In that main effort by the 21st Army Group the British Second Army would maintain pressure while the Canadian First Army would attack, no later than 8 February, in Operation 'Veritable', advancing southeast down the left (west) bank of the Rhine River. By 10 February Simpson's American Ninth Army (under British control, with Montgomery's 21st Army Group) would attack to the northeast as the right arm of a pincer, in Operation 'Grenade'to link up with the Canadians along the Rhine. The 21st Army Group's British Second Army and American Ninth Army would then cross the Rhine in Operation 'Plunder', which would cut off the Ruhr industrial region from the rest of Germany. The Twelfth and Sixth Army Groups would later make secondary crossings of the Rhine. Thus there would be two main thrusts into the heart of Germany, the northern one across the North German Plain, the southern through the Frankfurt–Kassel corridor, converging to cut the great Ruhr industrial region off from the rest of Germany.

When the 21st Army Group's Operations 'Veritable' and 'Grenade' had reached the Rhine, Bradley's 12th Army Group was to launch Operation 'Lumberjack', in which Hodges' American First Army would cover the south flank of the Ninth Army, clearing the triangle of land between the Erft and the Rhine Rivers extending north from Cologne, take Cologne, and then turn south along the west bank of the Rhine. Other contingents of Hodges' First Army were to launch a narrow thrust from near the road center of Euskirchen southeast to the Ahr River, converging with a thrust by Patton's Third Army through the Eifel, thereby cutting off more German forces west of the Rhine. Subsequently Devers' Sixth Army Group would launch Operation 'Undertone'

In Operation 'Veritable' the Canadian forces crossed the Dutch – German border south of Nijmegen, which they had captured in Operation 'Marketgarden', the failed attempt to gain the Arnhem bridge. They advanced southeast, just inside of and parallel to the German border with the Netherlands, through good terrain for armoured operations between the two rivers, hemmed in by flooded terrain. As part of Crerar's Canadian First Army, General Horrocks' British 30th Corps opened the attack, the 2nd Canadian Corps then being committed on the left.

Just inside the German frontier was the Reichswald forest, with only two north-south paved roads and, for east-west travel, no more than cleared rides, a few marginally paved for logging operations. A dozen miles to the east, two more forests, the Hochwald and the Balberger Wald formed another barrier on the approach to Xanten.

Marienbaum, where the *Panzer Lehr* units mentioned below detrained, is at the northern limit of the Hochwald. Goch, at the southwest end of the Goch–Kalkar road, lay on the edge of flooded ground of the River Niers, which flows into the Maas near Gennep. The Goch–Kalkar (Calcar) road, so important in the action described below, extended almost due northeast to Kalkar, which was on the margin of the extensive flooded area adjacent to the Rhine. Uedem was approximately two miles southeast of the straight line of the Goch–Kalkar road. The Uedem – Weeze road, mentioned below, paralleled the Goch–Kalkar road, extending southwest from Uedem to Weeze, Weeze being situated on the margin of the flooded land adjacent to the Maas River.

On 14 February *Oberbefelshaber West* released *Panzer Lehr Division* to *Heeresgruppe* H for commitment on the Maas front in the area west of Xanten. *Panzer Lehr* was attached to the XLVII *Panzerkorps* to join in a counterattack along with the 116th *Panzer Division,* in the action described below After the failure of the counterattack the *Panzer Lehr Division* was transferred to Erkelenz in the Mönchen-Gladbach sector during the night of 24–25 February.

# MS # B–768

## PANZER LEHR DIVISION (15–25 FEBRUARY 1945)

**PART ONE**

**By**

**Major a.D. Helmut Hudel**

See MS # B–830 for Part II

**Historical Division**
**HEADQUARTERS**
**UNITED STATES ARMY, EUROPE**

MS # B–768
[tr. note – This document was only available as the English copy. Spelling and grammar, including the dubious punctuation, are left as in the original.]

**PART ONE**
**PANZER LEHR DIVISION**
**(15–25 Feb 1945)**

### INTRODUCTION

There is little data available regarding the operations of the 130th Panzer Lehr Division west of the Rhine in the Uedem Rheindalen – Muenchen-Gladbach – Krefeld – Wesel area 15 – 25 February 1945. It was one of the few mobile reserve units of the High Command West and as there was a general shortage of troops on the entire Western front at that time, the division was constantly moved. The uninterrupted activity of the enemy air forces, lack of fuel, destruction of signal communications, traffic difficulties often necessitated splitting up the division units. Because of the above reasons it is very difficult to write an accurate report on the division as a whole. There are bound to be certain inaccuracies. Figures given must be considered as only approximate.

At the beginning of February 1945 I was transferred west and appointed commander of the Panzer Lehr Regiment of the 130th Panzer Lehr Division.

As ordered, I first reported to the Commander in Chief, Panzer Troops West, General Stumpf, at Daumenau near Bad Ems. As nothing accurate was known there regarding the where-abouts of the 130th Panzer Lehr Division I was ordered to report to Headquarters Army Group B.

The newly appointed operations officer (Ia) of the 130th Division, Major GS [*i.G., im Generalstab*=trained for General Staff], Koch-Erpach, happened to be at General Stumpf's Headquarters at the time and I drove north with him. We met the division marching from the area of Euskirchen to the area west of Xanten. [tr.(FPS) note – Shortage of fuel and danger of air attack delayed the march, which was carried out in separated march serials.]

On 15 February 1945 we both reported to the division commander, Colonel Niemack, at Schiefbahn, who was in command of the division during the march.

Since the end of January there had been important command changes in the Panzer Lehr Division. On 25 January the former division commander, Lt Gen

Fritz Bayerlein [*sic.*-lack of comma] had turned over his command to Colonel Niemack. At the same time the chief of operations (Ia) was transferred and at first Major, GS [*i.G.*] Fuhrmann was appointed chief of operations and later, after 15 February, Major, GS [*i.G.*] Koch-Erpach was assigned the duty. At the same time Major Hudel was appointed commander of the Panzer Lehr Regiment.

These changes naturally caused some initial difficulties which later showed up rather disturbingly in the various critical situations.

After the Battle of the Bulge, where the division had suffered very great losses, the division had been moved to the Neuerburg – Bitburg (Eifel) area and there it had been briefly reorganized. The various units had been filled out numerically almost to the authorized T/O strength, however, the combat value of the replacements was bad, as was usually the case during the last years of the war. The new leaders [officers] had no combat experience, the non-commissioned officers and the men had not had sufficient training. This was particularly noticeable in the transmission of orders and the inadequate execution of tactical orders. However, it must be emphasized that the readiness and willingness to fight were there and that up to the very end there was no lack of discipline. Because of this the division could keep on going and was able to carry out its missions.

Compared with other divisions, the materiel of the 130th Panzer Lehr Division, was still good. We had an adequate supply of weapons but the general lack of vehicles was clearly noticeable. We had no spare parts with which to repair vehicles heavily damaged during preceding actions.

The independent battalions of the division – reconnaissance, engineer, signal, antitank – were on the whole in a pretty good condition as far as personnel and materiel. The transmission of orders, however, was often handicapped by lack of signal equipment.

The 901st Panzer Grenadier Lehr Regiment had sufficient weapons and vehicles and its great number of armored personnel carriers was a particularly favorable factor.

The 903d Panzer Grenadier Lehr Regiment had about half of the vehicles required but its other equipment and weapons were sufficient.

The condition of the Panzer Artillery Regiment was very bad. It consisted for a time of only regimental headquarters and a very weak and light battalion of panzer IV. [tr.(FPS) note-Although this paragraph says it refers to the Panzer Artillery Regiment, the comments appear to apply to the Panzer Regiment, since a later paragraph describes the Panzer Artillery Regiment in quite different terms.]

Most of our tanks were either being repaired or were laying out on the roads somewhere. Because of lack of fuel and spare parte [*sic.*] towing and repair work took a very long time. A sufficient number of tank crews with combat experience were available.

A panzer battalion, organized by special orders, was entrained, enroute to join the division.

One battalion of the Panzer Artillery Regiment, which had originally consisted of three battalions, had been disbanded. Therefore the division had only two battalions equipped with [a] satisfactory amount of guns. It lacked vehicles to the same extent as the Panzer Grenadier Regiments.

There were far from enough supply trains and the striking power of the division was often badly handicapped by this factor.

(For the 130th Panzer Lehr Division's order of battle see appendix 1.)

## ACTION IN THE UEDEM – XANTEN AREA

On 18 February 1945 the 130th Panzer Lehr Division moved into the concentration area assigned it for the intended counter-offensive in the Xanten Forest. The hazy and rainy weather was favorable for the movement of the units but because of the expected strong enemy air activity they were widely dispersed. After the commanding officers had been briefed on the situation they were ordered to start reconnaissance.

Fighting methodically, and fully exploiting the superiority of their weapons and ammunition, the Canadian First Army advanced into the area southeast of the Reichswald Forest as far as, and beyond, the road Kalkar – Goch. From the direction of their attack it could be seen that they intended advancing in a southeastern direction and gaining the left bank of the Rhine. They were going to try in cooperation with the American forces advancing from the area of Aachen to roll up the German front to the south in order to encircle and destroy the German forces.

At the beginning of February the 130th Panzer Lehr Division had been moved into the area of Euskirchen to be employed as mobile reserve of Army Group B facing the expected major American attack. As the situation toward the north became more and more critical the division was attached to Army Group H for a short operation within the First Parachute Army. It was to be used only for counterattack and not to be inserted into the defense front and was to be returned as soon as possible to Army Group B.

During 18 February the 1st Battalion of the Panzer Grenadier Lehr Regiment [part of *Kampfgruppe v. Hauser*, consisting of *Panzergrenadier-Lehr Regiment* 901, *Panzerjäger-Lehr-Abteilung* 130 and an artillery *Abteilung*.] arrived and was unloaded without enemy air interference at various railroad stations in the Marinebaum [Marienbaum] area. The battalion's equipment was very good – two companies with 14 V tanks [*Panzer V, Panther*][tr. (FPS) Note – Ritgen remarks that inadequate training of the tank-drivers resulted in inordinately high losses of the factory-new inadequately inspected and tested equipment. Despite reinforcement by the 8th *Kompanie* of *Panzer-Lehr Regiment* 130, which, consisting of mixed *Panzer IV* and *Panzer V*, was the only combat-ready company of the II *Abteilung*, only 22 combat-ready tanks, along with 10 – 12 *Panzerjäger* of *Panzerjäger Lehr Abteilung* 130] supported the attack of *Kampfgruppe v. Hauser* on 19 February. (Ritgen, *Die Geschichte der Panzer Lehr Division*, p. 273.] Because of lack of fuel the new tanks had not been broken in and there had been no time to give them the final check up and overhauling. On account of this tank losses were high from the beginning. These losses were all the more serious because the enemy always attacked with masses of tanks and tanks can only be repelled by tanks and assault guns.

On 19 February the 1st Battalion was reinforced by one company (panzer IV) and four antiaircraft tanks which had arrived from the direction of the Eifel. There were in all 22 tanks ready for action that day. (Appendix 2)

Since early morning very strong artillery firing could be heard at the front. Unlike American artillery fire this fire was concentrated on the front and the area close behind. The expenditure of ammunition was extraordinary; no one had ever heard anything like it before.

The division was organized in the following manner for the mission ahead of it:

*Kampfgruppe* Hauser under Colonel Baron von Hauser, commanding officer of the 901st Panzer Grenadier Lehr Regiment;

901st Panzer Grenadier Lehr Regiment;

1st Reinforced Battalion of the 901st Panzer Grenadier Lehr Regiment;

Antitank Battalion;

Artillery Lehr Regiment.

The 902d Panzer Grenadier Lehr Regiment [*Kampfgruppe v. Poschinger*] was concentrated around about and at Uedemerbruch as mobile reserve. The regimental commander, Lt Col von Pochinger was the local commander at Uedemerbruch.[tr. note – Ritgen, in *Die Geschichte der Panzer Lehr Division...* and von Seemen, in *Ritterkreuzträger* list him as von Poschinger.]

On orders from LVII Panzer Corps, the division command post was established at the forester's house, at Nachtigall, with that of the 116th Panzer Division.

The terrain was reconnoitered during the morning of 19 February and early in the afternoon the *Kampfgruppe* Hauser was alerted. The Division was attached to the LVII Panzer Corps. The division commander at the command post of the 116th Panzer Division received the following combat mission by telephone from the commanding general:

1) The enemy has gained deep penetrations into the sector of the 116th Panzer Division and has advanced as far as the farm buildings about 3 kilometres southwest of Kalkar at the Kalkar – Goch road.

2) The Panzer Lehr Division will attack the enemy today, pushing them back to the northwest and gain the road running in a northwestern direction parallel to the Kalkar – Goch road as first objective.

[tr. note – The Kalkar–Goch road runs northeast-southwest. The sketchmap in Ritgen does show a road running northwest at right angles to the Goch–Kalkar road. The Schwanenhof farmstead is located on this road about half a kilometre southeast of the junction with the Goch–Kalkar road. The Totenhügel is a bit over one kilometre due south of this road. According to Ritgen (p.224), after assembling in the area south of the Totenhügel [hillock, burial mound?], *Kampfgruppe v. Hauser* was to attack and regain the road located about 1 kilometre northwest of and running parallel to the Kalkar–Goch road at Luisenhof, restoring the former defensive front.

Stacey's history of the Canadian Army in World War II, *The Victory Campaign*, vol. 3, also has a detailed sketchmap of this action, his Sketch 37, p. 485, showing Battle Group Hauser's attack on the Royal Hamilton Light Infantry on 19 February, accompanied by an intense, detailed account of the fierce fighting.

His Sketch 37 clearly shows *Kampfgruppe von Hauser's* objective, though his map labels it as Louisendorf, rather than Louisenhof and indicates a built-up area surrounding a large square at the crossroads. The road parallel to the Kalkar – Goch road, which passes through Louisendorf, is approximately two kilometres northwest of the Schwanenhof, where *Kampfgruppe von Hauser's* attack bogged down.]

> The plan is for the division to advance further to the northwest after the first objective has been reached.
>
> The 116th Panzer Division with all available artillery and tanks will support the attack of the Panzer Lehr Division.
>
> It will be reported when it is planned to begin the attack.

Because of the difficulties in circulating orders and because not all commanders had returned from their reconnaissance missions, the departure to the concentration area was delayed. It was after 1900 before the *Kampfgruppe Hauser* had concentrated south of Todtenhuegel. [Totenhügel].

The attack was begun at 2000 in a western direction. Combat reconnaissance patrols went ahead. According to what some parachutists holding positions northwest of Todtenhuegel reported the Kalkar–Goch road was strongly occupied by the enemy with tanks and infantry.

When *Kampfgruppe Hauser* turned northward it was delayed several times by strong harassing fire. Reconnaissance patrols reported that they had almost reached the farm at Schwanenhof. By 2400 *Kampfgruppe Hauser* approached the farm buildings and the road about 1 kilometre south of the Kalkar–Goch road. Suddenly it ran into concentrated defense fire and a fire duel developed during which some enemy tanks were disabled. The attack, however, did not progress. It was impossible to break into the farm buildings of Schwanenhof. The enemy defense fire became stronger and stronger.

At dawn 20 February the *Kampfgruppe* resumed its attack and fought desperately to take the farm buildings, however, the enemy defense fire from tanks and artillery, which responded immediately, again proved too strong forcing the attack to come to a halt. Tanks of both sides were disabled by the artillery duel.

Since the terrain was flat and exposed and one had an uninterrupted view over the whole of it major operations, of any kind, during the day time were out of the question. The enemy would immediately resume strong artillery fire.

The positions reached were improved and the division was temporarily attached to the 116th Panzer Division with the *Kampfgruppe Hauser* incorporated into the line of defense.

During the day the reconnaissance patrols from *Panzer Lehr* Regiment and the 902d *Panzer Grenadier Lehr* Regiment combed the area north of Uedem and north of the Uedem – Weeze road. We anticipated an enemy attack from Goch southward and southwest.

One tank company took positions on both sides of the road at the fork 1 kilometre north of Uedem to act as a mobile reserve for antitank defense.

On 21 February *Kampfgruppe Hauser* remained in its positions. Strong harassing fire from the enemy artillery was laid down on the front and rear areas and twice the enemy tried to advance. Their weak attacks were repulsed. Heavy

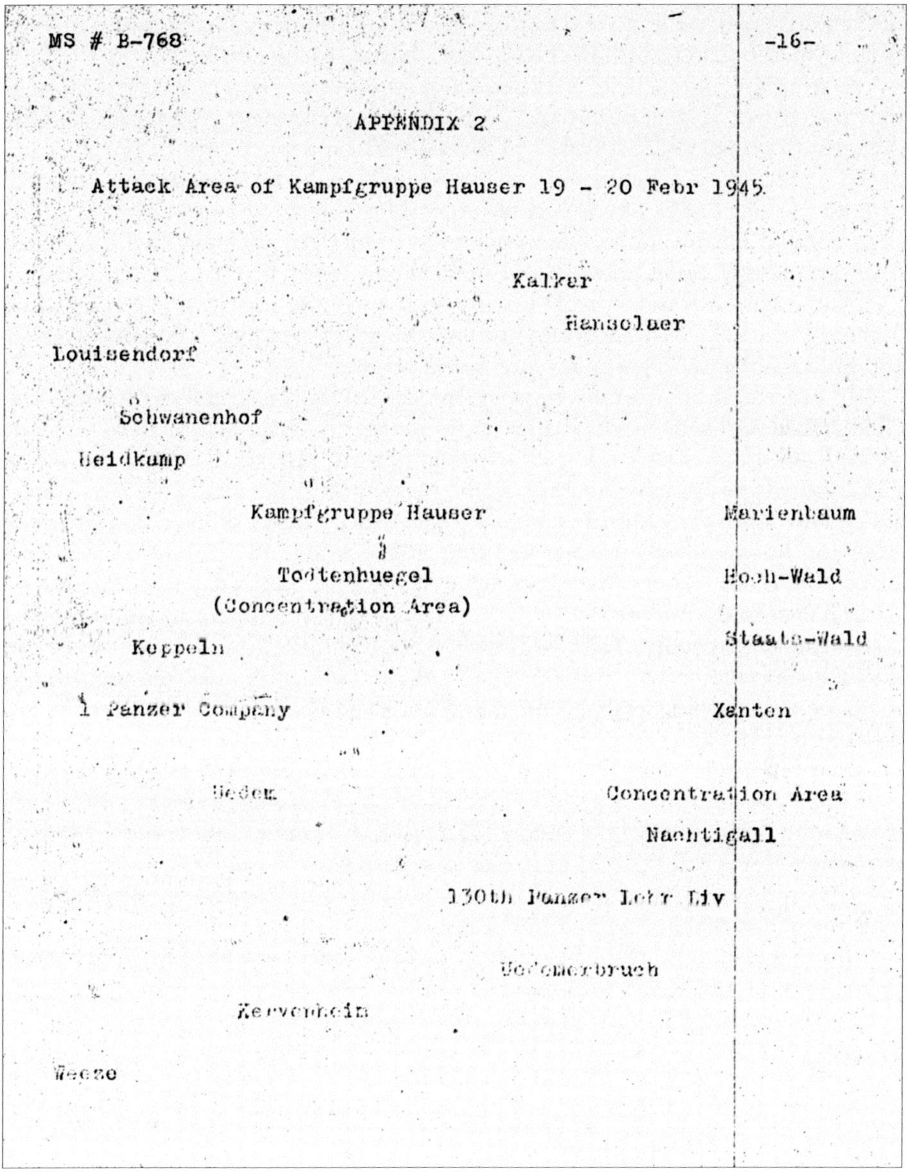

MS # B-768 -16-

APPENDIX 2

Attack Area of Kampfgruppe Hauser 19 - 20 Febr 1945.

Kalker

Hanselaer

Louisendorf

Schwanenhof

Heidkamp

Kampfgruppe Hauser

Marienbaum

Todtenhuegel
(Concentration Area)

Hoch-Wald

Keppeln

Staats-Wald

1 Panzer Company

Xanten

Uedem

Concentration Area
Nachtigall

130th Panzer Lehr Div

Uedemerbruch

Kervenheim

Weeze

Attack area of *Kampfgruppe* Hauser 19–20 February 1945

artillery drum fire was heard in the west. During the night the *Kampfgruppe Hauser* was relieved by elements of the 6th Parachute Division. The relief was considerably disturbed and delayed by an enemy attack which could not be repulsed. The division was assigned to the II Parachute Corps. The division command post remained at its former location south of the forester's hut at Nachtigall.

During the night 21–22 February the *Kampfgruppe* Hauser marched through the ruined town of Uedem and into the area south of the town. All preparations for the operation north of the Uedem – Weeze road sere set up. (Appendix 3).

By morning 22 February the reconnaissance battalion and the engineer battalion, which had been temporarily attached to the 15th Panzer Grenadier division, built up a thin security line in the forest south of the railroad line. They were hard pressed by frequent attacks and small enemy forces kept trickling through.

The terrain was unfavorable for any kind of counterattack. It was impossible because of the woods, swamps and brooks to commit any tanks. The rainy weather and mud made it hard going for any sort of vehicle.

In order to support units operating in the [.?..] line an assault company of the 901st Panzer Grenadier Lehr Regiment, mounted on personnel [carriers] was sent to the front, immediately upon its arrival in the area.. [tr. note— Due to extreme illegibility of the available document, the two words in brackets were indecipherable. ] During an early morning reconnaissance thrust north of the Babbe farm the company was involved in heavy fighting in the woods [with the Scottish 15th British Division] which caused considerable losses for both sides.

That evening the 902d Panzer Grenadier Lehr Regiment and units of the 901st Panzer Grenadier Lehr Regiment were committed for attack toward the north: their first objective to advance up both sides of Babbe and recapture the railroad line Uedem–Goch. After a fierce and bloody fight the attack was brought to a halt south of the line.

Early morning of 23 February the attack to recapture the railroad line was resumed. After some initial gain of terrain this second attempt failed because of the devastating defense fire of the enemy. *Kampfgruppe* Hauser withdrew to its former position and was able to hold it throughout the day.

On 24 February enemy attacks were repulsed mainly in close combat fighting. The line of resistance remained unchanged.

During the night of 24 February parachute units relieved the 130th Panzer Lehr Division and it was withdrawn from the First Parachute Army and Army Group H area and hurriedly marched to the Erkelenz sector.

**SUMMARY**

The British manner of fighting, as compared with that of other fronts, was characterized by the following features.

They fully exploited the whole of their superiority – artillery, tanks and aircraft. The British always used the same technique of attack. First uninterrupted artillery fire on the front of the sector concerned, lasting several hours, then a mass of tanks, advancing slowly and in phases. They withdrew if they encountered any strong resistance. Then again the artillery barrage was repeated and again the tanks attacked. Weather permitting the attack was supported by low-flying aircraft.

MS # B-768 -17-

APPENDIX 3

Counterattack Area of Kampfgruppe Hauser 22 Febr 1945

Todtenhuegel Marienbaum

Keppeln

Buchholt

1 Panzer Company Hoch-Wald

Uedem Nachtigall

130th Panzer Lehr Div

Concentration Area

Balbe Uedemerbruch

Kervenheim

Balberger Forest

Weeze

Counter-attack area of *Kampfgruppe* Hauser 22 February 1945

This method certainly reduced losses of men and equipment but on the other hand it was very advantages [advantageous] to the German command. It gave them time to shift their troops and seal up gaps that might have occurred. The German troops felt that the enemy does not attack he merely occupies.

British artillery operations also always followed the same technique. Their expenditure of ammunition was tremendous. Unlike the American technique of harassing fire, which was so extraordinarily disagreeable, the British laid theirs only on the front. One was practically safe in the rear.

As soon as the weather cleared the entire sector was controlled and dominated by the Allied air forces. During the night the sector was brightly illuminated with a great number of far-reaching searchlights. This handicapped our troop movements and prevented us from getting in our supplies.

The tank battles planned by the German commands never materialized. Mobile operations could not be carried out because the enemy did not allow themselves to be engaged in them. Our tanks could not make use of their speed and mobility and had to be used merely as mobile antitank guns or as artillery accompanying infantry.

All our attacks failed because of insufficient personnel and materiel. Enemy artillery and aircraft should have been at least partly eliminated in order that the attacks might achieve lasting success.

## APPENDIX I

### 130th Panzer Lehr Division
### Colonel Niemack, commanding
### Operations Officer (Ia) Major, GS, Koch-Erpach, Supply and administration officer (Ib) Major, GS, Klamroth

| | |
|---|---|
| 901st Panzer Grenadier Rgt | Colonel von Hauser commanding |
| 902nd Panzer Grenadier Rgt | Lt Col von Pochinger commanding |
| Panzer Lehr Rgt | Major Hudel |
| I (Panzer V) | |
| II (Panzer IV) | |
| Panzer Lehr Rgt | Lt Col Bartenwasser |
| I | |
| II | |
| III | |
| (HQ without troops) | |
| Lehr Rgt | Major Hoffman |
| Lehr Rgt | Capt Kuntze |
| Lehr Rgt | Capt Huebner |
| Lehr Rgt | Capt Bethke |
| Lehr Rgt | |
| Commander of div supply personnel | |
| The usual supply personnel | |

**APPENDIX 2**

*Attack Area of Kampfgruppe* **Hauser 19–20 Febr 1945**

See map on page 299

**APPENDIX 3**

*Counterattack Area of Kampfgruppe* **Hauser 22 Febr 1945**

See map on page 301

# *PANZER LEHR'S* INVOLVEMENT AGAINST SIMPSON'S AMERICAN NINTH ARMY'S 'OPERATION GRENADE'

*Panzer Lehr's* next mission was as part of the response to Operation 'Grenade'. Simpson's American Ninth Army's drive across the Roer River in Operation 'Grenade' to link up with the Canadian forces driving down the west bank of the Rhine in Operation 'Veritable' was delayed by the floodwaters released by the Germans from the Schwammenauel Dam. However, despite serious problems caused by the swift current or the swollen Roer and enemy artillery fire, Simpson's 23 February crossing of the last major water barrier before the Rhine was an outstanding success. The Ninth Army then swept forward irresistibly, reaching the Rhine north of Neuss on 2 March and linking up with the British on 3 March.

On 24 February *Oberbefehlshaber West* ordered the *Panzer Lehr Division* back to *Heeresgruppe* B, to the Schiefbahn area where it would be attached to the 15th *Armee*. Shortage of fuel caused considerable delays and made it necessary to entrain the tracked elements. After a strenuous night march the division had barely reached Schiefbahn when it received orders to proceed as rapidly as possible, bypassing Rheydt on both sides, to the Erkelenz area. Ritgen remarks (p. 281) that it was 'in light of the situation, a difficult task.'

Heavy pressure from the Allied air forces forced the road march to be made in small groups of vehicles hastening from cover to cover. It was 28 February before the division reached the Rheydt area.

# MS # B–830

## PANZER LEHR DIVISION
## (25 FEBRUARY–7 MARCH 1945)

Hudel
Frankfurt, 21 May 48

**Employment of *Panzer Lehr Division* 130**
**in the Areas of**
**Uedem – Rehindahlen – Muenchen [München]-Gladbach –Wesel**
**from 15 February – 7 March 45**

**Part II**
**25 February–7 March**

**Translated by Frederick P Steinhardt**

**MS # B–830**

**25 February 45**

The elements of the division that had been relieved during the night by *Fallschirmjäger* [parachute] units were ordered to concentrate and proceed to the Schiefbahn area. This was partially completed by morning, at which point strong enemy air activity prevented further movement by road. It was impossible to refuel the armour until darkness fell.

The division command post was moved to Schiefbahn. No final order was received for the division to move to the Erkelenz area.

The elements of the division were widely dispersed as a result of the long march to the Xanten – Uedem area and commitment there. What had, by now, become the usual shortage of fuel seriously delayed its reassembly. The same [lack of fuel] prevented the tanks of the II./*Panzer Lehr Regiment* that had been repaired in Neroth (Eifel) from rejoining [the regiment]. The I *Abteilung* of the *Panzer Regiment* had suffered relatively heavy losses due to mechanical problems. On 25 February about 15 tanks were available.

In other respects, the Division's losses had not been too bad, so, all in all, the Division was fully ready for action.

**26 February**

During the night additional elements assembled near Schiefbahn.

In the morning the Division received orders from the 1st *Fallschirmjäger Armee* to move to the Erkelenz area.

Two march groups were formed. One march group was to advance past Rheidt [Rheydt] on the west, the other to its east. Intense enemy aerial activity made it impossible for either group to move as a whole. Individual vehicles had to move independently, dashing from cover to cover. A liaison officer was sent to XII *SS-Armee Korps*. That evening he reported to the command post in Beeck and was briefed on the situation. The *Panzer Lehr Division* was urgently awaited, especially the armour as mobile antitank defense against the feared American armoured advance on Rheydt – München-Gladbach. In addition, elements of the Division were to launch an attack to the south to close the gap that had developed between the left wing of XII *SS-Armee Korps* and *Korpsgruppe Bayerlein*.

However, the first elements of the *Panzer Lehr Division* could not be expected to arrive before 27 February. The exact time of arrival depended on the enemy's air activity.

**27 February 45**

Due to problems with fuel supply and unforeseen difficulties in transmitting orders the leading elements of the Division did not move out until 0300 hrs.

As soon as it was light, enemy aircraft again patrolled the highways, producing further delays. *Panzeraufklärungs Lehr Abteilung* 130, reinforced with elements of *Panzer Pionier Batailllon* 130 and several *Panzerjäger* [tank destroyers] did not reach Rheidt until evening.

By noon the division staff arrived at XII *SS-Armee Korps* command post. The Division command post was to be established near the corps command post during the night. In the afternoon the Division was attached to XII *SS-Armee Korps*.

Assuming that the main body [of the Division] would arrive during the night of 27/28 [February] the Division received the following orders for the coming day:

1) Assemble and attack enemy forces advancing to the north and northeast from Erkelenz.

2) Establish a security line: Hardt – southern edge of Odenkirchen – Juchen.

3) Additional strong forces supported by armour were to be assembled to attack via Hochneukirch toward Garzweiler to close the gap between the left wing of XII *SS -Armee Korps* and *Korpsgruppe Bayerlein*. Since the first two tasks already involved division of forces, any attempt to carry out the third would involve such dispersal of forces that practically nothing could be accomplished. The Division Commander expressed this opinion emphatically.

[tr. note- Ritgen (pp. 281 ff.) remarks that the third task was typical of Hitler's wishful thinking and unreality at that point, since it envisioned the *Panzer Lehr Division* attacking toward the southwest in conjunction with a matching attack by the 11th *Panzer Division* to close the yawning gap in the front line north of Erkelenz, a task that, in itself, would have strained the abilities of a full-strength *Panzer* division in the best of times, and which was clearly unimaginable for what was left of *Panzer Lehr*. The Division Commander did his best to protest the fragmentation of his division and point to the urgent necessity of building a firm defensive front south of Rheydt in the face of the two enemy corps that were turning north, threatening the southern flank of the 1st *Fallschirmjäger Armee*, but to no avail.]

**28 February**

Additional elements of the Division arrived in Rheydt during the night. In the morning the Division was organized for the assigned mission as follows:

> [*Kampfgruppe von Hauser*:] Two battalions of *Panzergrenadier Lehr Regiment* 901, one battalion *Panzergrenadier Lehr Regiment 902*. Ten tank destroyers [of one *Panzerjäger* company] and one *Panzer* company with 12 tanks were ready at the southwest edge of Rheydt to attack toward Erkelenz. Its immediate objective was Hilderath.

*Panzer-Pionier-Bataillon* 130 held the security line from Hardt to the München-Gladbach – Erkelenz road; elements of *Panzergrenadier-Lehr-Regiment* 901 held from the road to the southeast edge of Odenkirchen; *Panzergrenadier-Lehr-Regiment* 902 held the line from north of Sasserath to Juchen. *Panzeraufklärungs-Lehr-Abteilung* 130 adjoined to the southeast, ordered to secure and reconnoiter to the southwest and south.

Enemy air activity was extremely intense from daybreak on. Nevertheless, assembly of the attack forces at the southwest edge of Rheydt was not significantly hampered, merely somewhat delayed. The group moved out at about noon and attained the Mennrath – Wickrath line. As it advanced further the leading elements ran into with strong enemy armoured forces attacking toward Rheydt [the American 5th Armored Division]. The enemy already held Hilderath and Wickrathhahn. Heavy fighting ensued, during which 15 enemy tanks were knocked out. The German assault group, however, was too weak in tanks and tank destroyers. It was forced back under enemy pressure. Wickrath was burning and was evacuated late in the afternoon. After an artillery preparation American tanks took Mennerath. Thanks to vast superiority in armour, the enemy could have advanced to Rheydt and München-Gladbach, but did not. The German forces went into position at the Rheindahlen – Rheydt railroad line and repulsed weak attacks until darkness fell.

In the *Panzer-Pionier-Bataillon* 130 sector several enemy attacks toward München-Gladbach were repulsed during the day.

*Panzeraufklärungs-Lehr-Abteilung* 130 identified strong enemy armoured forces in the area west and southwest of Juchen.

Since there was a gap between XII *SS-Armee Korps* and *Korpsgruppe Bayerlein* and, given the existing force ratio, there was no prospect of closing it, there was danger of envelopment.

Late in the evening the forces west, southwest and southeast of Rheydt were pulled back to the southwest edge of the city.

The Division command post was in the northeast part of München-Gladbach.

**1 March 45**

In the morning the American attack on Rheydt opened with heavy artillery fire. The defenders were forced back by the masses of armour advancing behind [the barrage]. Since there could be no thought of serious resistance in Rheydt and München-Gladbach, and to spare the cities from destruction, the Division fell back to the north. A planned counterattack failed to materialize since the enemy pursued closely and the enemy air force made assembly impossible.

In the morning the Division was ordered to form a line of defense via Viersen–Neersbroich–north bank of the canal to Neuss. However, this order arrived too late.

*Panzer-Pionier-Bataillon* 130 and one battalion of *Panzergrenadier-Lehr-Bataillon* 902 were already in contact with the enemy south of Viersen.

At about 1400 hours American armour attacked by surprise across the canal and captured Schiefbahn and Unterbruch. Low-flying aircraft suppressed isolated centers of resistance. Six German tanks were lost. Since the canal position was considered extremely valuable, an evening counterattack was planned to regain Schiefbahn and the north bank of the canal. At about 2000 hours one battalion (I./*Panzergrenadier-Lehr-Regiment* 901), supported by eight tanks, forced its way back into Schiefbahn. However, it could not hold its position there and, after an hour of fighting, was forced back to the north toward Krefeld.

It was apparent that the enemy would, on the next day, attack Krefeld – Uerdingen [Ürdingen].

During the night the Division fell back to the north and took over securing Krefeld to the west, southwest and southeast.

The Division command post was at the northern exit of Krefeld.

At this point the Division returned to the command of the 1st *Fallschirmjäger Armee* and, thereby, *Heeresgruppe* H.

**2 March 45**

The Division was too weak to form a continuous line of resistance. All of the roads entering Krefeld from the west, southwest, south and southeast were guarded by strong outposts reinforced with tanks or tank-destroyers.

Commencing at about 0900 hours the enemy exerted pressure from the southwest, then also from the south and southeast. His tanks advanced both on the roads and also across the terrain. Despite stubborn resistance, the detachments were continually forced back, slowly falling back to the city. Ten enemy tanks were knocked out during this fighting.

By late afternoon *Panzergrenadier-Lehr-Regiment* 901 had fallen back, fighting, to the southern edge of Krefeld, *Panzergrenadier-Lehr-Regiment* 902 and *Panzeraufklärungs-Lehr-Abteilung* 130 to the southeast edge of Krefeld and Ürdingen. The I./*Panzergrenadier-Lehr-Regiment* 901 secured at the railroad line southeast of Ürdingen. Fifteen tanks arrived at the railroad freight-yard for the division and were unloaded at the last minute.

The Division could not defend the city with the forces at its disposal. The several *Volkssturm* units that were available or that were in position had no combat effectiveness.

Damaged tanks, relatively immobile elements and trains units that were not vitally needed withdrew across the Rhine via the bridge at Ürdingen.

The enemy broke into the city at about 1800 hours. The problem now became preventing the Rhine bridge from falling into enemy hands. It was prepared for demolition.

However, artillery fire destroyed the demolition wires. [tr. note- As described in Cole *The Last Offensive*, p. 177, 'After dark {on 3 March} a six-man engineer patrol led by Capt. George L. Youngblood slipped past the defenders, gained the bridge, and crossed it, cutting all visible demolition wires in the process.'] Restoration would require extensive time. In the evening four tank-destroyers of *Panzerjäger-Lehr-Abteilung* 130 blocked the roads approaching [the bridge]. The next day the bridge was partially destroyed by a truck loaded with aerial bombs. [tr. note-The Americans thought they had missed some of the important wires to the demolition charges.] The commander of *Panzerjäger-Lehr-Abteilung* 130 assumed responsibility for securing the bridge until then and formed a makeshift line of defense on the right [east] bank of the Rhine. If the enemy had pressed hard on 2 and 3 March then he could have built a bridgehead like the one at Remagen.

During the night the Ia drove to the command post of LXIII *Armee Korps*. The Division was ordered to form a line of defense south of Moers [Mörs], in contact with the 15th *Panzer Grenadier Division,* which had fallen back to Mörs – Homberg.

The Division command post was established in Rheinhausen.

### 3 March 45

As, sector-by-sector, units fell back to the north fighting developed on the Ürdingen – Mörs road. The Division's tanks and tank-destroyers knocked out 24 enemy tanks on the countryside near Hochfeld.

The Division had lost considerable combat strength since departing the Uedem area on 26 February 1945, primarily for the following reasons:

> Commitment over a wide-ranging area led to supply difficulties, with the result that in a number of cases tanks and other vehicles had to be destroyed because they ran out of fuel. Constant withdrawal impacted maintenance and repairs. Shortage of communications apparatus and the constant presence of enemy aircraft patrolling the roads disrupted communications. Isolated resisting groups were captured. Frequently it took a long time for units to reform. The Division was constantly committed in the hot spots of the defensive fighting, thereby suffering heavy losses.
>
> The *Panzergrenadier* regiments had been reduced to the point where each had the strength of a reinforced battalion.
>
> *Panzer-Lehr-Regiment* 130 had only 20 tanks ready for action.
>
> *Panzerartillerie-Regiment* 130 had suffered the least losses and was still fully combat-capable.
>
> *Panzeraufklärungs-Lehr-Abteilung* 130, *Panzer-Pionier-Bataillon* 130 and *Panzerjäger-Lehr-Abteilung* 130 had suffered heavy losses.

Since replacements could not be expected and the *Feldersatz-Bataillon* [field-replacement battalion] had already been distributed [among the units], stragglers and small stray groups were rounded and used for reinforcements

In the afternoon the enemy pressed hard from the south and the Division had to fall back further to the north, toward Moers.

The Commander of *Panzer-Lehr-Regiment* 130 set out with a small staff to collect and organize the elements of the Division that were east of the Rhine in and east of the Muelheim [Mülheim]–Angermuend [Angermünd] area. Actually, the entire Division needed a short rest-period to more-or-less organize its elements. All such requests were turned down.

## Action in the Wesel Bridgehead

[tr. note- Contact was established between the British forces of Operation 'Veritable' and the American forces of Operation 'Grenade' on 3 March at Geldern, thus forming a continuous allied perimeter around the German forces remaining west of the Rhine in what now became the Wesel Bridgehead. *Panzer Lehr* had the dubious distinction of having first fought the Canadians in 'Veritable', as described in MS # B–768, and then the Americans in Operation 'Grenade' as detailed above. Now the Division's remnants would help defend the Wesel Bridgehead, which Hitler stubbornly refused to evacuate.]

Preliminary remarks:

I did not, myself, take part in this action. Therefore the description must be brief, limited to what is available from written and oral reports.

## 4 March 45

The unit adjoining the Division on the left had fallen back on Homberg and organized a defense at its south and southwest edge. Those elements of the *Panzer Lehr Division* that were still committed were withdrawn through Homberg in the morning. As ordered, they formed a line of resistance from Rheinkamp – west edge and south edge of the woods west of Lohmannsheide. The Division command post was in Vierbaum.

Before the withdrawal to this line the *Panzerartillerie-Regiment* 130 and *Panzer-Pionier Bataillon* 130 were sent across the bridge at Homberg to the right [east] bank of the Rhine. The artillery was ordered to follow the divisions from [the east bank of the Rhine] and to support the defensive battle. Forward observers remained on the left bank with the Division. The pioneers were, likewise, to follow [the division's movements] and, at any time, to be prepared to enable a crossing by constructing ferries.

The Division took these precautions on its own responsibility, since the end of the bridgehead was visibly approaching and the Division did not wish to uselessly lose its heavy weapons.

In the afternoon the enemy attacked with a strong artillery preparation. The Division was forced back In the evening it established a new line of resistance at Rheinberg — Eversael [Eversäl].

During this fighting the Division was attached to LXV *Armee Korps*.

## 5 March 45

Enemy artillery fire strengthened hour-by-hour. Attacks against the line of resistance were repulsed.

Adjoining the Division on the right was the 116th *Panzer Division*.

The Division command post was in Ossenberg.

## 6 March 45

The constant attacks greatly narrowed the bridgehead. The Division's combat strength constantly melted away. Its infantry strength was now down to that of a single battalion. Two tanks were still in action.

The bridgehead built by remnants of the 1st *Fallschirmjäger Armee* extend from Birten to Ossenberg. The Division was committed on the left of the 116th *Panzer Division* from the southern edge of Ossenberg to the Rhine. The Division command post was in the north part of Ossenberg.

The enemy artillery fire continued to mount.

It would be superfluous to describe the mood of the totally exhausted soldiers.

### 7 March 45

In the morning the Division's staff received orders to fall back with the remnants of the Division over the bridge at Wesel to the right [east] bank of the Rhine. The Division was again attached to *Heeresgruppe B*.

During the morning the remnants of the Division crossed the bridge. There were no further losses to enemy air activity.

In the evening the staffs and manpower, in approximate company strength, reached the area southeast of Mülheim.

The next day the *Panzer-Artillerie-Regiment* 130 and *Panzer-Pionier-Bataillon* 130 arrived in that area.

### Conclusions

It is no longer possible to recall all the many details that characterized the Division's actions from memory. Practically daily the same thing recurred one or more times: the Division received a mission, and when it arrived at the appointed place, the situation had already changed drastically. The Division's forces were far from adequate to accomplish all the missions assigned. The enemy attacked from all sides to gain the bank of the Rhine. Troops were everywhere in short supply. Therefore the Division was continually fragmented, and that under the most difficult conditions for logistical support,

The enemy was vastly superior. The constant low-level aerial patrols often delayed movement so much that the elements of the Division arrived quite late where they were committed. Heavy artillery fire in the restricted Wesel bridgehead caused heavy losses and had a severe effect on troop morale.

Superior enemy forces thrust the Division back to the northwest and north. Neither could it close the gap to *Korpsgruppe Bayerlein* nor could it significantly delay the enemy advance via Rheydt, München-Gladbach or Krefeld.

[Editor's note – Although much of the material in the following interview concerns events that took place after Panzer Lehr's action at the Remagen Bridgehead, I inserted MS # B–850 here, since it is the third in the series of interviews with Major Hudel and opens with the description of the formation and departure of the *Kampfgruppe* that was sent to Remagen. My notes on the events that took place after the Remagen Bridgehead until the surrender follow MS # A–970 on the Combat of the LIII Korps at Remagen Bridgehead from 10 to 22 March 1945.]

# MS # B–850

## 130th *PANZER LEHR DIVISION* 23 MARCH–15 APRIL 1945

MS # B–850
Helmut HUDEL
Frankfurt am Main, 25 June 1948

Major a.D. [retired]
former Commander
*Panzer-Lehr-Regiment* 130

**Employment and Combat of *Panzer Lehr Division* 130 at the Sieg [River] and in the Evacuation of Winterberg, Schmallenberg to Wardohl – Altena (Ruhr Pocket), 23 March–15 April 1945.**

### I. Foreword

There are no written records available from the time of the war for the following report. Through interviews with former members of the *Panzer Lehr Division* an attempt was made to write the most seamless possible account of the Division's action in the final fighting. The result leaves much to be desired because, as the war drew to an end, both officers and troops were exhausted. Constantly shifted from one hotspot to another in the turbulent rush of events there was no break from the rush of events and experiences. Memory alone does not suffice for a factual report. Accordingly, inaccuracies and omissions in this report could not be avoided.

### II. Preliminaries

On 7 and 8 March 1945 the remnants of the *Panzer Lehr Division* were withdrawn from the Wesel bridgehead. They assembled in the area south of Muehlheim [Mühlheim], where the elements [of the Division] that were immobile or in need of repair had gathered in the early days of March. With that the Division was, at the same time, again attached to *Heeresgruppe* B, which ordered hasty reconstitution with all available means.

The Division command post was in Ratingen.

On 9 March 1945 a *Kampfgruppe* [*Kampfgruppe Hudel*] had to be thrown together in all haste. That same evening it moved out for commitment under *Korpsgruppe Bayerlein* at the Remagen bridgehead. [tr. note–see MS # A–970, below.] It consisted of the following elements:

2 companies of the I./ *Panzer-Lehr-Regiment* 130 (about 18 tanks)

1 *Panzer-Aufklärungs Schwadron* from *Panzer-Aufklärungs-Lehr Abteilung* 130

1 company of *Panzer-Pionier-Bataillon* 130

1 *Panzer-Grenadier* company

1 platoon of *Panzer-Nachrichten-Abteilung* 130

1 platoon of *Panzerjäger-Lehr-Abteilung* 130.

The commander of the *Kampfgruppe*, [who was] the commander of *Panzer-Lehr-Regiment* 130, reported to the command post of *Kampfgruppe Bayerlein* in Oberpleis during the night of 9/10 March 1945.

For further information on the actions of the *Kampfgruppe* see reports of the 11th *Panzer Division* ands *Korpsgruppe Bayerlein* (MS # B–590, A–970). [tr. note-MS # A–970 is given below.]

At approximately 1000 hours the Division moved to the area north of Wuppertal. The time for reconstitution ended on 21 March. During that period the staffs and workshops laboured without a break. Along with the fact that the *Heeresgruppe* made no demands at all on the Division and gave it full support, it was only thanks to this industriousness that the Division was able to return to action in somewhat combat-ready condition.

During the fighting in the Wesel bridgehead the Division had suffered extremely heavy losses. Its personnel actually consisted of no more than staffs and small cadres [of its units]. During the period of reconstitution the Division was brought up to 60% [of its T/O strength] with [personnel from] disbanded homeland *Flak*-units, Hitler Youth and *Volkssturm*. [tr. note– *Volkssturm* units were the final emergency call-up of older men, youths and men physically unfit for or otherwise exempt from military service. Practically untrained and poorly armed with makeshift small-arms, these units were locally raised and committed. Some fought steadfastly, others were mercifully sent home by the commanders of the military units to whom they were assigned.] Practically no trained replacements were assigned. Naturally, there was no possibility of meaningful or effective training or instruction in the short time available to bring the Division to any sort of satisfactory combat-worthiness.

Materiel was lacking, especially vehicles of all sorts. About ten tanks were still in the repair shops. New armour was not provided. There were still about 20 tank-destroyers on hand. *Panzer-Artillerie-Regiment* 130 had suffered relatively light losses and was still combat-capable. The pioneers and, especially, *Panzer-Nachrichten-Abteilung* 130 [the communications section] had lost a tremendous amount of their equipment.

The *Panzergrenadier* regiments had only limited mobility. The weapons, for the most part, could be brought up to [usable levels].

During the period of reconstitution the Division was informed that the tanks of the *II. Abteilung* of *Panzer-Lehr-Regiment* 130 that had been left in the Eifel because of lack of fuel had been lost due to the sudden American armoured advance.

On 21 March, at noon, the Division received orders to move to the Siegburg area. Despite pressure from the *Heeresgruppe*, it was only on 23 March that the Division arrived in the area south of Eitorf. The reason for this delay was the inadequate nature of the replacements and deficiencies resulting from the short period of reconstitution. In addition, there was a shortage of fuel for this movement.

**23 March 1945**

The main body of the Division arrived in the area southwest of Eitorf during the evening, [where] it was attached to LXXIV *Armee Korps*. The command post was set up in Irlenborn, where the commander of *Panzer-Lehr-Regimnent* 130 reported back with the remnants of the *Kampfgruppe* that had been sent to Remagen.

The enemy constantly pushed to break out of the Remagen bridgehead. The Division was given the mission of preventing further enemy advance along the Sieg [River] by attacking to the west.

It became evident that *Heeresgruppe* B expected the enemy to turn to the north in order to roll up the German forces positioned at the Rhine.

**24 March 1945**

At about 0500 hours two *Kampfgruppen* of *Panzergrenadier-Lehr-Regimenter* 901 and 902, supported by tanks and tank-destroyers, launched an attack to the west from the Blankenberg – Uckerath line. *Schwere Panzerjäger Abteilung* 654 was attached to the Division for this attack. The Division had only six of its own tanks available. [tr. note- The war-diary of *schwere Panzerjäger Abteilung* 654, presented in Karlheinz Münch's 'Combat History of *schwere Panzerjäger Abteilung* 654', indicates it committed two *Kampfgruppen,* one with three *Jagdpanther,* the other with four. Due to shortage of fuel they were limited to local missions until fuel arrived.]

After considerable fighting the two *Kampfgruppen* reached their first objective, the stream south of Hennef, late in the afternoon. They were unable to cross the stream and were forced back that evening.

A small *Kampfgruppe* consisting of four tanks and two *Panzergrenadier* companies was committed under the 62nd *Volksgrenadier Division* to block the Sieg [River] road east of Hennef. No fighting ensued.

**25 March 1945**

In the course of 24 and 25 March the enemy advanced far toward Altenkirchen and broke through the defensive front south of the Division. Since it was not possible to close the existing gap with the available forces and there was no chance of stopping the enemy with an attack, the Division was withdrawn via Eitorf north of the Sieg [River] to form a line of defense directly east of Weyerbusch. As result of disruptions of the march and difficulties in transmitting orders not all the elements of the Division could be brought into action on time. The enemy pressed hard and delivered a lot of artillery fire. Towards evening he broke through the line of defense and advanced farther toward Altenkirchen. The repeated attempt to stop the enemy west of Altenkirchen failed.

The Division command post was at Breitscheid.

**26 March 1945**

Early in the morning the Division again attempted resistance north of Altenkirchen. Enemy armour, however, succeeded in advancing along the Altenkirchen – Wissen road. Isolated centers of resistance of the Division repeatedly attempted to halt the enemy. Only at the Sieg [River] south of Wissen could a more-or-less continuous line of resistance be formed.

That day the Division lost 14 tanks that were under repair in a workshop at Altenkirchen and which could not be moved because of lack of fuel.

**27 March 1945**

In accord with the further enemy advance south of the Sieg [River] to the east, the division was withdrawn during the night of 26/27 March 1945 via Friesenhagen – Freudenberg – Kirchen in order to form a new line of resistence along the Wilden - B[ach] [stream] between Betzdorf and the area south of Siegen [to secure the concentration of the corps south of Siegen]. There was no combat that day aside from the usual artillery barrages. The enemy continued to advance eastward south of the Division.

**28 March 1945**

Since a strong enemy thrust was expected from the south against Siegen, the Division established a new line of resistance directly south of the city. Aside from artillery fire and patrol activity there was no enemy combat activity.

Orders arrived in the afternoon for the Division to move out to the northeast to LIII *Armee Korps* in the Winterberg area.

During the night of and on 29 March 1945 the Division moved via Schmallenberg – Berleburg to the new area of commitment.

**30 March 1945**

The Division was supposed to join the 3rd *Panzergrenadier Division* and an infantry division in an attempt to burst the ring that was then forming around the troops in the Ruhr region and then break through to the east. Friendly forces were to meet [the breakout attempt] from the direction of Kassel.

Under the command of LIII *Armee Korps* the Division stood ready east of Winterberg with two *Kampfgruppen*, supported by a few tanks, which were to launch the breakout. The leaders of the *Kampfgruppen* were the commanders of *Panzergrenadier-Lehr-Regimenter* 901 and 902.

Towards evening an American attack, which could barely be held, hit the assembly position. The *Kampfgruppen* had to fall back to the edge of the forest area east of Winterberg.

**31 March 1945**

A new early-morning attack launched to the east against the general Hallenberg – Medsbach line also failed. Enemy resistance constantly strengthened. With their present personnel the *Kampfgruppen* simply could not do more. The practically untrained men and, in part, inexperienced officers were not up to such fighting.

At about noon the enemy attacked and locally caused an over-hasty withdrawal of the *Panzergrenadiere*.

**1 April 1945**

This day the attack to the east was temporarily halted. Apparently it was waiting until the German attack westward from Kassel took effect. The enemy carried out isolated reconnaissance thrusts, drawing a locally excessive response from our troops.

At an officer's conference at the Division command post (directly west of Winterberg) the commander, particularly of the *Panzergrenadier* regiments, expressed concern regarding the steadiness of their men. They based this on their most recent observations. The courageous deeds of individuals could not conceal the fact that the Division's former fighting spirit had finally been broken.

**2 April 1945**

Another attack to the east was planned for this day. The *Panzer Lehr Division* was to advance on the right of the 3rd *Panzergrenadier Division* toward Neukirchen – Sachsenberg. Again the Division readied its two assault groups. Before the attack could begin, however, the enemy attacked from the southeast and constantly increased his pressure from the Hallenberg area. By evening elements of the division had fallen back to the southeast edge of Winterberg. Such an extensive retreat was excessive.

The Division now attempted to form a line of resistance directly south and west of Winterberg. Due to the large number of military and civilian hospitals, Winterberg, itself, was evacuated.

During the night of 2/3 March [*sic.*,actually, as per Ritgen, 2/3 April] the staff of *Panzer-Artillerie-Regiment* 130 was surprised by the enemy in Mollseifen and captured.

**3 April 1945**

The Division extended its line of resistance to the south via the Kahle Asten. [Ritgen says (p. 305) that Alt-Astenberg, the highest-lying village in Germany, lay behind the new line, which he describes as running on both sides of the Kahle Asten. Jean-Claude Perrigault describes the Kahle Asten as the highest point in the Sauerland with an elevation of 841 meters, near Silbach. (Perrigault, *La Panzer-Lehr Division,* p.417).] The Division command post was moved to Rehsiepen, during which the Division Commander, *Oberst* Niemack, was wounded by an artillery fragment. The commander of *Panzergrenadier-Lehr-Regiment* 901, *Oberst* von Hauser, assumed command of the Division.

In the morning the Division received orders from the 15th *Armee* to recapture Winterberg. Since the condition of the troops precluded such an attack, the Division remained in its positions.

**4 April 1945**

Strong enemy forces attacked west and southwest from the Winterberg area. The Division's thin security line was forced back. The Kahle Asten was lost. The evening counterattack aimed at regaining the height failed. The forces that could be assembled for such a counterattack were very weak. Many times in this report the small counter-actions evoked by enemy penetrations have gone unmentioned. Often company and platoon leaders initiated such actions on their own initiative, but even when they had some initial success, they were forced back again because they lacked sufficient forces to hold the ground they had gained.

The Division command post was moved to Nieder Sorpe.

### 5 April 1945

During the day the enemy continued to advance westward. The Division's security line, which extended roughly from Alt Astenberg via Westfeld to Oberkirchen, could not be held with the scanty forces. The terrain offered numerous opportunities for the attacker to approach under cover, while the defender had only extremely limited fields of vision and fire. Tanks and tank-destroyers were limited to positions on the roads and were of limited effectiveness in the narrow valleys. As if that wasn't enough, the number of tanks and tank-destroyers had melted away to a very few. All in all there were only 15 left.

Alt Astenberg and Westfeld fell in the afternoon. Late in the afternoon the enemy captured the vital road junction of Oberkirchen. In the evening a *Kampfgruppe* was hastily assembled to recapture Oberkirchen (four tanks, one *Panzergrenadier* company, one *Landesschützen-Pionier* company and three tank-busting squads).

The attack along the Winkhausen valley road got off to a good start. Lack of the requisite radio apparatus precluded artillery support. After a short stay the German armour that had penetrated into Oberkirchen had to pull out as a result of effective enemy countermeasures from the houses and the fact that the friendly infantry was both too weak and too unskilled. As an example, all the men in the *Ladsesschützen-Pionier* company were over fifty years old.

At the army's continued urging three more vain attempts were made during the night and early morning to recapture Oberkirchen. The enemy put up an extraordinarily stubborn defense.

### 6 April 1945

The Division took up a line of defense on the heights between Almert and Rehsiepen. Early in the morning the 338th *Infanterie Division* took over the right portion of the sector east of Winkhausen – Grafschaft. During the relief the enemy attacked and captured the commanding forested heights south of Winkhausen. The immediate counterattack by a grenadier regiment collapsed under artillery fire with heavy losses.

In the *Panzer Lehr Division* sector there was no other significant action.

The Division command post was west of Fredeburg.

### 7 April 1945

The unit adjoining the Division on the right was forced back by an enemy attack from the south and east. Grafschaft was lost. To prevent the enemy from advancing to the north to Fredeburg a small *Panzer Lehr Kampfgruppe* was committed on both sides of Gleidorf. Other than a considerable amount of artillery fire there was no fighting.

### 8 April 1945

During the day the *Panzer Lehr Division* turned its sector over to the 338th *Infanterie Division*. The relief was irregular. The arrival of the elements of the 338th *Infanterie Division* took a long time. Typical of the entire condition of the troops was the fact that the officers of only a very few elements of the relief knew where they actually were.

The elements of the Division assembled in the area west of Fredeburg.

### 9 and 10 April 1945

The Division fell back before the pursuing enemy generally to the northwest. The units were severely lacerated by incessant aerial attack. It is impossible to form a coherent picture of these two days. There was no heavy fighting.

### 11 April 1945

The Division was ordered to the sector south of Werdohl with the mission of establishing a security line at the Plettenberg – Lüdenscheid road since a strong enemy attack was expected from the south.

Since there was not yet any sign of the enemy the Division had several hours to organize its units. The Division command post was established in Kleinhammer.

All that was left of the Division was one small *Kampfgruppe*. The two *Panzergrenadier* regiments had the strength of two weak battalions. The *Pionier* battalion and *Aufklärungs* battalion were at approximately company strength. About ten tanks and tank-destroyers were still capable of limited action. The artillery was notably short of ammunition and could hardly fire. There was still a limited amount of fuel consisting of a mixture of crude-oil and aviation petrol available from stocks remaining in the Ruhr region. Within a short time that [fuel mix] disabled many vehicles with engine trouble.

The Division constantly sought to recoup losses by rounding up stragglers of all origins and repair of all possible vehicles that were found standing driver-less on the roads. However, most of these efforts proved fruitless: the stragglers shortly vanished and, sooner or later, the vehicles had to be abandoned when they ran out of fuel.

### 12 April

During the day there was no immediate combat action on the Plettenberg–Lüdenscheid road in the Division's sector. In the afternoon the commander of *Panzer-Lehr-Regiment* 130 was ordered to Herscheid as *Kampfkommandant*. [tr. note -Appointment as *Kampfkommandant* gave him authority over any forces that happened into his specified area.] The forces at his disposal consisted of three tanks, one weak *Panzergrenadier* company and those elements of a *Flak-Sturmregiment* that were stationed in Herscheid. There was no way of holding [Herscheid], which was surrounded on all sides by commanding heights, with these weak forces. That evening in the face of an enemy who was primarily employing artillery, it had to be evacuated.

During the night the Division's *Panzergrenadiere* were ordered north to establish a line of resistance east of Werdohl–Neuenrade, since the enemy was pressing in from the east.

The remnants of the pioneer battalion and three tanks blocked the north-south valley road three kilometres northwest of Herscheid.

### 13 April 1945

During the night the enemy attacked from the east and took Neuenrade. There was imminent danger that he would continue to advance to the west to Lenne and would cut off the forces committed around Werdohl. Early in the morning the blocking group was pulled out of the north-south valley road (three kilometres northwest of Herscheid) and employed along with a weak battalion of *Panzergrenadier-Regiment* 902 in a counterattack north of Werdohl on Neuenrade. Repeated attempts were made to attack, but the forces were insufficient. What was accomplished was that, particularly thanks to the three tanks, the road at the southwest exit from Neuenrade was blocked by fire,

The remnants of *Panzergrenadier-Regiment* 901 and *Panzeraufklärungs-Lehr-Abteilung* 130 were committed east of Altena near Dahle to secure toward the east and southeast.

No significant fighting occurred at Werdohl. At times American artillery laid down heavy fire on the city.

### 14 April 1945

No significant fighting occurred in the sector east of Altena. Many stragglers collected during the day at the *Kampfgruppe* north of Werdohl. They, however, were of no use for fighting. In the evening the city had to be evacuated. The three tanks southwest of Neuenrade were cut off by American armour and, after expending their ammunition, had to be blown up.

Late in the evening the Lenne valley was blocked southeast of Altena with the elements withdrawing from Werdohl.

### 15 April 1945

Early in the morning all the remaining elements of the Division were immediately east and south of Altena. The enemy was only feeling things out. There was no more fighting.

The Ruhr pocket was split by the enemy's last advances. During the night of 14/15 April 1945 the Division command concluded that further resistance was senseless. At an officer's briefing at 0600 hours in the morning it was announced that the total destruction of Altena and the total disintegration of the Division were to be avoided. After firing off the remaining ammunition and destroying the heavy weapons, the Division would offer to surrender.

After the ammunition had been expended in the afternoon, the artillery pieces and the *Panzergrenadier's* weapons were destroyed. An order from the 15th *Armee* to continue resistance north of Altena was disregarded. For the last time the elements of the Division in Altena lined up before the Division Commander with their weapons. After a short speech he dismissed the Division. American tanks had already arrived. The remnants of the *Panzer Lehr Division*, which had been in constant action since June 1944, proceeded into captivity.

# PART IV

## *PANZER LEHR* AT REMAGEN AND AFTER

# *Kampfgruppe Hudel* at Remagen

Captured in an unexpected spur-of-the-moment coup on March 7, the bridge at Remagen was an accident of war and, despite the romance and drama of its capture, not entirely desired – at least ahead of time. Of all the possible crossing sites, it was at the bottom of the list for good reasons. At Remagen, the Rhine flowed through a gorge rather than an open valley. Directly east of the river the Westerwald, an area of sharply-compartmented wooded hills is at its most rugged and reaches right to the river.

Nevertheless, it was the only Rhine bridge to fall into allied hands in usable condition, though so damaged by the failed German demolition attempt, compounded by possible bomb damage, that it collapsed on March 17. Although Eisenhower was never tempted to shift from his strategy of making the main attempt in a massive thrust through the area north of the Ruhr, coupled with a lesser thrust up the Frankfurt – Kassel corridor, where, in both routes, excellent terrain for armour and good communications favoured rapid advance, the opportunity was exploited. The immediate response to, first the opportunity, then the fact of capture, was to push everything at hand across the bridge to build, defend and extend the bridgehead.

Rapidly, however, perspective returned and further development of the bridgehead was carefully regulated, the main emphasis continuing to be on crossing sites that, while lacking a surviving bridge, led to terrain and communications suitable for continuing the advance into the heart of Germany.

The German reaction was surprisingly slow, disorganized and inadequate. The fact that the American Ninth Army had made no immediate attempt on reaching the Rhine to cross over had lulled the Germans into thinking the Americans planned to mop up the west bank before crossing. Command relationships along the river were confused, cross-cutting (and under-cutting), a confusing jumble of competing responsibilities and claims of competence between party-controlled *Wehrkreis* jurisdictions that were supposed to be turned over to the army as the fighting approached, conflicts between regular field army and replacement army, *Luftwaffe Flak* units and, as if that was not enough, changes in assignment of responsibility between different army commands that came at a bewildering pace.

Much German attention was focused on getting the maximum number of units, the maximum amount of fighting-men and irreplaceable equipment, back across the river before they were cut off. That, of course, was in competition with the pressure to blow the bridges in time to deny an Allied crossing. Hitler's fear that preparation of defences to the rear would act like magnets and draw troops attention from defending the front, combined with the shortage of fighting units, meant that there were few if any usable combat units available for rapid response subsequent to the capture of the bridge.

The initial German response was fragmented and ineffective, allowing the Americans to get 8,000 men across the bridge before there was a significant German reaction. The German response was not up to the task it faced. The *Panzer Lehr Division* was already heavily involved, as described above, in combating, first the Canadian advance down the west bank of the Rhine in Operation 'Veritable', and then in battling the American Ninth Army's Operation 'Grenade'. It suffered extremely heavy losses in the Wesel bridgehead.

In MS # B–850, in his 'Preliminaries', Hudel details how, on 9 March, *Kampfgruppe Hudel*, (under his own command) was hastily thrown together and sent to Remagen.

# MS # A–970

## COMBAT OF THE LIII KORPS AT REMAGEN BRIDGEHEAD FROM 10 TO 22 MARCH 1945

**Index for MS A # 970**



Fritz Bayerlein, Ober Ursel 26 March 1946
former Lt. Gen.

To
HISTORICAL DIVISION
Section CENTRAL EUROPE
Captain S C O G G I N

In my work about 'Remagen Bridgehead', Appendix 1,[ tr. note-original letter in German included 'Course of the Combat Operations'] Sheet 5

I made a mistake by adding an incorrect sheet 5. Herewith I hand the correct sheet as Appendix a.

In the 'Explanations of Appendix 10 (Situation on 22 March)' the last sentence is to be replaced by the sentence in Appendix b.

(Signed) BAYERLEIN

**(handwritten) Appendix a**

**A – 970**

*Lehr Division*, with the 74th *Korps*. In addition, the *schwerste Panzergruppe* [extremely heavy *Panzergruppe*]. Change of commanders of the 53rd and 74th *Korps* – less staffs, except for the chiefs-of-staffs – was to take effect on the evening of 22 March or in the morning of 23 March, since the bulk of the armoured forces were now concentrated with the 74th *Korps*.

**22 March**

In the sector of the 53rd *Korps* there was no significant action.

In the sector of the 74th *Korps* the planned counterattack with the 11th *Panzer* [*Division*], the 3rd *Panzergrenadier* [*Division*] and *Kampfgruppe Panzer Lehr* took place with its objective of forcing the enemy that had crossed the PLEIS sector back.

**23 March**

Noon: Assumption of command in the 74th *Korps* sector by *General* Bayerlein.

For situation at the time of the change of command in the sector of the 53rd *Korp* see sketch-map, Appendix 10.

**(handwritten) Appendix b**

**A – 970**

Amendment to Appendix 10 (Situation in the evening of 22 March)

Situation in the Evening of 22 March:

Delete the last paragraph!

Replace with:

At noon of 23 March *General* Püchler's 74th *Korps* took over the sector.

**A –970**

Remagen Bridgehead 53rd *Korps* Appendix 1.

Course of Combat Operations.

**7 March**

Remagen bridge captured by U.S. troops, bridgehead built.

**8 March**

Commander of the 11th *Panzer Division, General* von Wietersheim takes over command at the bridgehead front. Troops: The forces of the former Rhine Defense and elements of the 9th *Panzer Division*.

**9 March**

Elements of the 11th *Panzer Division* arrived and stabilized the front.

At noon of this day *General* Bayerlein – formerly employed at DÜSSELDORF –was summoned to the command post of the commander of the Rhine Defense (*General* von Kortzfleisch) in OBER PLEIS. There *Generalfeldmarschall* MODEL briefed him on the situation at the bridgehead: UNKEL, BRUCHHAUSEN,OHLENBERG and OCKENFELS had been captured by the enemy, who was continuing to press his advance. Mission for *Korps BAYERLEIN*: Take over the bridgehead front and eliminate the bridgehead as quickly as possible. Available troops: 11th *Panzer Division, Kampfgruppe* 9th *Panzer Division,* remnants of *Brigade Feldherrnhalle* and one *Kampfgruppe* of the *Panzer Lehr Division* (this was to arrive during the night). Additional forces were expected in the immediate future. For strength of the troop elements see Appendix 2. Proposals for conduct of the operations to eliminate the bridgehead were to be presented in the shortest possible time to *Feldmarschall* Model.

After reconnaissance and determination of the situation *General* Bayerlein decided to deliver the attack to eliminate the bridgehead from ERL. Advance via

OHLENBERG to the heights of KASBACH and OCKENFELS to split the bridgehead and then, depending on the situation, to roll it up either to the south or to the north. The attack was to be delivered with *Kampfgruppe Panzer Lehr*. The attack was to be launched early in the morning of 10 March. For a sketch-map of the intended attack see Appendix 4.

Final discussion between Model, Bayerlein and Wietersheim at the command post of the 11th *Panzer Division* in KALENBORN. [spelled both 'Kalenborn' and 'Kahlenborn' on sketch-maps] The attack order was issued.

### 10 March

0400 hours in the morning, 53rd *Korps* assumed command on the bridgehead front.

*Kampfgruppe Panzer Lehr* arrived and was attached to the 11th *Panzer Division*. The planned attack, however, could not be delivered because elements of the *Panzer Lehr Division* arrived too late and the attack was forbidden by the *Heeresgruppe*.

In the course of the day the enemy attacked, penetrating HONNEF and significantly widening the bridgehead.

See the sketch-map in Appendix 5 for the evening situation.

### 11 March

Conference with *Feldmarschall* KESSELRING, who had just been appointed *Oberbefehlshaber* [Commander in Chief] *West* in OBERPLEIS regarding possibilities for eliminating the bridgehead. During the morning the 9th *Panzer Division* delivered a successful counterattack east of HONNEF. The enemy took the LEY-B[erg, hill]. Enemy tanks advanced via LINZ against HOENNINGEN [Hönnigen??-from Rawson–clearly Hönningen on Bayerlein's sketch map]. Thereupon the *Korps* sector was widened south to LEUBSDORFERBACH. HONNEF was lost in the evening.

Small counterattacks by the 11th *Panzer Division* forced the enemy back at a number of different positions. There was particularly fierce fighting for the HARGARTEN-peak. It remained in the hands of the 11th *Panzer Division*.

### 12 March

The lines of the previous day remained essentially unchanged.

### 13 March

The remnants of the 340th *Volksgrenadier Division* arrived and were attached to the *Korps*. For strengths see Appendix 2.

Strong enemy attacks from HONNEF to the northwest. The 9th *Panzer Division* was forced back. The superbly equipped 130th *Infanterie-Regiment* (brought in from Holland) arrived, complete. The Intention was to attack ERPEL with this regiment, reinforced with one *Panzer* company, from the AS-BERG [As-Hill] area via BRUCHHAUSEN-ORSBERG.. For Plan of attack, see sketch-map in Appendix 6. MODEL personally forbade this promising attack because he intended to give this regiment to the 340th *Volksgrenadier Division* in order to bring that division up to fighting strength. That put an end to any possibility of eliminating the bridgehead. The enemy then began to slowly but surely, steadily push forward. The German forces were worn down and gradually consumed until the enemy had gained favorable positions for his offensive to the east.

During the night of 13/13[*sic.*] [13/14] March the 340th *Volksgrenadier Division* took over the WINDHAGEN–ROTTBITZE [Sketch-maps 7 & 8 show a quite legible Robitze(?), sketch-map 9 is almost illegible, but might show it as Rottbitze, sketch-map 10 is small, but clearly Rottbitze] sector from the 11th *Panzer Division*. For the evening situation see sketch-map in Appendix 7.

### 14 March

In the sector of the 9th *Panzer Division* the enemy advanced to HIMBERG. The 340th *Volksgrenadier Division* and 11th *Panzer Division* essentially held their positions.

### 15 March

A counterattack by the 9th *Panzer Division* from the AEGIDIENBERG [Ägidienberg] area regained the HIMBERG–KOENIGSWINTER [Königswinter] road. Heavy enemy pressure shifted toward KOENIGSWINTER [Königswinter] in the adjoining (74th *Korps*) sector. In the center and southern portions of the *Korps* sector the enemy gained but little ground.

In the sector adjoining to the left (67th *Korps*) the enemy exerted heavier pressure on HOENNINGEN [Hönningen], and along the HOENNINGEN [Hönningen]–WALDBREITBACH road.

### 16 March

The enemy exerted heavy pressure on the right wing and in the center of the *Korps* [sector]. HIMBERG, VETTELSCHOSS and STROEDT [Strödt] were lost. There was fighting around ROTTBITZE.

In the sector adjoining to the right the enemy captured the DRACHENFELS and broke into KOENIGSWINTER [Königswinter]. For the first time he reached the AUTOBAHN near BRUENGSBERG [Brüngsberg]. The GROSSE OELBERG [Grosse Öl-Berg] was also lost. With that the enemy controlled all the commanding hills of the SIEBENGEBIRGES [Seven Mountains].

For the situation in the evening of 16 March see the sketch-map in Appendix 8.

### 17 March

In the sector of the 9th *Panzer Division* Aegidienberg [Ägidienberg] was lost, in the sector of the 340th *Volksgrenadier Division* ROTTBITZE [is this the ROBITZE shown on sketch-map 8? On sketch-map 9 the label is very tiny and hard to read but might well be 'Rottbittze'. On sketch-map 10 still tiny and hard to read but looks like 'ROTTBITZE'. ROTTBITZE is again mentioned with that spelling in the notes to Appendix 8.] was finally lost. The enemy extended his penetration in the sector adjoining on the right to the AUTOBAHN. The 3rd *Panzer Grenadier*

*Division* was committed in a counterattack from the north. In the sector adjoining to the left, the enemy reached the WIED [river] south of WALDBREITBACH.

**18 March**

Strong enemy attacks in the sector of the 9th *Panzer Division* and the 340th *Volksgrenadier Division* thrust forward between ORSCHEID and WINDHAGEN over the AUTOBAHN. WINDHAUSEN, STOCKHAUSEN AND WID[?]SCHEID were lost. The 11th *Panzer Division* held its positions.

**19 March**

The *Korps* front was generally quiet.

In the sector adjoining to the right the enemy continued to advance via KOENIGSWINTER [KÖNIGSWINTER] to OBERCASSEL.

In the sector adjoining to the left [the enemy] reached the WIED [river] on a broad front and built a bridgehead south of WALDBREITBACH.

**20 March**

Major attacks along the entire *Korps* front. The *Schwerpunkt* of the attack was in the sector of the 9th *Panzer Division*. The enemy penetrated near STOCKHAUSSEN [*sic.*] [Stockhausen] and captured the airfield north of GERMSCHEID. He achieved a penetration in EUDENBACH. GERMSCHEID, HUENGSBERG [HÜNGSBERG] and ROTT in the ELSAFFTHAL [Elsaff Valley] were lost. In the southern part of the *Korps* front the enemy reached the WIED [river]. What were, by now, only weak forces of the division somewhat delayed, but could not halt, the enemy's advance with small counterattacks.

The *Korps* received PREPARATORY ORDERS [Vororientierung] that the 11th *Panzer Division* was going to be withdrawn immediately for commitment with the 74th *Korps*. By order of the *Heeresgruppe 'Schwerste Panzergruppe HUDEL'* [Extremely Heavy Tank Group HUDEL] was formed, consisting of *Schwere Panzer Jäger Abteilung* 654, *Schwere Panzer Abteilung* 506 and *Schwere Panzer Jäger Abteilung* 512 (*Jagdtiger*). Immediately upon its arrival this armoured force was also to be employed in the sector of the 74th *Korps*. The focus of the enemy's offensive was expected to fall in that sector. The commanders of the 53rd and 74th *Korps* were to exchange commands, with *General* BAYERLEIN taking over the former sector of the 74th *Korps* and *General* PUECHLER that of the 53rd *Korps*. See sketch-map in Appendix 9 for the situation in the evening of 20 March.

**21 March**

The 11th *Panzer Division* was withdrawn from the front, minus *Kampfgruppe BUTTLAR*, to launch a counterattack in the 74th *Korps* sector. The *Heeresgruppe* believed that the main weight of the enemy's assault was directed at SIEGBURG. Remaining on the *Korps* front were: 9th *Panzer Division* (now no more than a weak *Kampfgruppe*), the 340th *Volksgrenadier Division* (approximately at battalion strength) and *Kampfgruppe BUTTLAR* (also at reinforced-battalion strength). At noon *Feldmarschall* MODEL, at the command post of the 74th *Korps* in OBERROTH (five kilometres south of EITORF), ordered that the planned counterattack be launched with the 11th *Panzer Division* and the newly brought up elements of the *Panzer Lehr Division*, along with the *Schwerste Panzer Gruppe* in the 74th *Korps* sector.

The exchange of commanders of the 53rd and 74th *Korps* – leaving the staffs behind, except for the chiefs of staff – was to take effect in the evening of 22 March, since now the bulk of the armoured forces was concentrated with the 74th *Korps.*

**22 March**

Assumption of command in the 74th *Korps* sector in the evening of 22 March.

New mission for 23 March: Attack in the morning of 24 March with all elements of the *Korps* to repulse the enemy advancing over the PLEIS STREAM SECTOR.

For the situation at the time of change of command (in the sector of Bayerlein's 53rd *Korps*) see sketch-map in Appendix 10.

Signed (actual signature) BAYERLEIN

[note-Bayerlein stated that the following 'appendix a' is to be inserted to replace the last part of the above entry for 21 March and what follows.]

**(handwritten) Appendix a**

**A – 970**

*Lehr Division*, with the 74th *Korps*. In addition, along with the *Schwerste Panzer Gruppe* in the 74th *Korps* sector. [the extremely heavy *Panzergruppe*].

Change of commanders of the 53rd and 74th *Korps* – less staffs, except for the chiefs-of-staffs was to take effect on the evening of 22 March or in the morning of 23 March, since the bulk of the armoured forces were now concentrated with the 74th *Korps.*

**22 March**

In the sector of the 53rd *Korps* there was no significant action.

In the sector of the 74th *Korps* the planned counterattack with the 11th *Panzer* [*Division*], the 3rd *Panzergrenadier* [*Division*] and *Kampfgruppe Panzer Lehr* took place with its objective of forcing the enemy that had crossed the PLEIS sector back.

**23 March**

Noon: Assumption of command in the 74th *Korps* sector by *General* Bayerlein.

For situation at the time of the change of command in the sector of the 53rd *Korp* see sketch-map, Appendix 10.

**A – 970**

## Appendix 2

## ORGANIZATION OF THE 53rd *KORPS* AT THE REMAGEN BRIDGEHEAD AS OF 10 MARCH 1945

11th *Panzer Division: General* von Wietersheim
Combat Strength: Manpower, 400; Armour, 25; Guns, 18.

9th *Panzer Division*: *Oberst* Dingler *
Combat Strength: Manpower, 600; Armour, 15; Guns, 12

*Kampfgruppe* of the *Panzer Lehr Division*: *Major* Hudel**
Combat Strength: Manpower, 300; Armour, 15, Guns, –

*Brigade Feldherrnhalle*
Combat Strength: Manpower, 100; Armour, 5; Guns, –

from 13 March
340th *Volksgrenadier Division*: *Generalmajor* Tollsdorf
Combat Strength: Manpower, 200 (without weapons); Armour, –; Guns, –

from 13 March
*Infanterie Regiment* 130: *Oberst?*
Combat Strength: Manpower, 2000

*Volksartillerie Korps* 208: *Oberstleutnant*?
Combat Strength: Two heavy, one light *Abteilung* with a total of about 20 guns

from 15 March
*Werfer Brigade?*. *Major*?
Combat Strength: A total of about 20 *Werfer* [see glossary note on *Nebelwerfer*]

*Schwere Panzer Jäger Abteilung* 651: *Major* Noak
Strength: About 15 *Jäger*

*Sturmgeschütz Brigade* 243: *Hauptmann*?
Strength: About 10 *Sturmgeschütze*

* from 17 March: *Obersti* ZOLLENKOPF

** later attached to *Kampfgruppe von BUTTLAR* as part of the 11th *Panzer Division*.

### Command Posts of the 53rd *Korps* and Attached Divisions 10–22 March 1945

| *Date* | *53rd Korps* | *9th Panzer* | *11th Panzer* | *340th Volksgrenadier* |
|---|---|---|---|---|
| 10 March | Walgenbach NW Asbach | NW Honnef | Kalenborn | — |
| 11 March | Walgenbach | Retscheid | Kalenborn | — |
| 12 March | Walgenbach | Retscheid | Günderscheid | — |

| | | | | |
|---|---|---|---|---|
| 13 March | Walgenbach | Retscheid | Günderscheid | Birken |
| 14 March | Kescheid NW Flammersteld | Retscheid | Günderscheid | Birken |
| 15 March | Kescheid | Quirrenbach | Günderscheid | Birken |
| 16 March | Kescheid | Germscheid | Bertenau | Birken |
| 17 March | Kescheid | Germscheid | Kloster-Ehrenstein | Hüngsberg |
| 18 March | Kescheid | Germscheid | Ehrenstein | Hüngsberg |
| 19 March | Kescheid | Oberscheid | Ehrenstein | Sessenhausen |
| 20 March | Kescheid | Oberscheid | Ehrenstein | Sessenhausen |
| 21 March | Kescheid | Oberscheid | Oberlahr | Sessenhausen |
| 22 March | Kescheid | Oberscheid | Oberlahr | Sessenhausen |

*Generalleutnant* BAYERLEIN
Ober Ursel 15 May 1946

53rd *Korps* Remagen Bridgehead.

**The Battle of the 53rd *Korps* at the Remagen Bridgehead from 10 to 22 March 1945,**
**(Worked up from the diary entries of *General* BAYERLEIN)**

1) Course of Combat Operations Appendix 1

2) Order of Battle and Combat Strengths Appendix 2

3) Command Posts of the *Korps* and the Divisions Appendix 3

4) Sketch-maps of Combat Operations Appendices 4 – 10

Signed (by hand) BAYERLEIN

**Table of Sketch-maps Appendices 4 through 10**

**Appendix 4**

1) Sketch of the Planned Counterattack on 10 March

**Appendix 5**

2) Situation, Evening of 10 March

**Appendix 6**

3) Sketch of Planned Counterattack on 13 March

**Appendix 7**

4) Situation, Evening of 13 March

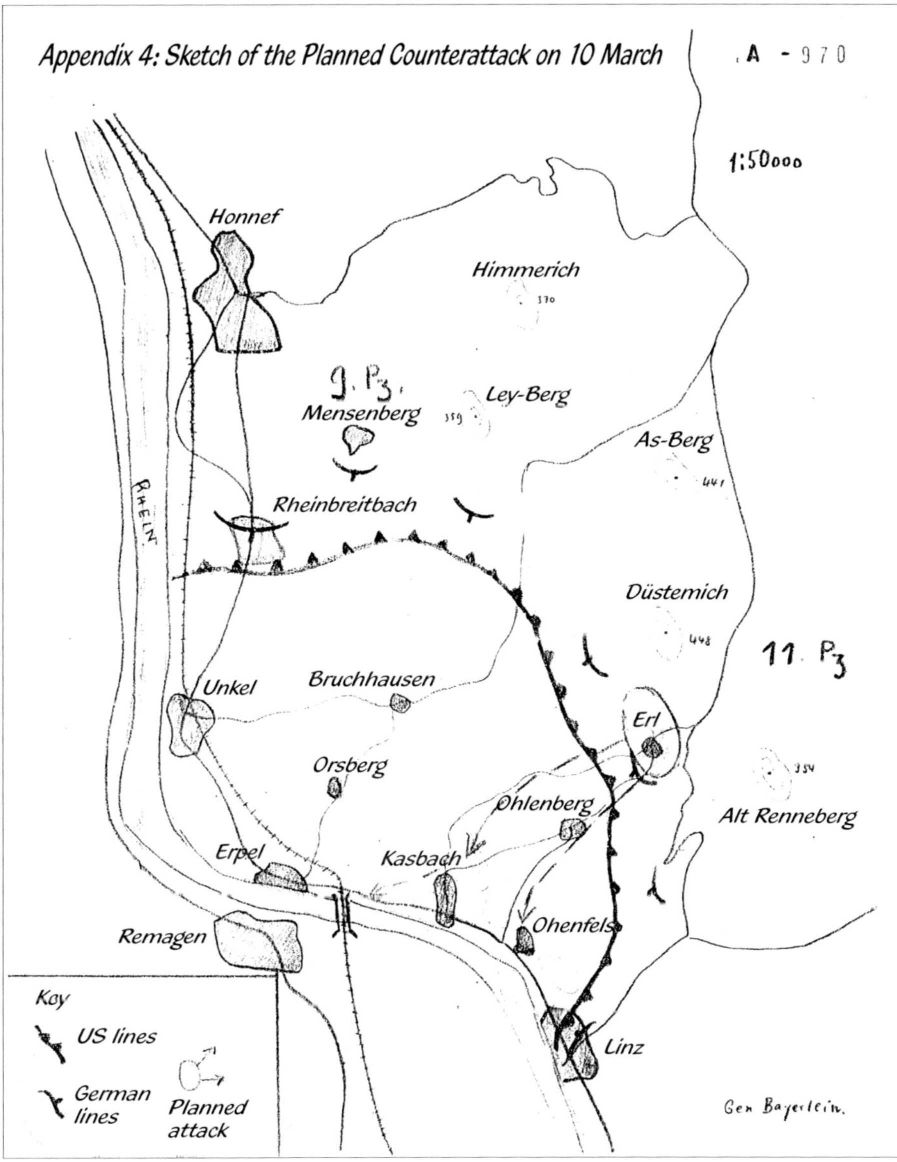


Appendix 4: Sketch of the planned counter-attack 10 March 1945

**Appendix 8**

5) Situation, Evening of 16 March

**Appendix 9**

6) Situation, Evening of 20 March

**Appendix 10**

7) Situation, Evening 22 March (Change of Command)

**Notes to Appendix 5, Situation, Evening of 10 March**[1]

German Lines
U.S. Spearheads
Boundaries between:
*Korps*
Divisions
Command Post, 53rd *Korps*
Command Posts of the 9th and 11th *Panzer Divisions*

**Situation, Evening of 10 March**

Enemy attacks took place throughout the entire day, thereby significantly extending the bridgehead. The LEY-BERG remained in German hands. The situation at DÜSTEMICH was unclear. The enemy was unable to take the HARGARTEN – Peak.

Elements of *Brigade FELDHERRNHALLE* and remnants of the former Rhine-bank garrison were attached to the 9th *Panzer Division*. (The positions of these elements are not shown on the sketch-map.)

Remnants of the former Rhine defense, an SS replacement battalion and other fragmented units were attached to the 11th *Panzer Division*. The positions of all these various elements are not shown on the sketch-map.

Adjoining to the right was the 74th *Korps* with the 3rd *Fallschirmjäger Division*. Adjoining on the left was the 67th *Korps* with the 26th *Volksgrenadier Division*. Elements of that division were nowhere to be found, so there was a gap in the LINZ area. This gap was closed in upcoming days by arriving elements of *Kampfgruppe Panzer Lehr*.

The *Korps* command post had to remain in OBERPLEIS, since communications had to be maintained with the COMMANDER OF THE RHINE DEFENSE [*Befehlshaber der Rheinverteidigung*] and, at that point, the *Korps* still had no means of communications of its own.

1 Publisher's note: for reasons of clarity it has been decided to reproduce the original pages from report A-970 showing pictorial symbols accompanying the maps, as well as translating the text within this book. For such a complex series of maps and appendices it was deemed better to offer the reader more rather than less information.

A - 970

**Erläuterungen zu Anlage 5. Lage am 10.März abends.**

deutsche Linie

US.Angriffsspitzen

Trennungslinien

zwischen denKorps

zwischen den Divisionen

Gefechtsstand 53.Korps

Gefechtsstände der
9.und 11.Panzer Div.

**Lage am Abend des 10.März.**

Während des ganzen Tages hatten feindliche Angriffe stattgefunden.Dadurch wurde der Brückenkopf erheblich erweitert. Der LEY-BERG blieb in eigenem Besitz. Die Lage am DUESTEMICH war ungeklärt. Der HARGARTEN-Gipfel konnte vom Feind nicht genommen werden.

Zu 9.Panzer gehörten Teile der Brigade FELDHERRNHALLE und Restteile der ehemaligen Rheinuferbesatzung.(Die Stellungen dieser Teile sind in der Skizze nicht angegeben).

Zu 11.Panzer gehörten Restteile der ehemaligen Rheinbesatzung ,ein SS Ersatz Bataillon und andere Splittergruppen. Die Stellungen aller dieser Truppen sind auf der Skizze nicht gesondert angegeben

Rechts schliesst 74.Korps mit 3.Fallschirm Div.,links 67.Korps mit 26.Volks Grenadier Div. an. Die Teile dieser Div waren aber nicht zu finden,so dass im Raume von LINZ eine Lücke offen stand. Diese Lücke wurde am nächsten Tage durch die in der Nacht eintreffenden Teile der Kampfgruppe Panzer Lehr geschlossen.

Der Korpsgefechtsstand musste in OBERPLEIS verbleiben,da die Verbindung mit dem dort liegenden BEFEHLSHABER DER RHEINVERTEIDIGUNG aufrechterhalten werden musste und da das Korps zu diesem Zeitpunkt noch keine Nachrichtenmittel bei sich hatte.

13

Reproduction of original notes to Appendix 5 from manuscript A-970 including pictorial symbols

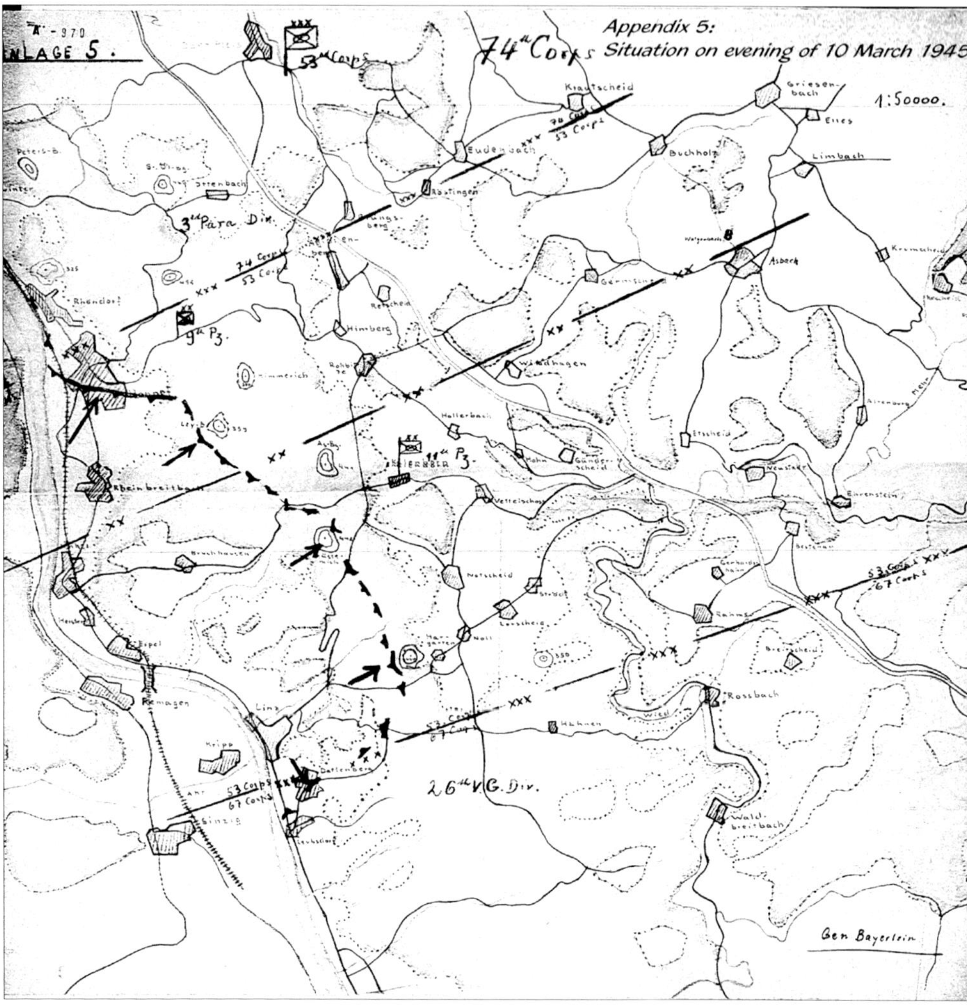


Appendix 5: Situation on the evening of 10 March 1945

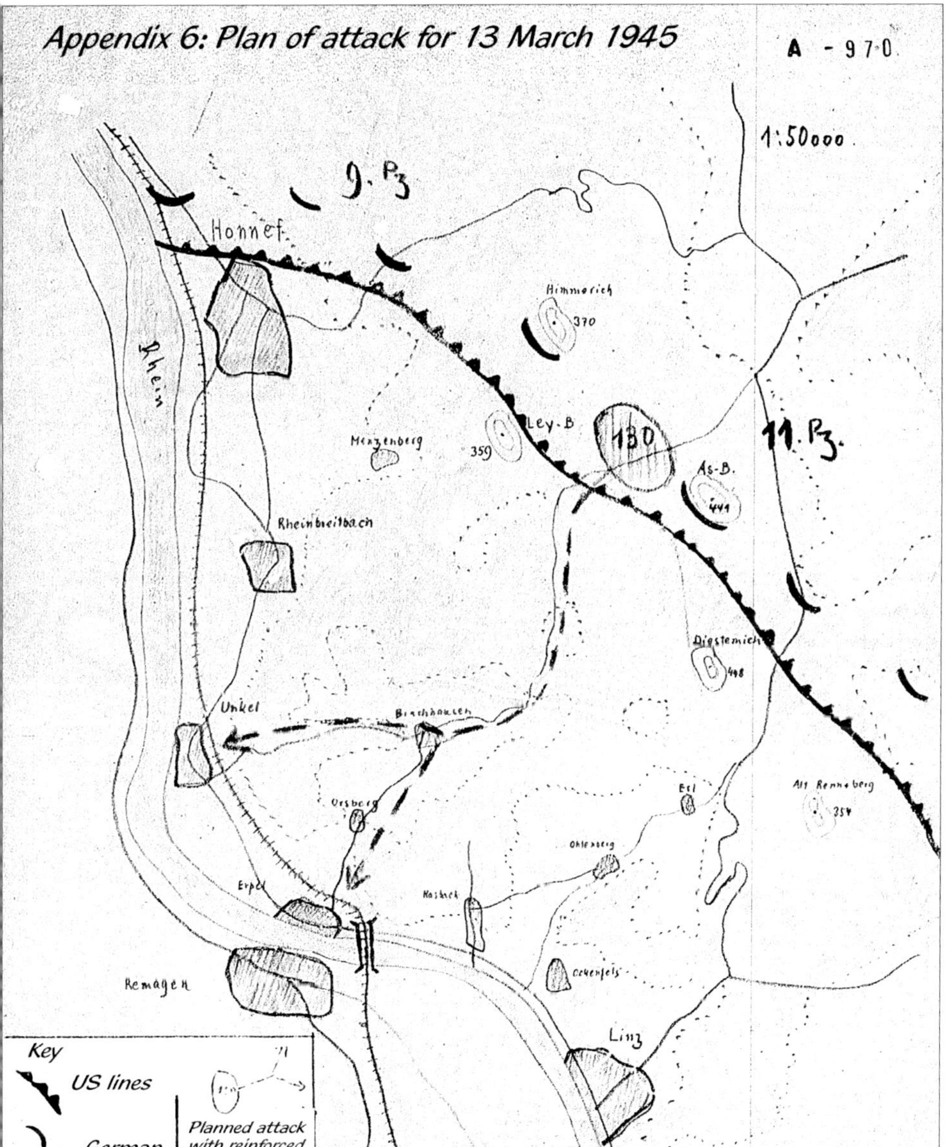


Appendix 6: Plan of attack for 13 March 1945

**Notes to Appendix 7 (Situation, evening of 13 March)**

German lines
U.S. Spearheads of attack
Boundaries:
Between *Korps*
Between divisions
Command Posts:
53rd *Korps*
9th *Panzer Division*
11th *Panzer Division*
Kampfgruppe von Buttlar

**Situation, evening 13 March:**

Between 10 and 13 March the enemy slowly but surely pressed steadily forward. He extended the bridgehead as shown on the sketch-map. In particular, the enemy gained control of the SIEBENGEBIRGE [Seven Mountains], the LEY-Berg (359 meters), HIMMERICH (370 meters) DUESTEMICH [Düstemich] (418 meters [elevation given as 448 meters on sketch map, Appendix 4]) HARGARTEN (441 meters), as well as the difficult high ground northeast of HONNEF. The AS-Berg(441 or perhaps 442 [strikeover] meters. Sketch-map is clearly marked 441.]) was the only commanding peak remaining in German hands.

Because of the difficult situation in the sector of the adjoining unit on the left (26th *Volksgrenadier Division*) the *Korps* had to take over a significant portion of that division's sector. Accordingly, *Kampfgruppe von Buttlar,* consisting of *Kampfgruppe Panzer Lehr,* elements of the 11th *Panzer Division* and fragmented elements of the Rhine defense units was committed on the left wing of the *Korps* on 12 March. *Kampfgruppe von Buttlar* was attached to the 11th *Panzer Division.*

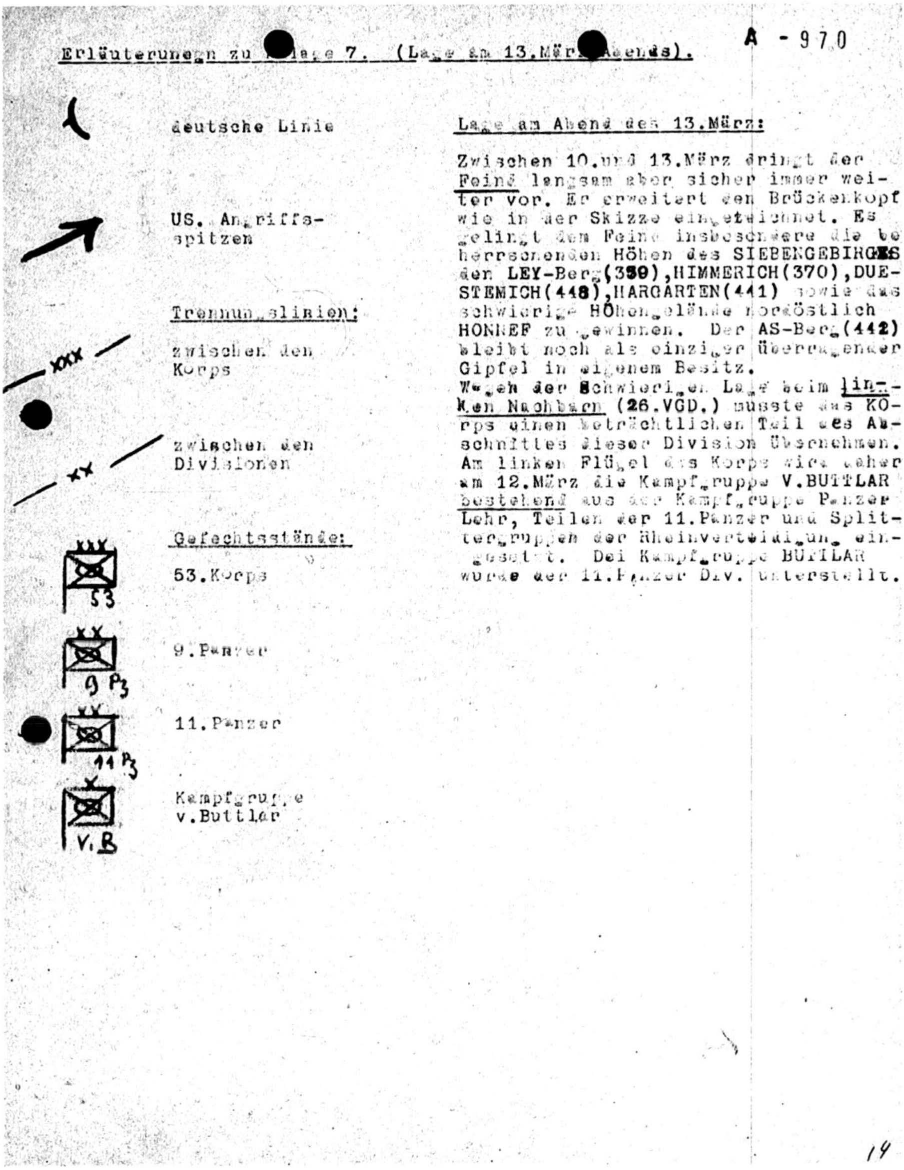

**Erläuterunegn zu Anlage 7. (Lage am 13.März Abends).** A - 970

deutsche Linie

US. Angriffs-spitzen

**Trennungslinien:**

XXX — zwischen den Korps

XX — zwischen den Divisionen

**Gefechtsstände:**

XXX 53 — 53.Korps

XX 9 Pz — 9.Panzer

XX 11 Pz — 11.Panzer

X V.B — Kampfgruppe v.Buttlar

**Lage am Abend des 13.März:**

Zwischen 10.und 13.März dringt der Feind langsam aber sicher immer weiter vor. Er erweitert den Brückenkopf wie in der Skizze eingezeichnet. Es gelingt dem Feind insbesondere die beherrschenden Höhen des SIEBENGEBIRGES den LEY-Berg(359),HIMMERICH(370),DUESTEMICH(448),HARGARTEN(441) sowie das schwierige Höhengelände nordöstlich HONNEF zu gewinnen. Der AS-Berg(442) bleibt noch als einziger überragender Gipfel in eigenem Besitz.
Wegen der Schwierigen Lage beim linken Nachbarn (26.VGD.) musste das KOrps einen beträchtlichen Teil des Abschnittes dieser Division übernehmen. Am linken Flügel des Korps wird daher am 12.März die Kampfgruppe V.BUTTLAR bestehend aus der Kampfgruppe Panzer Lehr, Teilen der 11.Panzer und Splittergruppen der Rheinverteidigung eingesetzt. Dei Kampfgruppe BUTTLAR wurde der 11.Panzer Div. unterstellt.

19

Reproduction of original notes to Appendix 7 from manuscript A-970 including pictorial symbols

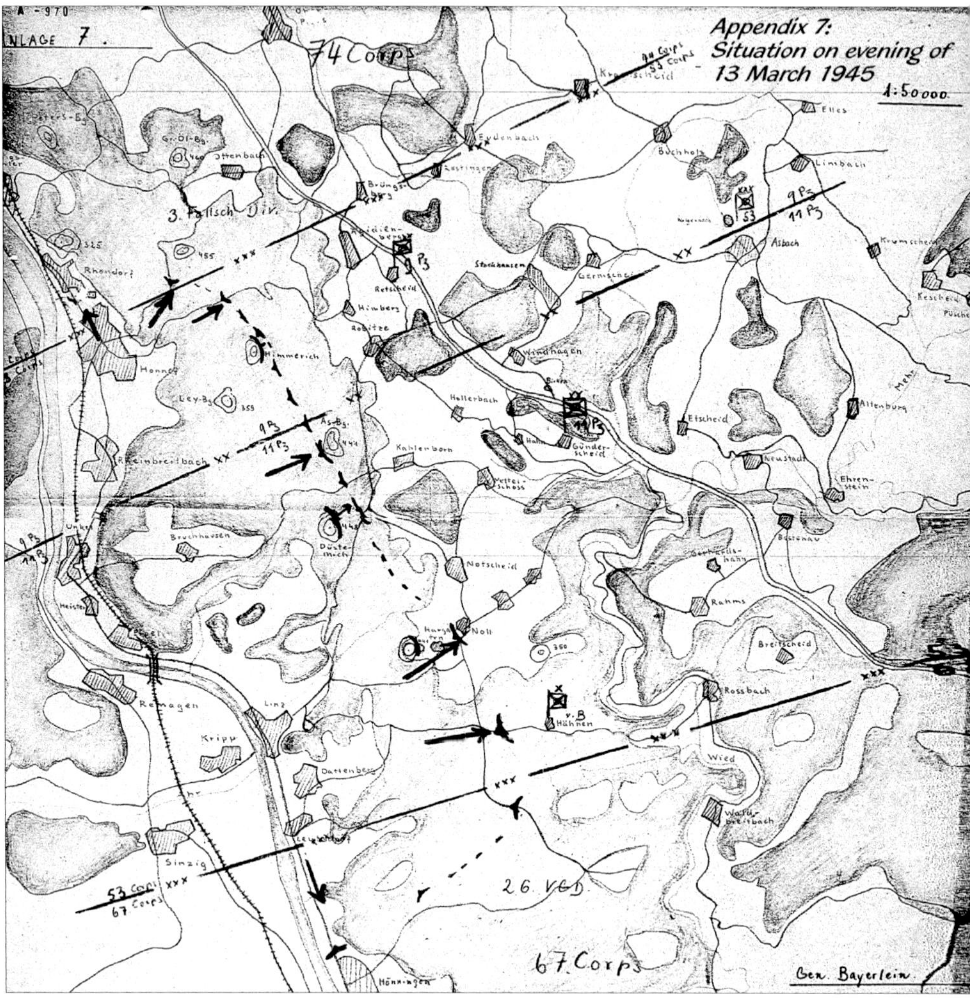


Appendix 7: Situation on the evening of 13 March 1945

**Notes to Appendix 8 (Situation, evening 16 March)**

German lines
German counterattacks
U.S. Spearheads of attack
Boundaries:
between the *Korps*
between the divisions
Command Posts:
53rd *Korps*
9th *Panzer Division*
11th *Panzer Division*
340th *Volksgrenadier Division*
*Kampfgruppe von Buttlar*

**Situation, evening 16 March**

In the sector of the unit adjoining to the right (74th *Korps*) the enemy reached and crossed the *Autobahn* west of BRUENGSBERG [Brüngsberg] on a narrow front. Thereupon the *Korps* had to take over the BRUENGSBERG sector. The 74th *Korps* also lost the commanding DRACHENFELS (southwest of KOENIGSWINTER [Königswinter]). With that, the *Korps* lost its last possible opportunity to observe the enemy bridgehead position. The GROSSE OEL-BERG [Grosse Öl-Berg] was also lost.

In the sector of the 9th *Panzer Division* the enemy took the HIMBERG hill and the locality itself, while AEGIDIENBERG [Ägidienberg] remained in German hands.

In the sector of the 340th *Volksgrenadier Division* ROTTBITZE was lost. The Division attempted a counterattack with armoured support in the evening, forcing the enemy back somewhat. RITTBITZE [*sic.*], however, remained in enemy hands.

In the sector of the 11th *Panzer Division* VETTELSCHOSS was lost. A counterattack was still in progress in the evening and led to its recapture. STROEDT [Strödt] was also lost, while the commanding Hill 341 remained in friendly hands. Hill 360 and STUEMPERICH [Stümperich] (395 meters) had already been taken by the enemy the preceding day. HAEHMEN [Hähmen] remained in friendly hands.

In the sector of the unit adjoining to the right the enemy advanced in strength to the WIED [river].

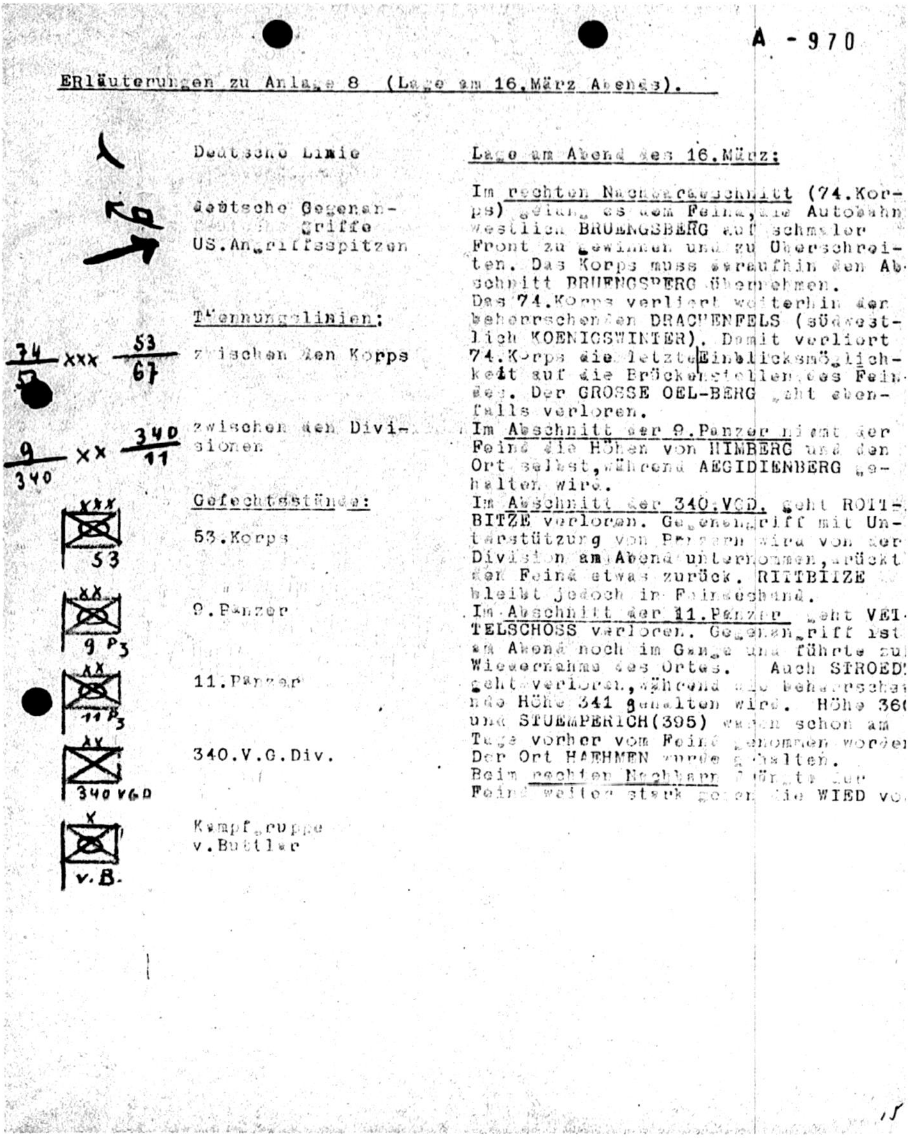

A - 970

ERläuterungen zu Anlage 8 (Lage am 16.März Abends).

Deutsche Linie

Deutsche Gegenangriffe

US.Angriffsspitzen

Trennungslinien:

zwischen den Korps

zwischen den Divisionen

Gefechtsstände:

53.Korps

9.Panzer

11.Panzer

340.V.G.Div.

Kampfgruppe v.Buttler

Lage am Abend des 16.März:

Im rechten Nachbarabschnitt (74.Korps) gelang es dem Feind, die Autobahn westlich BRUENGSBERG auf schmaler Front zu gewinnen und zu überschreiten. Das Korps muss daraufhin den Abschnitt BRUENGSBERG übernehmen.
Das 74.Korps verliert weiterhin den beherrschenden DRACHENFELS (südwestlich KOENIGSWINTER). Damit verliert 74.Korps die letzte Einblicksmöglichkeit auf die Brückenstellen des Feindes. Der GROSSE OEL-BERG geht ebenfalls verloren.
Im Abschnitt der 9.Panzer nimmt der Feind die Höhen von HIMBERG und den Ort selbst, während AEGIDIENBERG gehalten wird.
Im Abschnitt der 340.VGD. geht ROITTBITZE verloren. Gegenangriff mit Unterstützung von Panzern wird von der Division am Abend unternommen, drückt den Feind etwas zurück. RITTBIIZE bleibt jedoch in Feindeshand.
Im Abschnitt der 11.Panzer geht VETTELSCHOSS verloren. Gegenangriff ist am Abend noch im Gange und führte zur Wiedernahme des Ortes. Auch STROED[illegible] geht verloren, während die beherrschende Höhe 341 gehalten wird. Höhe 36[illegible] und STUEMPERICH(395) waren schon am Tage vorher vom Feind genommen worden. Der Ort HAEHMEN wurde gehalten.
Beim rechten Nachbarn drängte der Feind weiter stark gegen die WIED vo[illegible]

Reproduction of original notes to Appendix 8 from manuscript A-970 including pictorial symbols

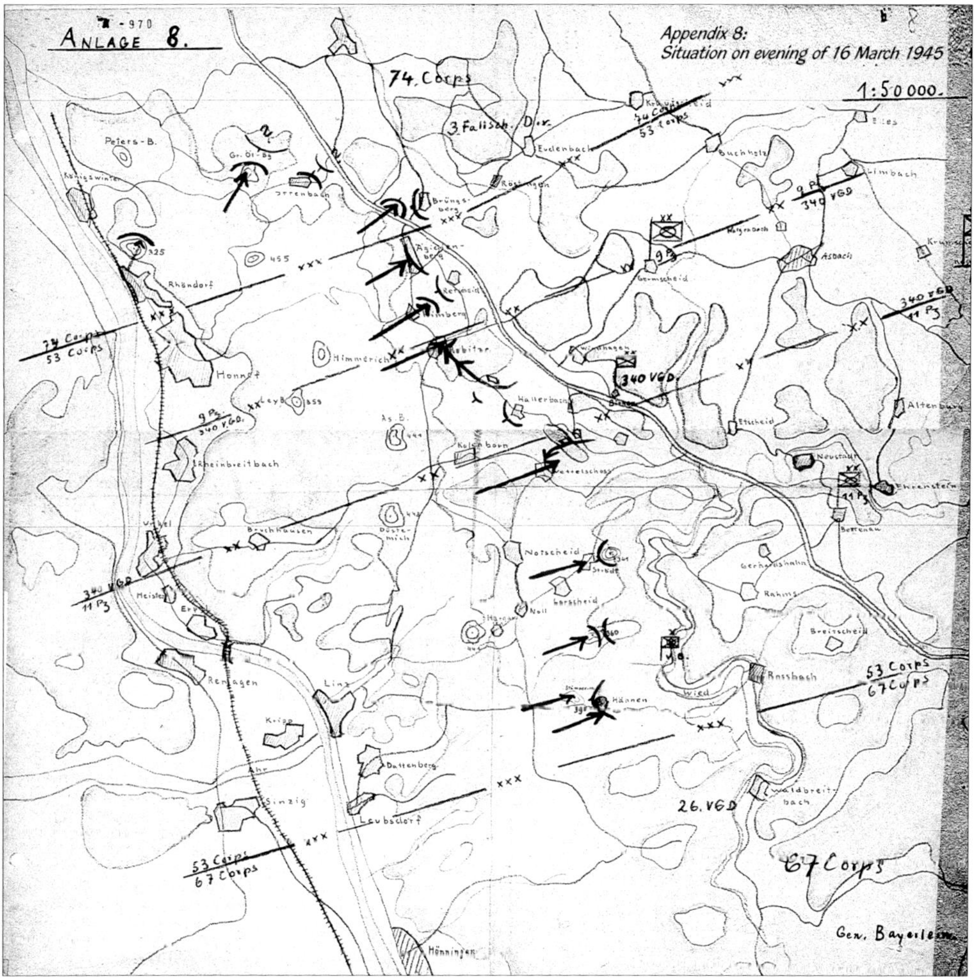

Appendix 8: Situation on the evening of 16 March 1945

**Notes to Appendix 9 (situation, evening of 20 March)**

German lines
German counterattacks
U.S. attack spearheads
Boundaries:
between *Korps*
between divisions
Command posts:
53rd *Korps*
9th *Panzer Division*
11th *Panzer Division*
340th *Volksgrenadier Division*
*Kampfgruppe von Buttlar*

**Situation, evening 20 March:**

In the sector of the unit adjoining on the right the enemy crossed the *Autobahn* on a broad front. OBER PLEIS was captured by the enemy. The enemy penetrated EUDENBACH.

In the sector of the 53rd *Korps*: The airfield north of GERMSCHEID was lost. GERMSCHEID, STOCKHAUSSEN [Stockhausen on sketch-map], WINDHAGEN, HUENGSBERG [Hüngsberg] and ROTT were in enemy hands. The enemy attained the WIED [River] – sector as far as west of ROSSBACH. The ROSSBACH bridgehead was held by *Kampfgruppe [von] BUTTLAR.*

In the sector of the unit adjoining to the left the WALDBREITBACH bridgehead was held by the 26th *Volksgrenadier Division*.

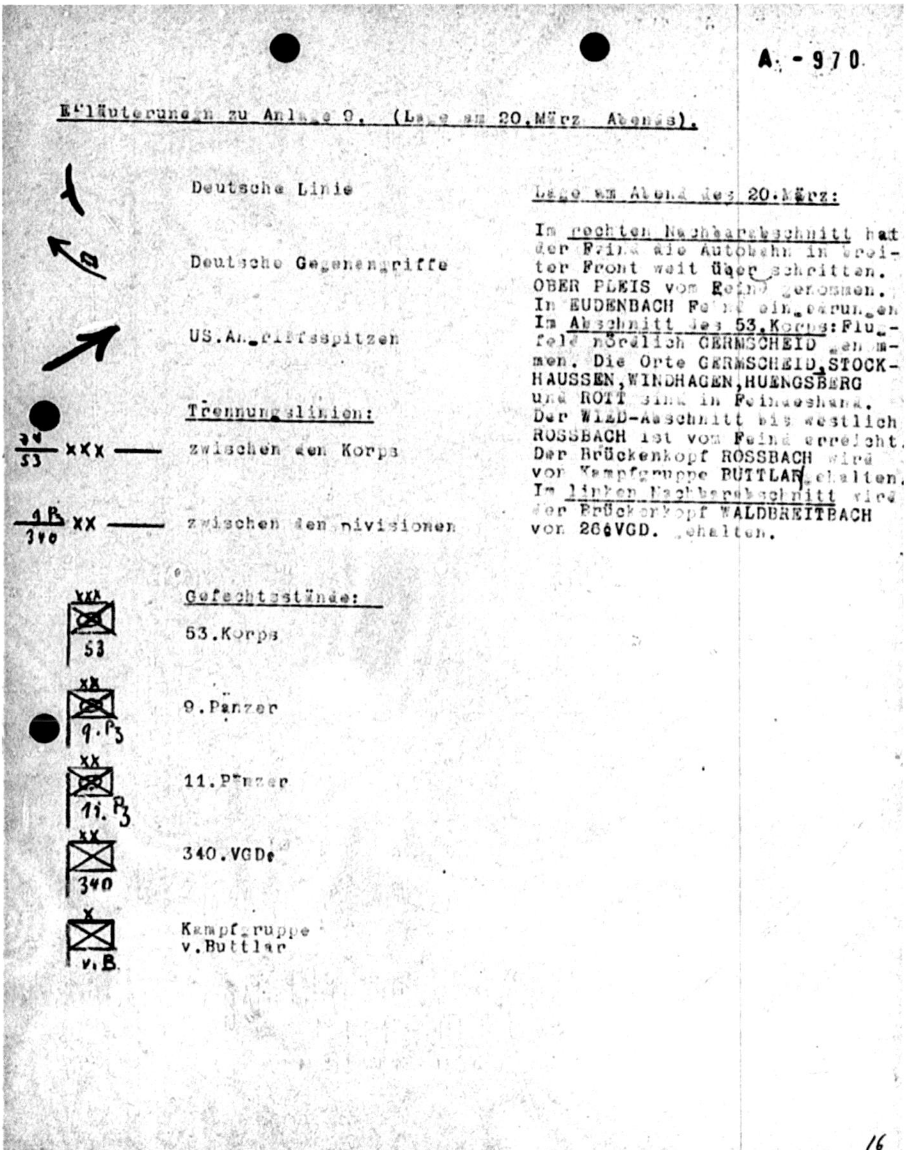

A - 970

Erläuterungen zu Anlage 9. (Lage am 20.März Abends).

Deutsche Linie

Deutsche Gegenangriffe

US.Angriffsspitzen

Trennungslinien:

$\frac{74}{53}$ XXX — zwischen den Korps

$\frac{9B}{340}$ XX — zwischen den Divisionen

Gefechtsstände:

XXX 53 — 53.Korps

XX 9.Pz — 9.Panzer

XX 11.Pz — 11.Panzer

XX 340 — 340.VGD.

X v.B. — Kampfgruppe v.Buttlar

Lage am Abend des 20.März:

Im rechten Nachbarabschnitt hat der Feind die Autobahn in breiter Front weit überschritten. OBER PLEIS vom Feind genommen. In EUDENBACH Feind eingedrungen. Im Abschnitt des 53.Korps: Flugfeld nördlich GERMSCHEID genommen. Die Orte GERMSCHEID, STOCKHAUSSEN, WINDHAGEN, HUENGSBERG und ROTT sind in Feindeshand. Der WIED-Abschnitt bis westlich ROSSBACH ist vom Feind erreicht. Der Brückenkopf ROSSBACH wird von Kampfgruppe BUTTLAR gehalten. Im linken Nachbarabschnitt wird der Brückenkopf WALDBREITBACH von 266VGD. gehalten.

16

Reproduction of original notes to Appendix 9 from manuscript A-970 including pictorial symbols

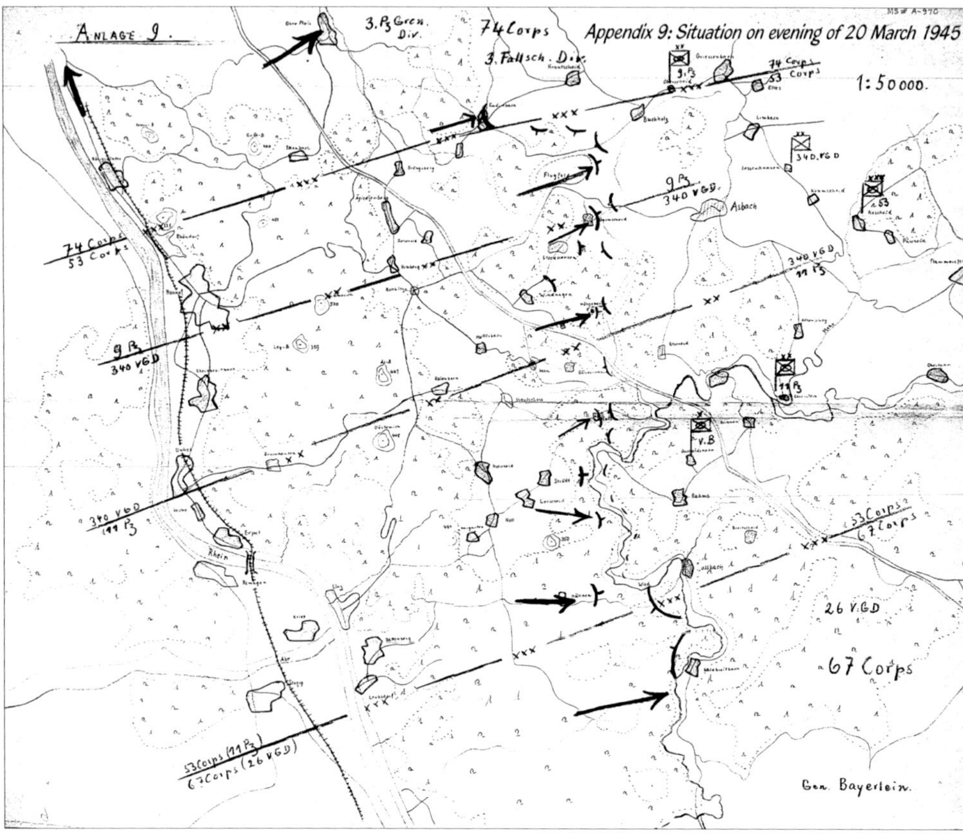


Appendix 9: Situation on the evening of 20 March 1945

**Notes on Appendix 10 (Situation evening 22 March)**

German lines
U.S. Lines
Boundaries:
between *Korps*
between divisions
Command Posts
53rd *Korps*
9th *Panzer Division*
310th *Volksgrenadier Division*
*Kampfgruppe von Buttlar*

**Situation, evening of 22 March:**

The enemy continued to advance on 21 and 22 March.

The *Schwerpunkt* of the attack was in the sector of the unit adjoining to the right.

In the sector of the 53rd *Korps* the only enemy success was near EUDENBACH, with the 9th *Panzer Division*.

The 11th *Panzer Division* and the newly formed *schwere Panzer Gruppe HUDEL* were withdrawn.

In the evening of 22 March the *Korps* sector was held only by weak forces of the 9th *Panzer Division*, the 310th *Volksgrenadier Division* and *[Kampf] Gruppe [von] BUTTLAR*. The position extended between GERMSCHEID and ROSSBACH along the stream sector.

The lines were very weakly held. Only a few tanks and *Panzerjäger* were still present, and they were built into the line of defense. The most endangered sector was that of the 9th *Panzer Division* in the GERMSCHEID BUCHHOLZ area where there was no natural obstacle and enemy armour could operate freely.

At noon *General* PUECHLER [Püchler] (74th *Korps*) assumed command of the sector. [note that last paragraph above is to be stricken out and replaced by 'Appendix b', below.]

**(Written in handwriting) Appendix b**

**Notes to Appendix 10 (Situation, evening 22 March)**

Situation, evening 22 March:
Strike out the last paragraph!
Replace with:
At noon on 23 March *General* Püchler*'s* 74th *Korps* assumed command of the sector.

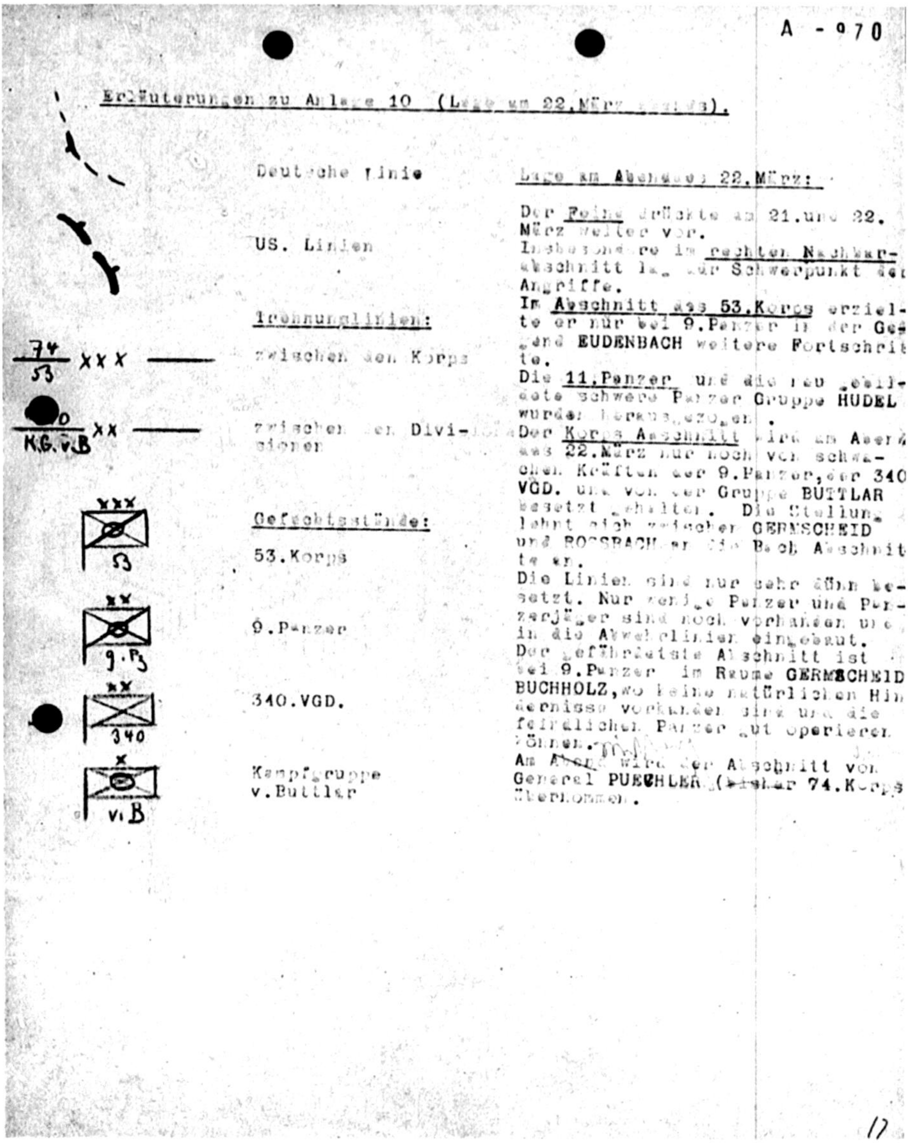

A - 970

Erläuterungen zu Anlage 10 (Lage am 22.März abends).

Deutsche Linie

US. Linien

Trennungslinien:

74/53 XXX zwischen den Korps

KG.v.B XX zwischen den Divisionen

Gefechtsstände:

53.Korps

9.Panzer

340.VGD.

Kampfgruppe v.Buttlar

Lage am Abend des 22.März:

Der Feind drückte am 21.und 22. März weiter vor.
Insbesondere im rechten Nachbarabschnitt lag der Schwerpunkt der Angriffe.
Im Abschnitt des 53.Korps erzielte er nur bei 9.Panzer in der Gegend EUDENBACH weitere Fortschritte.
Die 11.Panzer und die neu gebildete schwere Panzer Gruppe HUDEL wurden herausgezogen.
Der Korps Abschnitt wird am Abend des 22.März nur noch von schwachen Kräften der 9.Panzer, der 340 VGD. und von der Gruppe BUTTLAR besetzt gehalten. Die Stellung lehnt sich zwischen GERNSCHEID und ROSSBACH an die Bach Abschnitte an.
Die Linien sind nur sehr dünn besetzt. Nur wenige Panzer und Panzerjäger sind noch vorhanden und in die Abwehrlinien eingebaut.
Der gefährdetste Abschnitt ist bei 9.Panzer im Raume GERMSCHEID BUCHHOLZ, wo keine natürlichen Hindernisse vorhanden sind und die feindlichen Panzer gut operieren können.
Am Abend wird der Abschnitt von General PUECHLER (bisher 74.Korps übernommen.

17

Reproduction of original notes to Appendix 10 from manuscript A-970 including pictorial symbols

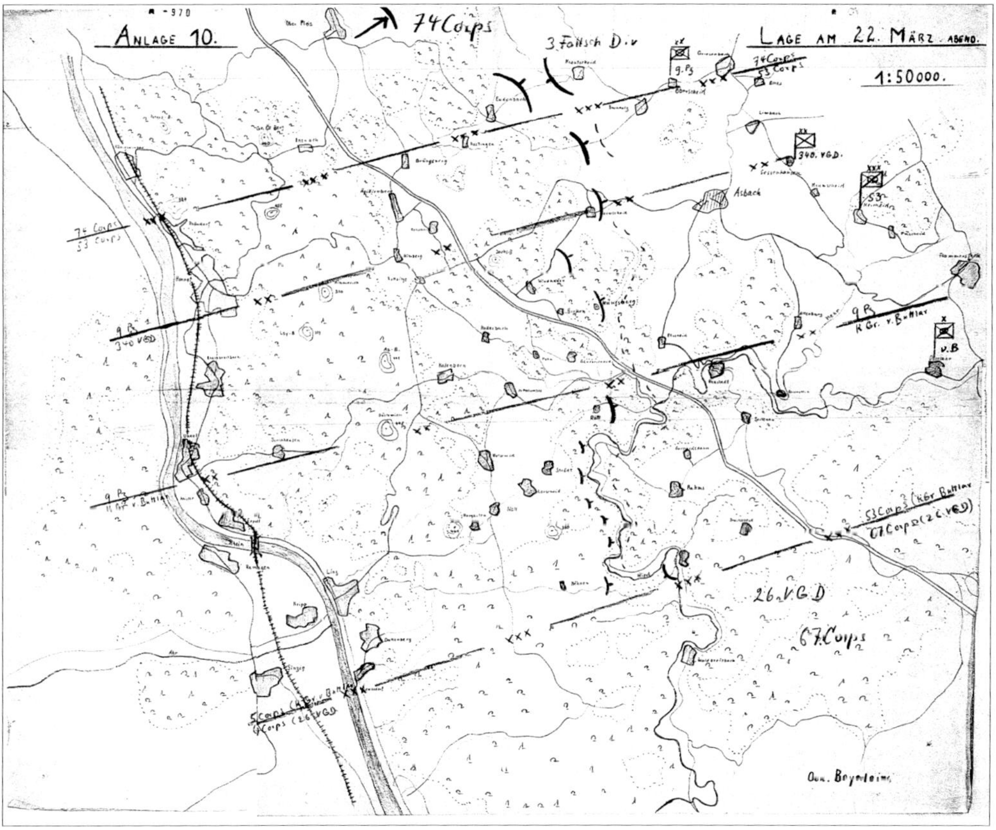


Appendix 10: Situation on the evening of 22 March 1945

# From the Remagen Bridgehead to the Ruhr Pocket

Despite the dramatic impact of the capture of the bridge at Remagen, the difficult terrain and poor communications east of that site did not tempt the allies to shift their main effort to that site. The main effort remained with Montgomery's 21st Army Group in the north, where the prize to be taken was the Ruhr industrial region, fifty miles wide at its base on the Rhine and extending sixty miles to the east as an approximate triangle. As the Russians captured Silesia and the Americans the Saar, the *Ruhrgebiet*, always Germany's strongest industrial region, was Germany's only remaining source of power and production.

General Hodges' American First Army in the Remagen Bridgehead was not permitted to break out of its bridgehead until after Montgomery's 21st Army Group had crossed the Rhine in the north. Then, however, Eisenhower's plans were that Hodges' First Army and Patton's Third Army were to build a ninety-two mile wide bridgehead between them extending from the Sieg River in the north to the Main in the south. The two armies would then advance up the Frankfurt – Kassel corridor along the Lahn River to Kassel, where the First Army would then turn northward to form the southern arm of a double-envelopment of the Ruhr.

The *Panzer Lehr Division* became embroiled in the futile efforts to combat the advance of the American forces as they broke out of the Remagen Bridgehead. At first it seemed confusing to the Division because the American forces (primarily the American 3rd Armored Division) kept on thrusting due east instead of making the expected northward turn to roll up the German forces on the east bank of the Rhine.

Then, as *Panzer Lehr* continually fell back, it found itself on the interior of the developing Ruhr pocket, the *Ruhrkessel*. By now reduced to weak remnants with totally untrained last-minute replacements, the Division finally surrendered to the Americans as the Ruhr pocket was cleaned up.

# BIBLIOGRAPHY


Agte, Patrick, *Michael Wittman, erfolgreichtster Panzerkommandant im Zweitem Weltkrieg und die Tiger der Leibstandarte SS Adolf Hitler*, Deutsche Verlagsgesellschaft, Rosenheim, 1994.

Bender, Roger James and Hugh Page Taylor, *Uniforms, Organization and History of the Waffen-SS*, R. James Bender Publishing, San Jose, California 1969 (five volumes)

Bernage, Georges and Georges Cadel, *La Guerre des GIs, Cobra, La Bataille Decisive*, Editions Heimdal, 1984.

Blumenson, Martin, *U.S. Army in World War II, European Theater of Operations, Breakout and Pursuit*, Office of the Chief of Military History, Department of the Army, Washington, D. C., 1978.

Carell, Paul,, *Sie Kommen*, Ullstein GMBH, Frankfurt/M – Berlin, 1964 reprint of 1960 edition.

Cole, Hugh M., *U.S. Army in World War II, European Theater of Operations, The Ardennes: Battle of the Bulge*, Office of the Chief of Military History, Department of the Army, Washington, D. C., 1965.

Cole, Hugh M. *The U.S. Army in World War II, European Theater of Operations, The Lorraine Campaign*, Office of the Chief of Military History, Department of the Army, Washington, D. C., 1950.

Davies, Arthur, 'Geographical Factors in the Invasion and Battle of Normandy', *The Geographical Review*, Vol 36, No. 4, pp. 613 – 631.

D'Este, Carlo, *Decision in Normandy*, E. P. Dutton, 1983, New York.

Donnhauser, Anton J. and Werner Drews, *Der Weg der 11. Panzer-Division, 1939 –1945*, 1982, Selbstverlag Traditionsgemeinschaft der 11. Panzer (Gespenster) Division

Dupuy, Trevor N., David L. Bongard and Richard C. Anderson, Jr., *Hitlers Last Gamble*, Harper Collins Publishers, New York, 1994.

Ellis, Major L. F., *Victory in the West, Volume I, The Battle of Normandy*, London 1962, Her Majesty's Stationary Office.

Elstob, Peter, *Hitler's Last Offensive*, Macmillan Company, New York, 1971.

Emde, Joachim, *Die Nebelwerfer: Entwicklung und Einsatz der Werfertruppe im Zweiten Weltkrieg*, Podzun-Pallas Verlag, Dorheim, 1979.

Engelmann, Joachim, *Deutsche Raketen-Werfer*, Podzun-Pallas-Verlag, Dorheim, 1977.

Fürbringer, Herbert, *9. SS-Panzer-Division Hohenstaufen, 1944: Normandie Tarnopol–Arnhem*, Editions Heimdal, 1984.

Gander, Terry and Peter Chamberlain, *Weapons of the Third Reich: An Encyclopedic Survey of All Small Arms, Artillery and Special Weapons of the German Land Forces, 1939 – 1945*, Doubleday and Company, Inc, Garden City, New York, 1979.

Guderian, Heinz Günther, *Das letzte Kriegsjahr im Westen: Die Geschichte der 116. Panzer-Division – Windhund -Division – 1944–1945*. Offsetdruck-Verlag, Herbert W. Schallowetz GmbH, Sankt Augustin, 1994.

Hahn, Fritz, *Waffen und Geheimwaffen des deutschen Heers 1933 — 1945, Band 1, Infanteriewaffen, Pionierwaffen, Artilleriewaffen, Pulver, Spreng- und Kampfstoffe* and *Band 2, Panzer- und Sonderfahrzeuge, Wunderwaffen. Verbrauch und Verluste* in one volume,, Bernard & Graefe Verlag, Bonn, 1998.

Harrison, Gordon A., *Cross-Channel Attack, United States Army in World War II, European Theater of Operations*, Office of the Chief of Military History, Department of the Army, Washington, D. C., 1977.

Hechler, Ken, *The Bridge at Remagen: The Amazing Story of March 7, 1945 – The Day the Rhine River was Crossed*, 2nd revised printing, 1995. Pictorial Histories Publishing Company, Inc., Missoula, Montana.

Hinze, Rolf, *Der Zusammenbruch der Heeresgruppe Mitte im Osten 1944*, Motorbuch Verlag, Stuttgart, 1980.

Hogg, Ian V., *German Artillery of World War Two*, Greenhill Books, London, 1997.

Isby, David C., *Fighting the Invasion, The German Army at D-Day*, Greenhill Books, London; Stackpole Books, Pennsylvania, 2000.

Isby, David C., *Fighting in Normandy, The German Army from D-Day to Villers-Bocage*, Greenhill Books, London; Stackpole Books, Pennsylvania, 2001.

Jung, Hermann, *Die Ardennen Offensive 1944/45, Ein Beispiel für die Kriegführung Hitlers*, Mester – Schmidt Verlag, Göttingen, 1971.

Kortenhaus, Werner, *Die Schlacht um Caen 1944: Caumont, Falaise, Seine, Der Einsatz der 21. Panzer-Division*, copyright 1989 by Werner Kortenhaus, Solingen.

Kurowski, Franz, *Die Panzer-Lehr-Division*, Podzun Verlag, Bad Nauheim, 1964.

Lehrmann, Rudolf and Ralf Tiemann, *Die Leibstandarte*, Bd. IV–1, Munin Verlag, Osnabrück, 1986 [available in translation]

Liddell Hart, B. H., *History of the Second World War*, G. P. Putnams Sons, Inc., New York, 1970.

Macdonald, Charles B., *A Time for Trumpets: The Untold Story of the Battle of the Bulge*, William Morrow & Co., New York, 1985.

MacDonald, Charles B., *The Last Offensive, United States Army in World War II, European Theater of Operations*, Office of the Chief of Military History, Department of the Army, Washington D.C., 1975 (repr.).

Manteuffel, Hasso-Eccard von, 'The Ardennes' in *The Fatal Decisions: Six Decisive Battle of the Second World War from the Viewpoint of the Vanquished*, Michael Joseph, London 1956.

Meyer, Hubert, *Kriegsgeschichte der 12. SS-Panzerdivision Hitlerjugend*, vol I, Munin Verlag GmbH, Osnabrück,1982. [available in translation]

Meyer, Kurt (Panzermeyer), *Grenadiere*, Schild-Verlag, 1953, München.

Münch, Karlheinz, *The Combat History of schwere Panzerjäger Abteilung 654*, J. J. Fedoroicz, Manitoba, Canada, 2002.

Nobécourt, Jacques, *Le Dernier Coup de Dés de Hitler*, Éditions Robert laFonte, 1962 (undated Éditions Rencontre edition with different pagination referred to in text).

Parker, Danny S. (Ed.), *Hitlers Ardennes Offensive, The German View of the Battle of the Bulge*, Greenill Books, London; Stackpole Books, Pennsylvania, 1997.

Parker, Danny S., *The Battle of the Bulge, The German View, Perspectives from Hitler's High Command*, Greenhill Books, London; Stackpole Books, Pennsylvania, 1999.

Pergrin, Col. David E. and Eric Hammel, *First Across the Rhine: The Story of the 291st Engineer Combat Battalion*, Athenaum, N. Y. 1989.

Perrigault, Jean-Claude, *La Panzer-Lehr-Division: Le Choc des Alliés Brise L'Arme D'Elite de Hitler, Normandie – Lorraine – Ardennes, Album Historique*, Editions Heimdal, 1995.

Pipet, Albert, *Mourir à Caen,* Editions Presse de la Cité, 1974.

Pipet, Albert, *La Trouée de Normandie*, Editions Presse de la Cité, Paris, 1966.

Rawson, Andrew, *Battleground Europe, Crossing the Rhine – Remagen Bridge, 9th Armored Division*, Leo Cooper, Barnsley, South Yorkshire, 2004.

Reynolds, Michael, *Men of Steel: 1 SS Panzer Corps, The Ardennes and Eastern Front 1944–45*, Sarpedon, New York, 1999.

Reynolds, Michael, *Steel Inferno: 1 SS Panzer Corps in Normandy*, Sarpedon, New York, 1997.

Reynolds, Michael, *Sons of the Reich: II SS Panzer Corps: Normandy, Arnhem, Ardennes, Eastern Front*, Casemate, Haverton Pennsylvania, 2002.

Rielau,Hans, *Geschichte der Nebeltruppe*, published by the ABC- und Selbstschutzschule [of the Bundeswehr] im Auftrag BMVtdg Fü H IV 1, 1965.

Ritgen, Helmut, *Die Geschichte der Panzer Lehr Division im Westen 1944-* 1945, Motorbuch Verlag, Stuttgart, 1979.

Ritgen, Helmut, *Westfront 1944*, Motorbuch Verlag, Stuttgart 1998.[available in translation]

Senger und Etterlin, F. M. von, *Die deutschen Geschütze 1939 — 1945,* Bernard & Graefe Verlag, Bonn, 1998,1999.

Senger und Etterlin, F. M. von, *Die deutschen Panzer 1926 – 1945,* Bernard & Graefe Verlag, Bonn, 2000.

Spayd, P. A., *Bayerlein, from Afrikakorp to Panzer Lehr, the Life of Rommel's Chief of Staff, Generalleutnant Fritz Bayerlein*, Schiffer, Atglen Pennsylvania, 2003.

*St. Lô, (7 July – 19 July 1944)*, American Forces in Action Series, Historical Division, War Department, Washington, D. C., 1946.

Stacey, C. P., *Official History of the Canadian Army in the Second World War, Volume III, The Victory Campaign, The Operations in Northwest Europe, 1944 – 1945*, The Queens Printer and Controller of Stationary, Ottawa, 1960.

Stöber, Hans, *Die Sturmflüt und das Ende: Geschichte der 17. SS-Panzergrenadierdivision Götz von Berlichingen*, vol. I, Munin Verlag, Osnabrück, 1976.

Tessin,Georg, *Verbände und Truppen der deutschen Wehrmacht und Waffen SS im Zweiten Weltkrieg 19339 – 1945 Zweite Auflage,* Biblio Verlag, Osnabrück, 1974 (18 volumes).

*The 28th Infantry Division in World War II*, 2000 reprint of 1946 original, The Battery Press, Inc., Nashville, Tennessee.

Tieke, Wilhelm, *Im Feuersturm Letzter Kriegsjahre: II. SS-Panzerkorps mit 9. und 10. SS-Division Hohenstaufen und Frundsberg*, Munin Verlag, Osnabrück, 1978 [available in translation]

Tiemann, Ralf, *Die Leibstandarte*, Bd. IV–2, Munin Verlag, Osnabrück, 1987. [available in translation]

Weidinger, Otto, *Division Das Reich*, Bd. V, Munin Verlag, Osnabrück, 1982.

Wilmot, Chester, *The Struggle for Europe*, Harper and Row, 1963 reprint of 1952 edition.

Ziemke, Earl. F., *Stalingrad to Berlin, the German Defeat in the East*, Center of Military History, United States Army, Washington, D.C., 1968.

Ziemke, Earl F. and Magna A. Bauer, *Moscow to Stalingrad, Decision in the East*, Center of Military History, United States Army, Washington D.C., 1987.